Topics in Signed Language Interpreting

Benjamins Translation Library

The Benjamins Translation Library aims to stimulate research and training in translation and interpreting studies. The Library provides a forum for a variety of approaches (which may sometimes be conflicting) in a socio-cultural, historical, theoretical, applied and pedagogical context. The Library includes scholarly works, reference works, post-graduate text books and readers in the English language.

EST Subseries

The European Society for Translation Studies (EST) Subseries is a publication channel within the Library to optimize EST's function as a forum for the translation and interpreting research community. It promotes new trends in research, gives more visibility to young scholars' work, publicizes new research methods, makes available documents from EST, and reissues classical works in translation studies which do not exist in English or which are now out of print.

Volume 63

Topics in Signed Language Interpreting: Theory and practice
Edited by Terry Janzen

Topics in
Signed Language Interpreting

Theory and practice

Edited by

Terry Janzen

University of Manitoba

John Benjamins Publishing Company

Amsterdam / Philadelphia

^{TM} The paper used in this publication meets the minimum requirements
of American National Standard for Information Sciences – Permanence
of Paper for Printed Library Materials, ANSI z39.48-1984.

Library of Congress Cataloging-in-Publication Data

Topics in Signed Language Interpreting : Theory and practice / edited by Terry
    Janzen.
       p. cm. (Benjamins Translation Library, ISSN 0929–7316 ; v. 63)
    Includes bibliographical references and indexes.
       1. Interpreters for the deaf. 2. Interpreters for the deaf--Canada. 3.
    Translating and interpreting. I. Janzen, Terry. II. Series.

    HV2402.T67 2005
    419--dc22   2005050067
    ISBN 978 90 272 1669 4 (Hb; alk. paper)
    ISBN 978 90 272 1683 0 (Pb; alk. paper)

John Benjamins Publishing Co. · P.O. Box 36224 · 1020 ME Amsterdam · The Netherlands
John Benjamins North America · P.O. Box 27519 · Philadelphia PA 19118-0519 · USA

To Josie

Table of contents

Contributors

Patrick Boudreault an Assistant Professor in the Deaf Studies Department at California State University, Northridge. He has an MSc from the School of Communication Science and Disorders, McGill University, and a PhD from the Faculty of Education, University of Manitoba. Patrick has been an American Sign Language-Langue des Signes Québécoise interpreter in Canada since 1996.

Patricia Conrad works as a freelance writer/editor. She has an MEd in Adult and Higher Education from the University of Alberta and was one of the earliest holders of the Certificate of Interpretation (COI) from the Association of Visual Language Interpreters of Canada. She has over twenty years experience as an ASL-English interpreter, taught for six years in the interpreting program at Grant MacEwan College, Edmonton, and is a past manager of Edmonton Interpreting Services at Connect Society.

Hubert Demers teaches in the ASL-English Interpretation Program, Red River College, in Winnipeg, Canada. He has a BA in English from the University of Winnipeg and holds the Certificate of Interpretation (COI) from the Association of Visual Language Interpreters of Canada. Hubert has over twenty years experience in ASL-English interpreting with a special interest in interpreting in legal settings.

Donna Korpiniski had a long and full career of nearly twenty years as an ASL-English interpreter in Canada and internationally, based in Edmonton. She had a BA in linguistics and was most recently enrolled as an MEd student in the Deaf Studies Program at the University of Alberta. Donna held the Certificate of Interpretation (COI) from the Association of Visual Language Interpreters of Canada, and for many years taught in the ASL-English interpreter education program at Grant MacEwan College, Edmonton. Donna passed away on September 2, 2007.

Terry Janzen has a PhD in linguistics from the University of New Mexico and now is an Associate Professor of linguistics at the University of Manitoba in Winnipeg, Canada. He has been an ASL-English interpreter for over twenty-five years and is a past board member of the Association of Visual Language Interpreters of Canada, for which he coordinated the development and implementation of the original AVLIC national certification process.

Lorraine Leeson is the Director of the Centre for Deaf Studies in the School of Linguistics, Speech and Communication Sciences, at Trinity College Dublin, Ireland. She has an undergraduate qualification in interpreting from the University of Bristol, UK. She also holds an MPhil and PhD in linguistics from Trinity College Dublin, and a Certificate in Feminism, Politics and the Economy from University College Dublin. She was one of the first cohort of professionally trained ISL-English interpreters in the Republic of Ireland (1992–1994).

Karen Malcolm is a faculty member of the Department of Sign Language Interpretation at Douglas College in New Westminster, British Columbia, Canada. Karen has a BGS (Bachelor of General Studies) from Simon Fraser University and an MS in Teaching Interpreting from Western Maryland College. She holds the Certificate of Interpretation

(COI) from the Association of Visual Language Interpreters of Canada and has twenty-five years experience as an ASL-English interpreter, currently specializing in interpreting in medical and mental health settings.

Debra Russell holds the David Peikoff Chair of Deafness Studies at the University of Alberta in Edmonton, Canada, and as well is the Director of the Western Canada Centre of Specialization on Deafness at the same university. Debra has a PhD from the University of Calgary. She has worked as an ASL-English interpreter since 1979 and is certified (Certificate of Interpretation) by the Association of Visual Language Interpreters of Canada. Debra is also a past president of AVLIC.

Barbara Shaffer is an Associate Professor in signed language interpreting in the Department of Linguistics, University of New Mexico in Albuquerque, USA. She has a PhD in educational linguistics from the University of New Mexico and has fifteen years experience in the interpreting field. Barbara holds the Certificate of Interpretation and the Certificate of Transliteration from the Registry of Interpreters for the Deaf (USA) along with Level V certification from the National Association of the Deaf.

Susan Stegenga is a freelance interpreter in Calgary, Canada. Susan works primarily in secondary and post-secondary educational settings and as well does community interpreting. She holds a Bachelor of Education from the University of Calgary. Susan has been an ASL-English interpreter for twenty-three years and is a past board member of the Association of Visual Language Interpreters of Canada.

Angela Stratiy is a frequent workshop presenter, entrepreneur (Deafutopia) and comedienne. She has an MEd from Western Maryland College and worked for fifteen years in the ASL-English interpreting program and the Sign Language Studies Program at Grant MacEwan College in Edmonton, Canada, in various capacities including instructor and program chair. Angela has been a Certified Deaf Interpreter, Registry of Interpreters for the Deaf (USA), since 1994. She has received numerous awards through her career, most recently the Deaf Albertan of the Year 2003 Award and the Governor-General of Canada's Queen's Golden Jubilee Medal, 2003.

Sherman Wilcox is Professor and Chair of the Department of Linguistics at the University of New Mexico in Albuquerque, USA. He has a PhD in educational linguistics from the University of New Mexico and holds a CSC from the Registry of Interpreters for the Deaf. He has been in the interpreting field for twenty-five years. Sherman is a co-author of *Gesture and the Nature of Language* and of *Learning to See*, which has recently been translated into Portuguese.

Acknowledgements

In July 2004 the Association of Visual Language Interpreters of Canada, the Canadian association of ASL-English interpreters, celebrated its twenty-fifth anniversary in Vancouver, British Columbia. Many of the organization's founders were there, reflecting on the exuberant beginnings and steady growth of the profession of signed language interpreting in Canada. In this officially bilingual country of French and English speakers, we also have two signed languages widely used in our Deaf communities, American Sign Language (ASL) and Langue des Signes Québécoise (LSQ). It is common at national level conferences and meetings to see all of these languages in use by a company of participants and interpreters. In twenty-five years the field of signed language interpreting in Canada has grown dramatically, largely through the efforts of many dedicated and hard working practitioners.

So too have educational programs to train interpreters evolved. In the mid-1970s almost the only opportunity to receive formalized training in Canada was a four-week summer program at Red River College in Winnipeg. While the number of educational programs is still small, training has advanced to programs two to four years in length, nation wide. To the students in these programs, and to the many hard-working interpreters across the country, this book is for you.

I recall that in the early days of full-time training offered at Red River College, when feeling the enormous challenges facing this developing profession and bringing my frustrations to my director, I was inevitably told 'but look how far the field has come!' It was always a reassuring reminder: in the thick of it, progress is sometimes difficult to see. For this encouragement, and many other such words of wisdom, I will always be grateful. I wish to acknowledge the hard work of my training colleagues at Red River College past and present, Janice Hawkins, David Still, Bonnie Dubienski, Marie Magirescu, Bruce Jack, David Burke, Cheryl Broszeit, Kyra Zimmer and many others, and especially Judy McGuirk, Hubert Demers, and Rick Zimmer. Your vision and dedication have opened many doors and led us to where we find ourselves today.

This volume is very much a collaboration. I would like to thank each author for their contribution, in believing so firmly in what they do, in continually guiding both interpreting students and practitioners, and in so graciously agreeing to commit their work to paper. This volume represents these contributors' numerous forward-thinking innovations and accounts of practices in the field; each will undoubtedly play a part in further moving the field forward. Without question we gratefully acknowledge the Deaf communities with whom we work. These communities have given us the gift of their languages; interpreters who work with signed languages owe much in return. As well I would like to thank the many students who have sat through my classes and participated in much fruitful discussion. These experiences have gone far to shape my own thinking. I have learned a great deal from you.

Many people have been instrumental in the development of this volume, but the contributions of some stand out. I am grateful to Linda Cundy, Marcella Demers, Rob Hagiwara, Donna Korpiniski, Lorraine Leeson, Liu Linjun, Denise Sedran, Elisa Maroney, Brenda Nicodemus, Barbara O'Dea, Arden Ogg, Debra Russell, Kevin Russell, Barbara Shaffer, Debbie Spindler, Susan Stegenga, Phyllis Wilcox, and Sherman Wilcox. Thank you for your inspiration, past, present and, most certainly, future. The anonymous reviewers of the book manuscript offered many comments and suggestions that have helped make the final version more readable and more complete. Thanks too to Liz Janzen for much support.

None of this would have been possible without the talents of Bertie Kaal, Isja Conen, and Miriam Shlesinger at John Benjamins. Thank you for your vision, numerous suggestions, and fine tuning.

On September 2nd, 2007, we lost our very good friend and colleague, Donna Korpiniski. Anyone who knew Donna was touched by her gregariousness and constant humour. And those of us who knew her as an interpreter, which includes almost every contributor to this volume, knew her as the model of professionalism – highly skilled at her craft, compassionate and fair in her work with both the Deaf and hearing communities, and fiercely ethical. I approached Donna at the AVLIC conference in Halifax in 2002 to ask her if she would write a chapter on ethics and professionalism with me, which she agreed to do immediately. As we wrote the first draft it became clear to me that much of what was going on paper was simply a description of Donna's way of working. Now, whenever I read through the chapter, I hear it in Donna's voice. But her contribution to this volume is even larger: there's a little bit of Donna in many of the chapters. For some, she lent a hand to get the words out of authors' heads and onto paper, for other chapters she provided me with good advice as the author and I worked out the direction of the writing, and still for others she is present in the ideas and words, because as these authors wrote about interpreters' best practices, Donna was most certainly one of the best models to draw from. Thank you, Donna. We miss you.

November, 20007

PART I

Introduction

CHAPTER 1

Introduction to the theory and practice of signed language interpreting

Terry Janzen
University of Manitoba

1. The task: Interpretation involving at least one signed language

Interpreters whose work includes at least one signed language began to formalize this work in the second half of the twentieth century in North America. The development of standard practices in this field, or more recently "best practices", thus has but a short history. Nonetheless, throughout this period the learning curve for interpreters has been very steep, beginning about the same time as William Stokoe's revelation that the signs that Deaf people made were more than rudimentary, instead comprising a complex, highly-principled language system. Interpreters' learning continues today with the intense pursuit of more knowledge of bilingualism, bi- and pluri-culturalism, the oppression of minorities and suppression of their languages, social and gender equality, and much more. The successful working interpreter requires a vast, almost encyclopedic, knowledge, it appears. And yet at times we still seem to be grappling with what Deaf people have most likely known intuitively for centuries, that signed languages are just that: languages. We are still working at understanding the complexities of their lexicons and grammars, because the skilled interpreter cannot only depend on intuitive knowledge (especially for many who have a signed language as their second language), but must know the structure consciously as well so that she can best understand what words and constructions represent within a given source text, and make informed choices about words and constructions that carry the same message in the target text.[1]

The chapters in this volume address many of the most fundamental aspects of interpreting involving signed languages. Here we have assembled a set of writings concerning both theoretical and practical components of the interpreter's work. The book is divided into two main sections entitled "Aspects of Interpreting Theory" and "Interpreting in Practice", and yet the reader will find that often these two ideas are interwoven. The perspective of many of the contributors is distinctly Canadian, that is, they reflect a Canadian sensibility toward language, multiculturalism and interpretation, as well as significant developments in the field of signed language interpreting in Canada, whether this is American Sign Language (ASL)-English, Langue des Signes Québécoise (LSQ)-French, or ASL-LSQ interpretation. Also included are several important contributions by authors outside of Canada, so that altogether this volume offers a collection of innovative views on signed language interpreting for students of interpretation, their instructors, and for practitioners already in the field.

2.   The intended reader

In the chapters that follow, the reader will find discussions on eleven different topics, chosen because they are some of the most likely topics to turn up in students' course curricula in interpreter education programs. However, we expect that the book will be of interest to students and practitioners alike.

2.1 Students of interpreting

This volume both promotes professionalization in the field and raises issues for practitioners. It is meant in large part for students of interpreting and their instructors, offering a blend of theoretical perspectives and practical application. Some chapters are more introductory in nature than others, but each addresses in some detail a topic that is necessary for interpreting students to grapple with, work at understanding, and apply into their practice as new professionals. Thus the book concerns some of the most fundamental aspects of interpreting involving signed languages, rather than attempting an overview of the field as is the case with, for example, Frishberg (1986), Humphrey and Alcorn (2001) and Stewart, Schein and Cartwright (1998).[2] The first half of the book is more theoretical, but often these writers make direct applications to practical considerations. Thus these chapters will be most accessible to more advanced students and practitioners who have already been exploring, and perhaps struggling with, many of the issues addressed. As well, interpreting program instructors will find this section beneficial in providing some theoretical bases for the approaches to the interpreting task they will be dealing with in the classroom, lab, and in supervising their students' practicum experiences. In the second half of the book, there are five chapters that address more clearly the practical aspects of the interpreter's work. This section is perhaps where less experienced student interpreters might begin their reading. The structure of the book situates theoretical discussions before practical discussions, but in actual fact there is no requirement that the chapters must be read in order. The material in each chapter should be considered (and taught) within the context of interpreting theory more broadly – as we advance further in our thinking, solutions to issues will surface but more often than not, so will more questions to consider. It is hoped that the material contained in this volume sparks discussion and learning, and promotes the pursuit of excellence in the classroom and in the field. Of course, on every topic more could be said, and thus further reading is always recommended.

Interpreters and interpreting students often seek rather immediate answers to the many questions that arise when studying the application of theoretical issues, and frequently lament that "it depends" is a frustrating response to almost every question about what to do in some interpreting scenario. It leaves one thinking that there is *never* an answer that can be pinned down. But it is important to consider that the response of "it depends" only makes sense in a hypothetical domain, that is, outside an actual interpreting situation when all contributing factors cannot be known. And for such potential, but not actual, scenarios, it is the *only* possible response.

In real situations, however, all the factors that can be known are known, so a decision can be made based on these; in a real situation "it depends" is not an option. This distinction is not made often enough, and interpreters who worry about there never being any actual answers to their questions are not considering the difference. This volume is bound to lead to numerous questions regarding possible interpreting situations with variable circumstances, and we encourage their discussion. It should not stop there, however. Rather, it is hoped that when approaching a real situation in which a real decision needs to be made, something read and discussed here will spark a more informed, principled decision on the part of the interpreter.

2.2 Working interpreters

For practitioners already in the field, this book will contain some familiar ideas but also numerous new approaches to consider, and so working interpreters are equally intended as a target audience along with student interpreters. It is doubtful that any graduate of an interpretation preparation program could rightly feel that there is nothing left to learn. The very essence of interpreting work and the careers we make out of it suggest the importance of career-long learning. In fact, certain of the theoretical chapters that follow may be best understood in the context of the experience a practicing interpreter has garnered. However, there are numerous ideas and suggestions made in the practical section of the book that may also benefit the interpreter in her work. The thinkers and writers who have contributed to the discussion in this volume have much to offer their colleagues in the field even when these practitioners have gained many years of interpreting experience. These chapters represent current trends and innovation in the field, but we recognize – and encourage – the continuation of much fruitful discussion and research.

3. Interpreters and their work

In this book we consider some of the fundamentals important to the interpreter who has at least one signed language in her repertoire of working languages. Many interpreters do work between a single signed and single spoken language (e.g., ASL and English), but as Boudreault (Chapter 12) and Leeson (Chapter 10) both demonstrate, a good number of interpreters work in situations not limited by a single language in each modality, something that may well become more common in the coming years. Then too we might consider similarities and differences between signed language and spoken language interpreters. For many reasons, it makes sense to suggest that differences are minimal, since interpreting theory applies to both groups and does not much depend on the specific languages being interpreted (See Roy 2000, for example, for a study based on general discourse and sociolinguistic principles but where one of the languages the interpreter uses is a signed language).

Despite this, having a signed language as one of the interpreter's working languages does mean that there are some specific, and critical, factors of the interpreter's work that need to be addressed. In particular, signed languages are indigenous languages of Deaf communities where community members interact with the surrounding non-Deaf community in every walk of life, and therefore interpreters can also be found working in almost every conceivable event and interaction type (see Frishberg 1986; Stewart et al. 1998; Solow 2000; and Humphrey & Alcorn 2001 as examples of surveys of work situations that attest to this). Second, including a signed language in the interpreting process means that a modality shift takes place (Cokely 1982), so that inherent in the process is a shift in auditory versus visual perception and message reconstruction. For reasons such as these, it is beneficial to focus on aspects of this group of interpreters who "specialize" in signed language interpreting.

Before the age of signed language interpreting professionalization, individuals showing promise where encouraged by Deaf community members to mediate interactions between Deaf and non-Deaf people, with the Deaf community relying on the integrity of each individual who did some interpreting for them. For those who began to practice this craft regularly, however, it eventually became evident that some standards were needed. The field has become more formalized in aspects of preparation, standards of practice, qualifications and certification, and even in specialization within the field. But having said this, it is also clear that interpreters' learning must continue. We still struggle with the complexities of many of the fundamentals, and it is these issues which the contributors in this text attempt to address.

4. An interpreter's resources in constructing a successful target text

How is the interpreter's target text shaped? (Recall here that "text" can mean any number of utterances in either a dialogue or monologue.) Ideally, the interpreter conveys *exactly* the source speaker's or signer's intended meaning, nothing more and nothing less. Interpreters' codes of ethics stress faithfulness to the source message and the interpreter's stance of impartiality. But producing a target text that is parallel in meaning can never be a direct transfer – the closest model we have of direct transfer is perhaps machine translation, the success of which is quite limited. It is interesting to note that the machine has been used as a metaphor for human interpreters' work: the interpreter as "conduit", discussed in detail in Wilcox and Shaffer (this volume), was the popular model espoused by ASL-English interpreters in North America from the late 1960s well into the 1980s.

Ultimately, however, this model fails. Except on an extremely rudimentary level, the interpreter cannot act like a machine[3] because the meaning of a source message is never directly accessible (once again, see Wilcox and Shaffer's discussion), and the interpreter cannot directly "convey" what is meant. As well, the linguistic building blocks available to the interpreter in the target language might be completely unlike those available in the source language.[4] Instead of directly conveying a message, the interpreter must gather evidence of meaning and construct a new text. Depending on what the interpreter knows and what her skills are, this new text more or less approximates the original – a great deal when the process works well, and very little when it doesn't. Thankfully, through a lot of hard work learning how to approach the task and with a lot of practice, our thoughtful approximations are often highly successful. The process is inherently complex, but various models of the process suggest a list of ordered sub-tasks to focus upon; Russell's model (this volume) is one cognitively based example that can help lead us to mastery.

In constructing the target text – the interpretation – I would like to consider three major aspects that might be thought of as the interpreter's "resources". In Figure 1 these are represented as three poles: meaning, linguistic form, and the interpreter's strategies. This rather simple model was first introduced in Janzen (2002), and is not intended to represent the myriad details of each cognitive process during the activity of interpreting. Each of these three poles, along with the significance of the model as a whole, is discussed in the sections that follow.

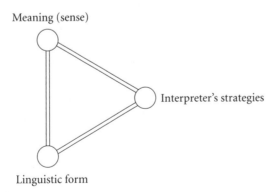

Meaning (sense)

Interpreter's strategies

Linguistic form

Figure 1. Three resources the interpreter holds in her approach to the target message.

4.1 Meaning

At all times, the interpreter strives first to find what the speaker or signer wishes to convey to her audience. Interpreters know that learning the meaning of a message is not a simple task. Clues to meaning are found in lexical words, grammar (which tells us how to read the relations between lexical words), the way the speaker or signer chooses to package her information (what Gile 1995 calls "secondary information"), the motives and goals of the speaker or signer, the intended effect of the text (thus "dynamic equivalence": Nida 1964), the context in which the text is uttered, and even in what is *not* said. Somewhere in all this the interpreter ascertains what the meaning of the message might be, but it is never directly accessible. Instead from these many clues the message meaning must be pieced together or constructed, as Wilcox and Shaffer point out in their chapter. Constructing meaning equally involves the interpreter's own experiences, because her understanding of message meaning depends entirely on what she already knows on many levels, and thus on her ability to synthesize the incoming information. It might be odd to think of meaning as one of the interpreter's "resources", but we might consider that it is in large part the meaning that the interpreter understands is intended that informs the interpreter's resulting text; following analysis of the incoming message in its context, the interpreter brings a constructed meaning to *her* text. Put another way, the interpreter relies on constructed meaning as only one part (one pole, in this model) of the text she produces, the other parts being structure and a strategized approach to the text's composition.

4.2 Linguistic form

It should be clear at this point that it is not the message itself that objectively "contains" meaning, but the interpreter's active interaction with the text that results in incrementally (Setton 1999) constructed meaning. Even though interpreters have long been cautioned to discard the linguistic form of the source early in the process (immediately, according to Seleskovitch 1978), interpreters must pay attention to form for several reasons. First, the form of the text is a resource where many important clues to meaning are found, so understanding how to read these clues is an indispensable skill for the interpreter. Second, particular forms, including grammatical constructions, are chosen precisely because they best reflect the speaker's or signer's intent (once again, secondary information). Finally, just as the source speaker or signer is necessarily tied to *some* form, so is the interpreter – linguistic form is chosen from available lexical and grammatical possibilities in the target language, and the interpreter *must* choose (Gile 1995). These aspects of language interaction are elaborated in Chapter 4.

Thus, not only is the interpreter's interaction with meaning obvious, so is her interaction with *linguistic form*. When the target text is being constructed, it is the interpreter's linguistic resources that will largely determine its structure, not the source speaker's or signer's, although the interpreter may "borrow" some aspects of the source text (form) if these can be carried over to enhance meaning.

4.3 The interpreter's strategies

The target text is also impacted by how the interpreter manages both the text and the interaction of discourse participants in the event as a whole.[5] To do this, the interpreter must strategize. Like the meaning and linguistic form poles, the strategies pole in Figure 1 represents complex interaction with the discourse on the part of the interpreter. The interpreter strategizes on numerous levels: what in the source message to profile, how best to represent the speaker's or signer's involvement with her own text across modalities (from a spoken to a signed form and vice versa), how to reconstruct portions of the interaction efficiently, how to understand bits of the source text when meaning is obscure, how to construct the target grammatically when there is much else to concentrate on, how to correct (inevitable) errors, and many others. These aspects of interpreting stress the interpreter's interaction with the discourse and management of the target text as the interaction proceeds. The process is thus dynamic, as suggested by Dean and Pollard (2001), who note that the aspects of the interpreting process that the interpreter has some control over are not static throughout the interaction.

Just as a number of chapters in this volume address both the resources of linguistic form and of meaning construction, many also deal critically with the interpreter's need to strategize, for example Malcolm on choosing language features, Russell on choosing to interpret consecutively or simultaneously, Leeson on both sociolinguistic variables and strategy types, and Boudreault on managing visual requirements of settings on one hand and communication variables for consumers with a range of linguistic skills on the other.

4.4 The three poles in balance

Even though there is push and pull among the three poles, they should not necessarily be considered as in opposition[6] but in balance. In other words, if the interpreter focuses her limited energy on the meaning pole, she draws from linguistic form to do so, and strategizes to build her understanding of the meaning. Similarly, if problems surface in reconstruction, she will work hard (that is, strategize) to find a solution, drawing upon meaning and appropriate linguistic form. All of this suggests that the target text clearly belongs to the interpreter and is a result of her own set of resources. And yet, it is of utmost importance not to unduly influence the text – the speaker's or signer's *message* – during the interpreting process. The interpreter has to learn how to minimize her own influences on the text (and interaction) that take away from what the source intends. This is no easy task.[7]

5. Emerging themes

With the model in Figure 1 above in mind, we might consider the three poles – constructing meaning, linguistic form, and the interpreter's strategies – as some of the themes emerging in the following chapters that link the diverse topics together. Even though each contribution addresses particular events, aspects of the field, or ways of thinking about interpreting, these viewpoints work together toward a realistic view of what the interpreter encounters and thus help us to better understand our role. For example, the various models used to understand the interpreter's position are presented from the viewpoint of communication expectations in Wilcox and Shaffer, from an ethical approach in Janzen and Korpiniski, and from a process management perspective in Russell. As well, the nature of communication, cultural influences, language specialization and expertise, critical strategizing, working closely with our communities of speakers and signers (instead of at arm's length), and professionalization also emerge as themes in the writing as a whole.

5.1 The contributions to the volume

The next six chapters make up the more theoretical part of the book. As mentioned earlier, at least some of these chapters require some basic understanding of the field. This is not to say that they are not accessible to new interpreting students, but they may require some guidance from more experienced instructors and interpreters as mentors. This set of chapters is presented first, considering that they provide an understanding of how the interpreter must approach her work, and from there work toward success.

Sherman Wilcox and Barbara Shaffer begin their chapter by providing an overview of how interpreters who work with a signed language have envisioned and explained the mental process of the task of interpreting over the years. As the field evolved in North America in the 1970s and 1980s toward a more professional status, the overriding model of the process became mechanistic, treating interpreters as conduits in the information exchange. And not without good reason: interpreting before this time was essentially *ad hoc*, with no set standards for behaviour and only a limited, and certainly not academic, understanding of the structure and status of signed languages and the cultures of Deaf communities. The earliest rigorous descriptions of signed languages began to appear in the 1950s and early 1960s with Tervoort's (1953) description of the Sign Language of the Netherlands and Stokoe's (1960) publication on what soon after came to be known as American Sign Language. As Wilcox and Shaffer demonstrate, conduit-model thinking has been somewhat difficult to shake. Even if interpreters have since preferred to see themselves as more closely allied with the Deaf community, and more actively participatory in the interpreted interchange, their view of language still treats it as a conduit for meaning. Wilcox and Shaffer instead propose a cognitively oriented view of communication in which the listener, in the case of a spoken language, or watcher, for a signed language, has access only to the material of language as cues to the originator's meaning, and must *construct* a meaning based on this perceptual evidence. Wilcox and Shaffer argue that understanding and accepting this cognitive model of communication is the only way that interpreters can truly move beyond a conduit approach in their overall role in the interpreted interchange.

In the first of **Lorraine Leeson**'s two contributions to this volume, she presents a view of the interpreter's task based primarily on the work of Daniel Gile (1995), and in doing so gives the signed language interpreter a look at an important perspective on their work. Leeson demonstrates first that Gile's Effort Model of simultaneous interpreting, intended for spoken language interpreters, applies equally well to interpreters working with a signed language. Essentially, Gile proposes that during the task of interpretation, various Efforts are distributed among components of the task, with the interpreter needing to master sets of skills related to each in order to carry out each component successfully. Over and above this, however, is the need to coordinate these components and the efforts expended in each direction – this coordination is the key to the interpreter being able to manage the process overall. Leeson then argues, once again following Gile, that success depends crucially on the interpreter's skills in strategizing. Strategizing is a necessary part of situation and interaction management, unavoidable because the task is large, interaction is complex, and the situation is never entirely predictable. Leeson iterates that interpreting is really decision making, which in many ways can be correctly considered as problem solving, the result of which is that the interpreter herself determines how to construct the bits and pieces of the target language text. The interpreter must thus learn how to strategize toward success. Leeson takes exception to labeling such processes as the interpreter adding to, omitting from, and substituting items in the text as "miscues". While these processes most certainly can be used inappropriately, Leeson argues that the well-trained and careful interpreter uses these (and others) in her text strategically to make the interpretation all the more successful. Thus Leeson's advice and suggestions add a practical component that complements the point of view taken by Wilcox and Shaffer.

In "Interpretation and Language Use: ASL and English" I present a discussion of language issues for interpreters who work between ASL and English. The chapter is not intended to be just a comparison of ASL and English grammars, which is sometimes the case when discussing the interpreter's languages in interpretation. Instead, here we examine what the interpreter's approach to her working languages should be, and how knowledge of language structure helps the interpreter in understanding what is going on in a source language text and how to construct a successful target language text. To this end, I look at language processes at four levels: words, constructions, text, and context, examining some examples where English as a spoken language and ASL as a signed language are similarly constructed (primarily because they are both languages), and where they differ. Where languages differ in these regards is where interpreters must pay attention in particular, because this is where work must be done to get the source and target texts to equivalently represent the ideas and intentions of the speaker or signer being interpreted. Linguistic transfer cannot be assumed, and neither will it be automatic, no matter how bilingual – how fluent – the interpreter is. Thus in this chapter I argue that the interpreter must pay attention to *both* form and meaning when analyzing the source text and constructing the target.

Karen Malcolm discusses the process of what has long been called "transliteration" in the field of signed language interpreting. In particular, Malcolm outlines basic differences in how this process is perceived in Canada and the United States, and how this is reflected in the two countries' evaluation and certification procedures. Malcolm makes the illuminating point that transliteration has been notoriously difficult to define, and instead if interpreters turn their attention to contact signing as described in Lucas and Valli's (1989, 1992) work, they can gain a more precise understanding of what successful interpretation should be like when the target text approaches a more English-like form.

Malcolm suggests that those who interpret using a contact variety of signed language (or even someone who may call herself a "transliterator" because this is the task that she performs regularly) do well to be fluent in ASL, precisely because the visual expression of language, even with English-like characteristics, can take advantage of signed language features such as the use of space and spatial relations – in other words, the *grammar* of ASL. Expertise in this appears to enhance the clarity of the overall target message.

There may be times when Deaf people's language use moves in the direction of more English-like forms in order to better accommodate (hearing) signers who do not have a command of ASL, or to better fit into a situation dominated by hearing English speakers when it is perceived that such accommodation would be somehow beneficial.[8] On the other hand, Deaf people may at times resist any English-like forms in the interest of solidarity among Deaf community members or when maintaining distance from hearing people's ways or influences is perceived as desirable.

Malcolm examines the times when some Deaf people are motivated to use a contact variety of signing and request transliteration, which must be respected by the interpreter, who cannot afford to stand in judgment. Many Deaf people decide otherwise, opting rather to maintain their use of ASL even when communicating interculturally, with the expectation that the interpreter will accommodate them in their language choice. But Malcolm also points to quite a number of Deaf people whose education has been facilitated by users of signed English, usually by hearing interpreters and teachers, and usually in public school programs, and thus who have had little exposure to the ASL-signing Deaf community. These people's general signed language use may be more English-like, and so for them it is less of a choice that depends on the situation at hand and once again, the interpreter has no call to judge the appropriateness of this language usage.

All of this points to the heterogeneity of the Deaf population that interpreters encounter (reiterated in Boudreault's chapter), and the flexibility needed to work in a wide variety of settings. As Malcolm rightly suggests, the interpreter must have the language skills to support this range of settings, and that because numerous features of ASL (the use of space, facial gestures, etc.) can enhance meaning in even the most English-like language use, a sound knowledge of ASL even for the transliterator is of huge benefit.

The Canadian perspective is that interpreters must have a range of skills as their goal, which includes ASL and more English-like signing, and that whether someone interprets or transliterates has more to do with the situation than with the role of the interpreter/transliterator generally. Malcolm ends her discussion with a number of recommendations, including that interpreters should continue to see target language options as ranging between ASL and more English-like signing rather than as discrete. Therefore in the process of interpreting, the target form is chosen situation by situation, not just consumer by consumer, and certainly not based on the preference of the interpreter.

Debra Russell examines critical questions regarding the use of simultaneous and consecutive interpreting in her chapter. Through a discussion of cognitive models of interpreting, and most notably through her own model first proposed in Russell (2000, 2002) and refined here, she suggests that the decision to interpret consecutively or simultaneously must be a part of the interpreter's fundamental assessment of the interaction and setting, and considered and reconsidered consistently as the interpreter progresses through the interpreted event. In other words, the interpreter may choose to interpret consecutively from the beginning, or strategically move to consecutive interpreting at some point during the interaction if that is determined to be the ideal way to maintain a high level of accuracy.

Russell notes that interpreters working with a signed language have traditionally not questioned the use of simultaneous interpreting, primarily because there is no direct interference between a spoken language and signed language when they are in use at the same time. This practice, however, has unfortunately created numerous problems for the interpreter. Russell claims it has led to a lack of skill development in the areas of message analysis and "translation skills" that would come with the discipline of practicing consecutive interpreting. Russell demonstrates that if these considerations are included in interpreters' professional preparation, the effect on message accuracy is profound. Including consecutive interpreting as a standard practice in the field, however, will take some adjustments at every level: the outlook of student interpreters, the terminology and methodologies that interpreter educators use, attitudes and practices of practicum mentors and working interpreters, expectations of employers, and agreement among consumers. In many cases, Russell states, interpreters have *taught* their consumers to expect simultaneous interpreting across the board, and convinced themselves that relying on consecutive interpreting signals that the interpreter is not up to the task. Clearly, this lopsided perspective must change: Russell cautions us that consistently defaulting to simultaneous interpreting can be damaging.

Russell illustrates the discussion with her detailed study of simultaneous and consecutive interpreting in the courtroom, in which she analyzed data from highly skilled interpreters and found that consecutive interpreting consistently yielded higher levels of accuracy in message transfer (Russell 2000, 2002). In the face of this evidence, it is clear that the field is in need of a paradigm shift to consider the value in choosing consecutive interpreting when that is most expedient, and simultaneous interpreting when the conditions are right.

Beyond linguistic competence and interpreting technique, interpreters must be adept at interacting with clients and consumers, working well together as colleagues, and approaching their consumers' texts and materials in an ethical and professional manner. **Donna Korpiniski** and I look at these issues in our chapter on interpreters' ethics. As we analyze many of the issues that confront interpreters, we see that almost invariably they involve a cultural component. In other words, ethical and professional issues cannot be examined and understood in isolation from the context that surrounds their circumstances, and this context includes cultural factors.

Interpreters who work with at least one signed language always work in situations where cultures meet.[9] There has been some awareness of this ever since the field began its formalization, but in recent years interpreters have sought to understand more clearly what this must mean for their work (see, for example, Mindess 1999). In this chapter, we argue that even though it is true that Deaf and non-Deaf consumers come together from different cultural points of view, the interpreter herself experiences many cultural conflicts that lead to so-called "ethical" dilemmas. Resolution, therefore, necessitates a cultural component as well.

From the beginning of the field's professionalization, interpreters have seen the need to lay out a set of principles to guide their behaviours and interactions while at work, a practice common to professional fields. Here we examine the rationale for interpreters' formalized codes of ethics, suggesting that while there is an obvious need for them, they tend to have been constructed during a period in our history when attempts were being made to standardize behaviour as the field moved away from the "helper" model. Thus underlying many of the principles in these codes is an "arm's length" approach to our consumers, their issues, and the texts they produce. But in this, we have been fooled into thinking we can be neutral, and further, into thinking that we understand what neutrality is.[10] This chapter on ethics and professional behaviour examines some of these questions, suggesting that the solution, at least in part, involves the need to understand cultural considerations at a much deeper level.

In the first chapter in the second section on practical aspects of interpreting, **Hubert Demers** introduces us to the interpreter on the job. His goal is to outline the steps required to put the interpreter in the best position for success at her work. Demers discusses a number of aspects of the interpreter's work generally, such as working freelance or as a salaried employee, working alone or in teams, and the kinds of skills an interpreter needs to develop both on and off the job to be a successful practitioner. Demers then describes a progression of eight steps to follow for each interpreting assignment, and makes the important point that such a structured approach to the work can lead to both efficiency and, over time, more rapid professional development. Perhaps the strength of this chapter, though, is Demers's vision of the expectations that are placed on new versus experienced interpreters. For this discussion, Demers focuses on two aspects: 1) the ability to predict what is likely to take place in the interpreted event along with the areas of knowledge and terminology the interpreter might encounter, and 2) the relative length of time it takes to prepare. Demers shows in a series of schematic figures how these two aspects typically play out both for new interpreters and those with more experience and as such points the way for newer interpreters toward a realistic expectation of how their work – and their relationship to their work – can progress.

An important, and very practical, question for interpreters who work with a signed language is how they relate to the communities within which they work. This is especially the case for interpreters working with the Deaf community, a community that often treats outsiders – for very good reason – with some suspicion. **Angela Stratiy** looks at several key aspects of the interpreter's relationship with the Deaf community and its members in her discussion of interpreters' behaviours. While Stratiy examines just a few aspects of this relationship in her chapter, it is obvious that interpreters cannot take what they do lightly. For those interpreters who come into contact with the Deaf community as they learn the local signed language, perhaps the best way to think of this community is as a "host" culture where they are "visitors": if they expect acceptance, they are going to have to learn the ropes. This means using the language of the community and buying into their cultural norms on Deaf people's terms.

Stratiy discusses this challenge based on three considerations: cultural, linguistic and interpreting phenomena. Each of these considerations merits discussion on its own, and yet each has implications for the others. For example, how culturally appropriate a person is will affect her acceptance in interpreting situations. In terms of language use, the interplay between language and culture will be quite obvious to members of the culture – if the interpreter's linguistic choices are appropriate, she will be seen as accepting of cultural norms. But nowhere is the effect of cultural appropriateness seen more than during the interpreted event. Here the interpreter's choices will critically determine whether or not she is seen as trustworthy. Stratiy makes the point that interpreters need to carefully consider the impact that their choices have – choices sometimes based on years of learning and practice – on the recipients of their interpretation. Quite often the true sentiment of the consumer is overlooked, and in fact has never been fully understood. Stratiy asks for serious discussion among interpreters and Deaf community members, suggesting there are still numerous issues left unresolved.

In **Lorraine Leeson's** second contribution to this volume, she addresses the case of language variation within the Deaf community in Ireland. Even though Leeson's study is somewhat localized to the Irish situation, the implications are very broad, well beyond the region where the Irish Deaf community lives.

Variation in the way that people use language is a fact of life. We might say that no two people have exactly the same mental "grammar", even if they speak or sign the same language. No two people have exactly the same mental lexicon. No two people would choose the identical phrasing or construction type in the same way all of the time. We may expect, however, that if two people are frequently in close contact, share many of the same experiences, have similar goals in their daily lives, watch many of the same programs on TV, etc., and truly want to communicate clearly with each other, they will share many similar language features. On the other hand, two people without much in common, with very diverse interests and so forth, will likely also diverge in their language use.

For the most part, this is not particularly problematic. We tend socially to spend more time around people we have much in common with, which can mean different people according to the setting, such as at work, at home, at the daycare, or while playing a team sport. For the interpreter, however, the differences between language users can range from minimal, such as when interpreting for a conference presentation where everyone shares a body of information and has similar interests, to maximally different, such as is the case in many social service, medical, legal, and other settings. In these cases, there may be great differences in two people's background, age, purpose, culture, and of course, language.

Leeson's study is illuminating because she describes for us the breadth of heterogeneity in language use. Irish Sign Language (ISL) signers are influenced not only by forms of signed English from various educational experiences, but by the signed languages of their closest Deaf neighbours who use British Sign Language, and even to some extent by ASL and French Sign Language (there is a historical connection between ISL, ASL and LSF, and modern world travel means that these languages are coming into contact anew). But perhaps even more striking is that the education system in Ireland historically has meant that for decades Deaf boys and Deaf girls did not interact, not until they finished their schooling and met in the Deaf community as young adults. The result of this has been the use of ISL strongly influenced by gendered differences. This situation has changed in the later part of the twentieth century, but this means that there is now an added generational component to these differences – the language use of older Deaf people can be quite different from that of younger Deaf people. Further, Leeson demonstrates that there are significant regional differences in the use of signed language around the country, so that interpreters are faced with dialectical differences as well. And finally, in this chapter Leeson places Ireland on the European stage, where a number of signed languages are coming increasingly into contact.

In all of this, interpreters are in a position where they must respond, both individually and collectively. For many interpreters in other countries where variation in signed language use appears less problematic, a valuable lesson can still be learned from Leeson's discussion: variation can occur around any corner, and the interpreter must either be prepared with the linguistic capabilities to handle the discourse or with strategies to handle the situation (or, of course, a good dose of both). It may be tempting to think that the interpreter's responsibility is to diminish the differences between two individuals who have come together to communicate through interpretation, but as Leeson, Malcolm, and Janzen and Korpiniski all point out, language differences that mark a particular speaker's or signer's discourse may be thoughtfully chosen, intended to make an impact on the communication event. Simon (1995) cautions us that culturally-laden discourse might be intended to signify identity (thus differences) just as easily as it might be meant to bridge cultures.

While this volume does not attempt to address the logistics of interpreting in the numerous specific settings that are often discussed in introductory works on the subject, one setting stands out as an environment that merits some attention. **Patricia Conrad** and **Susan Stegenga**'s chapter is on interpreting in educational settings. More interpreters work in education than in any other specialized setting, some full time, some part time while also working as interpreters in other placements, and others taking individual contracts as part of their freelance complement of work. Russell and Janzen (2004) found that 32.8% of respondents in a recent Canadian survey of ASL-English interpreters report either full-time or part-time employment in education at the kindergarten to high school level, and 35.8% of respondents report either full-time or part-time employment in education at the post-secondary (college and university) level.

Conrad and Stegenga's focus is on interpreting in the classroom, from kindergarten through elementary and secondary schools to college and university, including graduate programs. As such they address logistics and concerns facing the interpreter working with very young children to interpreting for self-directed adults in classroom situations. Conrad and Stegenga stress that while educational placements have often been thought of as good training ground for new interpreters, there are many reasons to think of these settings as highly specialized. Consider, for example, the responsibilities that come with being the linguistic link in a young child's education. An interpreter in this position must know a great deal about child development, language acquisition, and pedagogy – other professionals in this environment are required to do so and the interpreter should be no exception. In higher education, for example in a university environment, academic credentials are expected of anyone working with students, and again Conrad and Stegenga make the point that the interpreter's credentials should include her own university education.

Finally, **Patrick Boudreault** addresses the role that Deaf people themselves play as professional interpreters. In the last decade or so, Boudreault points out, Deaf interpreters have become increasingly recognized in the field of interpreting. In the beginning, they played a more peripheral role in the field as a whole, serving on evaluation teams leading to (hearing) interpreters' certification, teaching ASL in interpreter education programs (although hearing interpreters have quite frequently done this too), and occasionally assisting hearing interpreters with a Deaf consumer who is particularly difficult to understand. The value of Deaf interpreters, however, has been overlooked from the beginning of formalization within the field. In regard to interpreting for "low-verbal deaf persons" the authors of the first published manual of the Registry of Interpreters for the Deaf suggest that a Deaf person could be used as an intermediary if he was a "knowledgeable deaf individual with above average verbal ability" ("verbal" here is taken to include signed language) with much success, but that "in the case of the uneducated deaf adults who have had little contact with the deaf community but who respond well to natural gestures, a hearing acquaintance may sometimes prove the best person to serve as the intermediary" (Quigley & Youngs 1965:41).

Frishberg (1986) suggests the inclusion of Deaf interpreters in more settings where Deaf consumers' communication skills present problems for interpretation. Frishberg says, "Intermediary interpreters are those who have special communication skills for reaching deaf people who have idiosyncratic gestures or other signing varieties beyond the understanding of the originally scheduled interpreter" (Frishberg 1986: 164). This, however, illustrates that the expectation is that a hearing interpreter is first called in, and if her attempts prove unsuccessful, a Deaf interpreter may then be asked to assist. In more recent years, recognition of Deaf interpreters' abilities has improved, but more often than not, interpreting is still thought of as the purview of those who hear; Deaf interpreters are not yet equal partners. Bienvenu and Colonomos note that hearing interpreters have found it difficult to "*relinquish control* and request a relay team" (1992:76; emphasis added), which suggests this inequity.

Boudreault approaches interpretation and the role of the professional interpreter who is Deaf from a very different perspective. This approach is informed by his lengthy experience as an ASL-LSQ interpreter in Canada where the two Deaf communities, each using one of these signed languages, frequently interact. From here, Boudreault explores the many circumstances where Deaf interpreters might be found and the functions they perform, whether interpreting between two signed languages as bilingual experts, "mirroring" an interpreted text to an audience when the logistics of the situation require it, or as linguistic and cultural facilitators between Deaf and hearing consumers with or without a hearing interpreter present. Boudreault shows that with training and experience – much like what is expected of hearing interpreters – Deaf interpreters today bring a plethora of skills to the interpreting table, and these colleagues demand our utmost respect.

There are, however, some significant hurdles to overcome. Boudreault suggests that Deaf interpreters struggle with numerous ethical concerns. He notes that they desire to be ethical, but grapple with codes of ethics that were not written from a Deaf community perspective. Deaf interpreters are also members of Deaf communities, where certain expectations of them as community members are held. Thus they work to be ethical among members of their community on one hand, and in relation to the views on the role and functions of interpreters that their hearing colleagues have on the other. Boudreault concludes by suggesting that an important means of Deaf interpreters achieving a high level of skill along with a solid, respectful working relationship with hearing interpreters is more formalized training for both groups of professionals.

6. A final introductory note: Some text conventions

Throughout this volume we have chosen certain conventions in our descriptions of the activities of interpreting and the participants in the interaction, some of which are not commonly used by signed language interpreters, and so merit a brief explanation. In quite a number of works on signed language and interpreting research, these logistic topics are found in footnotes. They are addressed in slightly more detail here, however, simply because interpreters and interpreting students need to think carefully about how they use even seemingly simple terminology with each other and with their consumers or clientele.

6.1 "Signed language" vs. "sign language"

Readers will notice that we use the phrase "signed language" instead of "sign language" throughout the text. Although it is more common to see "sign language" in print and hear it in spoken English, there are at least two reasons why we do not use it here. First, grammatically, the adjective form "signed" aligns with the adjective "spoken". In other words, we are discussing languages that are signed and those that are spoken. Second, it is common for people to talk about "sign language" as *the* language they know and use, meaning ASL or another specific signed language, but "sign language" is not itself the name of any language, and in fact, many times people who are less in the know equate "sign language" with a few simple gestures, fingerspelling (only), and the like, without understanding that there is a sharp difference between using a few non-verbal signals or some means to spell out English and the full language systems of Deaf communities, whose languages are articulated with hands and bodies (i.e., signed) rather than through the vocal tract (i.e., spoken). Thus here, when authors wish to distinguish between languages that are spoken and languages that are signed, we use "signed language", and when we refer to a specific signed language, we use the name of that language (ASL, LSQ, etc.). This practice is beginning to appear in linguistic research as well, a few examples of which are Taub (2001) and Janzen and Wilcox (2004).

A final point regarding this convention is that readers will also see "signed language interpreter" and "signed language interpreting" which will be new for some. It has become rather conventional in interpreters' discourse to use the names of their working languages to describe themselves, calling themselves ASL-English interpreters as opposed to sign language interpreters, mostly as an attempt to give equality to each of the two languages they use and not to focus on one particular language group (and perhaps not to appear paternalistic). This convention of referring to the two languages the interpreter works with tends to be followed in this volume, although when authors refer to interpreting between signed and spoken languages more generally, the term "signed language interpreter" does appear.

6.2 The use of Deaf/deaf

It has become quite common practice to refer to culturally Deaf persons with an upper case "D" on Deaf, and when referring to audiological deafness to use a lower case "d" as suggested, for example, by Padden and Humphries (1988). We follow this practice in this volume. There are times, however, when it is not so easy to distinguish whether we are speaking about one group or the other. This is the case when discussing deaf children who have not yet become part of the Deaf community, but who are in the process of learning to sign, perhaps facilitated by an interpreter in a regular school classroom. There is a good chance that these children are *on their way* to becoming Deaf, but the question is, when do we recognize that they are not just deaf anymore, but have become Deaf? We do not attempt to answer such a question here, and instead adopt the convention that if there is any possibility that we may be referring to someone at any age who might be considered Deaf (with an upper case "D"), we will call her "Deaf", but if it is fairly clear that we mean someone who is "outside" the Deaf community, "deaf" will suffice.

6.3 Interpreters: SHE or HE?

Why can't pronouns be simple? There is a very longstanding tradition in English to use "he" when addressing a generic, singular third person, but this has changed dramatically in the last while. It's tempting to be inclusive, but slashes are hard to read: When someone is putting *his/her* thoughts on paper, *s/he* has to keep *his or her* wits about *him/her*! These days we are also witness to the alternative of the generic third person "they" and "their": When someone is putting *their* thoughts on paper, *they*... well, we can run into serious trouble here too; witness the reflexive: They were the only student in the class who could work by *themself*. There has to be a better solution.

We might be suspected of using "she" and "her" as generic pronouns in this volume because the majority of interpreters are women (as was thought by one of our early reviewers), but this is not the case. Our reasoning has just to do with grammar. A colleague of mine in linguistics suggested to me, when I asked for an opinion on whether we should use "he", "she", or to try and mix it up fifty-fifty, that writers of English have relied on "he" for hundreds of years – perhaps it is time to turn the tables. And that's what we have done. Whenever we are writing about a generic third person, we use the feminine gender, but of course, the reader should take that as really meaning anyone, male or female.

6.4 Interpreting as activity vs. interpretation as product

Throughout this volume, the authors consider various aspects of the process of interpreting, most critically whether as activity or in terms of the resulting target text. The question of which is being discussed is not trivial: focusing on the activity versus the product has far reaching implications both in how training the interpreter is accomplished, and how the practitioner conceives of her work overall. Per Linell (1997) addresses interpreting in terms of the text, the process and the practice, looking at how "texts" have typically been viewed in this way:

> As regards texts and translated texts, they may, at first sight, be seen as neutral with respect to monologism and dialogism. But there is a strong tendency to reify the text, to see texts as self-contained objects in their own right. Texts are thereby treated as decontextualized, which means that the perspective in practice squares more with monologism than with dialogism.   (Linell 1997:61)

It may be the case that traditionally we have taught interpretation mostly as a monologic task, focusing on *text analysis* once the interpretation has been completed, but in recent years there has been a movement away from this approach to a more activity-oriented, and thus more contextualized, approach. Generally in this volume we use "interpreting" to refer to the activity that interpreters undertake and participate in (see especially Wadensjö 1998) and "interpretation" to refer primarily to the product of the activity, although "interpretation" is also used as an overarching term for the field of practice. It is not uncommon these days to think of a setting as either "monologic" or "dialogic" in nature (see for example the contributions in Metzger, Collins, Dively, & Shaw 2003, and the orientation of training components as conceived by Cokely 2003 as discussed in Russell, this volume). As of late much theoretical discussion and research appears to have turned from interpreting largely as a monologic activity (an interpreter delivering a text from a single speaker to an audience in an uninterrupted manner) to interpreting as dialogue where participants are more or less equal interactants and the interpreter plays a significant role in the interactive discourse.

By and large the contributions here do not so much distinguish between working with monologic or dialogic texts, considering that in every case interpreters work in situations where communicative interactions take place. Even monologic discourse may be understood as a kind of discourse *among* interactants in a social context. As for the term "text", I point out in both this chapter and in Chapter 4 that texts may be thought of not as Linell notes has often been the case, that is, primarily as "products", but as any stretch of discourse the interpreter works actively with, either as input or output. Thus we are not treating "text" only as product, nor as strictly monologic.

However, it is worth making note of the two generalized ways of thinking about the interpreter's work – as "interpreting" (the activity the interpreter undertakes) and "interpretation" (the result of the activity), and what the interpreter is seeking to accomplish by looking at the task from either of these two perspectives.

Notes

1. The lexicon of a language consists of the total list of words of that language. People talking about signed and spoken languages have tended to refer to lexical items differently for each, that is, "words" for a spoken language and "signs" for a signed language. But this is not necessary – phonologically (how they are "pronounced") they are very different, but the lexicon of a signed language such as ASL is a list of the words of *that* language, with no intended reference to their translation into, say, English. Further, the label of "text" needs some clarification. It is probably common to think of a text as a fairly lengthy monologue such as a speech or lecture. Throughout this introduction, however, I use "text" to mean *any* utterance or string of utterances in either a dialogic or monologic context (cf. Linell 1997; Wadensjö 1998).

2. A second edition of Steward et al. appeared in 2004.

3. Mindess (1999) suggests that at times, the interpreter *can* work under such a machine model, but the only way this can be viewed realistically is in an emotional sense, in exceptional circumstances, and for only brief periods of time. But even a detached approach to the text is determined strategically and cannot be mindless, therefore just "carrying on like a machine" creates a particular kind of interpreter-effected, non-objective text.

4. Frishberg (1986) says the following: "We cannot assume that we can apply the results of research on spoken language interpreters' processing of language material to make predictions about how we expect sign language interpreters to behave. The structure of sign languages (at least American Sign Language) is sufficiently different, especially with respect to factors such as pausing and signing time, to warrant caution in applying findings directly" (1986: 38). Unfortunately, this may be taken to mean that the structure of a signed language such as ASL is unlike the structure of any spoken language. Certainly the modality difference creates some unique factors for interpreters, but it is clear that even for interpreting between two spoken languages, the two languages in the interpreter's language pair may be radically different structurally. When this is true, Gile (1995) suggests that certain of the interpreter's strategies, like maintaining a much longer process time, are critical. When interpreting using a signed language, factors such as this may be more meaningful than the actual modality difference effects.

5. Thanks to Hubert Demers and Judy McGuirk for pointing out to me that this aspect of interpreting is best described as managing the *interaction* rather than just managing the *message*. See also Wadensjö (1998: 108) on the interpreter's "coordinating function".

6. This is not to say that there are not intense oppositions at work which do push and pull the interpreter's target text in one direction or another; the interpreter must always contend with these. For example, Newmark (1983) outlines ten factors that can impact the direction of the text, e.g., to preserve the idiolect of the source language producer, or to make the target text entirely comprehensible within the target audience's cultural domain, or to align the text with the interpreter's own assumptions or beliefs about the text and its purpose. In all these cases, the interpreter, rightly or wrongly, must still actively draw from the three poles of this model to formulate the target text.

7. The interpreting process is vastly more complex a mental task than is laid out here. For an excellent review of models of interpreting processes based on a wide spectrum of disciplinary approaches, see González, Vásquez and Mikkelson (1991).

8. Bienvenu (1987) states that for many Deaf people "PSE [Pidgin Sign English] represents an attempt to match conversational partners at that point along the continuum where they are comfortable and competent. We call this 'language,' but a more appropriate term would be 'accommodation'" (1987: 2).

9. Although recall that interpreters working with more than one signed language can be the case, illustrated in Boudreault's chapter regarding ASL-LSQ interpreters and Leeson's chapter on dealing with language variation.

10. See Wilcox and Shaffer, this volume, for discussion on the difference between social neutrality and neutrality in the interpreter's approach to her linguistic text.

References

Bienvenu, M. J. (1987). Third culture: Working together. *Journal of Interpretation (RID)*, 4, 1–12.

Bienvenu, M. J., & Betty Colonomos (1992). Relay interpreting in the 90's. In Laurie Swabey (Ed.), *The Challenge of the '90's: New Standards in Interpreter Education* (pp. 69–80). USA: Conference of Interpreter Trainers.

Cokely, Dennis (1982). The interpreted medical interview: It loses something in the translation. *The Reflector 3* (Spring), 5–11.

Cokely, Dennis (2003). Curriculum Revision in the Twenty First Century: Northeastern's Experience. Keynote presentation for Project TIEM, on-line conference, March 10, 2003.

Dean, Robyn K., & Robert Q. Pollard, Jr. (2001). Application of demand-control theory to sign language interpreting: Implications for stress and interpreter training. *Journal of Deaf Studies and Deaf Education*, 6 (1), 1–14.

Frishberg, Nancy (1986). *Interpreting: An Introduction*. Silver Spring, MD: Registry of Interpreters for the Deaf.

Gile, Daniel (1995). *Basic Concepts and Models for Interpreter and Translator Training*. Amsterdam/Philadelphia: John Benjamins.

González, Roseann Dueñas, Victoria F. Vásquez, & Holly Mikkelson (1991). *Fundamentals of Court Interpretation: Theory, Policy and Practice*. Durham, NC: Carolina Academic Press.

Humphrey, Janice H., & Bob J. Alcorn (2001). *So You Want to Be an Interpreter?: An Introduction to Sign Language Interpreting* (3rd ed.). Amarillo, TX: H & H Publishers.

Janzen, Terry (2002). When Grammars Collide: The Language Interface in Interpretation. Keynote Address, the Fourteenth Biennial Conference of the Association of Visual Language Interpreters of Canada (AVLIC), Halifax, Nova Scotia, July 25, 2002.

Janzen, Terry, & Sherman Wilcox (Eds.). (2004). *Cognitive Approaches to Signed Language Research*. Special issue of *Cognitive Linguistics*, 15 (2).

Linell, Per (1997). Interpreting as communication. In Yves Gambier, Daniel Gile, & Christopher Taylor (Eds.), *Conference Interpreting: Current Trends in Research* (pp. 49–67). Amsterdam/Philadelphia: John Benjamins.

Lucas, Ceil, & Clayton Valli (1989). Language contact in the American deaf community. In C. Lucas (Ed.), *The Sociolinguistics of the Deaf Community* (pp. 11–40). San Diego, CA: Academic Press.

Lucas, Ceil, & Clayton Valli (1992). *Language Contact in the American Deaf Community*. San Diego, CA: Academic Press.

Melanie Metzger, Steven Collins, Valerie Dively, & Risa Shaw (Eds.). (2003). *From Topic Boundaries to Omission: New Research on Interpretation*. Washington, DC: Gallaudet University Press.

Mindess, Anna (1999). *Reading Between the Signs: Intercultural Communication for Sign Language Interpreters*. Yarmouth, ME: Intercultural Press.

Newmark, Peter (1983). Introductory survey. In Catriona Picken (Ed.), *The Translator's Handbook* (pp. 1–17). London: Aslib.

Nida, Eugene A. (1964). *Toward a Science of Translating*. Leiden, Netherlands: E. J. Brill.

Padden, Carol, & Tom Humphries (1988). *Deaf in America: Voices from a Culture*. Cambridge, MA: Harvard University Press.

Quigley, Stephen P., & Joseph P. Youngs (1965). *Interpreting for Deaf People*. Washington, DC: U.S. Department of Health, Education, and Welfare.

Roy, Cynthia B. (2000). *Interpreting as a Discourse Process*. New York: Oxford University Press.

Russell, Debra (2000). Interpreting in Legal Contexts: Consecutive and Simultaneous Interpreting. Doctoral dissertation. University of Calgary, Calgary, Alberta, Canada.

Russell, Debra (2002). *Interpreting in Legal Contexts: Consecutive and Simultaneous Interpreting.* Burtonsville, MD: Linstok Press.

Russell, Debra, & Terry Janzen (2004). Learning about Ourselves: Results of the First Canadian Demographic Survey of ASL-English Interpreters. Paper presented at the Association of Visual Language Interpreters of Canada (AVLIC) conference, Vancouver, Canada, July 2004.

Seleskovitch, Danica (1978). *Interpreting for International Conferences.* Washington, DC: Pen and Booth.

Setton, Robin (1999). *Simultaneous Interpretation: A Cognitive-Pragmatic Analysis.* Amsterdam/ Philadelphia: John Benjamins.

Simon, Sherry (1995). Delivering Culture: The Task of the Translator. In Marie-Christine Aubin (Ed.), *Perspectives d'avenir en traduction* (pp. 43–56). Winnipeg: Presses universitaires de Saint-Boniface.

Solow, Sharon Neumann (2000). *Sign Language Interpreting: A Basic Resource Book* (Revised ed.) Burtonsville, MD: Linstok Press.

Stewart, David A., Jerome D. Schein, & Brenda E. Cartwright (1998). *Sign Language Interpreting: Exploring Its Art and Science.* Needham Heights, MA: Allyn & Bacon.

Stokoe, William C. (1960). *Sign Language Structure: An Outline of the Visual Communication Systems of the American Deaf. Studies in Linguistics, Occasional Papers 8.* Buffalo, NY.

Taub, Sarah F. (2001). *Language from the Body.* Cambridge: Cambridge University Press.

Tervoort, Bernard T. (1953). *Structurele Analyze van Visueel Taalgebruik binnen een Groep Dove Kinderen.* [Structural analysis of visual language use within a group of deaf children.] Deel 1. Tekst. Amsterdam: North-Holland Publ. Co. Zugl.: Amsterdam, Univ. Dissertation.

Wadensjö, Cecilia (1998). *Interpreting as Interaction.* London and New York: Longman.

PART II

Aspects of interpreting theory

CHAPTER 2

Towards a cognitive model of interpreting

Sherman Wilcox and Barbara Shaffer
University of New Mexico

1. Introduction

> "If speaking *for* someone else seems to be a mysterious
> process that may be because speaking *to* someone does not
> seem mysterious enough."
>
> Stanley Cavell (Quoted in Geertz 1973)

Interpreting is, at its heart, about communicating. Although the interpreting situation is a unique communicative event, and the process of interpreting between two languages and two cultures places special constraints and demands on the interpreter, all acts of interpreting can ultimately be reduced to acts of communication. In this chapter, we propose that in order to understand the process of interpreting, it is necessary first to understand how we communicate with one another. Paraphrasing Cavell, we suggest that if *interpreting for someone* seems to be a mysterious process this is because *communicating with someone* does not seem mysterious enough.

Models of interpretation have developed over the years from an early view in which the interpreter was seen as a passive conveyor of information much like a telephone, to more modern conceptions such as communication-facilitator or bilingual-bicultural specialist in which interpreters are encouraged to acknowledge their active role. Although this development reflects a move away from conduit models in terms of how interpreters function in their role, conduit thinking often remains as an unquestioned assumption about how human communication works.

Here we suggest that interpreting is essentially communicating and that the cognitive processes required for communicating cannot be understood in terms of a passive, mechanistic conduit model. Rather, communication, and therefore interpreting, is an active process of constructing meaning based on evidence provided by speakers. Critical factors involved in this cognitive model are: (1) the nature of language, especially semantics (the nature of linguistic meaning); (2) production (how thoughts and meanings are expressed through linguistic messages); and 3) comprehension (the process by which we understand what another person means).

On the basis of a cognitively adequate model of language production and comprehension, we propose a cognitive model of interpreting. Further, we explore implications of this model for the preparation of interpreters and for how interpreters function in their daily work.

In Section 2 we review several models of interpreting that represent steps toward this shift in the paradigm of the interpreter's role. We pay special attention to how these models incorporate assumptions about the process of communicating. Our contention is that while interpreting scholars and educators have rejected conduit models of interpreting in favor of models that assume a more active role of the interpreter, they have nevertheless implicitly assumed conduit models of communication. Rejecting a conduit model of interpreting and replacing it with a more sophisticated model that still relies on conduit assumptions about how communication between people is achieved does little to further our understanding of how interpreters achieve success, how they should be trained, and how they should function.

In Section 3 we approach the understanding of communication from a perspective informed by recent findings in the field of cognitive science and cognitive linguistics. We find that concepts that play an important role in the interpreting models discussed in Section 2 reappear here. Finally, in Section 4 we offer some implications of our cognitive model for the field of interpreting and interpreter education.

2.   Interpreting models

We might observe, only half jokingly, that progress in the field of signed language interpreting can be measured in terms of how many models we have seen come and go. Although a relatively young profession, we have witnessed a panoply of models: helper, conduit, sociolinguistic, interactive, communication-facilitator, bilingual-bicultural specialist, and so forth. One driving force that seems to lead to the replacement of one model with another is a desire to rid our models of the interpreter's function of all aspects of conduit thinking. Models that described interpreters as telephones, or that constrained interpreters to not get involved, were replaced with models that accepted, encouraged, and eventually demanded that interpreters become active participants, even allies, with their Deaf consumers. Most of these attempts to eliminate conduit thinking from interpreting models have focused primarily on role models (Frishberg 1986; Roy 1993, 2000). Little attention has been devoted, however, to questioning conduit assumptions that are also presupposed in process models of interpreting.

Our contention is that despite our best efforts to rid the field of it, the conduit model remains, driven underground as interpreting models have focused attention less on the cognitive act of communication and more on political and cultural behaviours of the interpreter. In moving away from conduit models of interpreting to those in which the interpreter takes a more active role, interpreter educators have gradually eliminated any discussion of the cognitive process of interpreting and, more importantly, any discussion of what it means to communicate. Until we once again explicitly address how communication takes place, our models of interpreting run the risk of still being conduit in nature. Interpreters may no longer view themselves as neutral and uninvolved conduits of messages but, we hope to demonstrate, their models of interpreting still implicitly assume that language relies on the neutral encoding and decoding of messages by means of the conduit of words and signs passed between communicative participants.

2.1 A helper model

The helper model is arguably the earliest model of signed language interpreting. As Frishberg (1986) notes, interpreting has always taken place, but interpreters were not compensated for their time, nor did they receive formal training in interpreting. "Often the interpreters were family members, neighbors, or friends who *obliged* a deaf relative or friend by 'pitching in' during a difficult communication situation (1986: 10; emphasis added). The helper model was the norm. It was how Deaf people accessed the hearing world. But, as Roy notes, helping out in this way, while appearing admirable, reflected attitudes that Deaf individuals were not able to take care of their own personal, social or professional business "without the intervention of the helper" (Roy 1993: 139–140).

2.2 A conduit model

With the establishment of the Registry of Interpreters for the Deaf (RID) in 1964, people engaged in interpreting began to take a closer look at the process and at their role as interpreters. This increased awareness signaled the beginning of a shift in paradigm. "Helping out" was no longer always viewed as admirable, but instead as a potential intrusion. Deaf people, the new reasoning assumed, were capable of making their own decisions, and those providing access to communication should do nothing to interfere with that autonomy. Interpreters merely provided a professional service. Quigley and Youngs (1965: 52) note this when they state that "part of the interpreter's training and experience should include some self-discipline so that the interpreter always makes a strong effort to remain detached, neutral, and as completely impersonal and objective as possible." With this shift, the conduit model of interpreting had its beginnings. Solow (1981: ix) describes the interpreter's role as a communication conduit:

> The sign language interpreter acts as a communication link between people, serving only in that capacity. An analogy is in the use of the telephone – the telephone is a link between people that does not exert a personal influence on either. It does, however, influence the ease of communication and speed of the process. If the interpreter can strive to maintain that parallel positive function without losing vital human attributes, then the interpreter renders a professional service.

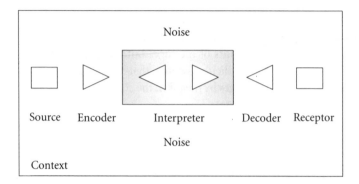

Figure 1. Ingram's semiotic model. Figure adapted from Robert M. Ingram, "A communication model of the interpreting process", *Journal of Rehabilitation of the Deaf, 7*(3), 3–9.

2.3 A semiotic model

While a step forward from the helper model, the conduit model did little to further
our understanding of what an interpreter *does*, that is, how an interpreter interacts
with language. Ingram (1974, 1978) took on this task with his semiotic model of
interpreting.

In Ingram's interpreting model, the interpreter is represented as a channel of
communication in a communication-binding context with a source and a receptor
(Figure 1). The interpreter "must decode, transfer, and re-encode not single, linguistic
messages at a time but a multiplicity of messages in a multiplicity of interwoven codes
with every single act of interpretation" (Ingram 1978:111).

In describing Ingram's model, Stewart, Schein and Cartwright (1998) state:

> A message is first coded for transmission – a process called *encoding*. The *code* may
> be English, ASL, or nonlanguages such as gestures, facial expressions, or grunts.
> The message is then transmitted over a *channel* (e.g., speech or writing). When
> received, it is *decoded* (i.e., put into a form accessible to the receiver). Any signal
> that interferes with transmission of the message is labeled *noise*.... . These are
> concepts familiar to engineers who develop and analyze communication systems.
> (1998:45–46).

2.4 A sociolinguistic model

Cokely (1992) attempted to shift our attention even further away from the conduit
model of interpreting with the publication of his sociolinguistic model of interpreting.
Stewart, Schein and Cartwright (1998: 47) provide a concise summary of Cokely's
sociolinguistic model, noting that it "indirectly implies the presence of a sender
and a receiver of the message. It also treats interpreting as linear, although it likely
involves parallel processing, with some aspects occurring simultaneously rather than

sequentially." As we will see in Section 4, these characteristics mark Cokely's approach as still well within the conduit model of communication.

2.5 A pedagogical model

Colonomos (1992) relies extensively on the work of Seleskovitch (1978) in her model of the interpreting process (Figure 2). The notion of "message" is a critical part of the Colonomos model, and so it deserves our attention here.

According to Colonomos, message "refers to the meaning of the speaker's message, represented through non-linguistic (ideally) means, which has been extracted by the interpreter during the analysis phase of the process. The absence of linguistic symbols frees the interpreter from the constraints of language meanings so that they [sic] may optimally recreate the message using target language forms that most appropriately convey message equivalence" (Colonomos 1992:4).

In other words, Colonomos believes that interpreters work with messages which *contain* the speaker's meaning; interpreters *extract* this meaning and *discard* all of its linguistic trappings, leaving a *formless* meaning which is then used to *recreate* the message in a way that conveys message equivalence. We contend that the underlying metaphor by which Colonomos understands communication is in fact a conduit model.

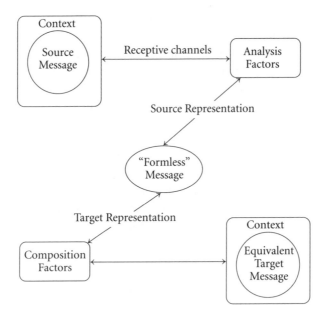

Figure 2. Colonomos's pedagogical model. Figure adapted from Betty Colonomos, workshop handout, © 1992.

2.6 A proposed cognitive model of interpreting[1]

Stewart et al. (1998) discuss what they refer to as "The Cognitive Model of Interpreting" in which the interpreting process is depicted linearly, moving from source
language, through reception and comprehension, analysis and encoding, expression
and evaluation, resulting in an interpreted message in the target language. Their model
is similar to the pedagogical model proposed by Colonomos, "but further simplifies
the process involved in interpreting. The first step of the model assumes that the interpreter understands the language in which the source message is presented. Once
comprehension of the message occurs, the interpreter then analyzes the message to
determine how the meaning will be encoded in the target language" (Stewart et al.
1998: 31–32). Stewart and his colleagues side step the issue of how communication
takes place by assuming that the interpreter comprehends.

2.7 The bilingual-bicultural model

Roy (1993) states that dissatisfaction with the conduit model led to the communication-
facilitation model, which itself gave way in the 1990s to a model of the interpreter as a
bilingual-bicultural specialist. This model was first proposed by Etilvia Arjona, a spoken language interpreter, and Ingram, who emphasize that language and culture are
inseparable: "As such, the translation process is considered as taking place within a sit-
uational/cultural context that is, in itself, an integral part of the process and that must
be considered in order to bridge, in a meaningful manner, this gap that separates both
sender and receptor audiences" (Arjona, in Roy 1993: 36).

   Humphrey and Alcorn (2001: Chapter 8, p. 10) note that within this model
the interpreter assumes responsibility for "cultural and linguistic mediation while
accomplishing speaker goal and maintaining dynamic equivalence." It is, they state,
the preferred theoretical framework from which an interpreter should work.

2.8 Text analysis and discourse analysis models

Recent attempts to elaborate process models of interpreting have incorporated knowledge from text and discourse analysis. Gish (1987) proposes an approach that provides
the interpreter with a set of guidelines, based on strategies for text analysis, for understanding the meaning of the message, the structure of the message, and for making
predictions about the next utterances and the ultimate goals of the speaker.

   For Roy (2000: 122), "the *basic* and *fundamental* interpreting event occurs when
two people who have particular intentions and expectations come together and talk
through an interpreter." This approach leads Roy to adopt a perspective that sees
interpreting as a discourse process, and she suggests that interpreter educators need
to re-examine the nature of communication. In the epilogue to her book, Roy touches
on this topic by introducing the work of Reddy (1979) and suggesting that we consider
the implications of his work for models of interpreting.

2.9 Summary of interpreting models

What we have seen over the last forty years is a slow but steady shift in conceptual paradigm – a shift in role from helper to passive, impartial conduit, and from conduit to active participant with some responsibility for the message.

During this evolution a body of terminology has developed. We now regularly use words such as "encoding" (what Stewart et al. call coding for transmission, as we saw in Section 2.3 above), "channel" (writing, speaking, signing), and "decoding" (what Stewart et al. refer to as putting the message into a form accessible to the receiver). A great deal of attention is given to what the interpreter does with the message, yet surprisingly little attention has been paid to the message itself. In this, interpreter educators have no clear foundation from which to teach.

2.10 The conduit model remains

What we have presented thus far is essentially a history of the field in an attempt to situate signed language interpreting within a contemporary context – one that has rejected the conduit model. While we acknowledge that the field has, indeed, moved away from conduit models of the interpreter role, our understanding of what is involved in interpreting messages remains largely unchanged. We continue to conceive of the interpreting process by means of a conduit model of communication.

In the following sections we suggest that the cognitive processes required for communicating cannot be understood in terms of a passive, mechanistic conduit model. Rather, communication, and therefore interpreting, is an active process of constructing meaning based on evidence provided by speakers. We begin by describing a cognitive model of communication, and then discuss how it informs our understanding of the nature of interpretation.

3. Cognitive models of communication

3.1 Language and communication

Our contention is that interpreting is communicating, and that unless our models of interpreting rest on a scientifically adequate foundation of what communication is and how it is achieved, our models will remain flawed.[2] The first order of business then is to ask: What is communication and how do humans communicate? One answer to that question is provided by Daniel Sperber and Deirdre Wilson in their book *Relevance*:

> How do human beings communicate with one another? For verbal communication at least, there is a sort of folk answer, suggested by a variety of metaphors in everyday use: 'putting one's thoughts into words', 'getting one's ideas across', 'putting one's thoughts down on paper', and so on. These make it sound as if verbal communication were a matter of packing a *content* (yet another metaphor)

into words and sending it off, to be unpacked by the recipient at the other end. The power of these figures of speech is such that one tends to forget that the answer they suggest cannot be true. In writing this book, we have not literally put our thoughts down on paper. What we have put down on paper are little dark marks, a copy of which you are now looking at. As for our thoughts, they remain where they always were, inside our brains.   (Sperber & Wilson 1995: 1)

The metaphors that Sperber and Wilson refer to are discussed at length under the rubric of the *conduit metaphor* (Reddy 1993).[3] According to Reddy, our talk about communication reveals that we conceptualize the process of communication to be one in which: (1) language functions like a conduit, transferring thoughts from one person to another; (2) in writing and speaking, people insert their thoughts or feelings in the words; (3) words accomplish the transfer by containing the thoughts and feelings and conveying them to others; and (4) in listening and reading, people extract the thoughts and feelings once again from the words (Reddy 1993: 170).

In order to investigate the pernicious effects of the conduit metaphor on how we understand human communication to operate, Reddy compares and contrasts the conduit metaphor of communication with what he calls the *toolmakers paradigm*. The *toolmakers paradigm* suggests that, in communicating with one another, we are "like people isolated in slightly different environments."

Imagine, if you will, for sake of the story, a huge compound, shaped like a wagon wheel. Each pie-shaped sector of the wheel is an environment... At the hub of the wheel there is some machinery which can deliver small sheets of paper from one environment to another. Let us suppose that the people in these environments have learned how to use this machinery to exchange crude sets of instructions with one another – instructions for making things helpful in surviving, ...
          (Reddy 1993: 171–172)

For understanding communication, the *toolmakers paradigm* suggests that each of us lives in our own world, and that ultimately no one can totally share in the experiences, thoughts, feelings, and perceptions of another. Reddy calls this "radical subjectivity" (1993: 172). Interpreters are well aware of the need to work from a position of radical subjectivity. We cannot and do not assume that we know what is going on inside the heads of those for whom we interpret. Even though Seleskovitch (1978: 32) says that interpreters are mind-readers, every interpreter knows that she was speaking metaphorically. We make assumptions about what people are meaning, but we do not *hear* their meanings and we cannot read their minds. Oddly, though, our interpreting models often incorporate assumptions about how language works that would make it seem that we do have direct access to people's thoughts.

The *toolmakers paradigm* is Reddy's model of how human communication *does* occur. In the toolmakers' compound, people have reasons for communicating with others. Since they do not have direct access to those people due to the compound walls, their only means of sharing their thoughts is through the machinery in the hub. But notice how communication must occur. A person in one sector, wishing to share something – for the purpose of the story we will call it some kind of tool, but recognize that it corresponds to a thought or intention – with a person in another sector, must make some marks on a piece of paper. The paper, but *not the tool itself* (that is, not the thought or meaning itself), is placed in the hub and transferred to another person.

What must the second person do in order to "understand" the first person – that is, in order to use the tool? The second person must first *construct the tool*. Notice what this means. The first person built her tool for certain purposes, with her particular intentions, and out of materials which were only available to her (recall the assumption of radical subjectivity). The second person, who must now make her own tool on the basis of instructions from the first person, does not share the first's purposes or intentions, and does not have access to the same materials. She receives only instructions for constructing a tool, hence the name *toolmakers paradigm*.

So the second person goes about building a tool. When she is finished she is left with a tool that probably does not look exactly like the first person's tool, and she has to figure out why and how this person used the tool, why she would want to share it with others. According to Reddy, this process is inherently active – the people involved are *actively constructing meaning*, quite literally *making sense*. The people involved in this process of communicating never actually share their tools with one another. All they share are the pieces of paper. It is on the basis of these metaphorical scraps of paper that people make sense of others, not through direct access to their thoughts but by means of "inference about each other and each other's environments" (Reddy 1993:174). Seleskovitch's metaphorical mind-reading is replaced with the cognitive ability of *making an inference based on perceptible evidence*.

At this point, we need to label two items in the story so that we can see how they are related to interpreting models. We must recognize first that the scraps of paper in Reddy's story correspond to the perceptible signals, the forms that are sent when people communicate – the "evidence". For spoken languages, these signals are the sounds that people utter, while for signed languages they are the optical signals that result from the movements of our hands and bodies.

We are often told as interpreting students, and we tell those who ask about the nature of the interpreting task, that interpreters deal not with words but with meanings. The task of the interpreter, Seleskovitch and Colonomos, among others, tell us, is to discard the form and retain the meaning. While it is true that interpreters work with meaning and not form, we cannot stop here. We must ask: how do interpreters gain access to meaning? How is meaning conveyed in form? We hope that our answer is now becoming clear: it is not. Meaning is not conveyed in form. Meaning is inferred from, constructed on the basis of, form.[4]

How is this different from the conduit understanding of how communication works? Returning to the toolmakers' compound, Reddy examines the process of communication as the conduit metaphor would see it, suggesting that "what the conduit metaphor does is permit the exchange of materials from the environments, including the actual constructs themselves. In our story, we would have to imagine a marvelous technological duplicating machine located in the hub" (Reddy 1993:174).

Instead of sending instructions for the construction of meanings, the conduit metaphor tells us that communication is achieved by actually passing meanings from one person to another. How is this achieved? What is the marvelous technological duplicating machine? It is language – rather, it is our conduit-influenced understanding of what language is and how it works. According to the conduit metaphor, words contain meanings. In speaking or signing, we put our meanings into words and messages; in understanding, we extract the meaning.

The terms that are often used for this process of "putting meaning into words" and "extracting meaning from words" – terms which are commonly used but rarely critically questioned by interpreters and interpreter educators – are *encoding* and *decoding*. As we have seen in Section 1, and as we just pointed out, interpreters are also concerned with the distinction between *form* and *meaning* or *message*. We hope to have begun to make clear the need to question the assumption that meaning is conveyed in form, that words or signs contain or hold meaning. We now need to explore a bit further the notion of message.

The notion of "message" is rife with confusion in the interpreting literature. Many interpreting texts forgo a definition or description of message, instead beginning with a description of how it is encoded and decoded. Some explain the extra-linguistic components of a message, without stating what a message is. Others simply dive in and describe how an interpreter accesses a message.

Humphrey and Alcorn (2001) discuss what they intend with the word "meaning" in their introductory chapter:

> Communicators must construct messages in a grammatically correct way in order to make sense. However, after the meaning being conveyed has been extracted from a sentence and understood by the listener, the specific grammatical structure no longer serves any purpose. This is because grammar is not needed to retain the information carried in an utterance. While interpreters must be fluent in their grammatical use of both languages they work in, *they work predominantly in the pragmatic realm to uncover the meaning of the message and the purpose intended by the sender.*
> (2001: Chapter 1, pp. 7–8)

Clearly this statement is laden with conduit assumptions. Meanings are "carried in" sentences, and listeners "extract" or "uncover" these meanings. Grammar plays only a minor role in conveying meaning, and it is categorically distinct from pragmatics – assumptions that we will reject in Section 4. Finally, it is assumed that interpreters have direct access to the purposes and intentions of the speaker (the sender). Nowhere are meanings constructed or intentions inferred. The meanings of messages and the intentions of speakers, it seems, are right there in the words waiting for the interpreter to uncover and extract.

Stewart, Schein and Cartwright also refer to the notion of "message" if somewhat indirectly. They state that messages can be divided into four parts: purpose, content, form and paralinguistics. "The content can include almost anything, although most can be subsumed under (1) information and description, (2) imperatives, (3) emotional expressions, (4) questions, and (5) casual comments" (Stewart et al. 1998:38).

While little is said about message or meaning, much has been written about how an interpreter accesses it. Humphrey and Alcorn (2001) refer to this as "deriving meaning". They state that if a person is "linguistically fluent" in the language they no longer need to "listen/watch each word/sign in a focused manner to determine meaning". This allows the interpreter to "analyze the context in which the exchange is happening and the way it influences the communication dynamics; analyze the incoming message at a deeper (textual) level; and make a switch into the target language without losing meaning or speaker goals" (Humphrey & Alcorn 2001:Chapter 9, p. 5).

We have clearly bypassed the notion of message here and instead moved on to aspects of the communication that can only be conveyed accurately in the target language if comprehension of the message in the source language has occurred. Comprehension of the message is assumed. The notion of the "message" appears to be uncontroversial, barely worthy of mention.

What exactly do interpreters believe the message is, then, and how do we access it? The problem arises from the misapplication of *information theory* (Shannon & Weaver 1949) to the understanding of communication by means of natural language. Once again, Reddy demonstrates how a misconception of what the term "message" means, when combined with the conduit metaphor, can lead to a total breakdown in our understanding of how communication works.

In order to understand how interpreters and interpreting models get into trouble with the concept of message, we start with yet another example from Reddy. Consider the word "poem" in the following sentences (Reddy 1993:178):

(1)   The poem was almost illegible.

(2)   The poem has five lines and forty words.

(3)   The poem is unrhymed.

Clearly, in these uses, "poem" refers to an actual text token, a signal which is legible or not, with countable words having language specific forms which can rhyme with each other, and so forth. Now consider the next three sentences (Reddy 1993:178):

(4)   Donne's poem is very logical.

(5)   That poem is so completely depressing.

(6)   You know his poem is too obscene for children.

Here, "poem" refers not to actual texts or signals, but to the "concepts and emotions assembled in the reading of a text" (Reddy 1993:178). In fact, the term "reading" here captures the point we are trying to make nicely. The word "poem" has multiple meanings in English: it can refer either to the signals of communication, or the meanings that people construct, their "reading" of a text.

The same problems arise in the use and understanding of "message" (Reddy 1993:183):

(7)   I got your message (MESSAGE₁), but had no time to read it.

(8)   Okay, John, I get the message (MESSAGE₂); let's leave him alone.

The confusion arises because interpreting theory, like information theory, does not clearly distinguish between a set of signals (MESSAGE₁) and the meaning that we assign to or construct from those signals (MESSAGE₂). As Reddy points out, "for conduit-metaphor thinking, in which we send and receive the MESSAGE₂ within the MESSAGE₁, the ambiguity is trivial. But for theory based totally on the notion that the 'message' (MESSAGE₂) is never *sent* anywhere, this choice of words leads to the collapse of the paradigm" (Reddy 1993: 183).

For interpreters the problem is compounded even further because we are keenly aware that we must work not only with forms (MESSAGES₁) in two languages, but with meanings (MESSAGES₂). Rather than leading us to see the damaging effects of conduit-metaphor thinking in our understanding of language more clearly, however, it has most often led interpreters to even further confusion about the nature of language.

The confusion is brought about by the polysemy, or multiplicity of related meanings, of the term "message". But polysemy is a natural condition of all language. In the case of "poem", polysemy leads from POEM₁ "an actual text" to POEM₂ "the meaning of the poem". This polysemy is based on metonymy. Metonymy is a type of meaning extension in which, when two entities frequently occur together in our experience, the name of one is used to refer to the other. The same metonymic process is surely what led from "message" being used to refer to the meaning of an utterance to also being used to refer to the signal that conveys that message. Notice, however, that this metonymic extension is intimately tied to the conduit metaphor. It is nearly impossible to explain the semantic extension without relying on the conduit metaphor, as we have illustrated in saying that the signal "conveys that message". If we were to attempt to express this in a way that does not rely on the conduit metaphor, we would have to use an entirely unwieldy expression, such as "the signal which the person receives and then uses, along with her background knowledge, to construct a meaning which she then infers was intended by the speaker who produced the signal".

We are not suggesting that such wording should be used in a zealous attempt to eradicate conduit metaphor expressions from everyday language. The use of conduit metaphor expressions in our natural language is perfectly acceptable. As interpreters, however, we must guard against believing that these expressions portray how language actually works. We will return to this point in Section 4, where we explore the ways in which the unquestioned acceptance of conduit metaphor thinking about language has pervaded interpreting models.

3.2 Cognitive science and communication

If human communication via language does not work as the conduit metaphor suggests, how does it work? How does modern linguistic theory explain the toolmakers paradigm? What do people do when they use and understand language?

To explore this, we turn to a body of research in the field of cognitive linguistics. The cognitive approach to language makes a number of assumptions about what language is and how language works that are radically different than those made in more commonly-known theories. For interpreters who are attempting to throw off the veil of the conduit metaphor and better understand what they do when working across languages and cultures, we believe that cognitive linguistics offers a far better framework.

Mark Turner, a cognitive linguist and professor of English, says this about how language works:

> In order to understand, we must bring to bear elaborate and detailed conceptual knowledge not referred to in the expression. This is the common situation of all language. Expressions do not mean; they are prompts for us to construct meanings. In no sense is the meaning of an utterance "right there in the words". When we understand an utterance, we in no sense are understanding "just what the words say"; the words themselves say nothing independent of the richly detailed knowledge and powerful cognitive processes we bring to bear.
>
> (Turner 1991:206)

Clearly, the cognitive linguistic approach to language does not accept conduit-metaphor thinking: words and expressions do not contain meanings, but instead they serve as prompts, as cues, for the construction of meaning. In explaining the process of communicating via language, cognitive linguistics does not assume a *code model* in which communication is achieved by encoding and decoding messages. Rather, it works from an *inferential model* in which communication is achieved by producing and interpreting evidence. As Sperber and Wilson (1995:12–13) note, "inferential and decoding processes are quite different. An *inferential process* starts from a set of premises and results in a set of conclusions which follow logically from, or are at least warranted by, the premises. A *decoding process* starts from a signal and results in the recovery of a message which is associated to the signal by an underlying code." Models of communication that rely on the conduit metaphor assume that language encodes meanings, and that understanding is the mechanical process of decoding. Models of communication that reject conduit thinking recognize instead that comprehending language is a process of constructing meaning, arriving at conclusions of what someone's meaning and intentions might be on the basis of the perceptible evidence that they produce – the sounds or the signs that they make when they use language.

3.3 Cognitive linguistics and interpreting

Our central claim is that while the field of interpreting has moved to reject conduit models of how the interpreter should function, our models of interpreting continue to rely on an understanding of language that implicitly assumes a conduit model of communication. In Section 3.1 we offered a first look at what a cognitive model of communication, which explicitly rejects conduit thinking, would look like. Here, we explore in a bit more depth what cognitive approaches to language have to offer the development of a cognitive model of interpreting.

A full exploration of the linguistic underpinnings of our proposed cognitive model of interpreting cannot be provided in this chapter. Readers interested in learning more about cognitive linguistics are referred to the work of Ronald Langacker (1987, 1991a, 1991b, 2000). For now, we want to address two questions that are essential to interpreting: what is meaning, and what is grammar.

The cognitive perspective is an alternative to the generative approach to language. Noam Chomsky, who pioneered the generative approach in his classic book *Syntactic Structures,* defined language in this way: "I will consider a *language* to be a set (finite or infinite) of sentences, each finite in length and constructed out of a finite set of elements" (1957: 13). Thus, generative grammar sees language as a device that *generates* grammatical sentences: "Assuming the set of grammatical sentences of English to be given, we now must ask what sort of device can produce this set" (Chomsky 1957: 18). For Chomsky, the answer was that the device must be some kind of mental organ, a language device that provided this grammatical ability, utterly distinct from other, more general cognitive abilities. On this point we will disagree with Chomsky. The difference in starting points – language as a grammar-generating device or language as a cognitive activity – is essential for interpreters.

Within the generative approach, meaning and grammar are absolutely distinct. Grammar does not in any way depend on meaning. As Chomsky put it, "the notion of 'grammatical' cannot be identified with 'meaningful' or 'significant' in any semantic sense. ... any search for a semantically based definition of 'grammaticalness' will be futile" (1957: 15). Chomsky demonstrated the autonomy of meaning and grammar with his famous sentence "Colorless green ideas sleep furiously" which, he claimed, was grammatical and yet meaningless.

Although the linguistic research of Chomsky, his students, and the many scholars who now work in the generative grammar tradition has evolved in complex ways, we would suggest that these basic claims – that the unique mental ability of language is distinct from other cognitive abilities, that grammar and meaning are unrelated – have become firmly embedded in the subconscious of many language practitioners such as interpreters.

The cognitive linguistic approach considers language to have two basic functions, "a *semiological function* allowing thoughts to be symbolized by means of sounds, gestures, or writing, as well as an *interactive function*, embracing communication, expressiveness, manipulation, and social communion" (Langacker 1998: 1). Cognitive linguistics challenges both of the major assumptions of generative grammar. It does not assume that language is a unique mental organ; rather, it claims that language is "neither self-contained nor describable without essential reference to cognitive processing" (Langacker 1991a: 1). Further, in the cognitive approach grammar is not regarded as independent of meaning. All of language – the lexicon, morphology, and syntax – is seen as inherently symbolic, having both form and meaning. Even the most abstract grammatical functions in language are regarded as pairings of form and meaning in cognitive linguistics.

Within the cognitive linguistic approach, meaning is equated with conceptualization. This *cognitive semantics* "posits a gradation between semantics and pragmatics, and also between linguistic and general knowledge. It views expressions as evoking (rather than containing) meanings, which emerge via an elaborate process of *meaning construction* drawing on all available resources – linguistic, psychological, and contextual" (Langacker 1998: 3).

Already we begin to see how cognitive linguistics explicitly challenges the conduit model of communication. Within the generative approach, the grammar of a language is seen as a device for generating the grammatical (regardless of whether they are meaningful) sentences of a language. Cognitive linguistics rejects this process metaphor and instead conceives of the grammar of a language as a **structured inventory of conventional linguistic units.** Each term in this definition is chosen carefully and must be understood in its precise technical sense: what is a linguistic unit, what makes a linguistic unit conventional or unconventional, what is an inventory, and how is it structured? This definition is important for interpreters because it views language as an inventory of symbolic resources shared by users of the language. Making use of these linguistic resources is what users of a language do when they express ideas, emotions, and feelings. This is a problem-solving activity on the part of the language user, who constructs expressions using the linguistic resources at her disposal, and on the part of the receiver, who constructs meanings on the basis of the cues provided by the speaker.

What does it mean to say that expressions evoke, rather than contain, meaning? We can demonstrate with a simple example. Consider the English expression *jar lid*. This is regarded in cognitive grammar as a minimal construction, an assembly of two component structures, *jar* and *lid*. Speakers of English know that there are many such noun-noun constructions, such as *garage door* or *table cloth*. This knowledge is reflected in speaker's grammars by means of *schematized expressions*, which can be thought of as "templates abstracted from a set of complex expressions to embody whatever commonality is inherent in them" (Langacker 2000: 110). That is, as we see specific expressions such as *pencil sharpener* or *letter carrier* used, we form generalizations that are then used to produce yet other expressions.

Speakers of English make use of their knowledge of these *constructional schemas* when they create a novel expression. The noun-noun constructional schema, for example, sanctions novel expressions such as *pencil sharpener, aqua farm, sewer pipe,* or *Pacific rim.*[5] The constructional schema provides the template for the construction, specifying the component structures (two nouns) as well as a composite structure that integrates the meanings of the two component structures into a *compositional value*.

The critical fact emphasized in a cognitive approach is that the compositional value of such novel expressions is merely latent: neither the constructional schema nor the component structures provide sufficient information to understand the expression's full contextual meaning. The constructional schema tells us only that a *pencil sharpener* is something that sharpens pencils. But this tells us very little about how this expression is actually understood, its conventional meaning in English being a very particular type of device that mechanically sharpens pencils.

In fact, sometimes the compositional value tells us very little about the conventional, contextual meaning. How many English speakers, on first hearing the expression *aqua farm*, know what it means? In our experience, almost no native speakers of English do understand the term on first hearing it. Their linguistic competence allows them to derive all that the constructional schema and word meanings provide, and when pressed they offer such anomalous meanings as, "It's a place where people grow water?" This is all that the language gives us. Meaning is clearly not encoded or contained in the words *aqua* and *farm*.

The implication for interpreters is that *what we are here describing is an essential fact about linguistic communication*. It is rare to find in any human language cases where knowledge of a constructional schema and the meaning of its component structures tells us everything we need in order to understand the conventional, fully contextualized meaning of an expression. Linguistic expressions are always vastly under-specified. This is in the very nature of language. And it is true whatever the size of the linguistic construction – multimorphemic words, simple expressions or phrases, sentences or utterances, and discourse. In the words of cognitive grammar, "novel expressions are not created by the linguistic system per se, but rather by the *speaker*, drawing on all available resources" (Langacker 2000: 111; emphasis added). Grammar is not constructive; speakers and hearers, or signers and watchers, are.

Notice that this conclusion derives from the cognitive view of language that we have been describing in this chapter. If we were to adopt, either implicitly or explicitly, a conduit model of language in which meaning is contained in words, then the full compositional value of an expression is simply the mechanical integration of the meanings of the component words. For example, Lawrence (1995) falls prey to a conduit model of language when she describes the differences between English and ASL and the importance of this difference in interpreting:

> "Couching" or "nesting" is when background or contextual information is added to a concept to make it clear. A particular adjustment occurs by virtue of the differences between the two languages. English is considered a "low-context" language. This means that with only a limited amount of information, speakers of English understand one another. There is a lot of implied information and only a minimal amount of context is required for understanding. In contrast, ASL is considered a "high context" language. This means that information is not easily implied and in fact, must be explicit. If an idea is presented in English which is "low context" in nature and it must be presented in ASL which is "high context" in nature, the "couching" or "nesting" of background information must be added to make the idea equally clear in ASL. This is probably one of the hardest features to identify in an ASL text because the idea is presented in a way natural to ASL. It is only when one focuses on how that same concept would be presented in English that we can identify the discourse as "couched". ... English examples of the need

to use this feature abound. Some examples might include the ideas of *primitive cultures, aqua farms,* or *the Pacific rim.*   (Lawrence 1995:212)

The terms "high-context" and "low-context" come from Edward T. Hall (e.g., Hall 1977), who uses them not to characterize entire languages and cultures as uniformly one or the other, but as tendencies which can vary according to situation, setting, participants, and so forth.[6] Lawrence also mischaracterizes the notion of "information" in this passage. It is not the case that ASL only permits utterances which "explicitly" state meanings. ASL users certainly can imply, suggest, equivocate, and otherwise state meanings in subtle, ambiguous, obscure, and other non-explicit ways. High- and low-context simply were intended to suggest that in certain uses, meaning resided primarily in the linguistically-encoded utterance (low-context) and in other uses meanings depended much more on context (high-context).

What is going on in Lawrence's example of "aqua farms" or "Pacific rim" is not a matter of whether English relies on "a lot of implied information" while in ASL information "is not easily implied." The difficulty for interpreters posed by expressions such as these is best understood as a matter of compositionality. All languages vary in the degree to which expressions are fully compositional. Full compositionality, in which meanings depend only on knowledge of component words and a constructional schema, is quite uncharacteristic of normal language use. The full, contextualized meaning of aqua farm is not given in the words, but neither is the full, contextualized meaning of pencil sharpener. The difference between aqua farm and pencil sharpener is not a matter of English being a high or low context language. Rather, it is that pencil sharpener is a conventional expression, and its conventional meaning now includes pragmatic or contextual aspects not included in the meaning of pencil, in sharp, in the verbalizing affix *-en*, in the nominalizing suffix *-er*, or in the constructional schema itself. The reason native speakers cannot construct an acceptable meaning of aqua farm is not because English is low or high context, or because English is implicit or explicit. It is simply because the term aqua farm is not yet conventionally understood in all of its contextual fullness. Speakers have access only to the vastly under-specific meanings available in the component words and in the very general meaning of the constructional schema.

We might note that the same can be said of ASL. A construction in ASL such as FEEL-EMPTY, which sometimes translates as 'oblivious-to', and in other discourse contexts as 'automatically, without conscious thought', cannot be understood by reference only to the meanings of the component words and the constructional schema verb+adjective. Here too, explanations that rely on describing ASL, as Lawrence does, as a "high context language" in which "information is not easily implied and in fact must be explicit" miss the point. There is nothing "explicit" about the meaning of FEEL-EMPTY as compared with *aqua farm*; both are in fact normal linguistic expressions, in that their full contextual meaning depends greatly on knowledge of their conventional meaning and not just their component parts.

4.   Implications

The problem is not interpreting. It is not that English is indirect and that ASL is direct as Humphrey and Alcorn (2001) and others would have us view it. It is not that translation equivalents are hard to find (indeed, they are, but that pales in comparison to the real problem). It is not that ASL is direct and elaborative and relies on expansion techniques while English is indirect and non-elaborative (Lawrence 1995; Humphrey & Alcorn 2001). The problem is that our models of interpreting simply do not do justice to the act of communicating. In trivializing the cognitive work that is done whenever we communicate with another we fail to prepare interpreters for the awesome and mysterious task that they perform: speaking for another.

As we have maintained throughout, the task of communicating is in construct-ing meaning, both in production and reception. The role of interpreter education programs now becomes clearer. Programs must address not only competency in two languages and the development of interpreting skills such as the use of memory and processing, they must also concern themselves with the general knowledge of their stu-dents. Interpreters should be encouraged to have at the very least a broad liberal arts background. Only with this broad background can they hope to understand and in-terpret the content with which they are faced. As Mark Turner so aptly puts it, which was mentioned earlier, "in order to understand, we must bring to bear elaborate and detailed conceptual knowledge not referred to in the expression" (1991: 206). Without a breadth and depth of knowledge, interpreters cannot construct meaning.

Another implication for both professional interpreters and interpreter educators concerns how we evaluate interpreting. The currently popular model relies on *error analysis* or *miscue analysis*. According to one proponent of miscue analysis, the process works like this:

> For an interpretation to be considered accurate or appropriate, the meaning of the source language message must be determined by the interpreter and conveyed in such a way that that meaning is intelligible in the target language. The very nature of the interpreting process makes it possible to determine accuracy or appropriateness by comparing the interpreted tL [target language] text with the source language text it is supposed to convey. … Comparison of sL and tL texts will necessitate an accurate understanding of the meaning of the sL text and the syntactic devices used to convey that meaning, as well as an accurate understanding of the meaning of the tL text and the syntactic devices used to convey that meaning. Only then is it possible to determine the extent to which equivalence in meaning has been achieved in the tL text.
>
> (Cokely 1992: 73)

The process being described here is akin to what a chemist would do when determining the weight of a compound: place a known quantity of weight on one side of a scale, the compound on the other side, and remove or add the compound as necessary to make the scale come into balance. But meaning is not so neat; communication is not chemistry. Meanings across languages cannot be weighed on a balance to determine objective equivalence.

The problem with this model for communication is that we do not have direct access to *the meaning* (as if there is only one!) of the source text and, if we are third-party evaluators of an interpreted text, neither do we have direct access to *the meaning* of the target text.

An even more profound problem lies in the basic premise of error analysis: it assumes successful communication and therefore requires only that failure to communicate be explained. A cognitive model approaches communication with the opposite assumption: if communication depends on the construction of meaning from cues, and if communicators do not have direct access to others' meanings or intentions, then what we should expect is partial communication. Successful communication requires our attention and explanation. In Reddy's words:

> In terms of the conduit metaphor, what requires explanation is failure to communicate. Success appears to be automatic. But if we think in terms of the toolmakers paradigm, our expectation is precisely the opposite. Partial miscommunication, or divergence of readings from a single text, are not aberrations. They are tendencies inherent in the system, which can only be counteracted by continuous effort and by large amounts of verbal interaction. In this view, things will naturally be scattered unless we expend the energy to gather them. (1993:175)

We see then that error analysis, by focusing on identifying and explaining failure, operates from a conduit model.[7] We propose that a more appropriate model for the evaluation of interpreting would be one that examines successful interpreting, that is, *success analysis*. By problematizing interpreting as successful communicating, we will learn more about how the interpreting process works than we ever will by assuming success and focusing only on failure to communicate.

A curious situation has arisen in the field of interpreting. At the same time that interpreters are advocating for their active participation and against outdated role models that see them as mere conduits, our models of communication objectify meaning as something that exists "out there" in the external world and thus downplay the active labor that we all undertake when we *make sense* with others. Once again, Reddy eloquently recognizes the implications:

> To the extent that the conduit metaphor does see communication as requiring some slight expenditure of energy, it localizes this expenditure almost totally in the speaker or writer. The function of the reader or listener is trivialized. The radical subjectivist paradigm, on the other hand, makes it clear that readers and listeners [and, we might add, interpreters] face a difficult and highly creative task of reconstruction and hypothesis testing. (1993:186)

We contend that because interpreters have relied on inadequate models of language and meaning, they have fundamentally misunderstood the process of communication and of interpretation. In an effort to address the real problems of understanding a person in one language and expressing what (we think) she meant to a third person in another language, interpreters have turned to models of the interpreter's role. It is as if interpreters, being highly sensitive to nuances of meaning, are aware that a problem faces them in their work to make sense across individuals and across languages. But when they turn to models of language, they are told that, if they will simply discard form and extract the internal meaning of messages, the problem does not exist. Faced with this predicament, interpreters develop new models of their role, hoping that this will resolve the problem. We suggest that the solution is for interpreters to discard the assumptions that we make about how language works. Only if we have an accurate understanding of how humans communicate through language, of how we understand each other, can interpreters approach their task fully aware of the essentially creative nature of what they are doing. In all cases, interpreters construct meanings, make sense, and hope that the sense they made somewhat captures the sense intended.

This does not mean that the interpreter's role is unimportant, and indeed we might ask what a cognitive model of interpreting suggests for the interpreter's role. If meaning is always constructed, if interpreters make meaning in the creative cognitive task we have been describing, then can the interpreter ever be neutral? Isn't all meaning construction necessarily coloured by our personal subjectivity?

The question is not new to the field of interpreting. Interpreter educators have written about the impossibility of achieving neutrality. Metzger (1999:23) writes, for example, that "[i]nterpreters have expressed the goal of not influencing the form, content, structure, and outcomes of interactive discourse, but the reality is that interpreters, by their very presence, influence the interaction".

Similarly, Baker-Shenk (1991), discussing the machine or conduit model that was for so many the prevailing approach to interpreting, points out that the model is "terribly naive. It is based on the false assumption that the interpreter can somehow avoid power, avoid taking a stand, and avoid influencing the outcome of the interaction" (1991:133).

We do not disagree in principle with any of these statements. It is unquestionably true that the interpreter is a significant presence in any interpreted discourse and that interpreters have access to tremendous power. We would only point out that what these and other authors appear to be addressing is more an issue of *social neutrality*: the impossibility of avoiding power, of taking a stand, and the fact that as parties to an interaction we influence that interaction.

What we have focused on is the issue of *communicative neutrality*, of whether there exists some meaning contained within words and expressions, which interpreters can somehow divine, extract, uncover, discover, or derive by "message analysis". We suggest that there is not an objective reality to socially communicated meaning, that all such communication operates in the face of radical subjectivity. If interpreters do engage in message analysis, the goal is not to extract meaning from words, it is to *put meaning into words*.

Notice, however, that it is entirely possible to advocate for the impossibility of social neutrality while still believing in a conduit model of meaning. It is here, we believe, that interpreters and interpreter educators have stopped mid-stream. The danger is not in recognizing that social neutrality is a myth, it is rejecting the myth without a firm understanding of what human communication is.

Rejecting the conduit model of communication in favour of a cognitive model requires interpreters to acknowledge that social neutrality is an impossibility. Communication is fundamentally social. Whenever humans come together and communicate, they are always trying to accomplish *something*, and that something usually reflects their social status. In saying that meaning does not have an objective existence, that it is constructed, we are really saying that it is co-constructed in dynamic interplay with our interlocutors. The conduit model is not only wrong when it claims that words contain meaning, but also when it suggests that meanings are sent and received in a strict "I give you my meaning, you receive my meaning, and then you give me your meaning in return" fashion.

If interpreters do not understand the dual problem of social neutrality and communication neutrality, they are doomed to two destinies. In one, they remain unaware of their social presence in interpreted interaction and unconscious of their acts of meaning construction. They believe that they are indeed mere neutral conduits of meaning, and they are blind to their role in the communicative situation. Such interpreters function in an unconscious, machine-like manner. They are ineffective as interpreters and are probably not even aware of it.

In the second alternative, interpreters reject the myth of social neutrality, but they nevertheless remain unconscious of the fact that they are engaged in socially constructing meaning. Instead, they believe that they have direct access to meaning, that as interpreters they are able to analyze messages to uncover and extract meaning and thus know others' intentions. These interpreters face the danger of even more egregiously abusing their power because they believe that if social neutrality is not possible, then they may become as involved as they like as omniscient allies. If this is taking place, and undoubtedly in some cases it is, how odd that our profession should have come full circle to such a paternalistic stance.

A third alternative is possible. Interpreters can become aware of their biases, aware of their power, and aware of their creative acts of meaning co-construction, and in so doing move towards an active and conscious neutrality. A cognitive model of interpreting helps interpreters to understand the true nature of how language works. In so doing, it also can guide the interpreter in charting a course through the pitfalls of maintaining social neutrality.

5.   A conclusion

The picture that the cognitive model thus paints is of an active interpreter, not one with direct access to the meanings and intentions of others, but of a maker of meaning on the basis of the cues provided by others. But the meanings made are the interpreter's own, not the product of an extractive process but of a creative, constructive meaning-making process. This requires a fully conscious, thinking interpreter. Further, because the interpreter is not only actively constructing meaning (this is unavoidable–it is simply the way communication really works), and is fully aware that she is constructing meaning, she can be more sensitive to the problem of her own social status. In fact, we would go so far as to suggest that the cognitive model of interpreting permits interpreters to break through the impossibility of achieving neutrality. If we accept the position that the interpreter, by her very presence, influences an interaction, then neutrality is by definition impossible. But this precludes any possibility of interpreting. Interpreters can never *not* be a part of the communicative setting. A more reasonable goal of achieving neutrality is for interpreters to recognize their role in making meaning. Once interpreters accept that they are makers of their own meaning, and not conveyers of discovered meaning, the goal of achieving neutrality becomes one of constantly monitoring their own understanding and taking ownership of it. When interpreters adopt this model, the enormous task of interpreting becomes at once more daunting and more rewarding.

Notes

1. See also Russell, this volume, for further discussion of cognitive aspects of the interpreting process.

2. Setton (1999) takes much the same approach, adopting a cognitive-pragmatic model of interpreting that draws heavily from cognitive semantics, speech-act theory, and relevance theory.

3. The first edition of Reddy's article appeared in 1979.

4. See Janzen (this volume, Chapters 1 and 4) for additional discussion of the relationship between form and meaning in the interpreting context.

5. We are assuming here that *aqua* and *Pacific* function here as nouns.

6. To get a better sense of what Hall meant by high-context versus low-context, consider the following: "A high-context (HC) communication or message is one in which most of the information is either in the physical context or internalized in the person, while very little is in the coded, explicit, transmitted part of the message. A low-context (LC) communication is just the opposite; i.e., the mass of information is vested in the explicit code. Twins who have grown up together can and do communicate more economically (HC) than two lawyers in a courtroom during a trial (LC)" (Hall 1977:91).
It seems to us that Lawrence has misunderstood the meaning of "explicit" in Hall's characterization of high-context and low-context. What this passage makes clear is that by "explicit" Hall is referring to the transmitted linguistic code. It is also obvious that Hall does not regard languages as HC or LC, as Lawrence seems to think. For example, it is entirely possible that the twins in their HC communication and the lawyers in their LC communication *are all speaking English*.

7. See Leeson (this volume, Chapter 3) for further, detailed discussion of error analysis versus meticulous strategizing on the part of the interpreter.

References

Baker-Shenk, Charlotte (1991). The interpreter: Machine, advocate, or ally. In Jean Plant-Moeller (Ed.), *Expanding Horizons: Proceedings of the 1991 RID Convention* (pp. 120–140). Silver Spring, MD: RID Publications.

Chomsky, Noam (1957). *Syntactic Structures*. The Hague: Mouton.

Cokely, Dennis (1992). *Interpreting: A Sociolinguistic Model*. Burtonsville, MD: Linstok Press.

Colonomos, Betty (1992). Processes in interpreting and transliterating: Making them work for you. Workshop handout: Front Range Community College, Westminster, Colorado.

Frishberg, Nancy (1986). *Interpreting: An Introduction*. Silver Spring, MD: Registry of Interpreters for the Deaf.

Geertz, Clifford (1973). *The Interpretation of Cultures*: New York: Basic Books.

Gish, Sandra (1987). I understood all of the words, but I missed the point: A goal-to-detail/detail-to-goal strategy for text analysis. In Marina L. McIntire (Ed.), *New Dimensions in Interpreter Education, Curriculum, and Instruction*. Silver Spring, MD: RID Publications.

Hall, Edward T. (1977). *Beyond Culture*. Garden City, New York: Anchor Books.

Humphrey, Janice H., & Bob J. Alcorn (2001). *So You Want to Be an Interpreter?: An Introduction to Sign Language Interpreting* (3rd ed.). Amarillo, TX: H & H Publishers.

Ingram, Robert M. (1974). A communication model of the interpreting process. *Journal of Rehabilitation of the Deaf, 7* (3), 3–9.

Ingram, Robert M. (1978). Sign language interpretation and general theories of language, interpretation and communication. In David Gerver & H. Wallace Sinaiko (Eds.), *Language Interpretation and Communication* (pp. 109–118). New York: Plenum Press.

Langacker, Ronald W. (1987). *Foundations of Cognitive Grammar: Volume I, Theoretical Foundations*. Stanford: Stanford University Press.

Langacker, Ronald W. (1991a). *Concept, Image, and Symbol: The Cognitive Basis of Grammar*. Berlin: Mouton de Gruyter.

Langacker, Ronald W. (1991b). *Foundations of Cognitive Grammar: Volume II, Descriptive Application*. Stanford: Stanford University Press.

Langacker, Ronald W. (1998). Conceptualization, symbolization and grammar. In Michael Tomasello (Ed.), *The New Psychology of Language: Cognitive and Functional Approaches to Language Structure* (pp. 1–40). Mahwah, NJ: Erlbaum.

Langacker, Ronald W. (2000). *Grammar and Conceptualization*. Berlin: Mouton de Gruyter.

Lawrence, Shelley (1995). Interpreter discourse: English to ASL expansion. In Elizabeth A. Winston (Ed.), *Mapping our Course: A Collaborative Venture, Proceedings of the Tenth National Convention, Conference of Interpreter Trainers, October 26–29, 1994* (pp. 205–214). North Carolina: Conference of Interpreter Trainers.

Metzger, Melanie (1999). *Sign Language Interpreting: Deconstructing the Myth of Neutrality*. Washington, DC: Gallaudet University Press.

Quigley, Stephen P., & Joseph P. Youngs (1965). *Interpreting for Deaf People, A Report of a Workshop on Interpreting*. Washington, DC: U.S. Government Printing Office.

Reddy, Michael (1979). The conduit metaphor: A case of frame conflict in our language about language. In Andrew Ortony (Ed.), *Methphor and Thought* (pp. 284–324). Cambridge: Cambridge University Press.

Reddy, Michael (1993). The conduit metaphor: A case of frame conflict in our language about language. In A. Ortony (Ed.), *Metaphor and Thought* (2nd ed.) (pp. 164–201). Cambridge: Cambridge University Press.

Roy, Cynthia B. (1993). The problem with definitions, descriptions and the role of metaphors of interpreters. *Journal of Interpretation (RID)*, 6 (1), 127–154.

Roy, Cynthia B. (2000). *Interpreting as a Discourse Process*. New York: Oxford University Press.

Seleskovitch, Danica (1978). *Interpreting for International Conferences*. Washington, DC: Pen and Booth.

Setton, Robin (1999). *Simultaneous Interpretation: A Cognitive-Pragmatic Analysis*. Amsterdam/ Philadelphia: John Benjamins.

Shannon, Claude E., & Warren Weaver (1949). *The Mathematical Theory of Communication*. Urbana: University of Illinois Press.

Solow, Sharon Newmann (1981). *Sign Language Interpreting: A Basic Resource Book*. Silver Spring, MD: National Association of the Deaf.

Sperber, Dan, & Deirdre Wilson (1995). *Relevance: Communication and Cognition* (2nd ed.). Oxford, UK/Cambridge, MA: Blackwell.

Stewart, David A., Jerome D. Schein, & Brenda E. Cartwright (1998). *Sign Language Interpreting: Exploring its Art and Science*. Needham Heights, MA: Allyn & Bacon.

Turner, Mark (1991). *Reading Minds: The Study of English in the Age of Cognitive Science*. Princeton, NJ: Princeton University Press.

CHAPTER 3

Making the effort in simultaneous interpreting

Some considerations for signed language interpreters

Lorraine Leeson
Trinity College Dublin

1. Introduction[1]

This chapter looks at several issues of theoretical and practical importance for signed language interpreters. We begin by considering some of the challenges that face interpreters before turning to investigate the constraints imposed by the interpreting process. From there, we will consider the strategies that interpreters use to maximize their performance, including some strategies that have hitherto been considered "miscues", a label that we suggest is inappropriate in certain contexts.

In considering the constraints imposed by the very process of interpreting, we draw on Gile's (1995) Effort Model of simultaneous interpretation to outline these constraints before exploring the range of strategies utilized by professional interpreters and translators to maximize their performance.

2. The challenges facing interpreters

Interpreters have to make decisions. As professionals we make decisions about the intent of the speaker or signer, the desired effect of their comments, the pragmatics of an event, the sincerity of the speaker, and the degree of definiteness of their utterances, among other things (e.g., Baker 1992; Gile 1995; Robinson 1997; etc.). Some of our decisions are influenced by what is said or signed, others by inferences made, and yet other decisions are formulated in response to the context that the interpreting occurs in, framed in part by the individual speakers and signers we find ourselves working with (Wadensjö 1998; Metzger 1999).

Having made those split second decisions, guided by our understanding of the language the speaker or signer is using, and how that language use is based in a specific cultural experience, we seek to find approximate equivalence in the target language. Of course, equivalence is a slippery concept that seems to be determined as much by the philosophical framework or "model" of interpreting that the interpreter may be working in. What counts as appropriate matching of equivalence in one context might be considered as too literal a transfer of meaning in another, for example when interpreting a narrative, a "free interpretation" (Napier 2002) that moves away from the form of the source language text might be considered highly acceptable while a more literal interpretation might not allow for a transfer of meaning couched in the appropriate cultural terms for the target language audience. However, what is considered as clear evidence of Napier's "free interpretation", or "dynamic equivalence" (Nida 1964), might be too removed from the form of the message in other contexts, for example in legal statements or in courts of law where accuracy of content in descriptions of events is critical. Indeed, the idea of "literal" translations (where the translator or interpreter remains as true as possible to both the form and content of the source language) versus "free" translations (where the translator or interpreter maintains the message of the source language, but abandons the form of the source) is one steeped in controversy that seems to have existed for as long as the issue of translation has been discussed (Hatim & Mason 1990).

While cultural viewpoint remains important in all interpreting settings, fact often takes precedence over "worldview". That this has consequences is clear (see Brennan & Brown 1997; Hertog 2001; Vernon, Raifman, Greenberg, & Monteiro 2001; and Miller & Vernon 2002 for further discussion regarding interpretation in legal contexts). For example, while signed language interpreters may ideally wish to produce a visual context and maximize use of classifier constructions in order to demonstrate how an act was carried out or how a window was opened, the source language may not encode the degree of information needed for an interpreter to accurately encode this information in the target signed language. Creating a visual representation that relates to the interpreter's visualization of how events unfolded is not offering "accurate" information in the target language, even though it may read like a more natural message to the target language client. Here, the only way that the interpreter can maximize accuracy in the target language is by preparation: asking to see a map of the area in which an accident took place, asking which direction vehicles were travelling (e.g., was one on the wrong side of the road, and if so, which one? From what direction was the witness viewing the event?), what kind of a door or window is being referred to (e.g., a sliding door, a door with a doorknob that must be turned to open it, a door with a handle that must be pushed down, a sash window or a window with a small opening at the top), etc.

Cultural encoding of information must also be considered in such ways – while an interpreter may seek to identify cultural equivalence in some contexts, legal contexts may dictate against this. An example is where a Deaf man was told by a judge that he "may not touch" his wife. She had said that he was harassing her physically. He said he was simply trying to get her attention in a culturally Deaf manner, that is, by tapping her on the shoulder, arm, or leg. It transpired that the man's wife would not look at him when he began to sign to her, so he would physically seek to gain her attention. For the court, a "cultural" translation such as 'I was getting her attention' would not work and could be construed as malicious on the part of the Deaf man (i.e., it could have been presumed that he was "getting her attention" in a semi-violent manner).

These kinds of tensions are central to the task of interpreting and interpreters must expect the challenges that they bring. Interpreting students are also typically aware of these factors and have considered them at length even before they ever graduate and implement them in practice.

However, if we accept that interpreting is not simply a task that depends on the movement of information from language A to language B by an unbiased and unobtrusive conduit (see also Wilcox and Shaffer, this volume), then we acknowledge that interpreters are participants in interpreting events and that their decisions influence the success or otherwise of their linguistic mediation. With this in mind, we begin to move towards a participant interaction framework (Humphrey & Alcorn 1996) where interpreters are seen as active third participants in a triadic (that is, three-party) exchange (Wadensjö 1998). Such a framework has consequences for our understanding of both the task of interpreting and the outcome of an interpreted event. As Napier notes, "an interactive model can only be applied successfully when interpreters adopt a sociolinguistic and sociocultural approach to their work and concede that every individual interpretation will vary according to the context of the situation" (2002:22).

The issue of the relative visibility or invisibility of the interpreter is one that we will return to later.[2] Here, we begin by considering the process of interpreting, outlining a model proposed by Daniel Gile (1995) called the "Effort Models" in interpreting. Following this, we look at some of the strategies that interpreters of spoken and signed languages use when interpreting to aid their decision making while on-task.

3.   Gile's Effort Models in interpreting

Gile (1995) proposes a set of models referred to as the Effort Models in interpreting. These set out to explain the difficulties inherent to the task of interpreting with the aim of facilitating interpreters' choices regarding the tactics and strategies that they could adopt to increase the success of their interpreting performance. Gile's model is based on two related concepts: first, that interpreting demands mental energy which is available in a limited supply and second, that interpreting takes up almost all of that mental energy and sometimes even requires more of this energy than is available. At such times, interpreting performance deteriorates.

Considering this, Gile presents a model of interpreting that is based on four Efforts, namely, the Listening and Analysis Effort (L), the Memory Effort (M), the Production Effort (P), plus a Coordination Effort (C). Each of these is summarized below.

3.1 The Listening and Analysis Effort

Gile defines this effort as entailing "all comprehension oriented operations, from the analysis of the sound waves carrying the source-language speech which reach the interpreter's ears, through the identification of words, to the final decisions about the 'meaning' of the utterance" (1995:162). As signed language interpreters, we can add to this definition the task of comprehending a visual-spatial language based on the identification of the visually received linguistic messages, followed by the identification of signed lexical items and phrases co-occurring with non-manual cues, through to decisions regarding the meaning of these items in context.

Gile suggests that while it is not yet clear just how far interpreters must comprehend a source language text in order to be able to interpret, he suggests that the underlying logic of sentences needs to be comprehended (i.e., is something a statement, a comparison, a question, etc.). This aside, conservative estimates suggest that at the very least, interpreters need to recognize words in the source language text. That is, if the interpreter doesn't understand the language that she is listening to, she cannot begin to transfer meaning to the target language. The understanding of both standardized and variable vocabulary items is of clear importance for interpreters in order to identify these items within a source language message and analyse their semantic content in context so that this contextualized meaning can be successfully reconstructed in the target language.

3.2 The Memory Effort

Short-term memory or working memory, as it is sometimes known, plays a significant role in simultaneous interpreting. Some short-term memory operations arise due to the lag between the expression of an utterance in the source language and the expression of an utterance relaying that concept in the target language. Other short-term memory operations may also arise because of the characteristics of a specific speech: a speech may be informationally dense or logically unclear, the linguistic structure may be unusual, or the speaker's accent or style may be unfamiliar. In such circumstances, interpreters may wish to increase their lag time (or "process" time; see Russell, this volume) in order to maximize the context available to them when attempting to comprehend and reformulate the message. Increasing lag time, that is, delaying the production of the target text, inevitably places increased demands on short-term memory.

The structure of the target language, including both linguistic constructions and overall information structure, can also place demands on memory. For example, if an interpreter is working from Irish Sign Language (ISL) into English and the source message signer introduces a "rhetorical question", the appropriate English output is arguably a declarative sentence in most instances. As an example, suppose the ISL signer presents the following:

(1) a.   CDS MEAN WHAT? CENTRE FOR DEAF STUDIES

In this case the interpreter may need to wait until she has recognized that this is a rhetorical question form whose function is to introduce an acronym to an audience. Having done so, she may choose to present an English equivalent such as:

      b.   'The Centre for Deaf Studies is also known by the acronym CDS.'

or,

      c.   'If you come across the acronym CDS, it is referring to the Centre
         for Deaf Studies.'

or, less formally,

      d.   'CDS stands for the Centre for Deaf Studies.'

Such production strategies depend to a great degree on the management of information in short-term memory, as well as the identification of syntactic patterns and their functions in the source language plus alternative patterns that convey appropriately equivalent information in the target language. This component of interpretation management is central, but given the burden that it places on processing, interpreters may reach "saturation" level quite quickly due to the pressure placed on memory in attempting to maintain the analyzed source language message components while seeking the appropriate target language structure in which to place them. For example, information about tense or aspect will be distributed differently in English than in ISL (Leeson 1996) and the interpreter will need to wait until she knows when an event occurred and whether it occurred just once or continually for a specific duration of time before she can adequately package this information in ISL.

Gile notes that the Memory Effort is also non-automatic in nature because it entails the storage of information for later use. He adds that "stored information changes both from one speech to another and during every speech as it unfolds, and that both stored information quantities and storage duration can vary from moment to moment, so that there is little chance for repetition of identical operations with sufficient frequency to allow automation of the processes" (1995:169).

3.3 The Production Effort

Gile defines the Production Effort in simultaneous interpreting as "the set of operations extending from the mental representation of the message to be delivered to speech planning and performance of the speech plan" (1995:165). As interpreters working into a signed language, we can also take the Production Effort to include the planning and performance of an output in the medium of signed language. Such production is not effortless in nature: Matthei and Roper (1985), cited in Gile (1995), make reference to the fact that listeners often have trouble decoding speeches and that speakers tend to make false starts and be ungrammatical when they speak. They take this as evidence that the speech production system makes great demands on our processing capacity. Indeed, Gile also cites Clark and Clark (1977) who report that "speaking is problem solving" (Gile 1995:165). Such problem solving may include, for example, finding the right word for some specific linguistic context or, as Gile notes, steering a sentence in a particular direction at a syntactic junction.

Such problems are common not only to interpreters working between two spoken languages, but are also clearly integral to the task of the signed language interpreter. Indeed, we might suggest that the fact that signed language interpreters must additionally deal with a shift in modality (i.e., from spoken discourse to signed discourse or vice versa) brings with it a special range of production issues relative to the way in which discourse is structured and maintained in signed languages vis-à-vis spoken languages. Such features include the tracking of referents through extended discourse via established spatial loci, appropriate use of non-manual features, and the use of simultaneous constructions.[3]

However, like other writers on interpretation and translation (such as Hatim & Mason 1990; Baker 1992; Robinson 1997), Gile notes that interpreters cannot afford to depend very heavily on the structure of the source language text in order to prepare the target language output. To do this leads to a number of potential problems for the interpreter, including:

–   If an interpreter follows the syntactic or lexical choices made by the source language speaker, the interpreter might become stuck at a certain point because the grammar of the target language differs significantly from that of the source language.

–   If the interpreter tries to closely follow the source language structure, she may limit her own resourcefulness as a speaker of the target language, which could be utilized if the interpreter had based her target language output on the meaning of the source language rather than on the actual linguistic structure of the source.

–   Where the interpreter stays close behind the speaker's or signer's production of the source language message while producing her target message, there is an increased likelihood of interference from the source language in the target language. Such interference might include mispronunciation of lexical items, grammatical errors, the choice of *faux-amis* or "false friends" (words that look or sound similar in the source and target languages but which have different meanings), or other subtler interferences that can make the target language less clear and less pleasant to listen to or to watch.

–   Finally, if an interpreter focuses too much on language form, she may potentially listen to the incoming source language speech more superficially than if she produced the target text based on meaning gleaned from the source language. Gile suggests that to focus more on the linguistic form of the source than the content may result in a greater number of errors being generated. In this case, the interpreter engages in less hypothesis testing to check the target language output for completeness than she would if she based her interpretation on the transfer of message meaning.[4]

These factors demonstrate why successful interpreting is guided by the general rule that whenever possible, the interpreter produces her target language output on the basis of the meaning and not the words of the source language message.

3.4 The Coordination Effort

The Coordination Effort is required to coordinate the Listening and Analysis Effort (L), the Memory Effort (M) and the speech Production Effort (P) (Eysenck & Keane 1995; Gile 1995). We might consider the Coordination Effort as the air-traffic controller for the interpreting that takes place, allowing the interpreter to manage her focus of attention between the listening and analysis task, the production task and the ongoing self-monitoring that occurs during performance. When smooth coordination is achieved, interpreters attain "flow" (Robinson 1997), the optimum state for interpreters (and translators) where their level of skill is in line with the challenge of the task at hand.

3.5 Gile's Effort Model of simultaneous interpretation

Gile's Effort Model of simultaneous interpreting comprises the elements that we have discussed above, namely, comprehension of the source language, maintenance of meaning in short-term memory, production of the target language and coordination of the task. This model is coded as follows (Gile 1995: 169):

(2) $SI = L + P + M + C$

Giles notes that:

> At each point in time, each Effort has specific processing capacity requirements that depend on the task(s) it is engaged in, namely the particular comprehension, short-term memory, or production operations being performed on speech segments. Due to the high variability of requirements depending on the incoming speech segments, processing capacity requirements of individual Efforts can vary rapidly over time, in seconds or fractions of seconds. (1995: 169)

For example, the Efforts are working on different parts of the interpreting message at any given moment: "Production acts on speech segment A, while Memory acts on segment B which came after A, and Listening and Analysis acts on segment C which came after B" (Gile 1995: 170).

Of course, sometimes the Efforts overlap, and at times interpreters may anticipate an utterance that has yet to be presented in the source language. The idea that Efforts deal with different segments is useful for us because it can help us to devise strategies and consider tactics that interpreters can use when coping with difficulties. In the next section, we consider some of the difficulties that interpreters face and outline a number of strategies commonly used to deal with these challenges.

4.   Coping strategies used by professional interpreters

Professional interpreters use a wide range of strategies to cope with the complexities of the interpreting task. These allow them to find "flow" while interpreting, the point in which the interpreting task is maximally effective and comfortable for the interpreter (Robinson 1997).

A primary skill required in interpreting, as we have already noted, is that of moving away from the surface form of the source language and corresponding meaning toward "free" translation or interpretation (Hatim & Mason 1990; Napier 1998, 2002). The well-known translation theorist, Eugene Nida, has called moving away from the form of the source language "dynamic equivalence" (Nida 1964) in that the target message must have the equivalent effect on the target audience as the original on the source language audience. Napier (1998:15) goes so far as to state that using free interpretation "requires the SLI [signed language interpreter] to focus entirely on the meaning, to ignore the form of the message, and ensure that any piece of information is made equally relevant to all parties involved". As was pointed out earlier, however, this approach of ignoring the form cannot be maintained in every case. Gile (2000) considers such "deverbalization", attributed to Seleskovitch (e.g., Seleskovitch 1968) as extreme. More realistically, interpreters must understand that the form of the source text should not interfere with constructing the target form, but that interpreters may consciously draw on source message form as they strategize to create the most meaningful target text possible (Gile 1995, 2000; Janzen, this volume, Chapter 4). Even Seleskovitch (1968) agrees that while interpreting is primarily meaning-based, "no interpretation, however freed from the constraints of the original linguistic system, is entirely devoid of code switching" (1968:96). This strongly suggests that interpreters need to draw on their knowledge of both the source and target languages in the discourse context where they occur, and with reference to the function of the message. This will guide the judgment of interpreters who may, with good reason, shift between degrees of formal equivalence and dynamic equivalence while working their way through a given text.

In any case, when attempting to represent the source message meaning, professionals make decisions about the relative weight of pieces of information in the source language text and whether each is essential to the production of a cohesive target language message. Interpreters consider whether a particular segment is redundant, whether an item is culturally relevant or accessible to the target language cultural audience as it stands, which is particularly true of metaphors, idioms and culturally embedded humour, or whether some re-phrasing is necessary in order to contextualize the interpreted message for the target language audience. It is clear that interpreters' decisions regarding the meaning in the text influence their structuring of the target text. Thus strategizing becomes increasingly important if the interpreter is to remain true to the source message, yet present the material in a cohesive, linguistically (grammatically) meaningful target text.

In the coming sections, we summarize strategies that are most widely reported for dealing with language transfer by professional interpreters. We draw particularly on Baker (1992) and Gile (1995) for this overview. For students of signed language interpreting familiar with Cokely's (1992) "miscue analysis", it may come as a surprise that the features that Cokely presents as miscues, or *errors* in a target language production, can be used strategically by interpreters with the aim of maximizing the strength of their performance, but in fact this is the case. Here, we are focusing specifically on generalized strategies that occur intra-sententially, but naturally, interpreters also make decisions about how they will manage long stretches of texts. Readers are referred to Baker (1992) for a discussion of equivalence beyond the level of the sentence and of cohesion across texts.

4.1 Strategic omissions

While omissions are considered miscues in Cokely's (1992) taxonomy, there are good reasons why an interpreter may consciously decide to omit an item from the target language text, most notable of which is the effect that redundancy of an item in the target language would have. A general rule of thumb guiding the choice to maintain or omit an item seems to be that the semantics and pragmatics of the original message should be conveyed in the target language (for example, see Baker 1992; Gile 1995; Robinson 1997). Omissions, then, can be appropriate and strategic (Hatim & Mason 1990; Baker 1992; Gile 1995; Napier 2003; Napier & Barker 2004). Recent research suggests that signed language interpreters make different types of omissions when interpreting and have high levels of metalinguistic awareness regarding their production of and reasons for omitting items in the target language (Napier & Barker 2004: 388). While Napier and Barker note that some omissions are problematic, they also stress the fact that interpreters make conscious and strategic decisions about certain types of omissions (2004: 372–388). This clearly differs from instances when interpreters omit information due to lack of adequate processing capacity for the Listening and Analysis Effort. However, as Janzen and Korpiniski (this volume) note, such strategic omissions can be successful only when interpreters deal critically with a text, guided by knowledge of their audience and the intentions of the source language speaker.

4.2 Strategic additions

Cokely (1992) also views additions as miscues. However, if an interpreter is aiming to mediate culture-specific terms, she may choose to "explain" a term by paraphrasing the meaning of the concept (for example, TTY or MINICOM in a signed source message may become 'a text telephone for the Deaf' in certain contexts). The function of the text and knowledge of the audience will guide an interpreter's judgment in this regard. Given that these additions are conscious on the part of the interpreter and function as a means of making the target language comprehensible to the target language audience, it does not make sense to consider these as "miscues". When working between a spoken source language and a signed target language, interpreters are also forced to make decisions regarding the relative locative positions of elements, the direction of movement or the relative size and shape of items. Information about these features may be inferred in an English source language text, but are not explicitly coded in the language to the extent that they are in a signed language. Similarly, the signed structure of numerous verb complexes, especially classifier-verb predicates, may require additions in the target English text. Inclusion of such information is central to ensuring that grammatical features are utilized appropriately in a comprehensive and grammatically sound target language message. This is where the fuzziness factor sets in: while interpreters must make decisions regarding these factors, they may be considered to be 'adding' to the target language message. Effectively, the interpreter is making explicit in the target language certain information that is often inferred or "gapped" in the source language (which can be necessary in either direction – into a signed *or* a spoken language target text). However, there are clearly other contexts where interpreters should not presume that their decision to add this kind of information is unproblematic: prime instances are contexts where information regarding location, size and shape of entities, relative positions of entities, etc. must be clarified, such as in legal domains (see Brennan & Brown 1997 for an excellent discussion of some of these issues for British Sign Language-English interpreters).

Preparation can aid the process of interpreting based on a real understanding of the event under description, but interpreters must be aware of the importance of context and allow that to guide their decision making at the linguistic level.

4.3 Strategic substitutions

Another of the miscue types identified by Cokely is the category of substitutions. However, substitutions are not always miscues: they are often guided by the need to coordinate a simultaneously interpreted message under pressure of time, as we have discussed above in Sections 3.4 and 3.5. If an interpreter is under pressure of time (perhaps because of the density of a text or the speed of the source language text delivery), they may choose the strategy of substituting specific information with less specific information providing that the core concept of the message is maintained. For example, if a rapidly produced source language text makes reference to a series of figures, but the core implied idea is that the number of students attending computer programming courses has increased over time in line with increased job prospects in that area, then an interpreter may choose to omit the actual figures, substituting them with a phrase that summarizes the core relationship between job prospects and interest in training in the field of computer programming. Again, if this is a conscious strategy chosen by the interpreter to aid performance, and where the figures that are omitted are indicative of the underlying concept of the causative relation between events, should we then say that this is a "miscue" or evidence of excellent dynamic equivalence?

We contend that to say it is a miscue is misleading, especially if acknowledging such an "error" suggests to the interpreter that she has been inadequate in her interpretation. Instead, under the right circumstances, utilizing the strategy of substitution (or perhaps more correctly, the combination of omission *plus* substitution) makes the meaningful transfer in the target text all the more accurate.

In this particular example, however, the wise interpreter, continuing to strategize in a skilful manner, would make a mental note that the specific figures occurring in the source text may in fact reappear down the line. If such further reference does take place, including the figures in question explicitly may become the appropriate tactic in the target text at that point; omission at this time may represent an inappropriate choice on the part of the interpreter. This highlights a further consideration for the interpreter: deliberate and careful strategizing is crucial, but each choice has certain consequences which the interpreter at best anticipates, and at the very least must be prepared to resolve in due course.

4.4 Paraphrasing

An interpreter may understand a term in the source text but may not know the equivalent term in the target language, or an equivalent term may not exist. In such instances, interpreters may choose to paraphrase the meaning of the source language concept, that is, they explain the concept in the target language. Gile (1995:198) gives an example whereby an interpreter successfully paraphrased the term *tableur* ('spreadsheet') as "the programme which defines rows and columns and allows calculations to be made". A similar example of not being able to retrieve an English vocabulary item comes from the following experience: when working from Irish Sign Language, I once could not retrieve the word *scrum*, which refers to the circular grouping that rugby players create when planning their tactics on the playing field. I paraphrased, which succeeded insofar as a rugby-playing member of the audience interjected with the exact word that was needed. However, this strategy can be inefficient in terms of processing effort (cf. Gile 1995). It also takes more time to produce a sentence than to produce a single word, affecting lag time by increasing the distance between the source speaker's utterance and the interpreter's output, and can thus negatively impact the interpretation of the message as it continues (flow is affected as additional attention is placed on the Production Effort, perhaps at the expense of the Listening Effort which should be focused on the next incoming segment). Further, this strategy can be distracting to the audience, as they must carry out the processing task of identifying the concept that the interpreter is attempting to refer to, perhaps distracting them from the following piece of the message. However, this strategy has the added benefit of allowing for the interpretation to continue without undue interruption of the source language presenter.

4.5 Other strategies used

While it is impossible to present a complete overview of the strategies used by interpreters here, Table 1 (after Gile 1995) is indicative of strategies that have been identified. Readers are encouraged to read Gile's own detailed discussion of these strategies and others in his (1995) Chapter 8, "Coping tactics in interpretation", pp. 191–208.

Table 1. Additional strategies for managing successful interpretation

Comprehension Tactics	Explanation	Consequences
These are used to eliminate potential consequences of problems in comprehending the source text.		
Delaying a response	Interpreters may delay beginning to work into the target language by up to a few seconds so that they can take on board further source language information.	This delay tactic leads to the accumulation of information in working memory, which means that there is risk of losing some of the speech segments in a "failure sequence".
Reconstructing a segment with the help of context	Interpreters may try to reconstruct a term (e.g., name, number, technical term) that they did not hear or see properly. They can try to reconstruct it on the basis of their extralinguistic knowledge of the subject.	While this can be a successful tactic, it may involve waiting until more source language information becomes available. This requires time and processing capacity. Like the delay tactic, it can lead to the loss of some of the following source language message.
Calling on a co-interpreter	Where an interpreter is working as part of a team, she may seek assistance from her (off-task) co-interpreter. The co-interpreter may give assistance with a term (e.g., the target language equivalent) or she can write down a source language term. When it is more difficult to "feed" a concept to a co-interpreter, a signed language interpreter may consider allowing her off-task colleague to take the floor for the purpose of rendering this concept before switching back for the remainder of her turn.	Problems include the fact that many interpreters work individually, so a co-interpreter will not always be available. Off-task interpreters often feel the need for rest from active listening or watching and this means that they may not be paying attention to the source language message. Another problem is that at conferences, papers may not be available in advance and so the off-task interpreter may be preparing for her turn while her colleague is struggling. Other difficulties include the fact that many interpreters are reluctant to indicate areas of difficulty to their colleagues for fear of losing face.

Table 1. *(continued).*

Altering lag time (process time)	Interpreters can lengthen or reduce lag time and thus, to a certain extent, control processing requirements associated with individual Efforts.	However, while shortened lag time decreases memory requirements, it increases the possibility for source language intrusion (Cokely 1992). Lengthened lag time may increase the potential for comprehension but may overload working memory.
Altering the order of items in dense texts (enumerations)	Gile (1995: 196) describes enumerations as high density speech segments. Interpreters may choose to reiterate the last component of a source language segment first in the target language output in order to free up working memory for other portions of the source language.	Gile notes that no analysis has been carried out as to why interpreters feel this is successful, but suggests that in reformulating the last elements first, they can be picked up before they have been fully processed, thus saving on processing effort. He suggests (for spoken languages) that this might work best with names, which can be reproduced from echoic memory and thus be produced phonetically in the target language.
REFORMULATION TACTICS *These are used to eliminate potential consequences of production problems or problems with working memory. In addition to the tactics outlined above, we can add the following:*		
Informing delegates of an interpreting problem	If an interpreter believes that she has missed an important piece of information she may inform her audience that this is the case.	This strategy takes up processing time and may thus jeopardize the reformulation of subsequent sections. Further, it may lead to the audience losing faith in the interpreter's ability to do her job, and to a loss of credibility. Gile suggests that while ethically, interpreters consider it their duty to inform clients if information has been missed, if this information is insignificant, or if informing clients would do more damage than good, the interpreter should choose another tactic.

(Based on Gile 1995: 191–201)

This chart demonstrates that interpreters have a range of strategies at their disposal. It also shows that every decision an interpreter makes has a consequence for the target language performance (e.g., delaying a response, calling on a co-interpreter, etc.), and potentially for how the interpreting profession is viewed by clients (e.g., informing delegates of an interpreting problem). While some common strategies work equally well for signed language interpreters, others do not. For example, Gile notes a strategy whereby the interpreter may render a name in the source language text phonetically in the target language (i.e., as it would be pronounced in the source language, but not the target – this strategy is used when the interpreter doesn't know how the name *would be pronounced* in the target language). However, signed language interpreters cannot simply reproduce the name orally – they probably need to fingerspell it (unless a sign name exists, but then this issue is not problematic). Of course, there is the added potential of misspelling a name, especially where the interpreter has not had recourse to written preparation or where the person or place name is introduced casually. Particularly hazardous are names that are spelled very differently from how they are pronounced (e.g., the Irish girl's name *Siobhan* (pronounced "shove-on") or the place name *Dún Laoighre* (an Irish name that is pronounced "Done Leery" in English). When working from a fingerspelled source, we could expect that additional attention would be needed to deal with these items. We should note that the list of strategies in Table 1 is not definitive in any way and that strategies used explicitly by signed language interpreters could be explored further.[5]

Gile (1995:201–204) notes that these strategies are not randomly selected by interpreters. Instead, they are chosen following certain rules:

1. MAXIMIZING INFORMATION RECOVERY. Interpreters aim to use tactics that aid information recovery such as reconstruction of information from the context, calling on the assistance of a co-interpreter and (if possible), consulting documents, rather than other forms of intervention.

2. MINIMIZING RECOVERY INTERFERENCE. Interpreters seek to recover information insofar as possible without jeopardizing the recovery of other segments of the source language message. Thus, tactics that require little time and processing capacity (e.g., omission, substitution or approximation of the information) are favoured over more processing-costly activities such as explanation or paraphrasing.

3. MAXIMIZING THE COMMUNICATION IMPACT OF THE SPEECH. Here, the interpreter must pay attention to how the information is being "packaged" by the speaker, and how re-packaging in the target language will affect the impact the speaker is attempting to create. As well, the credibility of the interpreter is an important facet of this rule. Gile (1995:202–203) gives the example of an interpreter who did not fully hear a name and believes that her potential mispronunciation of the name in the target text may be undiplomatic. Thus, the interpreter avoids attempting to reproduce the name but may not inform the delegates that there is a problem, because doing so could compromise the intent of the interaction. Ethical judgment plays a clear role in determining the appropriateness of this tactic.

4. THE LAW OF LEAST EFFORT. Gile regards this rule as an "unwelcome intruder" that crops up even when adequate processing capacity is available. Instead of maximizing effort, the interpreter may fall foul of the law of least effort which

results in the loss of information without good reason. That is, the interpreter simply avoids working as hard as she should with the consequence that her interpretation is not as complete or as elegant as it could be. Gile suggests that interpreters may consider strategies that assist in a kind of self-preservation to combat the effects of fatigue, but, especially when interpreters work in teams, rotation should allow for sufficient time to rest, making this rationale unjustified.

5.   SELF-PROTECTION. Interpreters may fail to reformulate the target message in a manner that they themselves consider satisfactory. Thus, they may be tempted to make use of tactics that minimize reflection on their performance (e.g., they don't tell delegates when problems arise in order to protect themselves, rather than for the legitimate aim of maximizing the impact of the speech). This is a "rule" to consciously avoid using.

These rules clearly apply to signed language interpreters too. While rules 1–3 are relatively straightforward (acknowledging that many signed language interpreters work in isolation, given the current shortage of interpreters), like Gile, we would recommend that interpreters reflect on why they would opt for following rules 4 or 5, which do little to promote the professionalism of signed language interpreting as a whole. Complacency seems to be at the heart of rule 4, and this is a difficult habit to break. New interpreters should set high standards for themselves and constantly strive to increase their skills. One way in which this can be achieved is by maximizing opportunities to work with respected and more experienced colleagues in the field, and seek their feedback on one's own performance. Mentoring by a seasoned colleague is a more formalized means of facilitating such professional development. Rule 5 may be a consequence of complacency too: as many interpreters work in isolation, in part because of the shortage of professional interpreters, some come to adopt an attitude which we might refer to as "it (my interpretation) is good enough".

Some interpreters may buy into the notion that self-preservation is all-important and that any demonstration of not understanding is a failure and should be avoided. But lack of understanding is not failure. Nor is making a mistake the end of the world. Interpreters must be able to admit openly when things go wrong, guided by ethical requirements. Thus, interpreters must constantly ask themselves if they are being honest, not just with the message that they produce in the target language, but with themselves, with colleagues, professional bodies, and with clients. This required honesty applies not only to what takes place in interpreted situations, but also to the decision to accept or decline assignments in the first place. If the interpreter does not have the prerequisite skills to do the work skilfully or will gain information that she should not be privy to for some reason, she should not accept the assignment.

5.   Summary and conclusions

In this chapter we have outlined just some of the challenges that interpreters must take into consideration when they engage in decision making processes, which are, as we have argued, essential components of the interpreter's task. In accounting for the process of interpreting, we introduced Daniel Gile's Effort Model of simultaneous interpretation and considered its applicability for signed language interpreters.

In discussing factors shaping interpreter performance, we have demonstrated that interpreters make decisions at every step of the interpreting process. Such decision making includes whether the interpreter addresses the task of interpreting in a literal or free manner, guided by a given context but also by her view of her role as interpreter,[6] how she chooses to omit or add information to the target language message strategically in order to maximize the completeness of the target language message, and how she deals with problems in comprehending the source language message.

In this chapter we have also discussed in some detail some of the strategies that interpreters use, though as Gile notes, not all of the strategies listed are as welcome as others, since certain of them tend to have a negative impact on the message or on the target language audience (notably, when inappropriately following the "law of least effort"). We also saw that there appears to be a preferred ordering to the strategies that an interpreter uses when attempting to manage her performance. Message management, where the interpreter solves a problem for herself, can take precedence over calling on a colleague for assistance. Co-opting a colleague, however, may take precedence over simply advising clients of a problem. We should bear in mind that when Gile discusses these strategies, he is referring to their frequency of use by spoken language interpreters, and then, typically in simultaneous conference interpreting situations. Empirical research is needed to determine the range of strategies (as opposed to "miscues") used by signed language interpreters in authentic situations as well as their frequency of use. We should further bear in mind that the strategies selected by an interpreter will be framed by the situation that she finds herself in. If an interpreter is working alone, for example, it is simply not possible to draw on the assistance of a colleague.

In short, we can say that interpreters make numerous decisions every time they interpret. While the core visible outcomes of these decisions are typically linguistic insofar as the interpreter's choices shape the form of the target language, the underlying rationale for many decisions made may be pragmatic in nature, framed by the context of the situation, and informed by the interpreter's understanding of her role (encapsulating models of interpreting, views regarding the role of ethics in shaping the interpreter's responses to interpreting situations, etc.). Interpreters are constrained by the interpreting process in that there is a limited amount of processing energy available to carry out the task. The effort of dealing with complex data can at times demand more processing energy than is in fact available. In such instances, interpreting quality may be affected. While we know that these factors impede interpreting generally, much remains to be learned about how interpreters who work with a signed language manage this situation. Further research is needed to identify the strategies used by interpreters to minimize processing overload, while maintaining the quality of their performance. Identifying the strategies that successful interpreters use is an important step in our understanding of maximizing performance on a consistent basis.

Notes

1. Thanks to the interpreting students at the Centre for Deaf Studies for their willingness to discuss the issues outlined in this chapter. Thanks also to Susan Foley-Cave for her thoughts on several of the ideas included here.

2. See Cokely (2005) for an excellent discussion of the consequences of interpreters' "shifting positionality" vis-à-vis Deaf community. See also Moody (2007) for an overview of the shifts in interpreter approaches to their task.

3. Because the signer has two hands that operate in three-dimensional space, it is possible for two constructions with distinct meanings to be articulated simultaneously. See Miller (1994) and Section 4.2.1 in Leeson (this volume, Chapter 10) for further description.

4. Although see Janzen (this volume, Chapter 4), who suggests that the interpreter must balance her focus on meaning *and* form, because some of the message meaning is in fact derived from particular structures used.

5. For example, see Leeson and Foley-Cave (2004) for a discussion of signed language interpreter decision-making in a postgraduate linguistics classroom.

6. See Wilcox and Shaffer, Russell, and Janzen and Korpiniski (this volume) for overviews of the models that have shaped interpreters' approach to their task.

References

Baker, Mona. (1992). *In Other Words. A Coursebook on Translation*. London and New York: Routeledge Press.

Brennan, Mary, & Richard Brown (1997). *Equality Before the Law: Deaf People's Access to Justice*. Durham: Deaf Studies Research Unit, University of Durham.

Cokely, Dennis (1992). *Interpretation: A Sociolinguistic Model*. Burtonsville, MD: Linstok Press.

Cokely, Dennis (2005). Shifting positionality: A critical analysis of the turning point in the relationship of interpreters and the Deaf community. In Marc Marschark, Rico Peterson & Elizabeth A. Winston (Eds.), *Sign Language Interpreting and Interpreter Education: Directions for Research and Practice* (pp. 3–28). New York: Oxford University Press.

Eysenck, Michael W., & Mark T. Keane (1995). *Cognitive Psychology: A Student's Handbook* (3rd ed.). East Sussex: Psychology Press.

Gile, Daniel (1995). *Basic Concepts and Models for Interpreter and Translator Training*. Amsterdam/Philadelphia: John Benjamins.

Gile, Daniel (2000). Issues in interdisciplinary research into conference interpreting. In Birgitta Englund Dimitrova & Kenneth Hyltenstam (Eds.), *Language Processing and Simultaneous Interpreting: Interdisciplinary Perspectives* (pp. 89–106). Amsterdam/Philadelphia: John Benjamins.

Hatim, Basil, & Ian Mason (1990). *Discourse and the Translator*. London and New York: Longman.

Hertog, Erik (Ed.). (2001). *Aequitas-Access to Justice across Language and Culture in the EU*. Antwerp: Lessius Hogeschool.

Humphrey, Janice H., & Bob J. Alcorn (1996). *So You Want to be an Interpreter: An Introduction to Sign Language Interpreting* (2nd ed.). Amarillo, TX: H&H Publishers.

Leeson, Lorraine (1996). The Marking of Time in Sign Languages with Specific Reference to Irish Sign Language. Unpublished M. Phil. dissertation. Centre for Language and Communication Studies, University of Dublin, Trinity College.

Leeson, Lorraine, & Susan Foley-Cave (2004). MEAN^DEEP BUT DEPEND CONTEXT Interpreting Semantics and Pragmatics at Postgraduate Level – Challenges to interpreter notions of impartiality. Paper presented at the Supporting Deaf People Online Conference. Direct Learn.

Metzger, Melanie (1999). *Sign Language Interpreting: Deconstructing the Myth of Neutrality*. Washington, DC: Gallaudet University Press.

Miller, Christopher (1994). Simultaneous constructions in Quebec Sign Language. In Mary Brennan & Graham H. Turner (Eds.), *Word Order Issues in Sign Language: Working Papers* (pp. 89–112). Durham: International Sign Linguistics Association.

Miller, Katrina R., & McKay Vernon (2002). Assessing linguistic diversity in Deaf criminal suspects. *Sign Language Studies, 2* (4), 380–390.

Moody, Bill (2007). Literal vs. Faithful: What Is a Faithful Interpretation? *The Sign Language Translator and Interpreter, 1* (2), 179–220.

Napier, Jemina (1998). Free your mind – The rest will follow. *Deaf Worlds, 14* (3), 15–22.

Napier, Jemina (2002). *Sign Language Interpreting: Linguistic Coping Strategies*. Coleford, England: Douglas McLean.

Napier, Jemina, & Roz Barker (2004). Sign language interpreting: The relationship between metalinguistic awareness and the production of interpreting omissions. *Sign Language Studies, 4* (4), 369–393.

Nida, Eugene (1964). *Toward a Science of Translating with Special Reference to Principles and Procedures Involved in Bible Translating*. Leiden: E. J. Brill.

Robinson, Douglas (1997). *Becoming a Translator: An Accelerated Course*. London and New York: Routeledge Press.

Seleskovitch, Danica (1968). *L'interprète dans les conferences internationals*. Paris: Minard Lettres modernes.

Seleskovitch, Danica (1976). Interpretation, A psychological approach to translation. In Richard W. Brislin (Ed.), *Translation: Applications and Research* (pp. 92–116). New York: Gardner Press.

Vernon, McKay, Lawrence J. Raifman, Sheldon F. Greenberg, & Brendan Monteiro (2001). Forensic pretrial police interviews of Deaf suspects: Avoiding legal pitfalls. *Journal of Law and Psychiatry, 24*, 43–59.

Wadensjö, Cecilia (1998). *Interpreting as Interaction*. London and New York: Longman.

CHAPTER 4

Interpretation and language use

ASL and English

Terry Janzen
University of Manitoba

1. Introduction[1]

Interpreting for people who don't share the same language involves understanding the ideas of one person inferred from one linguistic structure and re-constructing them into another linguistic structure, that of the language used by those intended to receive the interpreted message.[2] Clearly there is more to a speaker's or signer's message than linguistic structure, however; communication events of every kind include clues to meaning found in intonation behaviours, facial and body gestures, discourse patterns, and even in the situational dynamics surrounding the linguistic event. Seleskovitch (1976, 1978) goes so far as to say that the actual wording of a source message is largely immaterial, that interpreters must immediately discard the original wording and retain only the ideas, or sense, underlying the speaker's text (Seleskovitch 1978: 9). One reason for this claim is that word meaning can be variable – a word can often mean one thing in one context and something else in another, so that an interpreter cannot depend on what any word might mean when it is isolated out of a specific context:

> Interpretation focuses on the ideas expressed in live utterances rather than on language itself; it strictly ignores all attempts at finding linguistic equivalents (i.e., phrases that could be considered under any circumstances to carry the same meaning) and concentrates on finding the appropriate wording to convey *a given meaning* at *a given point in time* and in *a given context*, whatever that wording (i.e., the formulation used by the interpreter) or the original wording may mean under different circumstances.   (Seleskovitch 1976: 93; emphasis added)

What Seleskovitch is telling us is that the meaning of the source text is inextricably tied to the context of a single communication event, and the interpreter must look to features of this surrounding circumstance for clues to the particular meaning intended by the words as they are used this one time.

   This chapter is not intended to be a comparison of the grammars of ASL and English overall, but the fact that these two languages are strikingly different in their grammatical structure makes a discussion of how the interpreter manages the two language systems a necessity. In Section 2 I address some of the problems of linguistic differences between English and ASL, and in Section 3, link this discussion to the context of interpreting more specifically. Because the majority of ASL-English interpreters today have ASL as a second language, in Section 4 I address important aspects of the language learner's increasing linguistic competency. Following this, in Section 5 I examine how the interpreter deals with features of source and target texts on several levels, that is, at the level of morphology, lexicon, phrasing and sentence structure, and perhaps most importantly, at the level of discourse structure, by looking at "words, constructions, texts and context". Finally, in Section 6, I draw some conclusions – what might we learn from the ideas presented in this chapter?

1.1   Getting from source message to target message

Is there no value in the speaker's or signer's original words? Surely they have been chosen carefully, at least most of the time. And if a speaker has chosen to phrase something in a particular way, why wouldn't the interpreter attempt to replicate this phrasing in the target text? Nida (1964) identifies two approaches to translation that help address this question. FORMAL EQUIVALENCE in translation "focuses attention on the message itself, in both form and content" (Nida 1964: 159). This orientation is intended to allow the target text audience to learn as much as possible about the source speaker (or in written translation, the author) or source text, in other words the cultural and expressive features that characterize the original. On the other hand, DYNAMIC EQUIVALENCE is more oriented to the target audience. Here the focus is not on enabling the audience to experience the source speaker's culture or context, but instead the interpreter attempts to give the audience an equivalent experience housed within their own cultural context and "naturalness of expression" (Nida 1964: 159).

Another factor for the interpreter to consider when working with the source text has to do with information type. Gile (1995) suggests that information can be classed as PRIMARY INFORMATION and SECONDARY INFORMATION. Primary information is the content of the message itself, while secondary information includes background information, speaker style, information about the form and structure of the text, and even information about the speaker (e.g., idiosyncrasies and mannerisms). Often the interpreter has too much information of various sorts to be able to portray accurately in the target message, especially if the task at hand is simultaneous interpreting where time is highly constrained. According to Gile, when a choice must be made to convey only some of the information because there isn't time to do justice to every last piece, it is better to convey the primary information, sacrificing secondary information because it is less central to the theme. Of course, interpreters have a general goal of transmitting all the intended information of the source text in a manner that is fully accessible to the target audience, but in reality a "perfect" interpretation is not a reasonable expectation. In any case, what would a perfect interpretation look like? It is generally accepted that interpreting word for word does not usually produce a fully accessible target text, while attention to just the ideas, and not the source text form, may be more difficult to judge as "equivalent". In any case, the interpreter must make numerous subjective choices.

2. The problem of language differences

The view taken here is that while the ideas of the source speaker or signer are what interpreters attempt to apprehend and pass on to their target audience, it is the linguistic form of the source text[3] where many clues to meaning are found. Thus interpreters would do well in searching for the speaker's or signer's intended meaning in its entirety, while paying attention to how this meaning is framed within the linguistic system. Seleskovitch's objection is that the original wording is unhelpful in constructing a target text in an entirely different language and should therefore not be used as a guide for doing so. But Nida claims that the more similar the source and target languages are, the more one can take advantage of the original form. In other words, why would the interpreter do extra work which might be unnecessary if the solution to constructing a portion of the target text is evident because of this similarity in form?

I would contend that interpreters who interpret between English and ASL are working with two languages that have very differently constructed grammars, used by two groups of people whose cultures also differ greatly in at least some respects. One language is conveyed through auditory and vocal channels while the other takes advantage of the visual channel and is produced with movements of the hands, face and body, which adds a further complicating factor into the interpreting task. The impact of a visual modality of language on linguistic structure is not yet fully understood, but some linguists are beginning to pay more attention to this. Emmorey (2002a) suggests that evidence is mounting through cross-linguistic studies that there may be some typological features unique to signed languages because of their visual-spatial orientation. While it is clear that numerous features of language do extend over both signed and spoken languages, there are significant differences between the two types that do impact overall structure, for example regarding the distinct properties of the articulators (i.e., two hands, face, etc.) and the two perceptual systems (Meier 2002).

3. From source text to target text

The structure of the source text (words, phrases, sentences, and even discourse arrangement) may not be of assistance when the interpreter is working to construct the target text, especially if the languages are quite different. Because the language structure of the interpreter's audience differs from that of the source text, it is in the reconstruction phase that Seleskovitch's (1978) advice is most appropriate.

3.1   Source language structure as intrusion

When the interpreter inserts source language features into the target language phrasing, the result can often confuse the target audience. The interpreter is not completing her task. When the interpreter is sufficiently knowledgeable about both languages and their contexts of use, however, the choice to insert something from the source language form – usually quite rare – may be deliberate, because the interpreter understands the intentions of the speaker and expectations of the audience, and works hard to construct an interpreted message that balances these dynamics. More often, however, the interpreter just doesn't have a better idea of how to phrase something in the target text, and if compounded by factors such as stress or fatigue, inappropriate source language intrusions can become more frequent.

It is likely the case that inserting source language structure into the target text will happen more when the direction of interpreting is from English to ASL rather than from ASL to English, especially when ASL is the interpreter's second language. This might be for several reasons.

When one language is not a sound-based language, there is more potential for the interpreter to mentally overlay the spoken language onto the "silent" signed language. It is fairly common for non-deaf signers with ASL as a second language to continue thinking in (spoken) English words while signing ASL signs. The extreme of this is when people attempt to talk and sign simultaneously (often when they are addressing a mixed group of Deaf and hearing people). It is virtually impossible to speak proper grammatical English while signing proper grammatical ASL structure. This makes sense: ASL and English are two different languages, which overrides the perceived ease of communicating in a spoken and signed language mode at the same time. Something is going to suffer, and if the person's primary language is English, it is more likely that this is the language structure that will be followed both with speech and with signs. Problems regarding such simultaneous production have been examined by Johnson and Erting (1989) and Johnson, Liddell and Erting (1989). Perhaps when interpreting from English to ASL, interpreters don't always realize that the source language structure is creeping in. In this context, when they are not actually speaking out loud, they might assume that their signing is "more like" ASL when it is not.

A second problem is that many working interpreters have an incomplete grasp of ASL grammar as a whole (see Jacobs 1996 for a general discussion of difficulties in learning ASL, common entrance and exit expectations and practices of interpreter education programs, and a comparison to similar expectations of spoken language interpreting programs). There are several reasons for this and, undoubtedly, numerous effects. First, interpreters in training often get an insufficient education in ASL. Perhaps the biggest problem here rests with ASL-English interpreting programs themselves, which often don't include ASL fluency as an entrance requirement but then are too short to ensure that students attain an appropriate level of fluency while in school. The result is that graduates are sent into the work force without a great deal of confidence in their language skills. Second, the majority of interpreters learn ASL as a second language when they are already adults, when in fact the research on second language learning shows that native-like fluency in this circumstance is almost never reached. Studies have shown that for learning a first language (L1), the ideal learning period ends around puberty (Lenneberg 1967), after which full language fluency is less likely reached. Someone learning a second language (L2) may have a greater chance at fluency for somewhat longer beyond the L1 ideal learning period, but here too studies indicate that there is an advantage to acquisition of the phonological system of a second language at an earlier age, and both comprehension and production of morphological and syntactic systems of an L2 are better if the language is acquired earlier in life (Morford & Mayberry 2000). This should tell us that if interpreters are not balanced or "early bilinguals" (Moser-Mercer, Lambert, Darò, & Williams 1997:136), which would mean that the two languages are learned together when the person is very young, then attaining fluency in their L2 when they are older will require a lengthy and intense learning period. Interpreters who grow up with ASL as a first language are at an advantage because they have a better chance at being balanced bilinguals, although this does not automatically mean that they then have an ASL lexicon sufficient for the many contexts and registers they will be working in.[4]

The issue of bilingualism is an intriguing one for ASL-English interpreters. Moser-Mercer et al. (1997) suggest that an effect of "late" bilingualism is an imperfect pronunciation of the L2, which may not be particularly problematic for translators who work with written texts, or for interpreters who interpret from their L2 into their L1, a common expectation among spoken-language conference interpreters. These interpreters do not encounter difficulty in this regard because they only produce target texts in their native language.[5] It is rare, however, for an ASL-English interpreter with English as an L1 and ASL as an L2 to work primarily from ASL to English, which means that pronunciation difficulties or a heavy accent in her L2, along with other language deficiencies, will affect the quality of interpreting. Further, Moser-Mercer et al. (1997) suggest that stress during interpreting may lead to regression in L2 production (the interpreter's L1 may be similarly affected). Many interpreters say that they work mostly in the direction of English to ASL, so the overall impact in this field is likely to be considerable.

L2 pronunciation is one issue, but as well, how confident are interpreters that their L2 production is grammatically and semantically accurate?

4. The interpreter's acquisition of ASL as a second language

Interpreting involves the transfer of information from one speaker or signer whose message is shaped by intentional, situational, and cultural factors, to a recipient whose understanding is once again shaped by similar factors. These two discourse participants may have a great deal in common or be worlds apart. When ASL-English interpreters began to organize formally in the 1960s very little was known about ASL as a language. Although members of the Deaf community used a signed language as their primary language, it did not yet have status as a legitimate language in society. The wording in the early documents of the American organization, the Registry of Interpreters for the Deaf (RID), reflects the belief that proper "translation" requires English-like structure when signing:

> In *translating*, the thoughts and words of the speaker are presented verbatim. In *interpreting*, the interpreter may depart from the exact words of the speaker to paraphrase, define, and explain what the speaker is saying. ...When translating, the interpreter is recognizing that the deaf person is a highly literate individual who prefers to have his thoughts and those of hearing persons expressed verbatim.
> (Quigley & Youngs 1965:1; italics theirs)

Around the same time, William Stokoe began publishing research showing that ASL word and phrase structures have features in common with spoken languages, that is, the very same principles that determine the composition of words, phrases and sentences apply to all languages whether spoken or signed, even though the channel of delivery and perception may differ (Stokoe 1960; Stokoe, Casterline, & Croneberg 1965). Since that time much linguistic research has focused on investigating structural patterns in ASL phonology, morphology and syntax, and has extended more recently into the field of discourse structure. It is clear that ASL, along with all other signed languages, is a fully functioning language, although there is still much to learn about its grammar.

Students of ASL may at times be confused about what is grammatical, and this can be for a number of reasons. In part, because ASL is not a written language, and because it does not have a sound system that can be represented by strings of letters or symbols, it is difficult to represent on paper. This may not be as problematic for students interested in conversational ASL, for whom the goal of learning is mostly for interaction in social and family discourse. But for the interpreter, whose language proficiency must be at a high level in numerous contexts, language learning goes well beyond conversational skills. For vocabulary building, ASL dictionaries are good resources, but these benefit beginning interpreters the most. On-line dictionaries and those on CD are more helpful because they can include short clips of vocabulary showing movement and spatial features, but so far these tend to be limited in the number of items they contain. Numerous videotapes, CDs and DVDs of ASL (narratives, lectures, interaction samples, etc.) are also available giving interpreters access to connected discourse, and which are excellent resources for comprehension exercises and interpreting practice. But interpreters are still left with the problem of building their own language resource files for ASL. Inventories of ASL words,[6] especially in technical domains, are not easy to record and catalogue. How then do interpreters build their language repertoire at a sufficiently advanced level? There are three aspects to the solution to this dilemma: interaction with other proficient language users; the role of memory, especially for an unwritten language; and specific linguistic training.

4.1 Interaction

The importance of interaction with other ASL signers cannot be overstated. For users of an unwritten language, by far the most significant mechanism for information exchange is face to face interaction. For second language learners, and for interpreters in particular, this is doubly important. It is the best way to learn vocabulary and phrasing in context, and participating in interactive discourse (without the pressure of "performing" while interpreting) is the best time to get feedback on your own language use. Further, language skills must be practiced to be maintained, and challenged in order to develop. This can only take place in a variety of stimulating interactive settings.[7]

4.2 Memory

The ASL-English interpreter's memory for language must be sharp. Of course, an excellent memory is an important trait for any good interpreter, but in the case of learning and using an unwritten language, linguistic "files" will primarily be stored mentally.

Both long term memory (LTM) and short term memory (STM), or "working memory" as has been postulated (e.g., Baddeley 2000), are critical in language processing and interpreting. Most models of the interpreting process include memory components, for example Cokely's (1992) model proposes that Short Term Message Retention is an actual stage of processing, in which "chunks" of input remain until they are fully analyzed. What follows is not further discussion of the role of memory in interpreting, but an examination of the importance of memory in the interpreter's acquisition of an unwritten language (ASL, in this case), and in particular, how on-going acquisition relates to the interpreter's work. For extensive discussion and critique of models of language processing and interpreting, see González, Vásquez and Mikkelson (1991) and in particular for simultaneous interpreting, Setton (1999).

Can memory be improved? While this is difficult to quantify, it appears to be the case that memory activity strengthens memory ability. In the context of interpreter training, certain cognitive skills may be practiced that improve cognitive processing altogether, of which memory is a part. Moser-Mercer et al. (1997) report that *during* the activity of interpreting, memory for what is interpreted is rather poor, and as the interpreting continues such memory deteriorates further. However, over time the interpreter's semantic memory, that is, the build-up of encyclopedic knowledge, gradually increases as more and more new information is learned in the course of work. As interpreting students practice cognitive strategies and practical techniques, their overall ability to retain information can improve. An example of such a technique is note-taking during consecutive interpreting, where it is suggested that the "development and use of a particular note-taking technique (irrespective of its specific nature, i.e. with or without symbols) leads to the organization of a new cerebral language representation, which relies both on implicit and explicit memorization strategies" (Moser-Mercer et al. 1997:146).

Short-term memory capacity is central to both simultaneous and consecutive interpreting, although in somewhat different ways. Information from the source language text must be retained even if the exact form it takes is rapidly forgotten. Short-term memory "operations" occur continually while interpreting (Gile 1995:168) and the upper limit, "capacity" in Gile's terms, is constantly being tested. Gile refers to these operations as the short-term Memory Effort which is pushed and pulled along with others (the Listening and Analysis Effort and the Production Effort). It is evident that short-term memory is critical for recalling immediate aspects of the source message, and long-term memory gives us access to the source and target language lexicon, grammar and discourse structure information.

The role of long-term memory in language usage is evident in Gile's (1995) Gravitational Model of Linguistic Availability, given in Figure 1 (adapted from Gile 1995:217).[8] Individuals' linguistic knowledge is variable both in terms of what any single person understands and uses, and over the length of time that the person uses the language. In other words, a person's facility in a given language is never static, and no two people have an identical lexicon or pattern of usage.

While the interpreter must work at building a large inventory of vocabulary and constructions in her working languages, every part of her lexicon is not fully active all the time. Beyond the words and constructions that form a fairly basic, everyday usage (which shouldn't necessarily be taken to be small), the interpreter must focus on a specific sector of language use most critical for the subject matter she is interpreting

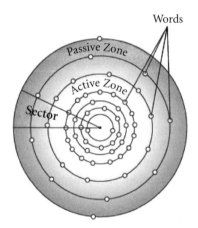

Figure 1. The Gravitational Model of Linguistic Availability. Gradient shading is added here to represent the indistinct division between Active and Passive Zones. From Daniel Gile, *Basic Concepts and Models for Interpreter and Translator Training* (1995:217). With kind permission by John Benjamins Publishing Company, Amsterdam/Philadelphia. www.benjamins.com.

at the time. For example, if interpreting a university course in psychology, terms pertinent to the discussion of psychology must be most readily available whereas terms related to tool and die (in manufacturing) are not so immediately important.

In Gile's Gravitational Model, words and constructions[9] exhibit some variability, that is, they may shift between the Active Zone and the Passive Zone. The closer they move toward the Nucleus, however, the more stable they become. Words (and constructions) in the Active Zone are those immediately available to the interpreter while those in the Passive Zone are less so. The closer the "orbit" of the word to the Nucleus, the more easily accessible it is; the farther out the orbit is, the more processing energy and time it will take to retrieve the word. The Sector is that content area in focus during interaction at any given time.

The significance of this model is found in a set of tendencies that Gile suggests describe the dynamics of word and construction availability, and which are helpful in understanding how our mental lexicon might work. These tendencies are given as rules, summarized from Gile (1995: 219–223):

> Rule 1: The Centrifugal Principle. If not stimulated, words and rules tend to drift outward (away from the center of the system).

Simply, when words are not used they slowly move out of the Active Zone. After a long period of time the speaker may lose access to them altogether.

> Rule 2: The Centripetal Effect of stimulation. When used, words and rules tend to move inward.

As words are read, heard, seen (for ASL), or used, they begin migrating toward the centre. This movement is more rapid than movement outward, and is increased by multiple stimuli. As Gile suggests, this may account for the rapid expansion of available terminology just prior to, and at the beginning of, an interpreting assignment when the interpreter undertakes intense preparation. This vocabulary is likely to remain available throughout the duration of the assignment, but in the days or weeks that follow, forgetting takes place.

> Rule 3: Stimulation frequency and the Centripetal Effect. The more frequently words and rules are used, the stronger the centripetal effect.

According to this rule, more frequently used words will be nearer to the Nucleus and will take the least amount of cognitive effort to activate. Interpreters who work in longer-term situations have the benefit of more frequent stimulation in a particular sector of words and constructions, which is one reason why preparation for each session can be easier and take less time.[10]

> Rule 4: The Centripetal Effect of active vs. passive stimulation. Active stimulation of a word or rule has a stronger centripetal effect than passive stimulation.

Words that are spoken, signed, or written have a greater effect on inward migration than those that are just heard or seen. Thus practice during preparation would seem to be a beneficial exercise. This rule also implies that language the interpreter uses outside the interpreting context is beneficial, especially in an L2 for which word and construction activation is likely to be less central overall in the Gravitational Model. This, of course, supports the notion of necessary interaction in the L2, discussed in Section 4.1 above.

Rule 4 also implies that if interpreters use incorrect or ungrammatical linguistic sequences repeatedly while interpreting without corrective feedback, they run the risk of having these erroneous patterns becoming learned, and thus activated over and over. This potential is yet another reason not to rely on L2 use while interpreting as the only practice one receives in using the language.

> *Rule 5: The Escort Effect and Interference Effect.* The centripetal migration of a word or rule generates the centripetal migration of other words or rules associated with it.

"When a Word becomes more available, other Words that sound or look similar, or that have been associated with it psychologically (through a learning situation, an emotional situation, etc.) also tend to become more available" (Gile 1995:221–222). That is, as words and constructions migrate inward, they bring their friends along with them. This principle has both a beneficial side and a deleterious side. The Escort Effect means that other related vocabulary may be more easily accessed on the basis of some specific word stimulus. Since other words in a target word's "neighbourhood" are also more likely to be needed while interpreting either because participants expand their information base throughout the discourse process or because interpreters employ strategies such as paraphrasing, using superordinate terms, etc., this rule suggests that there is a principled reason to expect that these other words will also be more easily accessed.

More problematic is the Interference Effect, meaning that linguistic interference may also result. Words that are similar in the interpreter's other working language, but which are not actually an exact match, may also be activated and if chosen, can create a less comprehensible target text. While more research on this phenomenon may clarify these effects, it is possible that Gile's Rule 5 helps to explain the extent of English intrusions when interpreting into ASL. Because of both the advantages of the Escort Effect and disadvantages of the Interference Effect, interpreters must remain alert to the consequences of their linguistic choices.

There are numerous ways to increase one's vocabulary. Gile advocates that students of interpreting spend time producing items over the more passive practice of listening to, or reading for, relevant vocabulary. For the ASL-English interpreter passive practice (in ASL) means watching someone else produce the items. But what if you need vocabulary that you don't know and are not likely to run across as you interact with others? Here we may strategize in several directions. It might first be assumed that very skilled interpreters have an advanced facility in their working languages altogether. Generally this means they have an above-average ability in language usage, with a solid, wide-ranging vocabulary. They interact linguistically in a broad range of settings, which affords both active production and more passive comprehension, and they read on a variety of topics. Readers are able to encounter situations and language use that differ greatly from their own experiences, and although this is a passive means of acquiring language, reading does introduce the interpreter to new ideas and words. Regarding ASL, which has no written form as yet, watching videotapes of ASL discourse exposes the interpreter to language and to the Deaf experience – equally as important as reading materials written in English.

Interpreters may increase the benefit from passive encounters with language by talking about, signing about, and even writing about what they read. This active production reinforces passive encounters with words, which encourages words to migrate inward to the Active Zone in the Gravitational Model. Such practices will help interpreters prepare generally for the work they do, but regarding specific content areas, attention must be paid to an appropriate sector of language use. Ideally, training programs will introduce student interpreters to sectors most common to their work, introducing appropriate vocabulary and discourse frames for these settings. Of course it is impossible to train for every conceivable topic (as some students would like), but there are certain topics and settings that ASL-English interpreters as generalists – how many interpreters begin their careers – are likely to encounter.[11] Specific and more intensive training can be given here.

It should be emphasized that interpreters, as language specialists, need to develop their language facility in *both* working languages; it is insufficient to put into practice the above strategies in only one, even though it is somewhat more critical for interpreters to spend time building their L2. But focusing on ASL development exclusively without regard to English is detrimental, especially when ASL to English interpreting requires the active availability of English words and constructions. Finally, the above discussion has focused on vocabulary and constructions specifically, but linguistic interaction involves much more than this. Proficient language users also have learned ways of structuring their discourse to portray a certain intended perspective or to produce some desired effect. They learn how to convince, argue, be polite, take and give up a turn, and many other things. In Section 5 below, we will extend the discussion with regard to interpreting in terms of "words, constructions, text, and context".

4.3 Linguistic training

There are two aspects to an interpreter's knowledge of language: intuitive knowledge and knowledge gained by careful study. These two aspects are not mutually exclusive. Conscious effort in studying the structure and meaning of language can reinforce intuitive knowledge, and sometimes challenge it.

Intuitive knowledge of language corresponds to the words and constructions nearest the Nucleus in the Gravitational Model of Linguistic Availability. While interpreting, especially when the delivery is simultaneous, word and construction retrieval must be quick, as there is very little time to consider choices. Such choices need to be logical and contribute to a target text that appears as conventional as possible to the audience. Intuitive knowledge of language is critical too because the interpreter's attention must be shared among several taxing efforts: taking in the source text, analysis, and production of the target.

Can an interpreter get by solely on an intuitive knowledge of language? The advantages to intuitive knowledge listed above are obvious. The longer a language is actively used, the more intuitions will build. This is especially the case for someone who begins to use the language early in life. But there are many reasons to think that a professional interpreter, no matter what background she has, must also engage in conscious study of that language. First, very few sectors of language use – in business, education, social services, the courts, religion, and many others – are gained through extended periods of everyday interaction. Inward migration of words in these sectors will take place through conscious learning; some items have a good chance of becoming strongly intuitive, but not all will. Therefore there will always be a balance between intuition and continued learning. Second, when forming a target text in any technical sense, it is irresponsible to "fly by the seat of your pants" as a general rule of practice. Rather, accuracy will depend on deliberate and wise linguistic choices, carefully chosen and carefully pieced together in phrases and sentences, which can only take place with much conscious effort. Intuitions here are necessary too, but these are not enough. Third, much of the interpreting process is evaluative. Analysis is an active, effortful process. Seleskovitch (1978:9) says that the interpreter must "apprehend" the source language of the message to understand "through a process of analysis and exegesis". The meaning of a message can only be apprehended (note the deliberateness and forcefulness of this word) when effort is expended in considering possible meanings and intentions, many times even by comparing what is being said to what is *not* being said. Further, at the text level, discourse frames and text structure are informative too. Here the interpreter must have text analysis tools at the ready to dissect what the text itself might reveal about the speaker's or signer's intent. All these tools of analysis, for a wide range of texts – not to mention the interpreter's own rendering of target texts – do take advantage of what is intuitive but can only be mastered through careful study and practice.

Fourth, intuitive language knowledge alone may be appropriate in certain contexts, but this cannot be generalized to all discourse settings. An interpreting student once habitually used the phrase "I *seen* that already/yesterday/etc." which may have been an acceptable usage for certain family members or a peer group when growing up (thus intuitive), but which would not be appropriate in most social and business contexts. For L2 learners of ASL, intuitive use comes only after a long period of practice, especially when learning takes place as adults. Intuitions may only be partial in this case, when they exist at all.

Because language facility is at the heart of interpreters' work, it is worth the effort to spend a good deal of time studying it. This is especially true for ASL, no matter if ASL is an L1 or an L2 for the interpreter. ASL and other signed languages have widely been taken seriously as legitimate languages only in the latter half of the 20th century. Today linguists generally consider this to be the case, but many have needed a great deal of convincing. More and more, however, information on the structure of signed languages is working its way into the course materials of linguistics departments. Many universities offer occasional courses on some aspect of signed languages, and some, like the linguistics department at the University of Manitoba, regularly offer upper level courses on the linguistic structure of a signed language such as ASL. The benefit to ASL-English interpreters of taking general linguistics courses lies in the fact that ASL morpho-syntactic structures pattern in many ways similarly to languages other than English. Some knowledge of these patterns is helpful in understanding how ASL is structured and what these cross-linguistic patterns mean. Comparison only with English can even lead to an ethnocentric view of ASL, something that no interpreter can afford to have.[12]

Interpreters are also able to take advantage of another branch of linguistics that has grown as of late, that of discourse analysis. Rather than focusing on theories of sentence-level structure based on constructed sentences, linguistic work on recordings and transcriptions of actual texts tells us much about how people *use* language, which brings the fields of linguistics and interpreting closer together. Such work often deals with how texts are constructed and why. For example, Taylor Torsello, Gallina, Sidiropoulou, Taylor, Tebble, and Vuorikoski (1997) show how the themes of a text can be tracked sentence by sentence as the dynamic text unfolds. The hearer (and more importantly, the interpreter) can therefore find clues regarding directions the discourse is taking, considerably helpful in the process of constructing a target text. Discourse analysis studies of ASL are an invaluable resource for ASL-English interpreters because they tell us much about how ASL texts are constructed as natural discourse. It might be cumbersome to learn transcription keys for how researchers have represented ASL in print form on paper, but such studies allow for the careful analysis of a stream of ASL discourse. An interesting application of this type of study is the analysis of interpreted discourse (see, for example, Metzger 1999; Roy 2000), where the source and interpreter's target messages can be compared for appropriateness, accuracy, error types, etc.

All in all, linguistics has much to offer the field of interpreting in terms of analytic tools to understand both linguistic structure and discourse sequencing. In turn, an interpretation offers an interesting discourse text type for linguistic dissection. The intersection of these two fields provides interpreters with more explicit ways to talk about linguistic aspects of their work, and most certainly any research directed at interpreted texts will further these practitioners' knowledge of their field.

5.   Words, constructions, texts, and context

Seleskovitch (1978:9) gives us a three-step model of the interpreting process that differentiates the form of both source text and target text from the essence of the message intended by the text. The model is as follows:

1. Auditory perception of a linguistic utterance which carries meaning. Apprehension of the language and comprehension of the message through a process of analysis and exegesis.
2. Immediate and deliberate discarding of the wording and retention of the mental representation of the message (concepts, ideas, etc.).
3. Production of a new utterance in the target language which must meet a dual requirement: it must express the original message in its entirety, and it must be geared to the recipient.

There is much about this model that is insightful. We know that the underlying sense (or meaning) of the source message is not completely tied to the original words and constructions because we can paraphrase, that is, we can use other words to say more or less the same thing. This has led to a profound belief among interpreters that linguistic form is unimportant and must be discarded as rapidly as possible. Umberto Eco, a semiotician and novelist, and himself a translator, says that "a translation can express an evident 'deep' sense of a text even by violating both lexical and referential faithfulness." (Eco 2001: 14). Statements such as these indicate that an intended sense of a message is indeed more than the sum of its words, but this does not mean that there is no relation between the linguistic material that makes up the message and the resulting sense being conveyed. Meaning can only be constructed based on the words and constructions used in the source text, combined with the context in which they are spoken or signed. Because of this, the form of the source message (again, the words and constructions) must be carefully scrutinized – they are the most direct source for clues to meaning the interpreter is apt to find and constitute the beginning point for the interpreter's journey of meaning construction for the text as a whole. Beyond the source message words and constructions, the interpreter will have to rely a great deal on inference: from the range of possible meanings that words carry, from the pragmatics of the situation in which they are uttered, and even from the surrounding political, economic, social, and cultural backdrop in which the situation and its participants are found.

In the following sections we look at the interpreter's text from the level of the word, through constructions, to whole texts and to context, keeping in mind that the interpreter has countless decisions to make in encountering and apprehending the source message and reconstructing it for the recipient of her interpretation. Some brief examples are included to illustrate each principle.

5.1 Words

Because of differences in phonetic properties and morphological processes between ASL and English, word building in each language requires different strategies. In part this has to do with differences in visual and auditory transmission of the linguistic signals. How much of an added cognitive effort switching between signed and spoken modalities is involved in ASL-English interpreting is not known, but researchers have speculated that this is an additional dimension for interpreters who have a signed language as one of their working languages. Cokely (1982) includes this "modality switch" as an added required step in his nine-step model of the interpreting process.

One effect of language being transmitted visually is that vision is more suited to "vertical processing" or the ability to process different types of input presented virtually all at the same time, whereas hearing is more suited to "horizontal processing" or the ability to process temporally ordered inputs. Both hearing and vision do allow for both vertical and horizontal processing, but not equally (Brentari 2002). The general effect in terms of language units is that processing through vision allows us to distinguish meaningful units that are produced simultaneously within the visual field, whereas auditory processing depends more on the sequencing of meaning-bearing units. Further, it is no evolutionary accident that the articulatory system for each type of language is well-suited for the modality. Sounds are produced as a stream via a single vocal tract and are combined more or less sequentially into meaningful language units, whereas linguistic units in a signed language are produced by two independently functional hands along with facial and body gestures all of which can operate simultaneously in the visual field (for detailed discussion see Armstrong, Stokoe, & Wilcox 1995).

In English, words are built in a number of ways, most of which involve adding morphological units made of strings of sounds to a base or root. A single lexical word might have a root (such as *book* – a noun or verb) along with one or more affixes that add specific meanings (*book-s, book-ing, book-ing-s*). Such affixes usually add grammatical meaning, for example the *-s* in *books* adds either plural meaning onto the noun or third person singular present meaning onto the verb (these are two distinct morphemes that happen to have the same phonological shape). Bound morphemes can also serve to change the word class in English, as in (1):

(1)   a. nation   *(noun)*
      b. national   *(adjective)*
      c. nationality   *(noun)*

Words can be built by compounding, a fairly common occurrence in English. In compounded words, two lexical items combine to form a single word with a predictable stress pattern that is different from the same two words as a phrase, illustrated in (2). The compound also has a meaning that is substantially different from that of the two-word phrase.

(2)   a. green house'   = (adjective + noun: a phrase) a green-coloured house; second word has the heaviest stress
      b. green' house   = (noun: a compound) a building, usually constructed of glass; first syllable has the heaviest stress[13]

English is not considered to be a very "morphologically rich" language however, compared to some languages for which the main mechanism of building complex meaning is affixing. In English, words are frequently added at the phrase level, even when the added meanings are grammatical in nature. A number of aspectual categories, which are units of meaning that say something about the temporal "internal" structure of the action coded by the verb, are realized as a phrase. The PROGRESSIVE in English, for example, is formed by the combination of verb stem, the inflectional suffix *-ing*, and the separate auxiliary *to be*. Progressive aspect indicates that the action is on-going, with tense added to the copula, as in (3):

(3) a. **is** walk-**ing**   *(present)*
     b. **was** walk-**ing**   *(past)*
     c. **will be** walk-**ing**   *(future)*

The action can be further described by the addition of elements that comment on the manner of motion. In English this is accomplished by including adverbs in the phrase:

(4) a. She was walking **slowly**.
     b. She was walking **slowly** and **carefully**.

English, then, has several ways of combining meaning, but for the most part words that are themselves not particularly morphemically complex are strung together to make up phrases and sentences.

  Some languages, on the other hand, add numerous meaning units to the word by affixing, rather than by adding more and more distinct words in the phrase. These languages are often called "polysynthetic" languages, in which it is common for a single word to also be a whole sentence. Example (5) is from Tiwi, an aboriginal language spoken in Australia (from Crystal 1987:293):

(5) a. ngirruunthingapukani
     b. ngi -rru   -unthing   -apu -kani
         I   PAST TENSE for some time eat repeatedly
         'I kept on eating.'

Signed languages typically have a combination of words with little or no inflectional or derivational bound morphology along with very morphologically complex words. The more complex forms are thought to have a verb as the root, although there is still much debate regarding how the roles of various parts of the complex relate to one another. These very common complexes lead some researchers to regard ASL as a polysynthetic language (e.g., Brentari 2002).

  A striking difference between polymorphemic words in signed and spoken languages is that rather than morphemes of various kinds being affixed in a linear pattern, as in the Tiwi example in (5), morphemes in a signed language are commonly combined by a type of fusion, that is, by an alternation to the internal structure of the verb stem. This results in a complex form that is not lengthened by affixing morphemic units and thereby increasing the number of syllables of the word, but by increasing the number of meaningful parts that co-occur more or less simultaneously.

An internal change to the shape of the word when meaning units are added does take place in English, but this is somewhat rare. Some examples are *goose/geese* in which a vowel change signals plurality, and *run/ran* which signals a tense alternation. Another type of internal change in English is shown in *prove/proof* in which the final fricative consonant is either voiced or unvoiced. This difference doesn't add specific meaning to the stem, but it does signal a verb/noun word category difference. The plural form *geese* means that in a single word of one syllable there are two morphemes: the noun itself (a content word) and plural-marking. In this case the two morphemes are said to be "fused", that is, they are not separable pieces.

Because of the nature of the articulation system in ASL and other signed languages, coupled with vertical processing that vision allows for, the potential for such simultaneous morpheme combining appears to be much higher than for spoken languages (Brentari 2002). In an example from Brentari (2002:58) shown in Figure 2, six morphemic units[14] combine while maintaining the shape of a single syllable.[15] This potential may represent a unique typological feature of signed, as opposed to spoken, languages.

The predicate represented in Figure 2 shows the complex way in which meaningful parts are combined. The handshape on each hand articulates a classifier morpheme for an upright figure, in this case the flexion means the figures are hunched. Because both hands articulate the classifier we understand that there are two of them (combinations of extended fingers on one or both hands indicate number in certain nominal forms). The two hands in a spatial relationship indicate that the figures are side by side, and the palm orientation signals that they are both facing front (in many object nominals

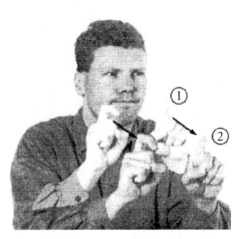

Figure 2. An example of a polymorphemic structure in ASL. Numbers in the figure refer to the beginning and end points of the movement. From Diane Brentari, "Modality differences in sign language phonology and morphophonemics". In R. P. Meier, K. Cormier, and D. Quinto-Posoz (Eds.), *Modality and Structure in Signed and Spoken Languages.* (2002:58), Cambridge University Press, Cambridge.

the faces of the hand represent the front and back of the object if these are salient inherent features of the item itself). Movement in the direction of the palm orientation here indicates that the figures are moving forward as well. The co-articulated facial gesture, also considered morphemic, signals a manner of movement, in this case careful movement. This predicate would normally be embedded in a larger discourse segment, so that the specific identity of the figures, for example, would have been specified, and so forth. But given this to be true, the predicate in Figure 2 represents a stand-alone sentence composed of a single polymorphemic word.

In word building across language boundaries, then, the ASL-English interpreter must use radically different grammatical knowledge of the two languages in order to transfer such information from one to the other. In working from English to ASL, the interpreter must determine what information coded by separate nouns, verb, adverbs, prepositions, etc. (some of which may have some morphological complexity) can be transferred to bound morphemes that make up the semantically complex predicate structure, and vice versa. Without this understanding, it might be tempting to think that a great deal of expansion or elaboration is taking place in working from ASL to English, and a great deal of reduction when interpreting from English to ASL, but this is not the case. Semantic information can be equally conveyed, even though the linguistic form ultimately chosen differs radically. A further factor involves usage conventions, that is, for each cultural group the level of specificity expected in conventional discourse may differ and the interpreter must consider these factors as well when formulating the target text.

The effects of different word-building strategies between English to ASL are felt most when combining items into constructions, which is discussed in Section 5.2 below.

5.1.1 *Meaning transfer in terms of (complex) words*
There are obvious ways in which word meaning does not transfer from language to language, for example words that have some connection to cultural or social phenomena in one language community are not likely to carry this significance to a target language text. It is possible that some words have a fairly equal counterpart in both source and target languages, and if so, and if the context of use permits, these make the interpreter's work less difficult. The problem, though, is that some such words may seem to equate, when in fact they do not. At a national interpreters' conference in Canada some years ago a conference host, speaking English, announced on the first morning that coffee would be *available* a little later during the morning break. The French-speaking audience members were disturbed (or perhaps a bit relieved) to hear from the English-French interpreter that the coffee was "*avalable*", that is, *swallowable*. Gile (1995: 167) refers to words that look similar in both languages "but do not have the same meaning, connotation, or usage" as "faux amis" (false friends).

The effect of morpheme combining in ASL in the way described above can also be problematic for constructing meaning, especially for interpreters with ASL as an

L2. Quite often, when watching an adept signer construct a complex predicate in ASL, many of the meaning units – on the (two) hands, facial gestures, body movements and positions – must be apprehended as they co-occur. But without sufficient language experience, some may be missed. On the other hand, the more linear, phrase by phrase encoding of meaning in English, especially during simultaneous interpreting, may lead to a complex target ASL predicate form that encodes *some* of the corresponding meaning units, but not quite all. What then does the interpreter do with the "leftovers"? Repeat and reconstruct the predicate? Add the additional pieces on to the end (which may not result in a grammatical construction in ASL)? Move to more English-like phrasing?

In a signed language, where articulation takes advantage of the three-dimensional space around the signer, the orientation and spatial distance of the hands to the signer's body conveys meaning as well. In the next example, we see an alternation in the structure of a single classifier predicate that changes the sense of the resulting sentence. Suppose that the interpreter wishes to convey the message, with English as the source language and ASL as the target, that a stranger had approached and frightened Sally, a third person referent. At least two choices are available to the interpreter as signer when articulating the verb construction and each has a very different effect. In one the signer could locate Sally with a third person indexical marker (PRO.3$_a$),[16] which is a point to a location in some space, or by signing Sally's name at that spatial location. Then the signer could give the classifier predicate form CL:1(*person*) with the movement beginning at another spatial location and ending abruptly at the first location chosen for Sally. Here the signer would most likely look toward the location for Sally at the same time. This might be followed by another pointing index to Sally's location, and then the sign AFRAID, as represented in (6):

(6) S-A-L-L-Y PRO.3$_a$, **CL:1(*person*)b→a**, PRO.3$_a$ AFRAID.EMPH
     Sally   3s   person.approach.3s 3s   frightened
     'Someone approached Sally and frightened her.'

A second choice would be for the signer to incorporate a slight body shift in the direction of the location for Sally, and reorient the predicate toward their own body, a kind of "first person as third person" construction, as in (7):

(7) S-A-L-L-Y PRO.3$_a$, body.shift→a, **CL:1(*person*)b→1**, AFRAID.EMPH
     Sally   3s   (signer as 3s)   person.approach.1s 1s.frightened
     'Sally was approached by someone and was frightened.'

Both of these are grammatical, but each conveys a markedly different message having to do with perspective or empathy.[17] In (6) the signer has "empathized" (grammatically) with the stranger; this is a sentence about what this person did to Sally. The sentence in (7), however, takes Sally's viewpoint. It's a statement about what happened to her and her reaction to being approached. The basic information doesn't differ, but the intended message – who the signer would like the audience to side with, perhaps – differs significantly.

These few examples give us only a hint of the attention interpreters must pay to complex forms in language, whether this is of the more sequential type of spoken languages or the simultaneous "fused" type of signed languages. In any case, this difference between English and ASL is a significant factor in considering these two grammar systems as structurally quite distinct.

It should be clear by now that passive knowledge of language is insufficient by itself for a responsible interpreter undertaking the work. Intuitive knowledge of language, built by early experience or by conscious effort, is but the first step on the way to accurate interpretation. The interpreter's language learning process is never complete. When faced with acquiring expertise in a signed language such as ASL, a concerted effort over a long period of time is needed to bring the interpreting student's language abilities up to the level required to work in the multitude of settings where professionals in various other fields work and interact. These same comments could equally describe the interpreter's facility with English. For both languages, a combination of intuitive knowledge and conscious knowledge will be the best way to make careful and correct decisions about how to rephrase the source language message into a top-notch interpretation.

5.2 Constructions

It is not possible in a signed language to incorporate every aspect of meaning in a single syllable word, even if "vertical processing" allows for a higher potential of simultaneously articulated morpheme combinations. For any language it is usual to find morphemes with meanings closely related to either a noun or verb clustered around that word or stem (Bybee 1985). Thus in English we find auxiliaries (e.g., *have*, *be*, etc.) next to the verb and tense inflections suffixed to the verb stem, not somewhere far apart from the verb in the sentence. Similarly we find articles (*a*, *an*, *the*) and adjectives close by the noun. A similar iconic pattern is the case for ASL too, although ASL has many more classes of bound morphology than does English.

Still, there are limits to what can be combined with a single ASL verb stem, especially by fusion. Many morphological units that can be added alter the shape of the movement of the verb stem (Klima & Bellugi 1979), such as CONTINUA-TIVE aspect which changes a straight path to a circular path (e.g., LOOK.AT → LOOK.AT.CONTINUOUS), DISTRIBUTIVE aspect which changes the shape of the path along with features of the final path location (e.g., $_1$GIVE$_2$ ('I give X to you') → $_1$GIVE$_2$.DISTRIBUTED ('I give X to everyone of you')), or one kind of completion meaning which effects a change in handshape along the path movement (e.g., flattened [O] handshape → open [5] handshape as in $_1$GIVE$_3$ ('I give X to him/her') → $_1$GIVE$_3$.COMPLETION ('I give X away (to him/her')). But other kinds of meaning addition can lengthen the word or result in a phrasal construction. Continuous aspect, noted above, not only changes the shape of the movement, but necessitates a repetition of the entire circular movement pattern as a reduplicated form. A somewhat different meaning results from a differently shaped and reduplicated movement, that is, a straight path in the forward direction followed by a circular path moving down and back to the beginning point, usually called ITERATIVE aspect. The difference in English would be *I looked at X for a long time* (continuative) versus *I kept looking at X over and over* (iterative). Note that in English the added meanings are given primarily by adverbial phrases following the verb.

A more complex example of sequencing in ASL is found in Supalla (1990) regarding certain verbs of motion. Supalla argues that for these predicates information about the path of motion and manner of motion cannot occur on the same articulated classifier+verb stem. If the signer wishes to convey the meaning 'he limped around in a circle', this is accomplished by CL:1(*person*) moved in a circular path followed by CL:('*legs*')[18] in a limping manner articulated in the space in front of the signer but with no path movement at all. These two forms are serialized (in sequence), but together they convey a single action. Supalla claims that this represents an upper limit on the number and type of morphemes that can be combined in a single verb stem.

A helpful approach to understanding the nature of constructions in language is outlined in Goldberg (1995, 1998), aptly labeled "Construction Grammar". According to Goldberg a construction is any word or phrase that pairs form with meaning. In this sense the size of the paired linguistic unit is inconsequential – either a single word or a string of words qualifies as a construction. I have already discussed single words, whether mono- or polymorphemic, above. Here I will focus on forms (phrases, sentences) that tend to be larger than single words. The division between words and phrases is somewhat artificial, however, especially when dealing with a language with large, polymorphemic forms. Many predicates in ASL incorporate subject and object agreement, classifier and verb stems, aspectual categories, etc. in a single form with no need to include separate noun phrases in the sentence.

An important claim of Goldberg's is that the construction type itself carries meaning over and above lexical meaning provided by the individual words in the phrase. Goldberg illustrates this claim with an example from English: the ditransitive. Note the example in (8) from Goldberg (1998:203):

(8)   Pat baked Chris a cake.

Goldberg notes that the sense of transfer that takes place is not apparent from the semantics of any of the words in the sentence, and therefore must be apparent from the construction type as a whole.[19] Thus she states:

> The question arises, where does the semantics of intended transfer associated with [8] come from? It is not a necessary part of the meaning of *bake* ..., and it is not associated with any of the noun phrases. One possibility is to allow the additional meaning component, the semantics of 'someone (intending to) cause someone to receive something' to be attributed directly to the formal pattern, Subj V Obj Obj2.   (Goldberg 1998:204)

From this we understand that because the composite meaning of a construction depends on both the words *and* the construction itself, interpreters would do well to pay attention to both. Although many interpretation theorists stress that the source language form is of little importance and must be discarded soon after it is received, here I contend that such dismissal should not be too early, and that before it occurs careful attention to the source words and structure is critical. It is patently true that the source structure cannot inform the target language structure, especially when the grammars of the two languages differ greatly, which I have argued is the case for ASL and English. But in terms of meaning, the words and constructions (not to diminish the importance of text and context, discussed in the following sections) are the most tangible elements from which the interpreter can infer specific meaning. Thus apprehension of the source message also must entail a critical analysis of the form of the source text (which, incidently, takes time).

A good example of a construction type in ASL that signals a particular meaning or intended orientation to the information being discussed is the so-called "rhetorical question", that is, a question form inserted mid-sentence. Such a construction is often glossed as follows in (9) taken from Valli and Lucas (1992: 280):[20]

rhet

(9)   PRO.1 TIRED WHY STUDY ALL-NIGHT
      'I'm tired. Why? Because I studied all night.'

Problems interpreters may have with this type of construction are first, how to understand what is intended by the inserted rh-question and second, how to reconstruct it in English, the target language. It is not uncommon to hear an interpreter working from ASL to English follow a phrasing similar to the ASL construction (statement + rh-question + statement) with rising yes-no question intonation on the rhetorical phrase. More often than not this reconstruction sounds forced and unnatural. The interpreter has missed the point.

The complete range of functions of such "rhetorical questions" in ASL grammar has not yet been studied (cf. Wilbur 1995 for a structural perspective on this topic), although it is clear that the construction serves to focus a particular piece of information in an unexpected way. The so-called rh-question here does not function as a real question of any sort, but rather has a grammatical function as a focus marker. It is often suggested that events are typically given in a chronological sequence in ASL discourse, that is, what happened first, second, third, etc., or cause first, effect second. But a cause-effect sentence that includes this (re-)focus marker, as in (9), reverses the combination to an EFFECT − FOCUS MARKER − CAUSE construction where the pragmatic focus is on the cause (the effect phrase may also be "shared" information, and marked with topic marking, but this is not a requirement for every context). Armed with this knowledge, the interpreter can recognize the intention of the signer from the construction type, and fill in the content from the lexical material. It should be noted that there appear to be several additional related functions of such focus marking in sentences other than the cause-effect case. Goldberg (1998) suggests that similar to many words, constructions can sometimes be polysemous, having a "family" of related meanings or functions. Nonetheless, in the construction discussed here, the focus marker is typically the ASL word WHY with co-articulated yes/no question marking (raised eyebrows, a possible forward head-tilt, followed by a pause),[21] which in English is commonly translated as 'because' or a paraphrase thereof.

The above discussion is just a glimpse at the role that constructions play in apprehending the meaning of a text, with some examples from English and ASL. But just as it can not be taken for granted that words will translate simply from one language to the next, it cannot be assumed that the interpreter's two working languages will have the identical construction for a given meaning (in a given context). This may be true in some cases, for example a yes/no question in one language usually translates fairly easily into a yes/no question in the other, even if the structures of the two are not the same, but even here there might be certain pragmatic contexts where a yes/no question in the target language does not express the intended sense. Once again it must be stressed that when interpreting, careful analysis of the source text and reconstruction into the target necessitates a strong conscious knowledge of lexical and grammatical components of both languages so that the interpreter can make informed choices in representing the speaker's or signer's intentions. But intuitive knowledge of language is important too, since the interpreter's time to work is extremely short, and the more accessible the lexical and construction choices are in the interpreter's mental store, the more quickly decisions can be made and an interpretation formulated.

5.3 Texts

Words and larger constructions appear in discourse segments which I will call TEXTS. Texts can be interactive or dialogic (Wadensjö 1998), as in a conversation or interview, or can be more like a monologue – the discourse of a single speaker or signer. In fact, it is misleading to think of only some types of texts as interactive and not others. A primary function of language is that of interaction among people, and even monologue deliveries have a purpose, such as to inform, persuade, or to entertain, all of which assume another participant as the recipient of the message. In other words, a source message is inevitably oriented toward a recipient. The source text speaker or signer chooses various features of the text, that is, particular vocabulary, construction types, discourse markers and discourse framing, stops and starts, etc., based on their perceptions of the audience, and what they must do to accomplish their communicative goals. They may allow for the audience to participate actively or passively, but language use rarely, if ever, occurs without some interactive purpose (Linell 1997). Thus the interpreter is well advised to scrutinize *both* the message sender and receiver when formulating her interpretation.

In many ways, the interpreter is caught in between the source speaker and target recipient. The two participants have some relationship to each other, which may be fairly close or quite distant, and yet they do not share the same set of language and cultural experiences or expectations. The interpreter must juggle both. We have already seen examples of this regarding linguistic content and structure at the word and construction level in the sections above, but it is also true that text structure is a crucial component of successful communication.

5.3.1 *Registers, genres, and the language style of texts*

It is fairly common to hear ASL-English interpreters talk about "register" as divisible into five general areas from least to most formal: intimate, casual (or informal), consultative, formal, and frozen (see, for example, Humphrey & Alcorn 1996). This paradigm stems from Joos's (1961) early work on language style differences in the book *The Five Clocks*. Since then, however, register variationists in the field of sociolinguistics have made numerous inroads in understanding the complex domain of language usage. It is much too simplistic to consider that actual discourse can be categorized in terms of the intimate to frozen paradigm.[22] For an interpreter to conclude that a certain text will be "consultative", for example, is only so helpful. What does such a term mean? Is there *one* consultative way of speaking? Of signing? Are they similar cross-language? Cross-culturally? How does a speaker or signer choose a particular language style in these terms? Once chosen, does this limit the type of language that can be used? And what in fact characterizes the language style in each given category?

Ferguson (1994) defines REGISTER as a communication situation within a society that occurs regularly such that participants develop particular patterns of language use that become identified with this setting. Used in this way, register is taken to mean the situation itself, not a language style that may be found there. The advantage to thinking of registers as situation types (e.g., a classroom, doctor's office, boardroom, etc.) is that it allows language use found there to *vary*, such that there will be a tendency to see a given language style associated with the register, although participants are not constrained by this style. Ferguson states:

> People participating in recurrent communication situations tend to develop similar vocabularies, similar features of intonation, and characteristic bits of syntax and phonology that they use in those situations. Some of these registral features, such as special terms for recurrent objects and events, and formulaic sequences or 'routines', seem to facilitate speedy communication; other features apparently serve to mark the register, establish feelings of rapport, and serve other purposes similar to the accommodation that influences dialect formation.
>
> (Ferguson 1994: 20)

A GENRE, on the other hand, is a message *type* that similarly emerges as a regularly occurring phenomenon with an internal structure identifiable by community members as different from other message types (Ferguson 1994). Thus members of a community will be able to recognize and produce a casual conversation, a prayer, directions to a location, a debate, lecture, and numerous other genres, having a sense of what belongs in, and does not belong in, the form of each. A text, in this sense, is a single instantiation of some genre produced in a corresponding register. The term LANGUAGE STYLE characterizes the language features found in the text.

In a given register, a post-secondary classroom for example, numerous genres are possible. The participants – teacher and students – are prone to moving from one genre to another. They may have discussions, present theories and arguments to support them, describe and explain the nature of a complex machine or some other structure, the teacher may give advice or help students through a difficult dilemma, etc., with each text type having particular characteristics. Similarly the tone of the discourse can change from formal and even controlling, to relaxed interaction, to arguing differences of opinion or perspectives. For each such situation, participants, by virtue of their shared knowledge of registers, genres and language styles, know more or less what to do. Interpreters in these situations must have this knowledge in two languages and cultural contexts. When a strong intuitive knowledge of the languages being used plus conscious knowledge (which allows for analysis) are in place, the interpreter can focus more on transferring material across these potential differences in whole-text features, without which recipients are not likely to get an accurate portrayal of what is going on around them. (Think, for example, of the effects of receiving a message in casual terms that is meant as a carefully constructed set of instructions, or of a target message given in short, sharp sentences that was actually something meant to put students at ease, like a series of puns.)

Therefore in any given register (i.e., situation) we will find a range of possible genres, exemplified by specific texts. The language style of participants may not remain the same throughout the interaction being interpreted; rather, the interpreter can likely count on the language style being quite variable overall, and the genre can change too, depending on the complexity of the situation and the interaction. Deciding that a register will be characterized as "consultative" at the onset of an interpreted situation, for example, can prevent the interpreter from understanding and conveying what is actually going on between discourse participants.

Interaction and language structure are related on yet another level. Social interactions and the various motivations behind them can spark particular patterns of language use, which solidify over time into expected and conventional linguistic structures for that context. The point here is that grammar has some "social relevance" in that it is pushed and pulled by the interaction of discourse participants. This is perhaps most evident in highly interactive discourse like conversation:

> The fact that talk in interaction is produced in the presence of active coparticipants brings into play the constant relevance of how and when addressees produce responsive behaviors. There are at least two far-reaching implications of the socially distributed nature of talk-in-interaction: The first has to do with the grammar of turn construction as a resource for the predication of upcoming points for speaker change. The second involves the input of addressees and how a speaker can use that input as a source for revision and extension in the production of a single turn.   (Ford, Fox, & Thompson 2003:123)

This is how individual texts (whether dialogue or monologue) get the shape they have. At present, we have very little formal understanding of the effects of these processes for ASL, but as researchers focus more and more on the properties of dynamic texts, our knowledge of both ASL grammar and features of genres within registers is growing. This knowledge would seem especially crucial to interpreters. Nonetheless, what I have tried to show in this discussion is that text "frames" have importance too, which must be examined by interpreters as they analyze the message as a whole.

5.3.2 *Culturally motivated text structure differences: A problem for interpreters*

The structure of a text overall can conventionalize for a specific genre. An important question for interpreters to consider is how these structures differ in various discourse contexts for English and ASL. It would seem that for English, some headway has been made regarding discourse registers and genres (cf. Ferguson 1994, discussed above), but this is not yet the case for ASL, for which very little such work has been undertaken. Speakers and signers from different cultures approach their subjects in different ways, many of which have cultural principles guiding them. It is one thing to understand the cultural motivations behind a text and the conventions of text structure in a particular genre, it is another to attempt a satisfactory interpretation when differences are striking. This continues to be a challenge for interpreters, with no easy solution. However, the first step is to understand the principles that guide text structure and their implications for the interpreter. Several examples are discussed here to illustrate the problem, but it is clear that interpreters will need to continue to work at appropriate ways of dealing with these text conflicts.

Differences in text structure between English and Arabic are illustrated in Hatim (1997), especially with regard to what the translator needs to know:

> Pending further quantitative and qualitative research, my own investigations into the argumentative text type in English and Arabic from the perspective of translation points to a noticeable tendency in English towards *counter-argumentation*. Furthermore, of the two counter-argumentative formats, English seems to prefer the Balance (thesis-opposition-substantiation-conclusion) to the Explicit Concessive (e.g. although…). Modern Standard Arabic, in contrast, tends more towards *through-argumentation* (thesis-substantiation-conclusion). No doubt, counter-argumentation is also in evidence in Arabic, but when this occurs, it is usually the Explicit Concessive which seems to be the more preferred option stylistically.
>
> (Hatim 1997: 44; italics added)

In other words, Hatim suggests that when English-speaking westerners argue a point, they will likely present their point, followed by a potential counter-argument to what they believe, and then present evidence that discounts the counter-argument and supports their claim. Note that this is a very common progression in presenting research findings in western cultures. Arabic speakers, however, appear to use more direct argumentation without contrasting their point with some counter-argument. Both speakers would have the same intention of convincing their audience to accept their thesis, but the effect of each of these text styles on the interpreter's target cultural group may not be equal. The Arabic–speaking audience may feel affronted by the English speaker's inclusion of a counter-argument, while the English–speaking audience may feel that the Arabic speaker hasn't satisfactorily completed the argumentation. Framing a translation from one to the other in the style of the source text type would render an incongruity in the resulting target text.

Interpreters may feel, with some justification, that they cannot be expected to alter the text in a major way to accommodate this difference in style, that source speakers should understand that they are addressing an audience with a different cultural perspective. But interpreters are often hired with the expectation that they have the means to bridge cultural differences, something ASL-English interpreters perpetuate by ascribing to a "cross-cultural" or "bilingual-bicultural" model of interpreting. Deaf interpreters, who inevitably identify more closely with Deaf community members than with hearing "outsiders" often see it as their responsibility to shape the target text to fit the cultural experience of their Deaf target addressees (cf. Boudreault, this volume).

When interpreting between western English speakers and Japanese speakers, the interpreter faces another dilemma. Kondo (1988) suggests that Japanese speakers value a culturally motivated principle of "less is more", that saying few words when making an argument garners respect from the Japanese addressee. Westerners, on the other hand (Kondo points to American speakers in his example), tend to say more, to continue talking until they feel their argument is complete. A refusal to participate fully in lengthy discussion can even be seen by westerners as anti-social. In interpreted situations, when the interpreter frames a Japanese target text in the American style, or an English text in the Japanese style, the result can be ineffective at best, disastrous at worst.

An example might be drawn from ASL-English interpreting as well. It is commonly thought that at least some English genres (such as a formal speech) begin with very general introductory comments and gradually narrow their focus until the main thesis is stated at or near the end of the text. In contrast, ASL texts are sometimes thought to be "diamond shaped", that is, the signer begins with a clear statement of the point, develops arguments or elaborates, and concludes with a reiteration of the main thesis (cf. Cristie, Wilkins, Hicks McDonald, & Neuroth-Gimbrone 1999).[23] If true, then constructing a target text in ASL with the organization of an English source text would cause a conflict, perhaps resulting in confusion on the part of the addressees.

What does the interpreter then do? As mentioned, there is no easy answer to this question. It is helpful, however, to consider the source and target texts as two parallel but distinct texts. The target audience has more or less no actual access to the source text structure and does not compare and evaluate the target text against the source text. In reconstruction, therefore, the target language text must stand on its own.

Several additional strategies can help alleviate some of the difficulty suggested here. First, the interpreter who is well-prepared will be at an advantage. Preparation should include considering the register, along with likely genres that will be encountered. Written texts or text summaries that might be available can be scrutinized for argumentation formats and plans laid for how to best restructure the material according to target text conventions. It is common, however, for interpreters to have limited written materials to prepare with, but frequently the speakers or signers can be approached prior to the event for some information about the soon to be delivered text. Knowing something about the elements discussed in this section can help interpreters direct their questions and planning to better accommodate the speaker, text and audience or recipient.

Second, the interpreter may consider the advantages that consecutive interpreting provides, where more complete understanding is possible prior to reconstruction. A primary advantage to consecutive interpreting is that often a sufficient amount of source text is encountered before reconstruction to enable the interpreter to reorganize the information with the target audience in mind. Not every situation lends itself to consecutive interpreting, however. In these cases, especially when less is known beforehand about the source text, the interpreter may choose to lengthen her processing time to allow for incoming information to be examined before committing to target text structuring.

This section has provided some discussion of text features over and above the words and constructions interpreters must consider as they work. It is evident that numerous levels of meaning occur that require scrutiny in a source message. The unifying factor for these three pieces – lexical words, constructions that include both lexicon and grammatical information, and text – is that the clues to meaning are found in the actual material of the message, and these clues should be taken advantage of whenever possible. Yet, one additional piece to the puzzle must be addressed, that of context.

5.4 Context

The interactions of speakers and of signers are not self-contained units, completely meaningful without reference to the communicators or their surroundings. Thus language cannot be seen as an entirely objective thing. Rather, an intention conveyed by linguistic means (i.e., a *message*) can only be correctly apprehended in relation to its CONTEXT.

Context is multi-faceted. Here I will discuss only a few important aspects of the relation between a message and its context, but in fact, the importance of context to an utterance's meaning is a consideration that occupies much of the interpreter's time as she works, and affects how a message is perceived and how it is reproduced. The two aspects discussed here are DISCOURSE CONTEXT, which refers to how the current utterance fits into the stream of discourse taking place, and PRAGMATIC CONTEXT, or the influence of the situation itself, the backgrounds of participants and their relationships to each other, the expectations they bring to the setting, and the global circumstances surrounding the situation altogether.

These two contextual dimensions cannot entirely be considered independently. Just as aspects of the pragmatic context shape what is said or signed in interaction, so what is uttered in turn shapes and changes our perceptions of things, surroundings, and each other. What someone says, for example, contributes to our opinion about him or her. The interaction of linguistic structure and social context is illustrated in Ford et al. (2003), discussed in Section 5.3.1 above. Pausing, as one example, can be understood as contributing to overall message meaning too. Ford et al. suggest that while traditional views of linguistics treat pauses as having no linguistic importance, and cognitive views of language consider pauses primarily to be moments of processing time during a speaker's discourse, interlocutors in fact use and react to pauses from a social perspective. Pauses can have just as much meaning as words do. It is not very clear how interpreters incorporate source message pausing "information" into their target texts, but it has been noted that they do pay at least some attention to pauses in the source text (Siple 1993; Ressler 1999; Winston & Monikowski 2003). Interpreters note speakers' pauses marking divisions between topics, for example, and reflect these boundaries in their target texts. These authors show that in some cases interpreters use pauses differently than the source speakers they were interpreting, such as "extralinguistic" pauses (Winston & Monikowski 2003) where the interpreter clasped her hands for a period of time. While these interpreters were quite consistent in pausing in this way to reflect topic boundaries, they did so even if the speaker had not used a pause for that purpose, and they also appeared to use this time to listen to a further stretch of the continuing source text. Thus we might assume that the target text recipient would perceive some pauses as part of the source speaker's intended message and some pauses that reflected the interpreter's approach to the process of interpreting itself.

5.4.1 *Discourse context*
When people interact in a given setting, the interpreter is safe to begin with the assumptions that the discourse will be both meaningful and connected. Participants build meaning as they interact, and each contributes to it. This is reflected in word, phrasing, and framing choices the interpreter encounters. For example, once some information becomes topical, discourse participants tend to switch from using full noun phrases to refer to or label the information, to using pronouns to refer to it further. After a certain amount of intervening discourse, an item loses topical functionality and a simple pronominal reference to it will not be sufficient to (re)identify the intended referent (Givón 1995). An interesting take on this phenomenon in linguistic interaction is the referential use of space for signers. ASL signers use points in space as co-referential with entities they are discussing. Once an entity has been established as a topic of discourse, a point to a particular location in space evokes the entity as topical, much the same as a pronominal word does in a spoken language (Winston 1995). Emmorey (2002b) shows that interacting signers can reach into each other's established spaces to refer to something topical, and given the size of the three-dimensional space in between two signers engaged in discourse and the potential for distributing references to items around this space, the potential for manipulating numerous topical elements in a single discourse setting seems to be great. The limits on such use of space, however, are far from clear.

The interpreter is somewhat at a disadvantage in this regard because she is often not as familiar with the entities being referred to in the discourse, and may require additional mental effort to keep them straight. However, the interpreter has the advantage of the above mentioned assumptions, so that with some effort and strategizing, referential meaning can be kept clear. In reformulation, the interpreter must work to keep the discourse equally meaningful to the target addressee. This means that effort must be put into judging the degree of explicitness or implicitness required to make the interpreter's utterances meaningful without overstating or over-elaborating.

Discourse itself can become part of the pragmatic context, which can be a difficult aspect of interpreting to deal with. Participants often refer to topics from past discourse events which the interpreter was not privy to. In such cases, there is the likelihood that participants will refer to things elliptically, assuming they do not need to say much at all to be understood, so that some information that is not known directly by the interpreter is not explicitly stated, making meaning difficult for her to construct in the present discourse setting.

5.4.2 *Pragmatic context*

Extralinguistic knowledge is considered by Gile (1995) to be one of the three core areas of knowledge required by the interpreter (the other two are linguistic knowledge and knowledge of interpreting technique). Numerous errors are made while interpreting not because of an incomplete knowledge of linguistic form and function, but because the interpreter does not understand the subject area or the context in which the discourse is placed.

The fact that context determines the meaning of words and utterances rather than dictionary definitions is clear from Seleskovitch's (1976) discussion suggesting that interpreting is about finding appropriate wording to convey a specific meaning at a particular point in time and in the present, unique context (discussed more fully in Section 1 above). Words can often have a range of meanings, but a speaker has one meaning in particular in mind when the word is used, evident from the context surrounding it. The significance of utterances is tied to when and where they are used.

On one hand, the experiences of both source text speaker or signer and the interpreter's target text recipient are bound to be quite different – they are not from the same language community, which means that they likely have different cultural practices and spend their time in somewhat different ways. Therefore when understanding a message from either group, or formulating a target text for either group, the interpreter must consider how each utterance (either uttered by others as the input text or by the interpreter as the output text) fits within that group's contextual experience. Ultimately, this is how utterances will make sense.

But on the other hand, the interpreter is interpreting because the two groups have come together in a *shared* context, which means that the immediate experience in which the interaction takes place is contributed to by both. Thus even though participants in the event may bring vastly different experiences to it, utterances as part of the event are situated within this immediate context and in the shared experience that is built up as the event unfolds. This is welcome news for the interpreter who can rely on witnessing, if not completely sharing in, the developing contextual clues to meaning, and therefore judge the necessary implicitness and explicitness by which to formulate target text utterances. But not every problem is solved; the interpreter often finds herself a visitor in other people's contexts. These people may have shared experiences outside of those for which the interpreter is present, and the interpreter must take care not to skew the message based on what her own experiences have been, and not assume that a participant doesn't know something because she herself doesn't know it (see Shaffer & Janzen 2005 for more detailed discussion on the interpreter's perceptions of what requires contextualization in interpreted discourse).

This description of pragmatic context is barely a glimpse at the issues related to language in its context of use. Space, unfortunately, does not permit a more extensive discussion here. However, throughout an interpreter's training and beyond into her career, she will focus much energy on understanding the pragmatic contexts of experience that people whom she interprets for bring to the situation, and the extralinguistic motivations behind the utterances that become the material she must grapple with.

6.   Some conclusions

A reasonable assumption made both by interpretation and translation theorists (e.g., Seleskovitch 1976; Gile 1995) and by many clients and consumers of interpreting is that interpreters' skills in their working languages are superior. For these theorists, this does not mean that the interpreter won't struggle with language related issues, but in Gile's discussion of the interpreter's knowledge base, language skills might be considered most basic. Proficiency in language then puts interpreting students in a position to *begin* to learn their craft. There is too much to take care of during the activity of interpreting – managing information flow and content, the dual processing of incoming and outgoing texts, representing signers and speakers well, cultural and cross-cultural factors, situational concerns, etc. – to risk much linguistic inadequacy.

What I have attempted to outline in this chapter are some key considerations in thinking about what place language has in the interpreting process. While it might seem more than obvious that interpretation is about language, understanding the specifics of language structure and the transmission of information across languages is not automatic and simply intuitive. Good interpreters are thinking interpreters. This chapter is intended to address many of the language related considerations that lead to appropriate strategizing in apprehending the message and formulating a target text of quality. Key to this process is knowing that there are decisions to be made at the level of word, construction, text, and context. There is much about language that we still need to learn as we hone interpreting skills. This chapter is an attempt to identify these issues and suggest some ways of thinking about them. It will be the case, in fact, that the interpreter never stops adding to his or her store of linguistic knowledge – it's a career-long investment: basic to the work, often excruciatingly complex, but inevitably rewarding.

Notes

1. This chapter has benefited from numerous discussions with many colleagues, in particular Hubert Demers, Barbara O'Dea, Deb Russell, and Barbara Shaffer, and with the students in my course Introduction to Interpretation Theory at the University of Manitoba. Helpful comments from two anonymous reviewers are gratefully acknowledged.

2. Here I subscribe to Wilcox and Shaffer's (this volume) notions of inferring and (re)constructing meaning.

3. I use "text" broadly to mean any speaker's or signer's discourse, whether long or short, and whether a monologue or as contributions to a dialogue.

4. This is in fact a problem for most interpreters whether or not they have ASL as an L1 or L2. Generally, both ASL classes (prior to interpreting training) and learning ASL informally in the community typically give the ASL learner conversational skills that are much below what is needed for the professional workplace. And it's not just lexicon that is problematic; as the discussion below will show, the language styles expected in, and even required for, various registers (i.e., situations) include certain types of sentence constructions and discourse frames which must be acquired as well.

5. The American Translators Association recommends that translators work only *into* their native language (see the "Getting It Right" link at http://www.atanet.org/bin/view.pl/52076.html. This notion has been questioned by some, for example Barik (1975) and de Bot (2000). Barik notes that two of his subjects, bilinguals with no interpreting experience, seemed to have an easier time simultaneously interpreting from their "dominant" to their "weak" language, yet Barik notes that their attempts are much more awkward and less intelligible than those of his professional interpreter subjects, often consisting of word for word "verbal transpositions" (Barik 1975:286). Overall, Barik's study includes too few subjects and too many variables to conclude anything definitive regarding an appropriate direction of interpreting work. Gile (1995:209) distinguishes between A languages (in which interpreters possess native-like proficiency), B languages (mastery at a near-native level) and C languages (understood at a native level). Gile refers to A and B languages as those the interpreter can expect to work into, that is, the interpreter's target languages.

6. It might be unusual to think of signs as "words" but there is no reason to believe that the idea of words belongs exclusively to the domain of spoken language. The lexicon of ASL is a list of ASL words. This in no way implies any link to English words, meaning that here we are not talking about English words being signed.

7. It is true that some language can be learned on the job, that is, while engaging in the activity of interpreting itself. There are two problems, however. For one, interpreters often work alone, and it is inappropriate to expect that the interpreter's clients will "teach" her as she works, even though many Deaf people are very willing to do so to an extent. Rather, her clients will more likely expect that she has the language abilities to handle the discourse; after all, by being contracted to work in this context, she is claiming some level of expertise as a language specialist.

Second, while interpreting the interpreter must by and large rely on what she already knows – there is usually little time for discussion or corrective feedback. These more likely will take place either before or *after* the interpretation has been completed, when the correction can help the interpreter build skills but won't help the consumer whose interpreted situation is over. In other words, the interpreter's language building takes place primarily during interaction, not during actual interpreting. "An interpreter must know his languages thoroughly before he begins to practice the profession, because he cannot learn or improve his knowledge of a language while expressing the meaning of a message at 150 words a minute" (Seleskovitch 1978:77).

8. The shading in the model pictured in Figure 1 is gradient, whereas in Gile's diagram the Passive Zone is shaded and the Active Zone is not. Gradient shading more accurately reflects Gile's position that word availability is dynamic. Gile (p. 218) suggests that the distinction between the Active and Passive Zone areas is somewhat artificial – in fact, no clear dividing line between the two zones actually exists.

9. Gile uses the term "rules" here, which he suggests are "syntactic and other linguistic rules" (Gile 1995:216). For our purposes, however, I will use "constructions" broadly meaning how any string of morphemes or words are put together. For more on the place of constructions in grammar, see Goldberg (1998).

10. Interpreting students are often confused when their training program stresses active preparation for interpreting assignments but as they enter practicum periods, and after that the workforce, they encounter more experienced interpreters who don't seem to spend much time in preparation activities. It is certainly the case that some interpreters get in the unfortunate habit of going into assignments "cold" (see Demers, this volume), but features of the Gravitational Model over an extended period of time may account for what new interpreters are observing in their colleagues.

11. ASL-English interpreters usually begin their careers as community interpreters, either freelance or for an agency, or in educational settings. Few training programs, and none in Canada, exclusively train educational interpreters as one type of specialist. Many ASL-English interpreters work in educational settings, however, perhaps even the majority, and thus these specialists encounter a sector of experience and language use that is quite wide. For more, see Conrad and Stegenga, this volume.

12. ASL is frequently discussed in relation to English, specifically regarding what ASL doesn't have that English has, for example that ASL doesn't mark tense, or doesn't have the "little words" (i.e., grammatical or function words) that English does. The implication is that ASL lacks the grammatical complexity of English. Even though it is often said that ASL has *its own* grammar, it is still regularly viewed from the point of view of English grammar (e.g., Isenhath 1990), which distorts the perception of grammatical detail that does exist in ASL.

13. Not all compounds are written as single words: note the differences in writing convention for *greenhouse* (single word), *movie-goer* (hyphenated), and *hot dog* (two words). Stress is on the first syllable in each of these compounds.

14. Brentari refers to these as "affixes".

15. The notion of syllable in ASL has received more attention as of late (see e.g., Brentari 1998 for a detailed discussion). Basically, it is thought that a syllable in ASL represents a single movement unit, seen for example in the movement path from one location to another in GIVE. A two-syllable word in ASL, much rarer, is CANCEL with two movement paths.

16. In the following examples, notation is as follows. For the transcription line (glossing, top line), PRO.1 is first person singular, and PRO.3 is third person singular, with a subscript, e.g., PRO.3$_a$ identifying the location in space, location "a". Letters and dashes (e.g., S-A-L-L-Y) means fingerspelling. Classifier predicates are indicated by CL: plus a symbol representing the handshape. Letters with an arrow (e.g., b→a) mean a movement from location "b" to location "a". "Body.shift→a" means the signer leans toward "a". Emph means additional emphatic stress on the sign. In the transliteration (middle) line, 1s and 3s mean first and third person respectively. Words with periods between them (e.g., person.approach.3s) mean that more than one word is needed to give the full meaning of the sign.

17. Most grammatical descriptions interpreters are familiar with claim that ASL does not have a passive, but see Janzen, O'Dea and Shaffer (2001) for an account of passivization much like that described here.

18. Index fingers on both hands extended and pointing down.

19. For a fuller discussion of construction grammar, see Goldberg (1995).

20. The overline with 'rhet' indicates the rhetorical question phrase. The translation given in (9) is the one suggested by Valli and Lucas, but is not advocated for here.

21. Janzen (1999:294) refers to these as "topic-marked WH words" with connective function. They align with the notion of "topic" because they share some of the functions of marked topics in ASL, e.g., they are pivots that link some prior stated information to what follows, they have a similar focusing function, and they have the same facial marking as more prototypical topics.

22. Joos (1961) never does use the term "register" himself. The work, however, represents a beginning point for examining variation, and while this is not explicated further in his book, Joos does suggest that speakers may easily move from style to style in their discourse within a given situation, although typically not up or down more than one level. Biber (1994:53) refers to Joos's paradigm as descriptive of language style "at a high level of generality".

23. These ASL and English text organization descriptions are attributed to MJ Bienvenu and Betty Colonomos. Zimmer (2001) argues, however, that such a text template for ASL has been considered much too broadly, and that ASL narrative texts don't quite conform. Certainly, more research is needed in this area.

References

Armstrong, David F., William C. Stokoe, & Sherman E. Wilcox (1995). *Gesture and the Nature of Language*. Cambridge: Cambridge University Press.

Baddeley, Alan (2000). Working memory and language processing. In Birgitta Englund Dimitrova & Kenneth Hyltenstam (Eds.), *Language Processing and Simultaneous Interpreting: Interdisciplinary Perspectives* (pp. 1–16). Amsterdam/Philadelphia: John Benjamins.

Barik, Henri C. (1975). Simultaneous interpretation: Qualitative and linguistic data. *Language and Speech, 18*, 272–297.

Biber, Douglas (1994). An analytical framework for register studies. In Douglas Biber and Edward Finegan (Eds.), *Sociolinguistic Perspectives on Register* (pp. 31–56). New York: Oxford University Press.

Brentari, Diane (1998). *A Prosodic Model of Sign Language Phonology*. Cambridge, MA: MIT Press.

Brentari, Diane (2002). Modality differences in sign language phonology and morpho-phonemics. In Richard P. Meier, Kearsy Cormier, & David Quinto-Pozos (Eds.), *Modality and Structure in Signed and Spoken Languages* (pp. 35–64). Cambridge: Cambridge University Press.

Bybee, Joan L. (1985). *Morphology: A Study of the Relation Between Meaning and Form*. Amsterdam/Philadelphia: John Benjamins.

Christie, Karen, Dorothy M. Wilkins, Betsy Hicks McDonald, & Cindy Neuroth-Gimbrone (1999). GET-TO-THE-POINT: Academic bilingualism and discourse in American Sign Language and written English. In Elizabeth Winston (Ed.), *Storytelling and Conversation: Discourse in Deaf Communities* (pp. 162–189). Washington, DC: Gallaudet University Press.

Crystal, David (1987). *The Cambridge Encyclopedia of Language*. Cambridge: Cambridge University Press.

Cokely, Dennis (1982). The interpreted medical interview: It loses something in the translation. *The Reflector, 3* (Spring), 5–11.

Cokely, Dennis (1992). *Interpretation: A Sociolinguistic Model*. Burtonsville, MD: Linstok Press.

de Bot, Kees (2000). Simultaneous interpreting as language production. In Birgitta Englund Dimitrova & Kenneth Hyltenstam (Eds.), *Language Processing and Simultaneous Interpreting: Interdisciplinary Perspectives* (pp. 65–88). Amsterdam/Philadelphia: John Benjamins.

Eco, Umberto (2001). *Experiences in Translation*. Toronto: University of Toronto Press.

Emmorey, Karen (2002a). *Language, Cognition, and the Brain: Insights from Sign Language Research*. Mahwah, NJ: Lawrence Erlbaum Associates.

Emmorey, Karen (2002b). The effects of modality on spatial language: How signers and speakers talk about space. In Richard P. Meier, Kearsy Cormier, & David Quinto-Pozos (Eds.), *Modality and Structure in Signed and Spoken Languages* (pp. 405–421). Cambridge: Cambridge University Press.

Ferguson, Charles A. (1994). Dialect, register, and genre: Working assumptions about conventionalization. In Douglas Biber and Edward Finegan (Eds.), *Sociolinguistic Perspectives on Register* (pp. 15–30). New York: Oxford University Press.

Ford, Cecilia E., Barbara A. Fox, & Sandra A. Thompson (2003). Social interaction and grammar. In Michael Tomasello (Ed.), *The New Psychology of Language: Cognitive and Functional Approaches to Language Structure*, Volume 2 (pp. 119–143). Mahwah, NJ: Lawrence Erlbaum Associates.

Gile, Daniel (1995). *Basic Concepts and Models for Interpreter and Translator Training*. Amsterdam/Philadelphia: John Benjamins.

Givón, Talmy (1995). Coherence in text vs. coherence in mind. In Morton Ann Gernsbacher & T. Givón (Eds.), *Coherence in Spontaneous Text* (pp. 59–115). Amsterdam/Philadelphia: John Benjamins.

Goldberg, Adele E. (1995). *Constructions: A Construction Grammar Approach to Argument Structure*. Chicago: University of Chicago Press.

Goldberg, Adele E. (1998). Patterns of experience in patterns of language. In Michael Tomasello (Ed.), *The New Psychology of Language: Cognitive and Functional Approaches to Language Structure* (pp. 203–219). Mahwah, NJ: Lawrence Erlbaum Associates.

González, Roseann Dueñas, Victoria F. Vásquez, & Holly Mikkelson (1991). *Fundamentals of Court Interpretation: Theory, Policy, and Practice*. Durham, NC: Carolina Academic Press.

Hatim, Basil (1997). *Communication Across Cultures: Translation Theory and Contrastive Text Linguistics*. Exeter: University of Exeter Press.

Humphrey, Janice H., & Bob J. Alcorn (1996). *So You Want to Be an Interpreter? An Introduction to Sign Language Interpreting* (2nd ed.) Amarillo, TX: H & H Press.

Isenhath, John O. (1990). *The Linguistics of American Sign Language*. Jefferson, NC: MacFarland & Company.

Jacobs, Rhonda (1996). Just how hard is it to learn ASL? The case for ASL as a Truly Foreign Language. In Ceil Lucas (Ed.), *Multicultural Aspects of Sociolinguistics in Deaf Communities* (pp. 183–226). Washington, DC: Gallaudet University Press.

Janzen, Terry (1999). The grammaticization of topics in American Sign Language. *Studies in Language, 23* (2), 271–306.

Janzen, Terry, Barbara O'Dea, & Barbara Shaffer (2001). The construal of events: Passives in American Sign Language. *Sign Language Studies, 1* (3), 281–310.

Johnson, Robert E., & Carol Erting (1989). Ethnicity and socialization in a classroom for deaf children. In Ceil Lucas (Ed.), *The Sociolinguistics of the Deaf Community* (pp. 41–83). San Diego: Academic Press.

Johnson, Robert E., Scott K. Liddell, & Carol Erting (1989). *Unlocking the Curriculum: Principles for Achieving Access in Deaf Education*. Washington, DC: Gallaudet Research Institute Occasional Paper, pp. 89–3.

Joos, Martin (1961). *The Five Clocks*. New York: Harcourt, Brace & World, Inc.

Klima, Edward S., & Ursula Bellugi (1979). *The Signs of Language*. Cambridge, MA: Harvard University Press.

Kondo, Masaomi (1988). Japanese interpreters in their socio-cultural context. *Meta, 33* (1), 70–78.

Lenneberg, Eric H. (1967). *Biological Foundations of Language*. New York: John Wiley and Sons.

Linell, Per (1997). Interpreting as communication. In Yves Gambier, Daniel Gile, & Christopher Taylor (Eds.), *Conference Interpreting: Current Trends in Research* (pp. 49–67). Amsterdam/ Philadelphia: John Benjamins.

Meier, Richard P. (2002). Why different, why the same? Explaining effects and non-effects of modality upon linguistic structure in sign and speech. In Richard P. Meier, Kearsy Cormier, & David Quinto-Pozos (Eds.), *Modality and Structure in Signed and Spoken Languages* (pp. 1–25). Cambridge: Cambridge University Press.

Metzger, Melanie (1999). *Sign Language Interpreting: Deconstructing the Myth of Neutrality*. Washington, DC: Gallaudet University Press.

Morford, Jill P., & Rachel I. Mayberry (2000). A reexamination of "early exposure" and its implications for language acquisition by eye. In Charlene Chamberlain, Jill P. Morford, & Rachel I. Mayberry (Eds.), *Language Acquisition by Eye* (pp. 111–127). Mahwah, NJ: Lawrence Erlbaum Associates.

Moser-Mercer, Barbara, Sylvie Lambert, Valerie Darò, & Sarah Williams (1997). Skill components in simultaneous interpreting. In Yves Gambier, Daniel Gile, & Christopher Taylor (Eds.), *Conference Interpreting: Current Trends in Research* (pp. 133–148). Amsterdam/Philadelphia: John Benjamins.

Nida, Eugene A. (1964). *Toward a Science of Translating*. Leiden, Netherlands: E. J. Brill.

Quigley, Stephen P., & Joseph P. Youngs (1965). *Interpreting for Deaf People*. Washington, DC: U.S. Department of Health, Education, and Welfare.

Ressler, Carolyn I. (1999). A comparative analysis of a direct interpretation and an intermediary interpretation in American Sign Language. *Journal of Interpretation,* (RID), 71–102.

Roy, Cynthia B. (2000). *Interpreting as a Discourse Process*. New York: Oxford University Press.

Seleskovitch, Danica (1976). Interpretation, A psychological approach to translation. In Richard W. Brislin (Ed.), *Translation: Applications and Research* (pp. 92–116). New York: Gardner Press.

Seleskovitch, Danica (1978). *Interpreting for International Conferences*. Washington DC: Pen and Booth.

Setton, Robin (1999). *Simultaneous Interpretation: A Cognitive-Pragmatic Analysis.* Amsterdam/Philadelphia: John Benjamins.

Shaffer, Barbara, & Terry Janzen (2005). Contextualization or Expansion? Compensating for Interpreter Inadequacies. Manuscript. The University of New Mexico and the University of Manitoba.

Siple, Linda A. (1993). Interpreters' use of pausing in voice to sign transliteration. *Sign Language Studies, 79,* 147–179.

Stokoe, William C. (1960). Sign language structure: An outline of the visual communication systems of the American deaf. *Studies in Linguistics, Occasional Papers 8.* Buffalo, N.Y.

Stokoe, William C., Dorothy C. Casterline, & Carl G. Croneberg (1965). *A Dictionary of American Sign Language on Linguistic Principles.* Washington, DC: Gallaudet College Press.

Supalla, Ted (1990). Serial verbs of motion in ASL. In Susan D. Fischer & Patricia Siple (Eds.), *Theoretical Issues in Sign Language Research, Volume 1: Linguistics* (pp. 127–152). Chicago: University of Chicago Press.

Taylor Torsello, Carol, Sandra Gallina, Maria Sidiropoulou, Christopher Taylor, Helen Tebble, & A. R. Vuorikoski (1997). Linguistics, discourse analysis and interpretation. In Yves Gambier, Daniel Gile, & Christopher Taylor (Eds.), *Conference Interpreting: Current Trends in Research* (pp. 167–186). Amsterdam/Philadelphia: John Benjamins.

Valli, Clayton, & Ceil Lucas (1992). *The Linguistics of American Sign Language: A Resource Text for ASL Users.* Washington, DC: Gallaudet University Press.

Wadensjö, Cecilia (1998). *Interpreting as Interaction.* London and New York: Longman.

Wilbur, Ronnie (1995). Why so-called 'rhetorical questions' (RHQs) are neither rhetorical nor questions. In Heleen Bos and Trude Schermer (Eds.), *Sign Language Research 1994* (pp. 149–169). Hamburg: Signum Press.

Winston, Elizabeth A. (1995). Spatial mapping in comparative discourse frames. In Karen Emmorey & Judy S. Reilly (Eds.), *Language, Gesture, and Space* (pp. 87–114). Hillsdale, NJ: Lawrence Erlbaum Associates.

Winston, Elizabeth, & Christine Monikowski (2003). Marking topic boundaries in signed interpretation and transliteration. In Melanie Metzger, Steven Collins, Valerie Dively, & Risa Shaw (Eds.), *From Topic Boundaries to Omission: New Research on Interpretation* (pp. 187–227). Washington, DC: Gallaudet University Press.

Zimmer, Rick (2001). The role of digression in ASL discourse. Paper presented at the Fourth Annual Conference of the High Desert Linguistic Society, University of New Mexico, March 30–31, 2001.

CHAPTER 5

Contact sign, transliteration and interpretation in Canada

Karen Malcolm
Douglas College

1. Introduction

In broad definitions of interpreting, the interpreter is understood to be working between two languages, conveying an equivalent message from the source language into the target language. The task of the signed language interpreter working between English and American Sign Language (ASL) is made more complex because of the additional, and often very confusing, dimension of English-like signed language varieties used by some members of the Deaf community in North America.

While the Registry of Interpreters for the Deaf (RID) in the United States has historically treated interpreting and transliterating as two different tasks, testing and awarding certification separately for each, the Canadian experience has been primarily focused on educating and testing for interpretation skills between ASL and English. The Association of Visual Language Interpreters of Canada (AVLIC) offers one certification process only, which evaluates an interpreter's ability to work between the languages of ASL and English. However, a need also exists within Canada for interpreters who are able to work with more English-like forms of signing, and therefore the education programs that prepare interpreters arguably should address this need.

This chapter will first address the occurrence of varieties of contact signing used by members of the Deaf community and the reasons why they exist, followed by definitions of the term "transliteration", also referred to as "interpreting into a contact variety of language". I will address how the term "transliteration" is used, and whether or not it is an effective way to describe what an interpreter does when processing and producing a message into a contact variety of signed language. Finally, implications for training and certification within Canada will be discussed.

2.   Contact sign: What *is* it?

Before beginning a discussion of transliterating, a description of contact varieties of language that exist within the Deaf community is warranted. The two languages coming into contact that are considered here are ASL and English. Lucas and Valli (1989: 12) state that "the varieties of language available to participants in a contact situation range from ASL to spoken English or Signed English, and to a variety of codes for English that have been implemented in educational settings". Lucas and Valli coined the term "contact signing" which is one result of language contact: "A fifth unique outcome of language contact in the American deaf community is what we have called contact signing, a kind of signing that incorporates features of ASL and English and may include other phenomena we have described such as loan translations, fingerspelling and mouthing" (Lucas & Valli 1992:48). Some of the varieties which result from this contact are more English-like in syntax and vocabulary while others more closely resemble ASL (Humphrey & Alcorn 2001).

The term Pidgin Sign English (PSE) has been used in the past to refer to these forms, although current research demonstrates that contact sign does not fit the criteria of a pidgin (Reilly & McIntire 1980; Lucas & Valli 1989, 1992). Throughout this discussion, I will use the terms "contact sign" or "contact signing", as coined by Lucas and Valli, and "contact variety of language" interchangeably to define the signed message created when features from ASL and English are combined.

2.1   Features of contact sign

There are a number of features which can guide an observer in determining whether a person is using a form of contact sign rather than ASL. The following discussion will highlight some of these, but for a more in-depth sociolinguistic treatment of the topic, readers are referred to Lucas and Valli (1992).

The structure of an utterance is one way of identifying a message constructed using contact sign. Contact sign often follows the grammatical order found in English. For example, wh-questions (e.g., WHO, WHAT, WHERE, WHEN, WHY, HOW) in ASL have a specific combination of non-manual signals (NMS) that includes furrowed eyebrows and a slightly backward head tilt, along with a possible forward movement of the shoulders. One wh-question form has the wh-word occurring only at the end of the sentence, but this form does not occur when a signer follows English word order for a similar question. Sentences in ASL that would usually be expressed in topic-comment format or as conditionals would also look different when following English structure.

Specific vocabulary items that are used are another way to identify contact signing. For example, manual codes for English often have invented signs, some of which violate the constraints of sign production in ASL, such as a sign for ''track and field' that builds on the ASL sign COMPETE, using the letter "T" on one hand and "F" on the other. ASL requires that when both hands move simultaneously in a sign, the handshape must be the same (Lucas & Valli 1992), but in invented signs where both hands move, the two handshapes may be different, as the above example shows. Another identifying feature is the use of pronouns. ASL has pronouns that are formed with an extended index finger handshape to indicate referents placed spatially, while manual codes for English have developed specific pronoun forms (e.g., HE, HIM, SHE, HER) signed near the head with no such spatial component. Signers may also use more initialized signs (i.e., using the fingerspelled first letter of an English word on a base ASL sign) such as the letter "D" for DESCRIBE, "I" for INSTRUCTOR and "R" for RABBIT.

The use of prepositions is another area where contact sign and ASL differ. ASL uses spatial referencing and classifiers to establish the relationship of objects one to another, while English uses prepositions such as *next to, under, on, beside,* and so forth. ASL signs do exist to represent these concepts, but they are not used frequently in an ASL utterance. Signers who use signs for prepositions rather than establishing relational objects in space are often using a contact variety of signed language rather than ASL (Lucas & Valli 1992:11).

The frequency of fingerspelling is a feature that also assists in identifying contact signing. Davis (1989) notes that fingerspelling is a way to represent the orthography of English, but the appearance of fingerspelling itself is not sufficient to determine that a text is a contact variety of language, since fingerspelling is also an integral part of ASL. ASL uses lexicalized fingerspelling, often referred to as "fingerspelled loan signs" (Battison 1978), where the combination of handshapes becomes an actual sign and the overall phonological form is a much reduced version of the fingerspelled word (e.g., #CAR, #BACK, #BANK).[1] The use of fingerspelling in contact sign is instead often marked by fully formed handshapes to represent letters. The occurrence of words that are not usually fingerspelled in ASL can help to identify contact signing, but as mentioned, the presence of fingerspelling alone is not sufficient to classify a language sample as a contact variety.

One of the clearest markers of contact signing is that of mouthing English words. Lucas and Valli (1992) note this as a central feature. ASL also incorporates some mouthing, although it is typically reduced (Davis 1989). An example of mouthing in ASL is the mouth movement that accompanies the sign FINISH, which is a reduced form that clearly originates in the English word *finish*. The mouthing found in contact signing differs from that in ASL in that it is usually fully produced and continues consistently throughout the text.

The combination of ASL and English features that characterize contact signing will vary from text to text because there is no one standard form of contact sign. The features described here, however, are useful in assisting the transliterator or interpreter in determining the mix of features needed to produce a target message comprehensible to the Deaf audience.

As well as identifying the features of contact sign, it is necessary to consider the various reasons for its existence within the Deaf community, along with social judgments often made about its use. These factors influence the members of the Deaf community and subsequently affect transliterators working with contact signers.

2.2 Why does contact sign exist?

A number of factors have led to the existence of contact sign within the Deaf community. First, the majority of Deaf people have had the experience of growing up with parents who are hearing, and who often have not signed to their children. As a result, these Deaf children have had to rely on some form of English to communicate in the home. Second, Deaf children who have Deaf parents do acquire ASL as a first language, but some are educated in a mainstreamed setting using a sign system developed to make visible the grammatical structures and features of English. Third, for those Deaf children who acquire ASL at residential schools, it is usually acquired from peers during social interaction, while the system used for educational purposes is often some form of English-like signing (Lucas & Valli 1992). The historic lack of recognition of ASL as a full, natural language has meant that only recently have some schools used it as the language of instruction and offered opportunities for students to study it. Consequently, the majority of Deaf adults have been educated by teachers and interpreters using a manual code intended to represent English.

These systems, broadly referred to as Manually Coded English, include such methods as Seeing Essential English (SEE 1), Signing Exact English (SEE 2), Signed English and Conceptually Accurate Signed English. SEE 2 has been the most widely used in the United States (Lane, Hoffmeister, & Bahan 1996).[2]

Many Deaf people have the ability to shift between ASL and contact signing that incorporates features of English, although their language of preference is ASL. There are some Deaf people who differentiate the variety of signing they use depending on the setting. They may use ASL for social interaction, and prefer a more English-based sign interpretation in professional settings or for educational purposes. As one respondent explained in a survey regarding transliteration, conducted in 2000, "I want to learn the language my (hearing) peers are using so that I can respond in-kind. If I reply using their language, my peers know that I understand them. It also lessens any negative perceptions they may have about my ability to function with hearing people" (Viera & Stauffer 2000: 90–91).

Deaf people will often make a shift from ASL into contact sign in order to facilitate communication with hearing people who are not fluent in ASL. Even if a hearing person is a near-native ASL signer, a Deaf person may shift to more English-like signing upon realizing that the person can hear, often unconsciously (Lucas & Valli 1992). In this case, Deaf people's experience of interacting with hearing people has often led them to respond automatically by shifting to contact sign whenever conversing with hearing people.

Another factor in the development of contact varieties of signed language concerns people who learned English as a first language before experiencing a hearing loss. These people's use of sign is profoundly influenced by their first language, and most prefer to use English modified for visual, rather than auditory, presentation. Lucas and Valli even suggest that the earliest historical manifestation of contact signing may have begun with late-deafened signers. They state in their discussion of the earliest studies of signed language in the United States, beginning with the establishment of the American School for the Deaf in 1817, that "contact signing didn't incorporate features of English necessarily because the hearing people couldn't understand ASL. It might have incorporated features of English because the first language of some of its users *was* English, even though they were now learning ASL" (Lucas & Valli 1992:14; italics theirs).

A further influencing factor on the use of contact sign is that a number of Deaf people are educated in mainstreamed settings without access to an ASL-signing Deaf community. Public Law 94–142, passed in the United States in 1975, mandates public education in the "least restrictive environment", which has been interpreted to mean Deaf students being placed in their local public school, rather than re-locating to attend a program specifically designed for them (Stewart, Schein, & Cartwright 2004:166). While Canada does not have the same legislation, similar practices are followed which result in students often having little or no contact with the larger Deaf community throughout their childhood educational experiences. Upon reaching adulthood, many of these Deaf people begin to interact in the ASL-signing Deaf community and often develop a contact variety of language that incorporates features of both the English-based code used in their education and features of ASL which they acquire through their community interactions.

A final reason for the existence of contact signing, it has been suggested, is that it "serves to prevent significant intrusions of dominant language patterns into a Deaf community, and that it, therefore, functions as a device for maintaining an ethnic boundary between hearing and deaf people" (Burns, Matthews, & Nolan-Conroy 2001:192). That is, members of the Deaf community preserve their identity through reserving their language, ASL, for use among themselves.

Having identified some of the features present in contact sign, let us next consider several studies of contact signing and their implications for transliterators.

2.3 Studies of contact signing

Among the studies of contact signing there are two studies particularly instructive for transliterators which I will address briefly. One is a study conducted by Sam Supalla (1991), which considered whether the structure of a spoken language could be incorporated successfully into a signed message. Supalla studied a group of SEE 2 signers who had only been exposed to SEE 2, to see "whether children exposed exclusively to SEE 2 produce signing with a grammatical system similar to that of SEE 2 or with a devised grammatical system more like that of a natural signed language (similar to, though not precisely like, that of ASL)" (1991:91). Supalla was interested in how the children marked subject versus object, hypothesizing that they would use spatial devices to indicate these relations, and that the devices would have to have been developed by the children themselves since they did not know ASL. He studied eight children, ages 9 to 11, who had no exposure to ASL at home or in any educational program.

Specifically, Supalla analyzed the devices used to mark tense and case (e.g., *he*, *him*). SEE 2 adds tense markers to verbs in a manner similar to how English marks tense, such as adding the marker -ED for past tense on the end of a signed verb. It also has specific lexical items for case-marked terms such as *he* and *him*, while ASL assigns spatial locations to each and indexes these to indicate the case.

Supalla's findings indicate that "SEE 2's non-spatial grammatical devices were replaced with essentially spatial ones" (1991:101). Even though the children's SEE 2 model did not include spatial modifications, the children produced them. These results suggest that the children spontaneously converted a system devised to manually and visually represent English into a system that took more advantage of the visual and spatial modality.

Another study that is instructive in the consideration of contact sign in the Deaf community was that conducted by Lucas and Valli (1992). They were interested in examining linguistic and sociolinguistic features of contact signing. To that end, Lucas and Valli studied the language patterns of six dyads of white signers, and four dyads and two triads of black signers. The participants (or "informants") in the study had a mixture of backgrounds. Some had Deaf parents, some hearing parents, and some had attended residential schools while others attended day programs. Participants grouped in each dyad or triad were strangers to each other. They were brought into an interview situation and videotaped throughout (with their knowledge and consent). Each group began conversing and then after some time a Deaf interviewer entered and began asking the participants questions. The interviewer was then called away on the pretext of an emergency, and the participants were instructed to continue their discussion. After 8 to 10 minutes, a hearing interviewer arrived and took the Deaf interviewer's place for a time. Then the hearing interviewer left, ostensibly to check on the Deaf interviewer, and the dyad or triad were left alone again until the Deaf interviewer returned and completed the interview.

Lucas and Valli had assumed that "Deaf native ASL signers would produce ASL with other Deaf native ASL signers, being either the Deaf interviewer or the other informant" (1992:62). While they did indeed find that the Deaf people used ASL with each other and contact sign with the hearing interviewer, they also found to their surprise that some Deaf ASL native users employed contact signing when no hearing people were present, some used ASL with the hearing interviewer, and sometimes as many as three different participants used three different modes simultaneously (Lucas & Valli 1992:63). It is evident that the choice to use contact sign, even among Deaf participants with ASL as their first language, was affected by a number of complex sociolinguistic factors. For example, the formality of an interview setting, Lucas and Valli suggest, led some participants to use contact sign instead of ASL. Others appeared to use ASL consistently to establish their identity as true members of the Deaf cultural group.

Lucas and Valli's study highlights the complex nature of contact sign use within the Deaf community, and that various factors are at play when a Deaf person determines, however consciously or unconsciously, what form of language to use. This is an important point for transliterators to consider when determining what variety of language they might use that best suits the Deaf person they are working with.

An interesting corollary to this study is the variability in Deaf viewers' assessments of the language samples in the videotapes. Lucas and Valli asked a group of viewers to watch clips from the study and determine if they were clearly ASL or not. Those who had studied ASL formally, either as linguists or teachers of ASL, had a high degree of agreement. However, naive judges without a metalinguistic awareness of ASL differed from the more aware group of judges. Valli and Lucas reason that, at least in part, "the disagreement in judgments has to do with the status of language in the Deaf community" (1992:72). They suggest that many adult Deaf ASL signers, who are competent users of the language, have a difficult time distinguishing between ASL and contact signing as a result of no formal education being provided for them to study their language during their schooling.

Lucas and Valli's study highlights the complexity of contact varieties of language in use within the Deaf community. They note that individuals vary in the ways they combine features of ASL and English in producing a message characterized by contact signing. There is no single standard structure for these contact varieties of language. Signers draw from both English and ASL to create individual blends of language features. Additionally, some Deaf people shift between using ASL and a contact variety depending on the setting. These findings are important for transliterators in determining what their own target language output should consist of to best meet the needs of individual Deaf consumers. These considerations are addressed later in the chapter, but for now let us turn our attention to how transliteration is defined, and how it is conceptualized within the broader field of signed language interpretation.

3.   Efforts to define transliteration

Most interpreters, at some point in their careers, are asked to transliterate, although the Deaf person often does not use that specific term. Instead, the interpreter may simply be asked to sign in English word order or to mouth more of the English source message. As Kelly (2001) describes in her text on transliterating, Deaf people would request of her to "show me the English" (2001:xi). In the United States, RID offers a test for certification in transliteration, and the term is used throughout the RID Code of Ethics. Given that this service is requested, it would seem logical to work from a commonly understood definition of the term.

However, the term "transliteration" continues to elude a standardized, unambiguous definition, although it is used as if one were commonly understood. While the term is not used as frequently in Canadian literature, we are nonetheless affected by American policies and practices due to our geographic proximity and the use of American research and publications, and thus could also benefit from such a common understanding.

Several definitions for transliteration have been proposed. Humphrey and Alcorn define transliterating as "the process of taking a message and expressing it in a different form of the *same* language" (2001:7.6). They note that while the modality may change from auditory to visual, only one language is involved.

AVLIC's original Code of Ethics, which was ratified in 1983, defines a transliterator in its preamble as "one who facilitates communication between persons who share the same language but not the same language mode". The current AVLIC Code of Ethics and Guidelines for Professional Conduct, ratified in 2000, makes no explicit reference to the term "transliteration" whatsoever. Instead, under Section 2.1 of the code, entitled "Qualification to Practice", it is noted that members work with a variety of consumers, and that they must be able to meet the linguistic needs of these consumers. Assumed in this statement is the reality of the range of communication options which interpreters will encounter within the Deaf community.

Siple (1997) points out that definitions of transliterating, while changing some-what over time, have retained certain fundamental features. Siple discusses a more current, and widely used, definition taken from Frishberg (1986), which states that it is "the process of changing an English text into Manually Coded English (or vice versa)" (1986:19).[3] RID's most recent attempt to define transliteration refers to Win-ston (1989), who also cites Frishberg (1986) but elaborates the process (discussed in some detail below in Section 4).

The term "transliteration" has also been used to describe the processes that occur when using systems such as Cued Speech and oral interpreting. Those using Cued Speech or oral interpreting to render a target message experience some similar cognitive challenges to those of the transliterator working between English and contact sign, but they are not faced with choosing which features of ASL and which of English to combine to create the target language message, and it is this challenge which is addressed specifically throughout this chapter.

In Canada, the term "transliteration" is not widely used by interpreters, educators of the Deaf or members of the Deaf community, but as mentioned, literature from the United States references it frequently, and for this reason it is familiar to Canadians in the field. None of the interpreter preparation programs in Canada use it in their course descriptions, and the AVLIC Test of Interpretation does not specifically test transliterating skills. The Program of Sign Language Interpretation at Douglas College, New Westminster, British Columbia, instead uses the term "interpreting into a contact variety". However, given that much of the existing literature does use "transliteration", I will continue to refer to it in this chapter and then address its usage in Section 8 which discusses some recommendations.

The definitions of transliteration cited above emphasize that the language being used is consistently English, and that only the form or modality changes. Transliterat-ing that strives to represent all features of the English source (for example, including tense markers and gender specific pronouns) may be best conceived of as a form of transcoding, and it may therefore be that the above definitions that stipulate two modes of the same language most accurately reflect that process. However, studies that analyze actual transliterating samples, while few in number, point to the fact that the transliterator incorporates features of *both* English and ASL, and is constantly deciding which combination of features will most readily convey meaning to the Deaf consumer (Winston 1989; Siple 1993, 1996). Thus, definitions focusing only on the modality change (i.e., two modes of the same language) are insufficient in addressing how incorporation of ASL features takes place.

4. Research on transliteration

The first attempt to outline the tasks necessary for transliterating took place at the 1984 gathering of the Conference of Interpreter Trainers in Asilomar, California.[4] Educators of interpreters sought to better understand the tasks inherent in both interpreting and transliterating, with the goal of more successfully teaching these skills. Participants who were engaged in the analysis highlighted the challenges of transliterating due to the lack of a standardized form of English-like signing (McIntire 1986: 94). They noted that in order to ensure that the target message makes sense, the transliterator often adjusts her output so her signing is more like ASL and less like English (1986: 95). They also commented that transliterating often requires the use of a number of processing strategies to be successful, that is, some information may need to be omitted due to the temporal pressure of attempting to convey every English word into a signed form. Articles, for example, are usually deleted, as are redundancies. As well, modulations of many ASL verbs may make it possible to omit some English words from the target text. For example, in a sentence such as *I helped him*, when the referent "him" has previously been established in visual space, the verb HELP can be signed moving from the signer towards the spatial referent, thus eliminating the need for a specific sign for "him".

Additions form another category of changes which can be found in the transliterated target language message. Cokely (1992) used the term "addition" in his discussion of interpreting to refer to certain miscues that occur, but the term is typically used differently in transliteration.[5] The additions present in transliterating clarify the intent when simply conveying the English word into contact sign would not. An example is the English phrase *when we bring young and old together*, when the transliterator adds the sign PEOPLE (i.e., YOUNG AND OLD PEOPLE) to clarify what is meant (Kelly 2001: 25).

Winston (1989) notes the use of some of these features in her study of the output of a transliterator working with a Deaf student in a university class. The student was an English-based signer in the process of learning ASL, who wanted the signed message to employ semantically accurate ASL signs while also retaining the structure of English. Winston analyzed the transliteration of a lecture, and noted some strategies used to create a clear message: sign choice, addition, omission, restructuring and mouthing. Each of these categories is described briefly below.

Winston's first category, sign choice, involves the selection of signed vocabulary that conveys the meaning of an English lexical item rather than a gloss which matches the English lexical item but does not convey the appropriate meaning for a conceptual interpretation of that source message.[6] An example often cited is the word *run*. The ASL sign, glossed as RUN, has the meaning 'to run' as in track and field, but it does not convey the meaning of water running, a run in a stocking, or running a meeting. An interpreter who heard a sentence using the word *run*, with the meaning of 'running a meeting', would select a different ASL lexical item to convey the intent, rather than the sign glossed as RUN.

Winston (1989:155) cites the following examples using the English word *got*, and suggests how they would be signed differently if meaning is the intent of the transliterator.

(1) a. I got sick   → BECOME
     b. She got hit   → Something HIT her
     c. They got there   → ARRIVE
     d. I got it (I understand)   → UNDERSTAND

These examples illustrate that transliterating is more than either a process of transcoding or simply a change in modality, but rather requires the analysis of intent similar to the analysis required when interpreting between English and ASL.

In instances of addition, Winston found times when the transliterator provided a more conceptual sign before or after a literal interpretation. She cites an example where the English phrase *don't want* is rendered as a two-sign phrase DON'T WANT followed by the ASL form of the verb with negative incorporation, DON'T-WANT. As mentioned earlier, this type of addition in transliteration refers to information added to the source language message in order to clarify the intent. The use of space, a prominent ASL feature, is another type of addition occurring in the transliteration. Winston found as well that facial expressions are used to assist in clarification of the message. For example, the transliterator in Winston's study signed SELF RESPECT with an expression of pride and an expanded chest (1989:160).

Winston also found instances of restructuring, where the transliterator would change the order of items in the message to increase the clarity. When Winston asked the transliterator why she restructured, she was unable to state explicitly which features of English prompted her to do so, but felt that the message, if preserved in its exact English form, "would not provide a clear visual message when recoded in the target form" (1989:162).

Finally, Winston looked at the use of mouthing. Of significance is that at times the transliterator mouthed the source English word but chose a different target sign that more conceptually matched the meaning.

Winston's study documents a sample of transliteration that includes many features of ASL along with features of English retained from the source text. This study provides evidence that transliterating involves message analysis: "Analyzing the source message and producing a target form that is both functionally equivalent and structurally similar to the source is a complex process and requires more than the simple recoding of English words" (Winston 1989:163).

How pauses in the source message are used in constructing a transliterated target message was investigated by Siple (1993). Siple studied twenty interpreters who transliterated an eleven-minute monologue produced with normal pausing in the speech stream, and then asked them to transliterate the same passage, this time produced with random and incorrectly placed pauses. Siple was interested in studying how these interpreters would show auditory pauses in a visual form. Would the pausing pattern of the source text be reproduced in the target message, even when the pauses occurred at unnatural moments and created difficulty in comprehending the message? Or would the transliterator ignore the incorrectly placed pauses and analyze the source message for its meaning, inserting pauses in the target transliteration that aided the Deaf consumer in understanding the meaning of the message?

The monologue was read and recorded twice by the same actor, once with natural inflection and an animated voice, and once with random speech pauses inserted and delivered in a monotone. There was a one-week time period between transliterating the first text and the second. The transliterators were asked to imagine they were producing the target text for the same Deaf student for each rendition.

Siple was able to demonstrate that transliterators do insert appropriately placed pauses in their transliterations to provide overall coherence in the target message. In showing that this paralinguistic element is used meaningfully in the target message, Siple's research supports the claim that transliterating involves more than just a modality shift or a word-for-word representation. Siple notes that further research is needed regarding other paralinguistic features such as vocal stress and vocal qualities conveying emotion, and how these also might affect the process of transliterating.

Winston and Monikowski (2003) also considered pausing, in both interpreting and transliterating. They compared the work of three interpreters who worked from the same English source text, interpreting it into ASL and transliterating it into contact sign. They found that the transliteration did indeed incorporate ASL prosodic features, such as the "use of space for sentence boundaries, lengthened final holds for signs, and head and torso shifting" (2003:189). Winston and Monikowski emphasize that ASL prosodic features are required for a dynamically equivalent transliteration (2003:195). They found that while pausing occurred in both the interpreted and transliterated texts, there were noticeably fewer extra-linguistic pauses (pauses where the interpreter or transliterator clasped hands and appeared to be thinking) in the transliterated texts. Stops between segments were significantly shorter, even to the point of being nearly imperceptible, and a question raised for further discussion is whether this leads to difficulty for the viewer in identifying major boundary shifts in the text. The researchers note the need for further study, with the goal of ensuring that transliteration is ultimately comprehensible.

Another study of transliterating that set out to compare Deaf students' comprehension of college-level material when presented via interpreting or transliterating is Livingston, Singer and Abrahamson (1994). Livingston et al. presented both narrative and lecture material to 43 Deaf college students, who were divided into groups based on whether they stated a preference for interpretation into ASL or transliteration into a contact variety. The students were also grouped according to level of education. Matched groups then watched both a narrative presentation and a lecture, either interpreted or transliterated, and subsequently were tested for comprehension. The results showed that even students who stated a preference for a more English-like target text scored better when receiving the message in ASL.

In discussing their findings, the researchers comment that "the characteristics of ASL and some of the strategies employed by ASL interpreters are basic to visual/spatial language – that even being perhaps somewhat unfamiliar with ASL did not preclude understanding it; and that in fact the unique characteristics of the language and the way it was interpreted served to clarify concepts and make them more memorable for English-preferring students" (Livingston et al. 1994:34). These findings support those of Supalla (1991) noted above, and suggest that transliterating, even when requested, will be more successful when incorporating features of ASL such as the use of space and directional verbs, as well as employing strategies such as addition and restructuring as noted by Winston.

Livingston et al. ultimately comment that "transliteration is interpretation that has not gone far enough" (1994:39). By this they mean that when the transliterator attempts to retain the exact form of the source language text, this restricts the transliterator from employing features of ASL which tend to make the target text more easily understood in terms of its visual and spatial form. Livingston et al. thus encourage transliterators to make use of these features of ASL, and to not concentrate on retaining every aspect of the source text form.

Another study of note is Siple's (1996) study which builds on Winston's work on the use of addition when transliterating. Siple analyzed the work of fifteen interpreters who were interpreting for an imagined audience of Deaf consumers that they knew preferred a more English-like transliteration.

Siple noted five types of information added to the target language production that were not found in the source message, but which served to make the source message more comprehensible visually and spatially. The first type of addition she found had to do with cohesion, serving to link different parts of the discourse, such as conjunctions and spatial referencing. The second were additions for clarity, which were attempts to reduce ambiguity, such as by providing additional semantic information and stating something explicitly that the source text implied. Siple also found instances of "modality adaptation", which referred to information that was originally conveyed auditorially, such as intonation, subsequently conveyed in the target message visually. There were also instances of repetition which provided emphasis. Reduplication, a grammatical feature of ASL, was used in the transliteration to indicate pluralization.

Sofinski (2002) built on the work of Lucas and Valli by examining a signed narrative which combined features of ASL and of English. He details the types of English mouthing that were present: full English mouthing, where a complete English lexical item or phrase could be viewed on the mouth; reduced English mouthing, where part of the English lexical item or phrase was present; lexicalized mouthing, whereby the original English mouthing has been modified to co-occur with a particular ASL sign; and mouthed adverbials (such as CHA, MM or CS) (2002:37). Of particular interest was the co-occurrence of these features, that is, mouthed English while ASL is presented in the "manual channel". Sofinski comments that "many people base their perception of a product as being more 'English-like' or more 'ASL-like' on the features contained within the oral and manual channels because these channels are where they can most readily find the 'most clear evidence' of an English influence, often paying little attention to the existence of simultaneously co-occurring ASL features" (2002:46). This study flags an important consideration for interpreters in their analysis of a Deaf person's language use and the resulting language production required by the interpreter.

Another recent study examining the mix of ASL and English features in interpretation is found in Davis (2003). Davis looked at the output of four certified interpreters in order to describe the cross-linguistic transfer from English during an interpretation into ASL. Similarly to Sofinski, Davis notes the potential to utilize both the oral/aural and visual/gestural channels of communication, and does indeed find examples of such combinations in the interpreting samples studied. He notes that the four interpreters whose work was analyzed alternated between ASL mouthing patterns, "lexicalized" lip movements and English that was clearly articulated although not auditory. In addition, Davis notes the use of fingerspelling as another example of cross-linguistic transfer.

The research on transliterating cited above shares a common thread, which is the recognition that transliterating, or interpreting into a contact variety of signed language, still involves the use of ASL features. This means that, essentially, transliterators need to know ASL. Additionally, the research points us towards a deeper understanding of the complex process which an interpreter must undertake to successfully produce a message in contact sign. Interpreting into ASL requires the interpreter to understand and convey the meaning of a source text, while transliterating strives to represent both meaning *and* the source language form. Further research, however, is needed to better clarify this process for the interpreter or transliterator striving to produce a meaningful message in a contact variety of signed language. This includes research into what contributes to the unique mixture of ASL and English features in each individual's use of contact signing, as well as studies on community attitudes towards the use of contact sign. In addition, further study is needed to more fully understand the complex decision-making strategies available to the transliterator.

5.   Challenges of transliteration

In this section, some of the challenges that interpreters face when working into contact signing are addressed. Here, I primarily use the term "interpreter" with the understanding that whether the target text is produced in ASL or in a contact variety of signed language, both involve at least some similar cognitive processing. As well, the same individual may find herself working with consumers who have quite different language preferences, so that we cannot assume that "interpreters" only work into (and out of) ASL while "transliterators" only work with contact varieties.

5.1 Assessing consumer needs

One of the first challenges facing the interpreter is to determine the correct mix of ASL and English features that a particular Deaf person employs and understands so that she can match this in her target language message. For example, a person who became deaf later in life, and has only begun to learn ASL, may emphasize the importance of following English word order and mouthing English words, while a Deaf person who uses ASL for most social interactions, but who has requested that the interpreter use contact sign for an employment-related training seminar, may prefer that the interpreter's target text incorporates the use of space and classifiers found in ASL along with fingerspelled technical terms. Thus the interpreter is constantly balancing the need to represent the form of the English source text along with incorporating ASL features in conveying the message in a visual and spatial language.

In their formal education, interpreters learn to assess the language preferences of the Deaf consumer in order to determine whether the most appropriate interpretation should be in ASL or a contact variety of signed language. If the preference is determined to be a contact variety, the interpreter must further decide what that particular variety should look like – for example, how much fingerspelling, how much to mouth the source English words while articulating semantically accurate signs, and so forth. In making these assessments, interpreters must consider the following factors.

Upon meeting a Deaf person at an assignment and introducing herself, the interpreter begins to get a sense of the Deaf person's language use. However, many Deaf people will code-switch to a more English-like form of signing when meeting a new hearing person. As discussed in Section 2.2 above, such code-switching often takes place unconsciously as a result of years of interacting with hearing people who cannot understand them when they use ASL. Armed with this knowledge, interpreters commonly use the strategy of continuing to sign in ASL, to see if the Deaf person begins to use more ASL as she realizes the interpreter can understand her. Sometimes, a Deaf person will continue to sign her own discourse using a contact variety, but comprehend other people's discourse more easily when it is produced in ASL. Interpreters must therefore be prepared to incorporate a range of both ASL and English features, attempting to match the Deaf person's specific language use, and watching for subtle signs of comfort on the Deaf person's part that indicate ease of comprehension (for example, a more relaxed body posture, less obvious straining to try to use unfamiliar signs, head nodding or other facial gestures that indicate comprehension, etc.).

Some Deaf people state clearly what their preference is, and yet even this specific kind of direction can be problematic for the interpreter when considering the variety of language she should be using. Burns et al. (2001) cite the study in Lucas and Valli (1989)[7] in noting that "the choice of varieties 'other than ASL', and the view that ASL is not appropriate for certain situations, are the direct result of a sociolinguistic situation in which ASL has been suppressed, and in which the focus has traditionally been on the instruction and use of spoken and signed English" (Burns et al. 2001: 193). This sometimes results in Deaf people stating they want an interpretation into a signed form of English, even though the meaning is not actually as accessible to them as it would be in ASL. One personal experience involved a Deaf woman who told me she did not know the "old signs", she only knew the "new ones". As we continued to converse prior to the interpreted event, I realized that by "new signs" she meant the use of many initialized signs which she had been taught in school, but in fact the grammatical features of her signing were more heavily influenced by ASL than English.

More recently, the converse of the above situation has begun to appear. With the increase in awareness of ASL as a complete language, capable of fulfilling all the functions for which language is used, and with the growth of pride in Deaf culture and identity, some Deaf students entering college are now instructing coordinators of interpreting services that they require ASL interpretation. Marna Arnell, facilitator of the Interpreting Services Project in British Columbia, Canada, has noted that once the interpreters begin to work with these students, however, they realize that in fact, the students have been educated orally and are very new signers, comprehending a contact variety of signed language better than a strict ASL interpretation (Marna Arnell, personal communication, May 2000). Their desire to identify with the Deaf community leads these students to represent themselves as ASL users.

5.2 Attitudinal barriers

As stated above, attitudes within the Deaf community itself can lead to confusion when a Deaf person is describing her language use and preferences. Attitudinal factors do not only affect Deaf people however; interpreters and transliterators are also affected. It appears that in the past, interpreters have sometimes reflected the thinking of the dominant hearing community that ASL is not a full language and thus that more English-like signing has been preferred, an observation made by numerous experienced interpreter educators (Jan Humphrey, Risa Shaw, Debra Russell, personal communication). Currently however, interpreting programs in Canada concentrate on teaching ASL and developing the abilities of students to interpret between ASL and English. As students in these ASL-oriented programs struggle to gain mastery of the interpreting process, they often receive feedback that they retain too much of the form of the source language (i.e., English) in their interpretation, or have not expressed the idea in the most easily understood way in ASL, thus they work even harder to use ASL well.

Having received this kind of feedback repeatedly, it is difficult for the student to then attempt to deliberately *maintain* the English form and to mouth English words along with their sign choices. Students at Douglas College, British Columbia, report feeling concerned that their Deaf ASL teachers will see them practicing this and think that the students are not respecting the wishes of the Deaf community to use ASL.

Students also report fearing that the abilities they have mastered in interpreting from English into ASL will be lost when they practice interpreting into a contact variety.

It is important for educators of interpreters to address these concerns, and assist students in recognizing that their goal must be the development of control over the interpreting process, so that the product, or target message, will be an appropriate match for Deaf consumers with different language preferences. Specific suggestions for educators are addressed in Section 6 below.

Occasionally an underlying attitudinal issue is apparent when students and professional interpreters alike have decided that signing in a more English-like fashion is undesirable, or is not as valued as interpreting into ASL, and this attitude must be challenged within the profession as a whole. Some examples of this type of negative reaction on the part of interpreters are reported in Viera and Stauffer (2000). They conducted a survey of consumers of transliteration and received 61 responses to the 80 surveys sent out (two respondents were from Canada and the remainder from the United States). Respondents reported that when requesting transliteration, some of the reactions they received included being asked incredulously by a certified interpreter, "You want everything?", while another signed and said, "I know you want me to mouth the words while I sign like this" with greatly exaggerated mouth movements (Viera & Stauffer 2000:84).

These responses demonstrate either that the interpreter lacked an understanding of what was being requested, lacked the ability to match the request, or lacked respect for a Deaf consumer's language preferences. It is difficult to determine whether these two reported instances reflect a deficit in skill alone or also include attitudinal resistance to the request. However, the following example clearly shows profound attitudinal resistance.

Jean Teets, a Deaf woman in the United States who is very clear in her requirement for transliterating that follows English word order, recounts an incident where she requested that the interpreter work into an English-like form. In her videotaped narrative, she recounts that the interpreter replied, "Shame on you! Don't you know that ASL is your natural language?" (Teets 1989). It should be evident to every interpreter and transliterator that this kind of judgmental response to a consumer's request is unacceptable.

No matter how strongly interpreters support the Deaf community's struggle for recognition, language rights, and the need for ASL to be used as the language of instruction in schools, it is crucial that they also respect consumers' choices and produce a transliteration, or contact sign interpretation, if that is the wish of the individual. It is not the interpreter's right to place judgment on the Deaf person's language choices. Rather, the need is for an accurate assessment of the consumer's language choice, along with the skills and flexibility that allow the interpreter to control the target language message she produces to match the preference of the Deaf consumer.

Still, Deaf consumers who request transliteration can create challenges for interpreters by the descriptions they do use. As Stauffer and Viera note, consumer expectations may or may not be realistic in terms of what transliterators can and cannot do (Stauffer & Viera 2000). Stauffer and Viera's survey of consumers requesting transliteration revealed that some consumers described their needs and preferences in the following ways. One said that the preferred transliteration should be "verbatim, word-for-word transliteration...and that they should mouth and fingerspell (to the best of their ability) those words for which they do not know the sign equivalent" (Viera & Stauffer 2000:91). Another suggested a preference for a "Signed English interpreter with good lip movement. No ASL allowed" (2000:91).

These statements can present a quandary to the interpreter. Meaningful transliteration typically includes some elements of ASL, as demonstrated by the research cited earlier in this chapter, so requests for a "verbatim" interpretation or instructions to not use ASL pose a challenge. It could be that a verbatim rendition is possible, if the speaker's pace and the content of the text are such that the interpreter is able to keep up. In addition, if the speaker is willing to pause frequently, the interpreter may be able to closely follow the form of the source message. Many times, though, including numerous manual markers that indicate the English forms of tense, gender, pluralization and so forth requires too much time for the interpreter's target message to consistently mirror the form of the source message.

Some consumers making such requests may not be aware of the features of ASL that can be present when transliterating, and which greatly assist in the delivery of a signed message that makes sense. The interpreter needs to pay careful attention to the requests of her consumers and strive to incorporate the elements of the English form they prefer, while also determining which features of ASL will benefit the overall clarity of the interpreted message. Ultimately, interpreters need the skill to manage their interpreting process so as to produce ASL or a variety of contact sign as is called for, the wisdom to determine what the appropriate target form should be, and the respect to comply with consumer requests.

6.   Preparing interpreters to work into contact varieties of signed language

The goal for signed language interpreters must be the development of control over their interpreting process, so that the product, or target message, will be an appropriate match for the Deaf consumer. No matter what her political beliefs and alignment to the ASL-using Deaf community may be, the interpreter needs to respect the language choices of every Deaf individual for whom she interprets, and it is clear that there are Deaf people who prefer or require a contact variety of signed language.

Currently, the skills to transliterate, or interpret into a contact variety of signed language, are not addressed in any depth in interpreter preparation programs in Canada. Programs concentrate rather on preparing students to interpret between English and ASL, and vary in the amount of time they have to complete the task (from two to four years). In some cases, students complete a language and culture acquisition program prior to entry into the interpreting program. For example, the majority of students entering the Douglas College Program of Sign Language Interpretation, a two-year program, have completed a ten-month, full-time program in ASL and Deaf Studies at Vancouver Community College.

Even with this strong foundation in place, students tend to be relatively new language learners when they enter their interpreting program, and are in the position of continuing to learn one of their working languages while they are also learning to interpret. Their interpretation into ASL thus may often include English-like forms because of their incomplete mastery of their second language.[8] In addition, students struggling to master the complex cognitive tasks required for simultaneous interpreting will often produce more English-like interpretations due to their inability to process the meaning without considering the form of the source language.

Thus programs concentrate on strengthening the ASL-English interpreting skills of their students, and transliterating skills are not taught. In my recent conversations with faculty at programs in Canada on this topic, a common theme arose: contact varieties are acknowledged within the program, but are not specifically addressed.[9] Faculty members do address the topic of language variety within the Deaf community and the necessity of adjusting the interpretation to meet the needs of different consumers, however. Additionally, Deaf models representing a range of usage along the language continuum are employed for class practice, but as mentioned, specific instruction in transliterating skills is not offered.

Time constraint is not the only barrier to transliterating skills being taught in interpreting programs. There seems to be a prevailing belief among both some program instructors and working interpreters that interpreting into a contact variety of signed language is easy, since interpreters already know English. In the past, interpreters have often produced messages that retained much of the English form, perhaps due to a historic lack of training in ASL and an improperly sequenced education in interpretation. My own belief too when I began teaching interpreting in 1988 was that interpreting into a contact variety was easy. It was what I had naively done at the start of my own interpreting career before I learned more ASL and received instruction in the process of interpreting. Campbell McDermid, an instructor in the George Brown College ASL-English Interpretation Program, who similarly entered the field in the 1980s, echoes much the same sentiment (Campbell McDermid, personal communication). Interpreters who have supervised Douglas College students on practicum have reported, impatiently at times, that the students simply do not use enough English features in their target texts when requested to do so by Deaf consumers. The impatience underlying their comments leads me to believe that they, as well, assume that conveying the form of the source language should be an easy task, one that students at that stage should not have difficulty accomplishing.

However, interpreting students consistently report that they do *not* find it easy to make the transition from interpreting into ASL to interpreting into a contact variety. Their education has taught them to disregard the form of the source message and wait for meaning. ASL instructors have also repeatedly emphasized the need to decrease the amount of mouthing English words. When unable to make sense of the message, students are taught to wait a short time longer until they do understand, and while practicing, if it is impossible to keep up with the pace of the speaker when working simultaneously, to convey at least the main points. It seems contradictory to these students then to stay close to the source language structure and to convey the form while mouthing English words, even if at times it means that they are not comprehending the speaker's point.

Interpreting into a contact variety of signed language in fact requires the interpreter to attend to both the meaning and the form. Interpreters will usually shorten their process time to retain the form of the source message, that is, they will process at the lexical or phrasal level. However, they must still monitor the overall message to ensure that meaning is conveyed in their target text. This means they are still considering what the speaker's point of view and goals are, as well as connecting what is being said with what the speaker has said previously and mentally predicting what the speaker may address next.

Interpreters need to make quick decisions regarding whether or not the English source text needs to be restructured using certain ASL features in order for the target text to make sense. But knowing ASL and having skills in English-ASL interpreting are not enough. In Viera and Stauffer's survey of Deaf consumers requesting transliteration, almost 100% of the respondents agreed that someone who can interpret into ASL is not automatically able to transliterate (2000: 93). The interpreting skills needed to work between English and ASL form a necessary building block for successful transliteration, but they are not a guarantee of that ability.

Given that the time students spend in interpreting programs is brief, it may not be possible for programs to prepare students both to interpret from English to ASL and into a contact variety of signed language. However, programs can address the range of contact sign that exists within the community by inviting Deaf models to class who use a contact variety to communicate. Students also need to be educated regarding the role of contact sign within the larger Deaf community. Even simply stating that transliterating does not imply a sign-for-word transcoding can be enlightening to students.

It is useful for students to watch the same person first interpret and then transliterate the same text in order to demonstrate that it is a reasonable expectation for interpreters to be able to vary the language form of the target message. Students can also attempt signing in English word order, mouthing English words and using semantically accurate signs, so they at least have some preliminary idea of what they need to do mentally in order to eventually produce a transliteration. Class activities where students alternate between interpreting into ASL and interpreting into a contact variety are a useful way to help students gain a sense of the difference between the two, and to begin to control their output.

Ultimately, the skills required to produce quality transliteration could easily take a full semester course meeting three hours per week, although given the limited time available in interpreter education programs currently, programs may not be able to do this. At least some time, however, should be allotted for an introduction to the concept of contact varieties of signed language within the Deaf community, along with some discussion of the use of ASL features when transliterating. If this is not done, students will continue to first encounter the task of transliteration at the practicum site and on the job once they graduate, where they will be ill prepared to meet consumers' needs.

7. Certification and standards

When AVLIC was working to establish the Certificate of Interpretation (COI), the national certification implemented in 1990, a decision was reached in collaboration with the Deaf community to offer one certification only, which recognized skill in ASL-English interpretation. This contrasts with the certification offered by RID in the United States, which offers a separate Certificate of Interpretation (CI) and Certificate of Transliteration (CT). For RID, the definition of a set standard for the CT has been problematic, due to the lack of a standardized form of the target language when transliterating from English. RID has described three broad categories which are assessed during the English-to-sign portion of the test, which are grammar and vocabulary, processing, and mouth movement patterns (Friedenreich 1996:24). Several statements regarding what successful transliteration in the test would look like demonstrate that the incorporation of ASL features is desired. These are:

– use of space for role taking (characterization)
– conceptually correct sign choices (based on meaning rather than form), and
– some additions of ASL signs which enhance the clarity of the visual message (modals such as CAN, classifier constructions, indexing and listing structures) (Friedenreich 1996:24).

While this explanation does make it clear that a word-for-word, or even morpheme by morpheme transcoding is not expected, it is still difficult for the test taker to determine to what extent these features can be employed, with the result still considered a successful transliterating performance.

The difficulty in assessing transliterating skills lies in the non-standard form of the contact varieties of language in use. The transliteration required for an adult Deaf man who lost his hearing at the age of 20, for example, will most likely follow the English form very closely, and may include frequent fingerspelling and some sign choices that reflect source message words rather than ASL semantic features, along with consistent English mouthing, since the consumer in this case would be very familiar with English as a spoken language. This transliteration would likely be very different from that required for a culturally Deaf computer specialist who has requested transliteration at a training seminar and who is accustomed to receiving the message in a visual and spatial form, and is thus very familiar with the inherent semantics of ASL signs.

Within Canada, transliterating has not garnered the same attention it has been afforded in the United States. Supporters of sign systems designed to represent English have joined RID and sought organizational recognition for their transliterating skills, while AVLIC has predominantly represented interpreters working between ASL and English (and for a time, LSQ[10] and French), although recall that AVLIC expects its members to attain a wide range of language skills to accommodate diverse consumers. RID has consistently provided both an interpreter and a transliterator on stage at the same time for its meetings, which has not occurred in Canada. There does not appear to be a large cohort requesting interpretation into contact varieties of signed language in Canada in the same way that exists in the United States. As well there has been no organized consumer demand for separate certification for transliteration in Canada.

Screening tools that employers use across Canada also reflect the emphasis on ASL. The screening at the Ontario Interpreter Services tests for skills in ASL-English interpretation, as does the Medical Interpreting Services screening in British Columbia. The newly developed screening for community interpreters in Edmonton and Calgary tests for ASL-English interpretation skills as well, although some of the models of Deaf people appearing in the test materials use contact signing, and test takers are expected to match the language choice of the Deaf person.

The one screening currently in use that does require demonstration of the ability to interpret from English into both ASL and into a contact variety of signed language is the Post-Secondary Screening in British Columbia. Test takers need to demonstrate the ability to maintain a sense of control over their output so that there is a clear difference between work into ASL and work into the contact variety.

It is evident that screenings and certification tests used in Canada reflect the need in the community for ASL-English interpreting skills, and that the need for testing for interpreting into a contact variety has not been widespread. I continue to support testing and certification for ASL-English skills, and also support the inclusion of language models who use a contact variety of signed language as part of the screening tools, rather than the development of a separate certification system for transliteration.

8.   Recommendations

The research on transliterating suggests a common theme: quality transliterating requires the incorporation of both ASL and English features. ASL interpreting skills are required for a transliteration that conveys meaning in the target text (as opposed to a transcoding of the source language), and the interpreter must undertake cognitive processing that is fundamentally similar whether the target language is ASL or contact signing. Therefore, the field would be well served in referring to the work in this way, that is, interpreting into contact signing or a contact variety of signed language, rather than using the term "transliteration", which is ambiguously defined and poorly understood. Siple (1996) notes the reaction of interpreters when she asked them to transliterate. One described her understanding of the task in this way: "Well, there's word-for-word, and then there's what I consider to be a more effective form" (1996:31). Without the use of the confounding term "transliteration", this interpreter may have more quickly moved to a determination of the contact variety features best suited for the Deaf audience. As well, as Siple points out, "the perception that transliteration is simply the robotic task of assigning a sign to each word has led to a status difference between interpretation and transliteration" (1996:30). The term "transliteration" is thus too fraught with misunderstandings and judgments.

Interpreters need education in how to approach the task of interpreting into a contact variety. Even the explanation that their goal is not to be a word-for-word, verbatim presentation is reassuring to many beginning interpreters. The importance of incorporating ASL features needs to be emphasized, along with building skill in following the source text closely in order to present aspects of the form of the source message. Drawing on the research to date, training must emphasize the decision-making process the interpreter faces in using strategies such as addition, omission, restructuring, use of semantically accurate ASL signs, and use of mouthing English words, among others.

An important concern that interpreting programs must address as they teach students to interpret into a contact variety of signed language is the potential reaction of the Deaf community. Program faculty need to affirm their support for the primacy of ASL in the Deaf community and within Deaf education. They need to work with Deaf organizations to emphasize that they are not actively supporting the use of signed English, but rather are training interpreters who can serve the needs of various members of the broader Deaf community. Programs can consult with Deaf organizations, and in a very respectful way, bring to the attention of the Deaf community that there are members of their community and organizations who prefer to interact using contact sign in certain interpreted contexts. But faculty and interpreters should bear in mind the sensitive nature of language issues within the Deaf community, the oppression of the Deaf ASL-signing community that exists to the present day, and the role that hearing people and hearing institutions have played in perpetuating it.

A personal example may prove useful in illustrating my point. As I prepared this chapter, I consulted with interpreting programs across Canada to determine what their current practices were in terms of teaching transliterating and contact signing. One Deaf ASL instructor and I became involved in a long discussion where he raised concerns that students' signed language use is already too influenced by their first language, English, and that they do not produce ASL interpretations. He also raised the issue that the Deaf community supports the recognition of ASL as the language of that community. I agreed wholeheartedly with these points, but I could see that he was not convinced that I understood him. Finally, I thought of a Deaf leader who uses contact sign and who is well respected. I was able to say, "You know X? Well, we want the students to be able to interpret for him too". Finally the Deaf person responded, "Oh, okay, if it's for X, then that's okay".

The concerns this Deaf man raised in our conversation are legitimate ones, and as a non-Deaf person, I may not be able to address such community issues on my own. It is important for Deaf faculty members in interpreter education programs who are full members of the community and are respected by other members to also speak to these issues. It may be helpful to show samples of interpreting that achieve the desired goal, that of an interpreter (or interpreting student) who is able to adapt her output successfully for a variety of consumers' language preferences.

In Canada, AVLIC should continue to focus on certifying ASL-English interpreters. As stated earlier, a demand for separate certification of interpretation skills into contact signing has not emerged within Canada, and consumers of interpreting services are better served by a single certification process. A large number of employers of interpreters are relatively unfamiliar with ASL and the interpreting process, and are not able to determine if an "interpreter" or a "transliterator" is the most appropriate choice. Given that ASL skills are required for an interpretation into a contact variety of signed language as well, AVLIC's single certification process appears to suffice. Programs training interpreters, however, should ensure that the training includes work on interpreting into contact varieties. Finally, interpreters must also strive to demonstrate respect for Deaf people's choices of language and language varieties they use.

There is a great deal of research that could still be undertaken which would inform our understanding of contact signing and the processes required to use it successfully when interpreting. Further work building on Lucas and Valli's research, outlined above, would be instructive in identifying ways in which ASL features are incorporated into varieties of contact signing, and what features of the resulting message make it more acceptable to the ASL-using Deaf community. Further research into the sociolinguistic factors that influence an individual's use of contact signing would also be beneficial to interpreters.

More research on transliterating itself is also needed. We need to develop a common understanding of the process, whether it is called transliteration or interpreting into a contact variety of signed language, along with what cognitive processes the interpreter undertakes in producing a message characterized as contact signing. In addition, no research has yet been conducted on working from contact signing as the source text into spoken English as the target, and it would be instructive to identify the cognitive processes necessary for the interpreter to do so successfully.

Another area of research that would be useful to interpreters is that of investigating what cognitive processes take place for interpreters who can clearly distinguish between producing ASL or contact signing as appropriate target forms. Is their cognitive processing the same for each, or different? How have they learned to keep the two target forms distinct?

These research areas will serve to deepen our understanding of the role of contact signing within the Deaf community and the strategies that aid interpreters in their work with a variety of signers' language preferences. Further, such research will assist interpreter educators in preparing students to successfully meet this complex array of language usage they will encounter.

As ASL is increasingly used as the language of instruction in schools instead of systems constructed to represent English, younger generations of Deaf people may reach adulthood with a strong base in their first language without as much influence from English-based systems. Also, if interpreting programs continue to focus on teaching students to be able to interpret fluently into ASL, with an appropriate range of register, Deaf people may gain more confidence in the accuracy of the ASL interpretation they receive, thus preferring that even the most technical information be interpreted into ASL. As such it may be the case that the need for interpreting into contact varieties of a signed language will decline.

At this point in time, however, this has not fully taken place. Many Deaf children are still being educated using a range of English-based signing systems, and a significant minority in the Deaf community still uses and comprehends contact varieties. The enrollment at residential schools for the Deaf is declining across Canada, with many Deaf children now being educated in the public school system. Frequently in these cases, either their teacher or their interpreter uses a strongly English-based system for signing. Thus, it seems more likely that the need for interpreters who are comfortable with contact signing will continue to exist, at least for the time being.

9. Conclusion

The preceding discussion has addressed the existence of contact sign within the Deaf community, and the factors that have led to its existence and continuation. Given that many Deaf people do use it, it is important for interpreters to gain mastery of interpreting into contact varieties of signed language in order to meet the communication preferences of the entire diverse Deaf community. Skills in signing ASL and interpreting into ASL are prerequisites to successful interpretation into a contact variety, but do not alone guarantee success. Interpreters need to study and practice the skills of combining features of ASL and English to produce a coherent message in the target language or language variety, tailored to the specific needs of each Deaf consumer. Negative attitudes on the part of members of the Deaf community towards contact sign, as well as on the part of interpreters, can create barriers to interpreters respecting and mastering these skills, and yet the need within the community clearly exists. As contact varieties of signed language are studied further, along with the processes which the interpreter undertakes when working with these varieties, we will gain a better understanding of the educational needs of interpreting students, and the ways in which they can be ensured of their readiness for work within the broad Deaf community in Canada.

Notes

1. This notation for fingerspelled loan signs follows Battison (1978) and is intended to differentiate these from fully formed fingerspelled words.

2. SEE 2 follows a three-point set of criteria for determining what sign to use to represent an English word. If two out of three criteria (sound, spelling and meaning) are the same, then the same sign will be used, even if the meaning of the sign in ASL would not convey the same

semantic intent as that of the English word. As well, signed affixes and inflections are used, such as the use of -S to mark a plural (e.g., cat, cats) or the addition of -ING. Additional principles guiding the use of SEE 2 can be found in Gustafson, Pfetzing and Zawolkow (1980).

3. Siple (1997:87) also points out that Manually Coded English in this definition refers collectively to a number of different sign systems that represent English.

4. The Conference of Interpreter Trainers is an organization whose mission is the promotion of quality education for interpreters working with ASL and English, including English-influenced forms of signing. Conferences are held biennially and proceedings of the conferences are published.

5. Cokely defines an addition as information that may be added to an interpretation which has no corollary in the source language message.

6. A gloss is an English word, written in upper case letters, used as a label to express the meaning of a sign. ASL and English lexical items may share similar meanings in some contexts, but depart from each other in other contexts.

7. See Section 2 above on Lucas and Valli's contribution to the definition of contact signing.

8. For further discussion, see the videotaped teleclass presented by Betty Colonomos, entitled "Processes in Interpretation and Transliteration: Making Them Work for You" (1992).

9. Colleagues who were consulted include Donna Korpiniski, Grant MacEwan College, Edmonton, Alberta; Campbell McDermid, George Brown College, Toronto, Ontario; Judy McGuirk, Red River College, Winnipeg, Manitoba; and Denise Smith, Nova Scotia Community College, Halifax, Nova Scotia.

10. Langue des Signes Québécoise.

References

Battison, Robbin (1978). *Lexical Borrowing in American Sign Language.* Silver Spring, MD: Linstok Press.

Burns, Sarah, Patrick Matthews, & Evelyn Nolan-Conroy (2001). Language attitudes. In Ceil Lucas (Ed.), *The Sociolinguistics of Sign Languages* (pp. 181–215). Cambridge: Cambridge University Press.

Cokely, Dennis (1992). *Interpretation: A Sociolinguistic Model.* Burtonsville, MD: Linstok Press.

Colonomos, Betty (1992). Processes in Interpretation and Transliterating: Making Them Work for You. Front Range Community College: Interpreter Training Program teleclass.

Davis, Jeffrey (1989). Distinguishing language contact phenomena in ASL interpretation. In Ceil Lucas (Ed.), *The Sociolinguistics of the Deaf Community* (pp. 85–102). San Diego: Academic Press.

Davis, Jeffrey (2003). Cross-linguistic strategies used by interpreters. *Journal of Interpretation* (RID), 95–128.

Friedenreich, Kathy Matthews (1996). Report on the National Testing System. *RID VIEWS, 13* (2), 24.

Frishberg, Nancy (1986). *Interpreting: An Introduction.* Silver Spring, MD: RID Publications.

Gustason, Gerilee, Donna Pfetzing, & Esther G. Zawolkow (1980). *Signing Exact English.* Los Alamitos, CA: Modern Signs Press.

Humphrey, Janice H., & Bob J. Alcorn (2001). *So You Want to Be an Interpreter? An Introduction to Sign Language Interpreting* (3rd ed.). Amarillo, TX: H & H Publishers.

Kannapell, Barbara (1989). An examination of deaf college students' attitudes toward ASL and English. In Ceil Lucas (Ed.), *The Sociolinguistics of the Deaf Community* (pp. 191–210). San Diego: Academic Press.

Kelly, Jean (2001). *Transliterating: Show Me the English*. Alexandria, VA: RID Press.

Lane, Harlan, Robert Hoffmeister, & Ben Bahan (1996). *A Journey Into the Deaf World*. San Diego: DawnSign Press.

Livingston, Sue, Bonnie Singer, & Theodore Abrahamson (1994). Effectiveness compared: ASL interpretation vs. transliteration. *Sign Language Studies, 82,* 1–54.

Lucas, Ceil, & Clayton Valli (1989). Language contact in the American deaf community. In Ceil Lucas (Ed.), *The Sociolinguistics of the Deaf Community* (pp. 11–40). San Diego: Academic Press.

Lucas, Ceil, & Cayton Valli (1992). *Language Contact in the American Deaf Community*. San Diego: Academic Press.

Malcolm, Karen (1992). Transliterating: The interpreting no one wants to talk about. *Conference Papers of the Association of Visual Language Interpreters of Canada* (pp. 59–67). Saskatoon, Saskatchewan: AVLIC.

McIntire, Marina L. (Ed.). (1986). Task analysis of transliteration and response. In *New Dimensions in Interpreter Education: Task Analysis, Theory and Application* (pp. 70–102). Silver Spring, MD: Registry of Interpreters for the Deaf.

Reilly, Judy, & Marina L. McIntire (1980). American Sign Language and Pidgin Sign English: What's the difference? *Sign Language Studies, 27,* 151–192.

Siple, Linda (1993). Interpreters' use of pausing in voice to sign transliteration. *Sign Language Studies, 79,* 147–180.

Siple, Linda (1996). The use of addition in sign language interpretation. In David M. Jones (Ed.), *Assessing our Work: Assessing our Worth, Proceedings of the Eleventh National Convention of the Conference of Interpreter Trainers* (pp. 29–45). United States: CIT.

Siple, Linda (1997). Historical development of the definition of transliteration. *Journal of Interpretation* (RID), 77–100.

Sofinski, Bruce A. (2002). So, why do I call this English? In Ceil Lucas (Ed.), *Turn-taking, Fingerspelling and Contact in Signed Languages* (pp. 27–48). Washington, DC: Gallaudet University Press.

Stauffer, Linda K., & Judith A. Viera (2000). Transliteration: A comparison of consumer needs and transliterator preparation and practice. *Journal of Interpretation* (RID), 61–80.

Stewart, David A., Jerome D. Schein, & Brenda E. Cartwright (2004). *Sign Language Intepreting: Exploring its Art and Science* (2nd ed.). Needham Heights, MA: Allyn and Bacon.

Supalla, Samuel J. (1991). Manually Coded English: The modality question in signed language development. In Patricia Siple and Susan D. Fischer (Eds.), *Theoretical Issues in Sign Language Research, Vol. 2: Psychology* (pp. 85–109). Chicago: University of Chicago Press.

Teets, Jean (1989). Consumer's perspective (Video-recording). *Sign to Voice Modeling Tape #4F.* Sign Enhancers, Inc.

Viera, Judith A., & Linda K. Stauffer (2000). Transliteration: The consumer's perspective. *Journal of Interpretation* (RID), 83–98.

Winston, Elizabeth A. (1989). Transliteration: What's the message? In Ceil Lucas (Ed.), *The Sociolinguistics of the Deaf Community* (pp. 147–164). San Diego: Academic Press.

Winston, Elizabeth, & Christine Monikowski (2003). Marking topic boundaries in signed interpretation and transliteration. In Melanie Metzger, Steven Collins, Valerie Dively, & Risa Shaw (Eds.), *From Topic Boundaries to Omission: New Research on Interpretation* (pp. 187–227). Washington, DC: Gallaudet University Press.

CHAPTER 6

Consecutive and simultaneous interpreting

Debra Russell
University of Alberta

1. Introduction

Studies in the field of interpretation and translation have offered various models with which to explore the nature of the interpreting process, whether using simultaneous or consecutive interpreting. This chapter examines both simultaneous and consecutive interpreting, particularly as they relate to American Sign Language (ASL)-English interpreters, and argues for the increased use of consecutive interpreting. One of the unique features of working between ASL and English is that the languages are produced in different language modalities, one signed and one spoken, which has created a long-held view that because there is no auditory interference, as is the case with interpreting between two spoken languages, there is no need to work consecutively. Here we explore the role of consecutive interpreting in the education of ASL-English interpreters in North America, highlight some of the perceptions and myths held by interpreters and by consumers of interpreting services, and discuss the impact of choosing simultaneous or consecutive interpreting on the accuracy of the work. While the studies described in this chapter are largely based in Canada and the United States, the principles discussed will apply to interpreters working in other signed languages throughout the world.

2. Consecutive and simultaneous interpreting

The issue of whether or not to use consecutive or simultaneous interpreting is an important one in any discussion of how to achieve the most accurate interpretation in a format that works effectively for all participants in the interpreted event. It is important for all concerned: signed language and spoken language interpreters, interpreting students, interpreter educators and consumers of interpreting services. We begin our discussion by defining what consecutive interpreting means. There appear to be several perceptions of consecutive interpreting that interpreters hold, for example some interpreters see consecutive interpreting as having a processing time so as to stay several seconds behind the speaker, while others view it as a form that requires the speaker to stop speaking in order for the interpreter to deliver the message. This chapter, however, adopts definitions commonly found in spoken language and signed language interpretation research. That is, SIMULTANEOUS INTERPRETATION is defined as the process of interpreting into the target language at the same time as the source language is being delivered. CONSECUTIVE INTERPRETATION is defined as the process of interpreting after the speaker or signer has completed one or more ideas in the source language and pauses while the interpreter transmits that information.

Interpreting, whether simultaneous or consecutive, is a highly complex discourse interchange where language perception, comprehension, translation and production operations are carried out virtually in parallel. In addition, when the interpretation is delivered simultaneously, it is performed under severe time pressure (Tommola & Hyönä 1990). Early research on interpretation conducted by Gerver (1976) and Moser (1978) led to the development of several models of interpreting performance based on information processing. Empirical studies reviewed and described by Goldman-Eisler (1972), Gerver (1976), Barik (1973, 1975), Chernov (1979), and Lambert (1984) focus on the various aspects of input and output, such as the overlap between comprehension and production, the length of ear-voice span, also known as PROCESSING TIME,[1] the effect of source text delivery rates and hesitation pauses, and the recall performance of simultaneous interpreters. All of this research points to the numerous challenges of providing accurate simultaneous interpretation in the field of spoken language interpreting. During the 1980s, Cokely (1984), Colonomos (1987), and Ingram (1985) contributed to a body of literature on simultaneous signed language interpreting by describing models of cognitive processing and the impact of these on providing effective interpretation. All these research studies, and the models of the process that have been proposed, have served to draw our attention to some of the important stages of cognitive processing required to comprehend a message, analyze it for its salient features, and then determine the appropriate linguistic structure and features needed to convey the message accurately in the second language.

Humphrey and Alcorn (1995) summarize the common features of these models, which apply to both consecutive and simultaneous interpreting:

a) The interpreter takes in the source utterance;
b) lexical and semantic units are strung together and held until the interpreter has sufficient units to determine the meaning of what is being said or signed;
c) a string of lexical and semantic units (referred to as a chunk) is analyzed to identify the speaker's or signer's intent and communication goal(s), explicit and implicit ideas, and a multitude of sociolinguistic features that impact upon the meaning of the source utterance. This could include gender, power distance between the speakers, setting, and contextual factors such as the impact or significance of the message on the receiver;
d) cultural and linguistic equivalents are sought, observing cultural norms and the cultural overlays of meaning;

e) a search is made of the target language to identify the lexical and semantic units and communication behaviours that can be used to produce an utterance in the target language with an equivalent meaning;

f) the interpretation is expressed in the target language; and

g) the interpreter monitors internal and external feedback to check for errors or needed corrections.

Models of cognitive processing are critical to an interpreter's understanding of how to produce accurate interpretation, and how to assess whether a situation requires the use of either consecutive or simultaneous interpreting. What is clear is that interpreting is not an easy task, and this is especially true for interpreters who have ASL as a second language. There is much to learn about interpretation processes and this learning typically begins when the student enrolls in an interpreter education program.

3. The role of consecutive interpreting in the education of interpreters

By investigating the programs of study offered by interpreter education sites, it can be seen that approaches to teaching the cognitive models of interpreting in the curricula vary greatly. Russell (2002b) conducted a pilot study of fifteen interpreter education programs in both Canada and the United States. The purpose of the study was to explore the ways in which consecutive interpreting is taught in those programs and to invite interpreter educators to comment on their experiences of teaching consecutive interpreting and of using it in their professional practice. Also, interviews were held with fifteen interpreters who graduated from interpreter education programs between 2000 and 2002. The results indicate that ten out of the fifteen programs emphasize the need for students to gain a solid understanding of the cognitive processes involved in interpreting by acquiring text analysis skills and then to use these to build towards consecutive interpreting exercises. Subsequently, only after consecutive interpreting has been mastered do students begin to move toward simultaneous work. By contrast, other programs choose to teach cognitive models and consecutive interpreting through an informational approach, providing theory but little time for acquiring the foundational skills necessary for consecutive interpreting. The approach used and the length of time spent teaching consecutive interpreting varies from program to program, from one-half a semester, one full semester, two semesters, to one program where there are three semesters of consecutive interpreting taught to students.

Several problems arise for educational programs that do not thoroughly address cognitive models of interpreting or that teach consecutive interpreting primarily through an informational approach. This pedagogical approach can lead to difficulties that include the following:

a) Students approach interpretation as a transcoding activity, looking for the sign choice that may reflect a particular word, versus looking for deeper meaning and producing grammatically and semantically correct interpretation. For ASL-

English interpreters, this often means that the interpreter produces sign-for-word matches, and follows the structure of English when the task is to produce ASL.

b)   Students who lack a thorough grounding in consecutive interpreting immediately begin interpreting in a simultaneous mode, not recognizing the relationship between the use of processing time and the number of errors produced in the interpretation. Again, because ASL and English are two different language modalities, the languages do not interfere or overlap. This appears to have led to the long-held belief in the field of signed language interpreting that because there is no signal interference, there is no need to perform consecutive interpreting. Without the foundation of consecutive interpreting, interpreters frequently develop ingrained patterns whereby several of the tasks identified in cognitive models of interpreting have been missed, thus producing work that is consistently processed at the lexical level. The impact of this work on Deaf consumers is that they must assume the task of "translating" the interpreter's form-based message themselves, trying to determine the meaning behind the signed message. For consumers who use ASL this results in a situation where their linguistic preferences and needs are not met via the interpretation.

c)   Students are unaware of the benefits of consecutive interpreting, and lack a decision-making schema to guide them in determining when to use consecutive interpretation (for example, when the material is particularly complex or deleterious to consumers, or when the nature of the interaction lends itself to consecutive interpreting, such as an informational interview). As well, students lack the ability to articulate the benefits to colleagues and consumers in order to engage in meaningful dialogue about consecutive interpreting in the workplace.

Cokely (2003) reviews the theoretical and philosophical influences on North American interpreter education programs that led to deliberations at the 1983 biennial conference of the Conference of Interpreter Trainers, resulting in a document that organized the principles behind, and sequencing of, skill-sets necessary for interpreting. These make up the commonly accepted sequence of developing translation skills first, followed by consecutive interpreting and finally, simultaneous interpreting. Cokely acknowledges that the sequence is indeed helpful to students in acquiring the interpreting skills needed, however he questions the practice of teaching these skill-sets as distinct courses. By examining the work settings of recent ASL-English interpreter graduates in the state of Massachusetts, Cokely concludes that a redesign of the interpreting curriculum is needed. His suggestion is that each skill-oriented course should focus on the entire range of skill-sets: translation, consecutive interpreting and simultaneous interpreting. Cokely also recommends that the skill courses should have as their main focus the interaction types revealed in the work settings data, thus better meeting the needs of both interpreters and employers. The interaction types included inquiry, narrative, expository and persuasive interactions. In each course, however, the relative weight of each skill-set in the sequence varies. For example, in the first semester, the course "Interpreting Inquiry Interactions" has translation skills weighted at 50% of the classroom time, consecutive interpreting at 40% and simultaneous inter-preting at 10%. Such an approach to the teaching of interpreting skills would address the problem identified in Russell (2002b) that suggests some educators and recent graduates of interpreter education programs see consecutive interpreting only as a stepping stone to the development of simultaneous interpreting, not as a mode of in-terpretation to be used throughout an interpreter's career. The practice of consecutive interpreting in the education of interpreters will be addressed again in later sections of this chapter in more detail. The next section addresses some of the beliefs and myths that interpreters in the field hold regarding consecutive interpretation.

4.   Myths and perceptions

As stated earlier, the research indicates that some interpreter education programs focus on consecutive interpreting as a distinct skill-set, and others are not seeing it as an important area of focus (Russell 2002b). However, it is not only some interpreter education programs that dismiss the importance of consecutive interpreting. There are interpreters and consumers who also hold a number of myths and misperceptions that discount the effectiveness of consecutive interpretation. For example, one of the prevailing myths in the field is that if an interpreter interprets consecutively, it is an indication that she is less skilled than an interpreter who uses simultaneous interpretation. In the study outlined in Russell (2002b) the following comment illustrates this myth. The quote comes from one interpreter surveyed, but it was a consistent theme expressed by twelve out of fifteen of the interpreters who graduated between 2000–2002:

> I was told by my mentor that while the program stresses consecutive, that it isn't used in the "real world". She said Deaf people hate it and the best interpreters don't use it.   (Russell 2002b: 7)

When interviewing Deaf consumers for the study in Russell (2000) it was clear that these consumers can benefit from conversations with interpreters who use consecutive interpreting. Often, once consumers have seen consecutive interpretation used well, and have observed the benefits of it, they are open to its use. These Deaf consumers indicated, however, that they didn't want interpreters learning how to use consecutive interpreting during appointments. If the interpreter could set up appropriate signals and allow the Deaf and hearing participants to feel connected, consecutive interpreting was acceptable. Interrupting consumers in mid-thought, or making them wait for long periods for the interpretation, was not appreciated.

Such comments imply that if interpreters have strategies to process the message while attending to it, have a clear sense of when to ask speakers or signers to pause without being disruptive to the process, and can use note-taking strategies when it is not appropriate to interrupt, then Deaf consumers are willing to try consecutive in-terpreting. Some Deaf consumers occasionally view consecutive interpretation as the thing that hearing children of Deaf adults do when learning to communicate messages between non-deaf people and their Deaf parents. Another perception held by some interpreters and consumers alike is that it is too time-consuming to perform consecutive interpretation. However, this perception can be countered with the argument that if simultaneous interpretation is inaccurate and has be to repaired and clarified numerous times, it can take longer to provide the work than when using consecutive interpretation. Ultimately, interpreters have contributed to these myths. They have shaped the perceptions held by many consumers that simultaneous is the preferred mode of interpreting because they rarely use consecutive interpreting, rarely speak about it if they do use it in their professional practice, and they don't support other colleagues who are trying to learn to use consecutive interpreting effectively.

Beliefs and perceptions held about consecutive interpreting have also shaped the face of the profession's testing procedures, in that very few employment screening tools, quality assurance mechanisms, or national certification exams allow for the use of consecutive interpreting in contexts that may in fact lend themselves to the process, such as one-to-one interviews. Cokely (2003) suggests that the extensive use of monologue interpreting in interpreter education programs has influenced the testing procedures of the Registry of Interpreters for the Deaf (RID), which tested samples of monologue interpreting exclusively until 1988. After that year, RID introduced a dialogue situation as one-third of its testing condition. In Canada, the Association of Visual Language Interpreters of Canada (AVLIC) implemented their testing model in 1990. The test includes monologues and dialogues, and like RID, simultaneous interpreting has been required for all segments.

These beliefs, myths and misperceptions that have in many ways shaped the field are slowly being challenged through professional dialogue among practitioners and educators, through research findings that support the need for consecutive interpreting, and by interpreter education programs that include consecutive interpreting skills as a core skill-set, not just as a skill-set that supports simultaneous interpreting. Interpreters are increasingly using consecutive interpreting in a variety of settings, including courtrooms, interview appointments and counseling sessions. In Canada, employment screening mechanisms such as the British Columbia Medical Interpreting Screening Tool, the British Columbia Post-Secondary Interpreter Registry, and the Deaf and Hard of Hearing Services Interpreter Screening Tool used in Alberta, allow interpreters to choose consecutive or simultaneous interpretation or a combination of both in interview segments of the test. In June 2003, AVLIC passed several motions at their Annual General Meeting directed toward the creation of new test materials that allow the test taker the choice of using consecutive interpreting during interview segments.

These examples of testing practices reflect an awareness of recent research and the increasing practice of interpreting consecutively in settings such as one-to-one interviews. Such dialogue settings are well suited to consecutive interpreting or a blend of consecutive and simultaneous interpreting, given that the discourse is often a question and answer format or is informational. There are natural pauses after questions are asked that allow for consecutive processing, and typically an answer can be chunked into appropriate units so that it can be handled using consecutive interpreting. While this is helpful to interpreters at any stage of their career, it is especially helpful to novice interpreters who may need the extra time to process language. However, while there is an increasing awareness of the importance of consecutive interpreting among some interpreters, interpreter educators, Deaf consumers and test developers, the profession has a long way still to go before there is a more consistent understanding of the relevance of consecutive interpreting in a multitude of settings.

5. Models of interpreting and their role in consecutive interpreting

Pöchhacker (2004) provides us with an excellent overview of the theoretical and methodological paradigms that have shaped interpretation research and interpreting models. In his text *Introducing Interpreting Studies* Pöchhacker reminds us that no single model can illustrate interpretation as a whole. For each of the models that have emerged in the field of spoken and signed language interpreting research, one can trace the model back to the researcher's or scholar's epistemological position (2004: 107). Indeed, other authors in this text have discussed cognitive models and introduced new models in order to broaden the discussion and address some of the weaknesses of the previous models (see Janzen, Chapter 1; Leeson, Chapter 3; and Wilcox and Shaffer, this volume). Pöchhacker (2004) reports on models that reflect many levels of analysis within interpreting studies, and while all are relevant to the discussion here, I have chosen to examine some of the *cognitive, textual,* and *interactional* models that have impacted the field of signed language interpreting.

Some of the earliest models from the 1970s focused on *cognitive* processes. Seleskovitch (1978) was one of the first to posit a cognitive model of interpreting that focused on the interpreter's understanding and expression of "sense" as part of a three-part process. Her model, which was not based on empirical evidence, became the foundation of the Paris School and continues to be debated today. Her work also shaped the early stages of the education of signed language interpreters in North America via her writing and presentations. In the field of signed language interpreting specifically, Colonomos (1987) also described three stages of cognitive processing, each with its own cognitive tasks. Her model focuses on some of the tasks of accessing short-term and long-term memory for knowledge, making the target language switch based on linguistic and cultural knowledge including awareness of discourse frames in both ASL and English, and thus introducing communication norms into the discussion. During this same period, Cokely (1992) also offered the field a cognitive model of interpreting, based on a detailed breakdown of the mental processes that occur during linguistic analysis and reconstruction. His model highlights seven main processing stages, and many more sub-processes that reflect top-down processing.

Each of the cognitive models mentioned above has made contributions to the field of interpreting by articulating some of the concepts that can help interpreters find strategies to improve their work, and offering tools to interpreter educators in teaching interpreting. However, the models have also invited critique and further debate about the complexity of interpretation, which has resulted in further research into communication processes and the ways that interpreting affects communication among participants who do not share the same language. In the late 1980s we saw an increase in the discussion of the nature of *text* and *discourse* in interpreted interactions (Pöchhacker 2004). Pöchhacker's (1992) own model of interpreted interaction brings attention to the "perspective" of the individuals in the event, moving us away from a sole focus on text and content. Alexieva (2002) emphasizes seven parameters which influence the interpreted event, raising our awareness of distance vs. proximity between participants, equality, status and power of participants, setting dynamics, goals of participants whether shared or conflicting, and cooperativeness/directness vs. non-cooperativeness/indirectness.

Again, specific to the field of signed language interpreters we find some examples of *textual processing models* that have been discussed. For example, Smith and Savidge (2002) and Witter-Merithew, Taylor and Johnson (2002) have written about additional features that need to be considered within cognitive models of interpreting. They suggest that interpreters, no matter how competent, bilingual, and bicultural they may be, must constantly weigh choices in search of the best ways to convey shades of meaning and speaker intent. Interpreters must also deal with the cultural differences that are embedded in the linguistic structures. For example, narrative structures found in ASL, the depth of detail of a description, and the social fabric of a culture all differ from the language and culture of the majority creating incredible challenges for an interpreter when she is attempting to convey equivalent meaning so that all parties in the event can communicate effectively. This type of discussion parallels the models advanced by Pöchhacker (2002) and Alexieva (2002) and takes us away from the conduit models of simply encoding and decoding messages.

During the 1990s, Roy (1996) and Wadensjö (1998) led the field to examine interpreting as dialogic discourse-based interaction. Roy (1996) specifically studied signed language interpreters while Wadensjö (1998) examined the work of spoken language interpreters. Wadensjö explored interpreting from the perspectives of "interpreting as text" and "interpreting as activity", distinguishing between these different orientations that interpreters hold when they are working. Wadensjö uses the phrase "interactionally oriented" (1998:24) to describe interpreters who coordinate both interpreting at the textual level and at the level of situated activity as interaction within the interpreted event.

Given the numerous models and orientations of study that are prevalent in the field of interpreting, what are the benefits of using models in interpreter education programs, and how do these models reinforce consecutive interpreting skills? The value of some of these models to the field of ASL-English interpreting is that they offer guidance in understanding the nature of how communicators structure their messages and how interpreters try to capture that meaning in order to recreate it in a second language. They also offer us insight into how interpreters can practice the cognitive sub-tasks of interpreting so as to develop the short- and long-term memory and analysis skills needed to produce accurate target texts. Shlesinger (2000) suggests that simultaneous interpreting is such a complex task that we may never fully understand all of the components of the process and how they interact, but that interpreting may actually be a combination of cognitive processes and proceduralized strategies. As stated earlier in Section 2, interpreters who do not have a thorough appreciation of the cognitive processes involved in interpreting will not be able to provide consistently accurate, meaning-based work. It is also helpful for us to have models of interpreting as an activity where interpreters focus on the participants' understanding of various parts of the interaction and the progression of that interaction, drawing on the context that participants bring and the meaning that is created during the interaction (Wadensjö 1998).

In the sections that follow, I discuss one additional model that may aid interpreters in their work, whether working simultaneously or consecutively (Russell 2000, 2002a).[2] The model acknowledges differences in linguistic and cultural meanings between two languages and the need for meaning-based work as the desired interpretation product that is created throughout the interaction. As the field of interpreting has developed, other approaches have been introduced, such as Gish's (1986, 1992) work that is a goal-to-detail/detail-to-goal schema for information processing in interpreting and Isham's (1986) text analysis framework based on understanding the purpose of a message, along with features of content, context, register and affect. Neither Isham's work or Gish's model are cognitive models *per se*, but rather are very useful approaches to text analysis, and which form the foundation for the analysis stages of the model outlined below. In addition, the works of Wadensjö (1998) and Roy (2000) have shaped my awareness of context and the background information that the interpreter must possess in order to deal with the multitude of decisions they make when observing both the language and patterns of interaction within an interpreted event.

Interpreting students often feel overwhelmed with the goal of learning to interpret, and such a model can demystify the interpreting process, strengthen the interpreter's text analysis skills, and help her handle the multitude of aspects required to produce an accurate interpretation by constructing meaning between parties. The model will be helpful throughout the interpreter's career, as it can be used as a diagnostic tool to provide insight into the interpreter's strengths by identifying successful interpreting patterns as well as areas of need, which can then be translated into ongoing professional development. It can pinpoint where the processes may be breaking down for the interpreter and reveal the specific language tasks that need further development, for example semantic development in ASL or in English, or the ways in which the interpreter did not attend to the patterns of interaction that shaped the discourse, missing key contextual information.

Steps of a Meaning-based Interpreting Model

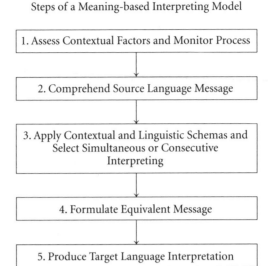

Figure 1. The Steps of the Model (adapted from Russell 2002a).

5.1   A meaning-based model of interpreting

The model developed in Russell (2000, 2002a) and refined in this section specifically identifies the need for the interpreter to assess and apply the contextual factors
impacting the interpretation, actively using her background knowledge about language, culture, conventional ways of communication in both English and ASL, and
to determine whether to use consecutive or simultaneous interpreting within a given
interaction. It is an attempt to build on the models that highlight text and language
analysis, and to incorporate the dynamics of the interaction via context. This model is
shown in Figure 1.

The steps of the Meaning-Based Interpreting Model include:

1. ASSESS CONTEXTUAL FACTORS AND MONITOR THE PROCESS: As the interpreter
    approaches the interpreting task, contextual factors need to be considered, but this
    activity does not stop here. Throughout the interaction, the interpreter constantly
    assesses contextual factors and their impact upon communication. Context helps
    the interpreter determine the speaker's or signer's particular meaning within
    the specific interpreted interaction. This includes assessing factors such as the
    relationship between the parties in the interaction, the formal and informal
    power structures represented, the similarities and differences in backgrounds and
    experiences of the participants, the emotional overlay of the interaction, and
    the impact that having an interpreter present has on the way the speaker and
    signer construct their messages. As well, throughout all phases of the interpreted
    interaction, the interpreter monitors the communication process because the
    participants are creating additional context and experience through their dialogue.

At times, the interpreter finds herself surrounded by topics, specific lexicon and jargon, and descriptions of events that the participants have shared knowledge of, whereas the interpreter lacks that content and contextual information. This is Step 1, but importantly it overlays each further step represented in the model.

2. COMPREHEND SOURCE LANGUAGE MESSAGE: During this stage, the interpreter must draw upon skills related to bilingual and bicultural awareness and text analysis in order to support comprehension of the original message. The interpreter draws upon her fluency in both English and ASL in the following areas:

    a. Syntactic knowledge;
    b. Semantic knowledge;
    c. Associated knowledge and background experience;
    d. Cultural awareness; and
    e. Contextual knowledge.

    It is at this stage that the interpreter is required to process information at lexical, phrasal, sentential and discourse levels to determine characteristics of the discourse frame that the speaker or signer is using. For example, this could include identifying register and style features such as the use of politeness markers, and structural items such as syntactic forms needed to convey particular question or answer styles, say in a courtroom setting.

    At this stage the interpreter needs to verify comprehension and seek clarification when needed and when appropriate. This also includes negotiating movement between simultaneous and consecutive interpreting as required. Lastly, this stage also includes checking for and correcting errors as appropriate, which are often created when the interpreter lacks sufficient contextual knowledge[3] about the content or the situation in which she is interpreting.

3. APPLY CONTEXTUAL AND LINGUISTIC SCHEMAS AND SELECT SIMULTANEOUS OR CONSECUTIVE INTERPRETING: This stage involves the application of the interpreter's ongoing assessment of contextual factors influencing the interaction, such as linguistic competence, the experiential and cultural frames of the participants who are interacting, along with their cross-cultural and cross-linguistic experience. At this stage the interpreter also determines whether to use consecutive or simultaneous interpreting for the message in order to support genuine communication for all participants and to maintain message equivalence.

4. FORMULATE EQUIVALENT MESSAGE: After processing the information at all levels, that is, lexical, phrasal, sentential and discourse, and applying cultural and linguistic frames in order to realize the goals of the speaker or signer, the interpreter then makes these cultural and linguistic choices – planning, formulating and reviewing the elements to be used to express an equivalent message in the target language. Elements of the target message may be rehearsed at this stage. Assessing contextual factors and monitoring the process continues to apply.

5. PRODUCE TARGET LANGUAGE INTERPRETATION: At this stage the interpreter produces the target message, based on the previous stages. Once again, at this step,

the interpreter continues to assess contextual factors and monitors the process to ensure the effectiveness of the interpretation among the parties.

This model brings together the roles of context, linguistic and cultural schemas and the decision-making processes that involve choosing consecutive or simultaneous interpreting. The Meaning-based Model presented above offers the interpreter and the interpreter educator a window into the tasks to be accomplished when analyzing interpreted interactions. The process of interpreting is very complex but by identifying and practicing some of the tasks of each stage, the student learning to interpret can develop the linguistic and interactional skills necessary to perform the work.

The Meaning-based Model builds on the need for honed text analysis skills dependent on careful contextual assessment. These processes applied to consecutive interpreting in particular will enable the interpreter to solidify skills that promote meaning-based work. The message analysis and message production time needed by a novice interpreter, who may still be acquiring bilingual fluency, is such that consecutive interpreting is likely the only way she will have success. Successful experience in consecutive interpreting will then lead the interpreter to be able to handle simultaneous interpreting because she can return to the processes that have been firmly established and adequately rehearsed in her consecutive practice. By contrast, the consequence of undertaking simultaneous interpreting prior to mastering the process of consecutive interpreting often results in inaccurate meaning construction or the production of strictly form-based work. If the interpreter has missed the stages that involve recognizing contextual factors and the intent of speaker-chosen discourse frames, she will likely develop a strong tendency to transcode in her work.

Typical errors that occur for interpreters who have not employed consecutive interpreting include semantic errors, source language intrusions, omissions of content, missing cohesive devices that link ideas as effectively as they were linked in the source text, and ultimately excessive repairing of the message as the interpreter realizes the errors that she is making while performing simultaneous interpreting (Berk-Seligson 2000; Russell 2002a).

5.2   Consecutive interpreting and signed language interpreters

A review of studies conducted in the field of spoken language interpretation shows an emphasis on consecutive interpreting during programs of training. Numerous descriptive studies have examined differences between consecutive and simultaneous interpreting, and provide support for students to be well trained in consecutive interpreting prior to moving to simultaneous interpreting. Consistently, the evidence suggests that consecutive interpreting results in much greater accuracy in the transmission of the message (Alexieva 1991; Bruton 1985; Cokely 1992; Mikkelson 1994; Seleskovitch & Lederer 1995). Alexieva (1991) found that regarding simultaneous interpreting, not all types of texts can be interpreted successfully under the difficult conditions characterizing the circumstance (e.g., simultaneity of the speaker's and interpreter's performance, speed of delivery of the source language, lack of knowledge about the context, and a single rendition of the source utterance). Barnwell (1989) concurs with this view, stating that simultaneous interpreting offers very little time to reflect on the linguistic choices needed for a precise rendering. Consecutive interpreting, in which the interpreter waits until a complete thought has been uttered and then begins interpreting, is the primary form of interpretation used in medical situations (Mikkelson 1994). Consecutive interpreting allows for the conveyance of the source message content, as well as critical information conveyed in the structural elements of that message that are not contained in the words: pauses, tone of voice, stress, etc. Nida (1964) and Seleskovitch (1978) note that a successful interpretation must not only include reformulation and "retranslation" into the target language, it must also produce the same impact or impression on the target language audience as that created by the speaker on an audience who understand the speaker directly. Further, there is agreement within the literature that interpreters using consecutive interpreting, who work from memory and notes, find it easier to break down the interpreting process and examine the skills required to cope with the process successfully (Alexieva 1991; Barnwell 1989; Bruton 1985; Gile 1988; Harris & Sherwood 1978; Mikkelson 1994).

Bruton (1985), Lambert (1984) and Seleskovitch and Lederer (1995) emphasize that through a progression of exercises aimed at teaching interpreters to grasp, analyze, remember, and only then reproduce the message of the speaker, it is subsequently possible to proceed to acceptable simultaneous interpretation where required or desired. This last point is an interesting one when contrasted with the practices of some signed language interpreter education programs, where students are placed in a position to interpret simultaneously without the foundation of progressive exercises designed to hone text analysis and consecutive interpreting skills.

As mentioned earlier, in a pilot study oulined in Russell (2002b), twelve out of fifteen ASL-English interpreter educators themselves had training in consecutive interpreting. Beyond this study, however, it is not known how widely interpreter educators across programs have received such training. It may be that educators default to how they were trained, and if their training has not included these methodologies consistently, including text analysis and consecutive interpreting, they may not be focusing on such skills with their own students. This also applies to the field, where recent graduates report that while on practicum they were discouraged from using consecutive interpreting by practicum mentors. The practicum mentors may also lack training and experience in consecutive interpreting, and hence they return to how they learned to interpret. The following comment came from an educator participating in the pilot study (Russell 2002b) regarding the teaching of consecutive interpreting. This quote invites us to consider how we can help practitioners in the field accept and then use consecutive interpreting when appropriate:

> Since we are working with existing practitioners the discussion is always dynamic and students are anxious about whether consecutive interpreting will be accepted. It is challenging – the interpreters are afraid, and they want to do what is familiar

> to them. I would estimate that 55–60% of the practitioners are able to successfully make the transition. The rest are not.   (Russell 2002b: 9)

Another educator's comments offer additional views:

> Some of our mentors model consecutive interpreting [CI] but the majority do not. Because our students are immersed in the CI perspective and practice it in role-plays, they are adept at analyzing situations in which they would prefer to use CI and explain the justification for it. So, even though some consumers may not want students to do it, the students can handle that and offer it as a mode when appropriate.   (Russell 2002b: 9)

She continued to say:

> All of our mentors are trained in the model and we have some taped modeling that reflects models of chunked/consecutive work. More importantly, students are taught to regularly prepare interpretation or rehearse portions that can be rehearsed in advance – even when doing simultaneous work.   (Russell 2002b: 9)

What is reflected in this information is that some programs are helping students to identify strategies to talk about consecutive interpreting with consumers and how to make effective choices about when to use it. As well, at least one program is working with mentors to help them understand the nature of consecutive interpreting. What would benefit students entering the field is to see instructors model consecutive interpreting, and to be able to engage working professionals in dialogue about its use.

The field of spoken language interpreting has benefited from the progression of learning translation skills, leading to consecutive interpreting skills, which then support simultaneous interpreting. Certainly Cokely (2003) argues for the inclusion of all of these skill-sets within each interpreting course. We would be well advised to revisit our approaches to teaching based on the literature from the field of spoken language interpreting and from recent research on the accuracy of consecutive interpreting for signed language interpreters in order to bring about significant change in this field.

Cokely (1992) examined simultaneous interpreting among ASL-English interpreters, and his findings demonstrate that when calculating interpreting errors there is a critical link to the length of time between a speaker's utterance and the target language production. Cokely reports that one of the primary causes of misinterpretation appears to be the lack of sufficient source language input, which is determined by the interpreter's "lag" or processing time. The shorter the processing time, the greater the probability of inappropriate syntactic constructions and lexical choices appearing in the target text, and the greater the tendency for the interpreter to adhere to source language syntax, resulting in word-for-word transcoding. Given these findings, consecutive interpreting must be reconsidered as a viable option by ASL-English interpreters working in a variety of settings.

The research is sparse when it comes to examining the differences between experienced and novice interpreters' work, or about possible differences in the way they carry out the task. One school of thought suggests models developed for skilled interpreters do not apply to novice interpreters, and that there are important differences in the ways that novice and experienced interpreters perform the task (Dillinger 1994). For example, Dillinger points out that some studies suggest that experienced simultaneous interpreters may short circuit the deeper semantic analysis (Gerver 1976), and that experienced interpreters have been found to include more source information and delete less, process larger chunks of the input, and give less literal translations (Barik 1969). However, research conducted by Russell (2000, 2002a) with experienced, certified interpreters working in courtrooms shows that even their simultaneous work was not as accurate as their consecutive work. This difference in accuracy occurred despite interpretation being performed by experienced interpreters working in teams, with the expectation that they would monitor each others' work for accuracy.

Despite the significant body of literature from spoken language interpreting which suggests that consecutive interpreting allows for a greater degree of accuracy, the predominant practice of ASL-English interpreters has been to provide simultaneous interpretation. A striking difference is that signed language interpreters not only work between two languages, but two modalities. This modality shift is noted in Cokely's (1992) model, but there appear to be very few studies examining its significance. This modality difference has contributed to the predominant use of simultaneous interpretation which can occur more readily in this circumstance because there is no need for technology such as interpretation booths and infrared systems, nor for pausing, in that the interpreter can sign while someone is speaking and speak while someone is signing without the signals interfering. But a question arising from the predominant use of simultaneous interpreting must be asked: are consumers, both Deaf and non-deaf, receiving accurate and effective interpretation when the majority of service is being provided simultaneously?

6. Consecutive and simultaneous interpreting in legal contexts

There are, most certainly, ASL-English interpreters who use consecutive interpreting successfully in their practice. How do these interpreters decide how and when to use consecutive interpreting? What is the impact of their decision on the quality of the interpretation product? Russell (2000) conducted a study that consisted of a comparative analysis of simultaneous and consecutive interpreting provided by ASL-English interpreters in courtroom interactions. Three distinct courtroom events were studied: expert witness testimony, the entering of direct evidence with a Deaf witness, and cross-examination of the Deaf witness. The study also explored consumer satisfaction with the two different interpreting methods.

Quasi-experimental design principles shaped the study. Specifically, the study used a factorial design, and manipulated one independent variable. Four mock trials were conducted with four ASL-English interpreters. The interpreters worked in teams of two, and participated in all three courtroom events. The interpreters were chosen from four areas of Canada, and were selected on the basis of the following criteria:

1) interpreters needed to be experienced practitioners who were identified by the interpreting and Deaf communities as interpreters respected for their interpreting skills in a variety of settings; 2) interpreters holding national certification were preferred (i.e., the Association of Visual Language Interpreters of Canada (AVLIC) Certificate of Interpretation); and 3) interpreters had a minimum of 500 hours of interpreting in legal settings. Three females and one male who met the criteria were chosen, with three of the interpreters holding national certification at the time of the study. Other courtroom participants included judges, lawyers, an expert witness and two Deaf witnesses. The lawyers and judges who participated in this study each had more than five years of experience in criminal law, and only one lawyer had previous experience working with signed language interpreters. The four ASL-English interpreters were videotaped providing consecutive and simultaneous interpreting in four mock criminal trials and subsequently a sociolinguistic analysis was conducted on the interpretation data to determine its accuracy. As well, all mock trial participants gave post-trial interviews, offering their reflections on the experience.

The mock trials were written by the British Columbia Criminal Trial Lawyers Association based on actual courtroom cases. Mock trials are often used in the education of lawyers and include all the elements of real trials. Two criminal trials were chosen, one regarding a sexual assault charge and the other a charge of assault causing bodily harm. Criminal trials were chosen for the study because the consequences of interpreters' errors are grave in these circumstances. Participants were prepared for court by reviewing key materials. For example, the interpreters received details that are standard when considering accepting a courtroom assignment. The lawyers prepared for the witnesses as they would in any trial, and interpreters met with the Crown Prosecutor and Defense Counsel prior to the trials.

The trials were taped at the University of Calgary, Faculty of Law, using the Moot Courtroom. This room is equipped with multiple video cameras built into the walls, and a professional technician operated all of the equipment. The Moot Court closely resembles a regular courtroom and as such added to the simulation. Multiple camera angles allowed for all witnesses and interpreters to be recorded.

During the trials, the interpreters were videotaped performing ASL to English and English to ASL interpreting, while working with a non-deaf expert witness, a Deaf witness, the cross-examination of that same witness, and the interactions between judges and lawyers. They performed their interpreting in a team context, each team composed of two interpreters. None of the discourse was scripted in order to capture natural language interaction in the courtroom.

Quantitative data collected on videotape were analyzed by contrasting the original messages with the interpreters' target language texts. An ASL linguist and interpretation expert each verified the analysis. Further, a chi-squared analysis was conducted using the linguistic data. The qualitative interview data were summarized and analyzed for common themes, recommendations and significant insights.

Trials conducted with consecutive interpreting produced significantly different results from the trials using simultaneous interpreting. The consecutive mode demonstrated a greater degree of accuracy than did simultaneous interpretation. The two trials where simultaneous interpreting was used achieved 87% and 83% accuracy rates, while the two trials conducted with consecutive interpreting realized 98% and 95% accuracy rates.

In all trials the number of interpreting errors across the discourse events was greater during expert witness testimony and when direct evidence was being given. For all four trials, there were fewer errors exhibited during cross-examination. The data were pooled and tested for significance using chi-squared tests. The three discourse events (expert witness, direct evidence, and cross-examination) were used as dependent variables, with type of interpreting (consecutive or simultaneous) as the independent variable. Tests of significance suggest that the consecutive mode of interpreting is superior to the simultaneous form, when used for all three legal discourse types. Tables 1 to 3 show the numbers of correctly versus incorrectly interpreted utterances (and percentages) over the three discourse event types.

From Table 1, we see that for the expert witness discourse, the number of correctly interpreted utterances during consecutive interpreting was 613/645, or 95%, whereas the number of correctly interpreted utterances during simultaneous interpreting was 362/415, or 87%. The chi-squared test shows that this difference is statistically significant. Tables 2 and 3 for direct evidence and cross-examination respectively, should be read in the same manner.

The following table (Table 4) shows the number of interpretation errors across each trial and each discourse event. Trials One and Four were conducted using simul-

Table 1. Accuracy of interpretation for the expert witness discourse event, consecutive versus simultaneous

Evaluation of Interpretation	Consecutive	Simultaneous	Total (N)
Correct	613/95.04%	362/87.23%	975
Incorrect	32/4.96%	53/12.77%	85
Total N/Total %	645/100.00%	415/100.00%	N = 1060

Chi Square = 20.188, df = 1, p < 0.001:Phi = 0.14, p < 0.001

Table 2. Accuracy of interpretation for the direct evidence discourse event, consecutive and simultaneous

Evaluation of Interpretation	Consecutive	Simultaneous	Total (N)
Correct	237/95.95%	290/77.54%	527
Incorrect	10/4.05%	84/22.46%	94
Total N/Total %	247/100.00%	374/100.00%	N = 621

Chi Square = 39.25, df = 1, p < 0.001:Phi = 0.25, p < 0.001

Table 3. Accuracy of interpretation for the cross-examination discourse event, consecutive and simultaneous

Evaluation of Interpretation	Consecutive	Simultaneous	Total (N)
Correct	241/98.37%	331/91.18%	572
Incorrect	4/1.63%	32/8.82%	36
Total N/Total %	245/100.00%	363/100.00%	N = 608

Chi Square = 13.55, df = 1, p < 0.001:Phi = 0.15, p < 0.001

Table 4. Ratio of interpretation errors over total number of utterances by trial and discourse event

Trial Number	Expert Witness	Direct Evidence	Cross-Examination
Trial One (S)	21/213*	39/189	15/188
Trial Two (C)	5/292	4/154	1/157
Trial Three (C)	27/353	6/193	3/188
Trial Four (S)	32/202	45/185	17/175

*To be read as 21 errors out of 213 total utterances

taneous interpreting (S) and Trials Two and Three were conducted using consecutive interpreting (C).

The results also show a greater number of errors when the target language was ASL. For many interpreters, ASL is a language they develop as a second language, after acquiring spoken English, and often during their adult years. Three of the four interpreters identified ASL as their second language, whereas one interpreter has Deaf parents and therefore ASL is a first, or native, language. This second language factor may have contributed to the number of errors made interpreting into spoken English, in that the majority of the errors appeared to be related to comprehending ASL utterances. This was not tested in Russell (2000) but would be an important factor to test in future study. When examining errors made while interpreting from ASL to English, it became clear that the interpreters could produce fluent English, but the *message* was inaccurate.

Across all four trials the cross-examination discourse events showed far fewer errors than the other discourse events. This was an expected result in that the evidence had already been entered via direct testimony, and cross-examination is an opportunity to refute that same evidence. At this stage in the trials, the interpreters had previously interpreted the witness's evidence, so were therefore more prepared for the cross-examination of the witness. There was nothing substantially new that arose during cross-examination, and hence the accuracy rate was higher across all four trials when contrasted with the other two discourse events.

An examination of the transcripts revealed that common patterns of errors emerged from all trials, including omission of content and summarized answers for the court when critical details were explicit in the source text, shifts in tense (mixing present and past tenses), shifts of register (more casual in ASL than indicated in the English source message), target messages produced in fluent English that included inaccurate content, ungrammatical ASL, source language intrusions which resulted in form-based or transcoded work, and interpreter-initiated utterances which were not interpreted for all participants. As well, there were patterns of "hedging" in the target spoken English when the answer had been complete and definitive in ASL. There were also times when the interpreters inappropriately used a previous question and linked it to the current question which resulted in an answer of "no" when the predicted response was "yes".

When using simultaneous interpreting, the number of errors was highest during the direct evidence discourse event, followed by the expert witness discourse event. Direct evidence is a critical part of any trial so errors made in that testimony are often discovered during cross-examination, resulting in a witness who appears to have changed her story when in fact the errors belong to the interpreters. Such errors have grave consequences for the judicial process, and interpreters and consumers should both be very concerned about such findings. In this study, simultaneous interpreting, even when performed by experienced and certified interpreters, resulted in dramatic errors that were not corrected during the trials.[4]

During post-trial interviews, interpreters were able to identify segments of the simultaneous trials where they believed the interpretation would have been more accurate if they had interpreted consecutively. In these segments, the interpreters indicated that they lacked the time to fully analyze the messages and find equivalent choices in the target language. When asked about how the simultaneous mode impacted upon their management of the interpreting process, two interpreters noted that during the expert witness testimony they felt the pressure of time and that seemed to push them from the first stage of attending to the source message to directly producing the target message, with very little time for analyzing the meaning, let alone the contextual variables that were influencing the message. The data show that when source messages were intricate in either English or ASL, and the interpreting was provided in a simultaneous form, there were numerous grammatical errors, omissions of essential content, as well as content errors.

However, there were times when simultaneous interpreting was used effectively. This occurred during the cross-examination process, in that the scope of questions re-lated only to the previous testimony, so the interpreters likely knew the information and the witnesses' responses were more predictable. When the answers were inconsis-tent, or introduced new information, the interpreters appeared to verify answers more frequently with the Deaf witnesses and also between themselves, and moved into us-ing consecutive interpreting for some of the ASL to English responses. This decision to use consecutive interpreting within the trials where simultaneous interpreting was to be used is an interesting one and appears to indicate that the interpreters were mon-itoring their work effectively and knew that a change in mode of interpretation was required for those specific utterances.

From a consumer perspective, the lawyers noted that the consecutive process was familiar to them based on previous experience with spoken language interpreters, but it was not the preferred mode of interpretation when conducting a cross-examination, as the pausing interfered with their cadence when questioning the witness. The lawyers also expressed concern about the signals used by the interpreters to ask participants to pause in order to deliver the consecutive interpretation. The interpreters and trial participants had reviewed signals such as holding up one finger to indicate that the interpreters needed to stop the speaker or signer for a moment. During the trials, however, interpreters reverted to using signals that had not been discussed and this was confusing to the lawyers. The interpreters also stopped lawyers or witnesses at inappropriate times, such as in the middle of an utterance, or they allowed participants to continue to speak or sign for long periods without using any signal for them to pause. This resulted in consecutively delivered interpretations that were very lengthy, or times when an interpreter would begin the interpretation and then ask for a restatement as they had forgotten the original message.

Deaf witnesses noted that they found the interpretation easier to understand when presented consecutively, especially during complicated questioning. They identified that the interpretation was more grammatically correct, used more of the natural features of ASL, and exhibited fewer false starts and less repetition in the message. They also observed that they felt more relaxed when the interpretation was presented consecutively, allowing them to participate more fully in the trial.

When presented with simultaneous interpreting the Deaf witnesses commented that they observed more frequent false starts and repairs, and found that the interpretation moved closer to the structure of English, the source language. The Deaf witnesses commented on how this move affected them, in that it heightened their anxiety about whether they were understanding the proceedings fully, and whether the interpreting team would understand their answers. Hence, their attention shifted from participating in the proceedings to worrying about the accuracy of the interpretation.

It is also interesting to contrast the judges' perceptions and experiences with those of the Deaf witnesses. The presiding judges were interviewed one week after the conclusion of the mock trials. They indicated that they appreciated the simultaneous interpreting, which seemed to help speed up the proceedings. However, when presented with information about the nature of interpretation, and potential impact of errors within the interpretation when performed simultaneously, the judges all agreed that the quality and accuracy of interpretation was paramount in the assessment of the evidence. They also admitted that in their time on the bench, they had never received information about the nature of interpreting and how best to accommodate Deaf people who appear in court. Based on these interviews, the judges subsequently requested professional seminars in order to educate lawyers and judges about the complexity of interpretation, and the best practices that could be employed in courtrooms when working with Deaf witnesses.

The interpreters in this study who were most successful in using the consecutive interpreting process knew how to segment or chunk messages effectively, and had a sense of the appropriate time and place to pause so that part of the overall text could be interpreted. All the interpreters who participated in the study had experience with consecutive interpreting, but despite their experience, not all the interpreters were well trained in how to use consecutive interpreting effectively, with the least disruption to the proceedings. For example, not all the interpreters had consistent strategies for chunking messages in appropriate ways, or effective note-taking skills to help retain complex utterances, nor did they have well-established signals to use with Deaf and non-deaf consumers. As well, only two out of the four interpreters had effective ways to explain the use of consecutive interpreting to consumers in both spoken English and ASL.

Interpreters who employed both consecutive and simultaneous approaches to interpreting identified the need to educate consumers regarding the rationale for consecutive processing and how it can enhance the accuracy of the work (Russell 2000, 2002a). In the study of courtroom interpreting, the interpreters were taped while conducting their preparation conversations with the lawyers. Interpreters who were viewed as successful in educating the lawyers about their work in the courtroom were those who had non-technical explanations, who were confident about expressing their needs, and who identified that the accuracy of the interpretation was paramount in making decisions about when to use simultaneous or consecutive interpreting. Educating consumers is critical because it is then that interpreters can address any fears or concerns that arise about the use of consecutive interpreting. The establishment of signals to be used between interpreters and consumers to request that discourse participants pause in order for the interpreter to produce the interpretation was another critical aspect of the preparation process leading to the consumers' acceptance of consecutive interpreting.

This section has described but a small portion of the results of the study in Russell (2000, 2002a), however the research clearly provides insight into the current challenges of providing accurate interpretation, and the results strengthen the argument to use consecutive interpreting in such settings.

7. Deciding factors in the use of consecutive interpreting

How do ASL-English interpreters determine when to use consecutive interpreting? The results of the pilot study in Russell (2002b) and subsequent consultation with two interpreter referral agencies in Canada reveal that consecutive interpreting is typically being used in several types of assignments, and the setting itself appears to be one of the determinants for choosing to interpret consecutively. For example, six out of fifteen interpreting program graduates reported that while on practicum their practicum mentors had modeled the use of consecutive interpreting and encouraged its use in one-to-one and small group settings. Still Interpreting Inc., an interpreting referral agency based in Vancouver, British Columbia, reported that consecutive interpreting was most frequently used in job interviews, counseling appointments, legal interviews, and in courtrooms during direct evidence or expert testimony (David Still, personal communication, August 2003). Still Interpreting, Inc. has full-time interpreters who report using consecutive interpreting daily, and these interpreters indicated that they base their decision to use consecutive interpreting on the density or structure of the message. These reports were matched by those at another interpreter referral agency, the Independent Interpreter Referral Service (IIRS)[5] of Winnipeg, Manitoba, who identified that increasingly consumers and interpreters alike are becoming more comfortable using consecutive interpreting in one-to-one interviews (Bonnie Dubienski, personal communication, August 2003).

Interviews with seven out of fifteen interpreters revealed that while they knew how to make decisions about consecutive interpreting, and had some confidence about describing their reasons in spoken English (to non-deaf consumers), thirteen out of fifteen interpreters said they lacked the same confidence to describe consecutive interpreting in ASL. Clearly, interpreters require strategies in both ASL and spoken English to describe their desire to produce accurate interpreting. Such strategies would help to influence change within the field. Most interpreter educators reported that they use consecutive interpreting in their own work as interpreters and use the following variables in making the decision to do so (Russell 2002b):

- Complexity and density of information
- Setting (e.g., one-to-one interaction where the discourse frame lends itself to natural chunking of information for consecutive work)
- Consumers' non-conventional use of signed languages
- Consumer is a child
- Consequences of interpreting errors are grave
- When working with a Deaf interpreter
- One educator added an additional factor: when she did not know the participants well and the newness of the situation or information was challenging for her. This speaks to the role of contextual variables and their impact on the interpretation.

This type of information, coupled with current research, is crucial for interpreting students so that they can understand when they should be using consecutive interpreting, along with the rationale that can be used to negotiate for consecutive interpreting in both spoken English and ASL in the work environment. It is also crucial that interpreter educators model consecutive interpreting for students.

Both IIRS and Still Interpreting Inc. indicated that interpreters who came into their employ had divergent experiences and understandings about the use of consecutive interpreting, depending on where and when they completed their interpreter education. For those interpreters not well trained in consecutive interpreting, the employers have had to provide additional education and opportunities for skill development, by having interpreters who are comfortable with consecutive interpreting mentor inexperienced interpreters, and by creating in-house learning opportunities.

Over the past twenty years, our field has been fortunate to have a number of interpreter educators offer workshops and publish papers on discourse analysis, text analysis and cognitive processing models. By noting the work of Roy (1996), Wadensjö (1998), Smith and Savidge (2002), Winston (1998), and Witter-Merithew et al. (2002), to name but a few, we are gaining a body of knowledge upon which to build consecutive interpreting exercises that are effective and educationally sound. The Model Curriculum edited by Baker-Shenk (1990) offers a framework for teaching and learning about consecutive interpreting. Witter-Merithew et al. (2002) provide an effective and comprehensive ten-step discourse analysis process leading to consecutive interpreting. For any interpreting student or practitioner who wants to develop her consecutive interpreting skills, these materials are crucial and offer very helpful information. As Witter-Merithew et al. (2002) remind us, students ideally come to the task already possessing bilingual and bicultural competence. Then, through systematic exercises designed to practice the cognitive processes necessary for translation and consecutive interpreting, we can help students to achieve mastery of the interpreting process. Such training, whether in the classroom setting or on the job, must include:

- experience with text analysis that includes identification and control of linguistic aspects such as genres, registers, affect, cohesion, semantics, grammar and prosody
- auditory and visual memory development
- mapping of texts for linguistic elements and patterns of interaction among communicators
- note-taking and mapping techniques
- the ability to identify and segment linguistic and meaning-based chunks within the interaction that are suitable units for interpretation
- creation of culturally appropriate signals to use in order to ask consumers to pause so that the interpretation can be given
- consecutively interpreted texts modeled by interpreters who demonstrate success
- live models for simulated one-to-one role-plays

When interpreters are faced with content that is complicated, detail laden, or presented using linguistic structures that are challenging for the interpreter to construct meaning from, consecutive interpreting should be used. Interpreters who use consecutive interpreting report that when working with Deaf children, who may not use standard language features or conventional discourse structure, or when working with Deaf people who are using non-standard varieties of signed language, they will often move toward consecutive interpreting. By doing so, they better ensure that they are comprehending the complete message, are able to apply text analysis principles and bring the contextual analysis into the creation of meaning, and then can restructure the message in the target language. This reduces miscommunication and false starts, and increases the use of conventional discourse strategies in the English to ASL work.

There are settings where an interpreter may choose to use a blend of both forms of interpreting within one assignment. An example of using both consecutive and simultaneous interpreting naturally within one interpreted event might occur during a police interview. The interpreter may begin the interview using simultaneous interpreting for some of the more predictable content (e.g., questions designed to establish rapport, confirming printed information such as name, address, employment details, etc.). Once the interviewer moves the discussion toward facts or details of an incident, the interpreter may choose to switch to consecutive interpreting, thus allowing for greater complexity in questioning style and the level of detail that must be accurately conveyed across languages. As the interview closes and the incident related information exchange portion of the interview ends, the interpreter may return to simultaneous interpreting for the leave-taking process, which once again may be more predictable in nature. The interpreter can rely on several criteria to help her make this decision during the assignment, such as the question and answer discourse style itself, the complexity of questions and answers, the density of information, and the consequences of interpreting errors on the communication event. Sometimes interpreters prepare the consumers for such a switch prior to the assignment, and others choose to let consumers know during the assignment if they perceive a need to alternate between consecutive and simultaneous interpreting. Both negotiating strategies can be effective, depending on how the interpreter presents the two possibilities both in English for the non-deaf participants and in ASL for the consumer who is Deaf. Ultimately, consumers are usually willing to make adjustments when they understand that it will ensure a greater degree of accuracy. It is clear from Russell (2002b) that Deaf consumers are more concerned with miscommunication among participants than they are about the use of consecutive interpreting.

Interpreters who successfully use consecutive and simultaneous approaches to interpreting are those whose practice includes:

- strategies to discuss and negotiate for the use of consecutive or simultaneous interpreting (in spoken English and ASL) with consumers in order to produce the most effective interpretation possible;
- the ability to establish culturally appropriate signals in spoken English and ASL to cue consumers when to pause for the interpreter to deliver the interpretation;
- strategies to manage the interpreting process, including how to chunk complete thoughts or fully-formed questions in the source language;
- knowing when to employ mapping and note-taking approaches and when to rely upon short-term memory;
- the ability to move between consecutive and simultaneous interpreting, based on the nature of the content (complexity, lack of familiarity with content or context, impact of errors, type of discourse, goals, etc.); and
- knowing how to monitor the work for success and for errors, and how to modify processing time in order to produce accurate work.

This list may seem daunting but these skill-sets can be honed if the interpreter develops strong text and contextual analysis skills and has the opportunities and time needed to create a solid foundation of consecutive interpreting skills. Less experienced interpreters can learn from watching more proficient models of consecutive and simultaneous interpreting, and from dialogue with colleagues about the benefits of approaching their work from within this framework.

There are divergent views among educators and interpreters about what constitutes best practices in interpretation. For example, Russell (2002b) reports that while fifteen out of fifteen interpreter educators in the sample agreed that consecutive interpreting could provide a more accurate interpretation, only eight out of fifteen practicing interpreters agreed with that statement, revealing different perspectives among educators and interpreters. When these educators and interpreters were asked about their experience talking with consumers about the benefits of consecutive interpreting, two out of fifteen interpreter educators felt it was difficult to speak to consumers about the issue, compared to ten out of fifteen interpreters. There is agreement among these two groups that their experiences have shown them that consumers of interpreting services do not like consecutive interpreting, however we might ask whether consumers don't like it because the interpreters are not performing it well, or because interpreters on the whole have thus far "trained" consumers to believe that they can consistently produce accurate simultaneous interpretation. My own experience working with Deaf interpreters leads me to believe that they are some of our best allies because it is these Deaf interpreters who are having important conversations within the Deaf community about how communication and meaning-building among participants occurs in the interpreting process, and why consecutive interpreting is needed in some situations. Clearly, if interpreters are committed to accurate interpretation, they must engage all stakeholders in discussions of what constitutes best practices altogether, incorporating research, educational practices and effective interpreting strategies.

8.   Implications for our field

There are several opportunities that emerge for the profession from recent research on consecutive interpreting. Educators and students have opportunities to explore methods of integrating research into the classroom, bringing new awareness of the role of cognitive models of interpreting and of consecutive interpreting as part of the critical skill-set that interpreters require throughout their careers. As the field changes, we have opportunities to examine our curriculum and the language we use to describe consecutive interpreting to students, practitioners and consumers. Over the past twenty years we have given consumers a strong message that simultaneous interpreting is somehow "better" than consecutive interpreting.[6] It is time to revisit what it is that informs our practice and perceptions, and to learn more about when consecutive or simultaneous interpreting can be used most effectively. Our goal must be to apply the knowledge that research brings us to our work as interpreters, and to question our motives for valuing one mode of interpretation over another.

9. Conclusion

This chapter has examined some of the models of interpreting which provide insight into the nature of the interpreting process and has emphasized the need to use such models when learning how to interpret. These models are useful in teaching interpreting, and have relevance for both spoken and signed language interpretation, especially when examining what defines successful practices regarding the relationship between processing time and the ability of the interpreter to realize meaning based on the interaction and context that all participants bring to the communication event. This chapter has also examined consecutive interpreting research that supports the use of consecutive interpreting in a variety of settings in order to improve upon accuracy during the interpreting process.

It is clear from the literature that there are advantages to teaching consecutive interpreting as a distinct skill-set that will be needed throughout the career of a signed language interpreter. It is thus critical that students receive solid training in the use of consecutive strategies, and learn to apply them effectively as they work. Managing processing time requires that interpreters develop strong visual and auditory memory abilities, and that they understand how to take meaningful notes, when appropriate, that can reinforce their memory of the source message. As well, they must learn how to effectively segment messages during interpreted interaction while applying text analysis principles to determine meaning that has been created throughout the dialogue.

Preliminary results from the study of courtroom interpreting demonstrate that interpreters can and do successfully employ both consecutive and simultaneous interpreting within an interpreted event. Regardless of the skill level of the interpreter, simultaneous interpreting is a very complex process, and the risk of errors and miscommunication increases when the content or context is challenging to the interpreter, when the rate of speech and signing is rapid, when interpretation is performed under tight time constraints, when speakers' and signers' utterances overlap, and when interpretation mediates interactions that are emotionally charged. The impact of an interpreter's choice to use only simultaneous interpreting is significant; it can have grave consequences for the accuracy of the interpretation, and thus adversely impact the lives of those whose discourse depends on that equivalent meaning.

Research supports the use of consecutive interpreting and emphasizes that accuracy is higher when it is used. But, are there times when the use of consecutive interferes with the pragmatic and interactional goals of the participants for whom we are interpreting? This is one question still to be examined by further research studies. Clearly, further research is needed that will offer important insights into the many facets of providing interpretation. These include cognitive approaches to our work, the nature of interpreting for those who do not share the same language, culture, social identity or world views in legal and health care settings, the ways in which technology impacts the delivery of services, and the role that interpreters play in shaping the events that occur in an interpreted interaction. Pöchhacker (2004) suggests that interpreting researchers can look to a number of disciplines that may advance our knowledge, such as those studying cognitive pragmatics and situated cognition, in addition to building on interpreting studies that incorporate linguistic analysis and discourse studies.

Learning what constitutes effective practice in the field of spoken language and signed language interpreting is an avenue for further exploration. Expanding the research in our field and learning to incorporate that knowledge into interpreter education programs and into interpreters' daily practice will move us forward. Given the consistent evidence suggesting that consecutive interpreting yields greater accuracy in the interpreted interaction, it is a practice that clearly warrants expanded use in the context of signed language interpreting. By exploring when and where consecutive interpreting might be used most effectively, we will be exploring ways to better serve those who rely on our professional services.

Notes

1. Ear-voice span is a term used in spoken language research that measures the period of time between when the ear receives the input and when the interpreter begins her interpretation. This period of time is also called "processing time", referring to the cognitive tasks that are occurring during that time. The term "processing time" implies an active process and is preferred over the phrase "lag time" which does not address the cognitive functioning required in order to understand and reformulate the message into the target language. However, when the intent is, in fact, to address the time differential between source and target utterances, "lag time" can be an appropriate term, as is the case in Leeson (this volume, Chapter 10).

2. Wilcox and Shaffer (this volume) present an additional cognitive approach to both communication in general and interpreting in particular. This work represents important new insights into cognitive models of interpreting, and the interpreter's direct involvement in constructing meaning. I encourage readers to consider the ideas that Sherman Wilcox and Barbara Shaffer present in their chapter.

3. For further reading on contextual knowledge, see Witter-Merithew et al. (2002).

4. It is of interest that federal legislation is in effect in the United States that requires consecutive interpreting for all non-English speaking witnesses giving direct testimony.

5. As of 2005 called the E-Quality Communication Centre of Excellence (ECCOE).

6. Perhaps this is a "self-preservation" strategy that buys into Gile's (1995) rule of Self Protection, discussed in Leeson (this volume, Chapter 3).

References

Alexieva, Brista (1991). The optimum text in simultaneous interpreting: A cognitive approach to interpreters' training. Paper presented at the Annual Meeting of the First Language International Conference, Elsinore, Denmark, May 31–June 02, 1991.

Alexieva, Brista (2002[1997]). A Typology of interpreter-mediated events. In Franz Pöchhacker & Miriam Shlesinger (Eds.), *The Interpreting Studies Reader* (pp. 219–233). London and New York: Routledge.

Baker-Shenk, Charlotte (1990). *A Model Curriculum for Teachers of American Sign Language and Teachers of ASL/English Interpreting*. Silver Spring, MD: RID Publications.

Barik, Henri C. (1969). A Study of Simultaneous Interpretation. Unpublished doctoral dissertation, University of North Carolina, Chapel Hill.

Barik, Henri C. (1973). Simultaneous interpretation: Temporal and quantitative data. *Language and Speech, 16*, 237–270.

Barik, Henri C. (1975). Simultaneous interpretation: Qualitative and linguistic data. *Language and Speech, 18*, 272–297.

Barnwell, David (1989). Court interpretation: A need for a certification process. Paper presented at the Annual Meeting of the Southeast Conference on Languages and Literature, Orlando, FL, February 24, 1989.

Berk-Seligson, Susan (2000). Interpreting for the police: Issues in pre-trial phases of the judicial process. *Forensic Linguistics: The International Journal of Speech, Language and the Law, 7* (1), 213–238.

Bruton, Kevin (1985). Consecutive interpreting – the theoretical approach. In Noell Thomas & Richard Towell (Eds.), *Interpreting as a Language Teaching Technique – Proceedings of a Conference* (pp. 19–36). University of Salford, England: Centre for Information, Language Teaching and Research.

Chernov, Ghelly (1979). Semantic aspects of psycholinguistic research in simultaneous interpretation. *Language and Speech, 22* (3), 277–295.

Cokely, Dennis (1984). Towards a Sociolinguistic Model of the Interpreting Process: ASL and English. Doctoral dissertation, Georgetown University, Washington, DC.

Cokely, Dennis (1992). *Interpretation: A Sociolinguistic Model*. Burtonsville, MD: Linstok Press.

Cokely, Dennis (2003). Curriculum Revision in the Twenty First Century: Northeastern's Experience. Keynote presentation for Project TIEM, on-line conference, March 10, 2003.

Colonomos, Betty (1987). Interpreting process: A working model. Unpublished workshop handout.

Colonomos, Betty (1992). Processes in interpreting and transliterating: Making them work for you. Riverdale, MD: The Bicultural Center.

Dillinger, Mike (1994). Comprehension during interpreting: What do interpreters know that bilinguals don't? In Sylvie Lambert & Barbara Moser-Mercer (Eds.), *Bridging the Gap: Empirical Research in Simultaneous Interpretation* (pp. 155–190). Amsterdam/Philadelphia: John Benjamins.

Gerver, David (1976). Empirical studies of simultaneous interpretation: A review and a model. In Richard W. Brislin (Ed.), *Translation: Applications and Research* (pp. 165–207). New York: Gardner.

Gile, Daniel (1988). An overview of conference interpretation research and theory. In Deanna L. Hammond (Ed.), *Language at Crossroads: Proceedings of the 29th Annual Conference of the American Translators Association* (pp. 363–371). Medford, NJ: Learned Information.

Gile, Daniel (1995). *Basic Concepts and Models for Interpreter and Translator Training*. Amsterdam/Philadelphia: John Benjamins.

Gish, Sandra (1986). I understood all the words, but I missed the point: A goal-to-detail/detail-to-goal strategy for text analysis. In Marina L. McIntire (Ed.), *New Dimensions in Interpreter Education: Curriculum and Instruction* (pp. 125–137). Silver Spring, MD: RID Publications.

Gish, Sandra (1992). A Vygotskian perspective on interpreter assessment. In Elizabeth A. Winston (Ed.), *Student Competencies: Defining Teaching and Evaluating. Proceedings of the Ninth National Convention of the Conference of Interpreter Trainers* (pp. 19–44). USA: Conference of Interpreter Trainers.

Goldman-Eisler, Frieda (1972). Segmentation of input in simultaneous interpretation. *Journal of Psycholinguistics Research, 1*, 127–140.

Harris, Brian, & Brian Sherwood (1978). Translating as an innate skill. In David Gerver & H. Wallace Sinaiko (Eds.), *Language Interpretation and Communication* (pp. 155–170). New York: Plenum Press.

Humphrey, Janice H., & Bob J. Alcorn (1995). *So You Want to Be an Interpreter? An Introduction to Sign Language Interpreting.* Amarillo, TX: H & H Publishers.

Ingram, Robert (1985). Simultaneous interpretation of sign languages: Semiotic and psycholinguistic perspectives. *Multilingua, 4*, 91–102.

Isham, William P. (1986). The role of message analysis in interpretation. In Marina L. McIntire (Ed.), *Interpreting: The Art of Cross Cultural Mediation, Proceedings of the Ninth National Convention of the Registry of Interpreters for the Deaf* (pp. 60–69). Silver Spring, MD: Registry of Interpreters for the Deaf.

Lambert, Sylvie (1984). An introduction to consecutive interpretation. In Marina L. McIntire (Ed.), *New Dialogues in Interpreter Education: Proceedings of the Fourth National Conference of Interpreter Trainers Convention* (pp. 76–98). Silver Spring, MD: RID Publications.

Mikkelson, Holly (1994). *The Interpreter's RX: A Training Program for Spanish/English Medical Interpretation.* Spreckels, CA: ACEBO.

Moser, Barbara (1978). Simultaneous interpretation: A hypothetical model and its practical application. In David Gerver & H. Wallace Sinaiko (Eds.), *Language Interpretation and Communication* (pp. 353–368). New York: Plenum Press.

Pöchhacker, Franz (1992). The role of theory in simultaneous interpreting. In Cay Dollerup & Anne Loddegaard (Eds.), *Teaching Translation and Interpreting: Training, Talent, and Experience* (pp. 211–220) Amsterdam/Philadelphia: John Benjamins.

Pöchhacker, Franz (2004). *Introducing Interpreting Studies.* London: Routledge.

Roy, Cynthia B. (1996). An interactional sociolinguistic analysis of turn–taking in an interpreted event. *Interpreting, 1* (1), 39–67.

Roy, Cynthia B. (2000). *Interpreting as a Discourse Process.* New York/Oxford: Oxford University Press.

Russell, Debra (2000). Interpreting in Legal Contexts: Consecutive and Simultaneous Interpreting. Doctoral dissertation. University of Calgary, Calgary, Alberta.

Russell, Debra (2002a). *Interpreting in Legal Contexts: Consecutive and Simultaneous Interpreting.* Burtonsville, MD: Linstok Press.

Russell, Debra (2002b). Reconstructing our views: Are we integrating consecutive interpreting into our teaching and practice? In Laurie Swabey (Ed.), *New Designs in Interpreter Education: Proceedings of the 14th National Convention of the Conference of Interpreter Trainers* (pp. 5–16). St. Paul, MN: Conference of Interpreter Trainers.

Seleskovitch, Danica (1978). *Interpreting for International Conferences: Problems of Language and Communication.* Washington, DC: Pen and Booth.

Seleskovitch, Danica, & Marianne Lederer (1995). *A Systematic Approach to Teaching Interpretation.* Paris: Didier Erudition.

Shlesinger, Miriam (2000). Interpreting as a cognitive process. In Sonja Tirkkonen-Condit & Riitta Jääskeläinen (Eds.), *Tapping and Mapping the Processes of Translation and Interpreting: Outlooks on Empirical Research* (pp. 3–15). Amsterdam/Philadelphia: John Benjamins.

Smith, Theresa, & Ellie Savidge (2002). Beyond knowledge and skills: Teaching attitude. In Laurie Swabey (Ed.), *New Designs in Interpreter Education: Proceedings of the 14th National Convention of the Conference of Interpreter Trainers* (pp. 17–32). St. Paul, MN: Conference of Interpreter Trainers.

Tommola, Jorma, & Jukka Hyönä (1990). Mental load in listening, speech shadowing and simultaneous interpreting. Paper presented at the Meeting of the World Congress of Applied Linguistics, Thessaloniki, Greece, April 15–21, 1990.

Wadensjö, Cecilia (1998). *Interpreting as Interaction*. London and New York: Longman.

Winston, Elizabeth A. (2000). It just doesn't look like ASL! Defining, recognizing, and teaching prosody in ASL. *CIT at 21: Celebrating Excellence, Celebrating Partnerships, Proceedings of the 13th National Convention, Conference of Interpreter Trainers* (pp. 103–115). Silver Spring, MD: RID Publications.

Witter-Merithew, Anna, Marty Taylor, & Leilani Johnson (2002). Guided self-assessment and professional development planning: A model applied to interpreters in educational settings. Appendix A. In Clay Nettles (Ed.), *Tapestry of our World: Proceedings of the 17th National Conference of the Registry of Interpreters for the Deaf* (pp. 177–196). Alexandria, VA: RID Publications.

CHAPTER 7

Ethics and professionalism in interpreting

Terry Janzen and Donna Korpiniski

University of Manitoba / University of Alberta

1. Introduction[1]

Among the areas of skills and knowledge needed for expertise in interpretation are those of fluency in the languages the interpreter works in, extralinguistic or world knowledge, and interpreting technique. These basic areas, themselves multi-faceted, are interlaced as the interpreter works. Overarching these three, though, is a further area of consideration for the interpreter – that of how she makes her way through the many potential conflicts that arise: between interpreter and client expectations, interpreter and text, clients' approaches and interactions, and between cultures that differ. As she works, the interpreter makes countless decisions that involve ethics and the pursuit of professionalism.

This chapter addresses what ethical and professional choices mean for the interpreter in her work and in her relationships with her consumers. Making ethical choices is important for the interpreter because these decisions greatly affect the consumers' understanding of what has transpired during their interaction both with each other and between the consumer and the interpreter herself. Our assumption is that an interpreter needs to adopt a philosophy of proactive ethical behaviour at the onset of her training, and this approach must continue throughout her career.

In Section 2 we examine some of the short history of the field of ASL-English interpretation, including the various models by which interpreters have attempted to understand their role over the years. This evolution has shaped the way interpreters think about the scope of their work. Each model has given interpreters insights but has also introduced new questions for which there have been no easy answers. In Section 3 we address the importance of interpreters' codes of ethical behaviour. As an example, we discuss some features of the Association of Visual Language Interpreters of Canada (AVLIC) Code of Ethics and Guidelines for Professional Conduct and how the interpreter can take advantage of such a set of guidelines. Following this we turn to ethics and culture more specifically in 4, a theme that is introduced early in the chapter and continues throughout. Section 5 looks at professional considerations and business practices on one hand, and cultural effects in the interpreter's interactions with consumers on the other. Section 6 considers some of the effects of interpreters' choices, both in terms of their language use and their behaviours and interactions. In 7 we briefly address the interpreter's involvement in the Deaf community and in the professional community of interpreters. The final topic we examine is that of neutrality in Section 8, considering the potential for interpreters to impact the situations and events they are attempting to facilitate. In 9 we draw some conclusions and suggest strategies for continued learning in the area of ethics and professionalism.

2.   How we got to where we are: A look at our history

It is common for ASL-English interpreters to define their position or perceived role in terms of models, such as the "conduit" model or the "bilingual-bicultural" model. These labels are used to capture certain attitudes and behaviours that are often associated with particular time periods in the development of the field. It is also common for interpreters to espouse the current philosophical model and to distance themselves from older ones which might be thought of as less enlightened or even oppressive to Deaf people. However, Mindess (1999) cautions interpreters to be slow to reject these older models altogether, suggesting instead that there may be good reason to adopt some behaviours associated with a number of models in particular circumstances while at work. Mindess takes the stance that none of these models – the "helper", the "conduit", the "bilingual-bicultural", and the "ally" – should be rejected outright. Rather, there are times when behaviours associated with each may be the culturally appropriate choice.

   To understand this, and to consider how we come to a discussion of cultural considerations and interpreter ethics, we can look back through the progression of how interpreters have seen themselves performing their role over the years. While there may be numerous models by which interpreters define themselves, the description here will be restricted to the several most commonly used labels, discussed in more detail in works such as Mindess (1999) and Stewart, Schein and Cartwright (1998). It should also be pointed out that another type of model is that of representing the interpreting process, which is not so much about the role the interpreter plays, but about how a message framed in one language can be accurately reframed in another. Such process models are usually psycholinguistic or sociolinguistic in nature (e.g., Cokely 1992), and are not the focus of this chapter.

2.1 Interpreters as helpers

We might make the reasonable assumption that as long as there have been Deaf people with signed languages as their primary languages, there have been people who have interpreted or translated. Most often these were family members – parents, siblings, and children of Deaf people – or they were teachers or members of the clergy who could sign. It would be unlikely, however, that throughout history many of these people were employed as interpreters such that they made a living at it.

There is little recorded history of interpreters who work with a signed language (recorded histories of social and linguistic features of Deaf communities are not very complete either), but there is some anecdotal evidence that interpretation has taken place in historic times, and because we know that Deaf people rarely live in total isolation from non-deaf communities, we can assume that people have interpreted incidentally in the past among friends and business associates, for meetings, and for formal occasions. Lane (1984) writes, for example, of the abbé Sicard interpreting for his Deaf pupils as he demonstrated their language skills to the intellectuals of the day around the turn of the nineteenth century. On Martha's Vineyard in the United States, where an unusually high number of Deaf people lived until at least the mid 1800s and where everyone, Deaf or hearing, seemed to know and use signed language, there were still times when someone was called upon to interpret (Groce 1985). There were plenty of hearing people who knew how to sign well enough, so that occasionally at a gathering, especially when someone was visiting from "off-island" who couldn't sign but who needed to communicate with Deaf islanders, there would be a willing person to help out. These facts suggest that the history of interpreters who use a signed language extends well beyond the beginning of a professional designation.

2.2 Interpreters as conduits

Around the middle of the twentieth century much began to change for Deaf communities in North America. Researchers in linguistics began investigating ASL, which has brought more recognition of signed languages as fully functioning languages on par with spoken languages. Deaf communities began to experience an invigorating sense of pride in their language and their culture, and more and more rejected paternalistic "help" from outsiders. Educational opportunities opened up, in part because of a trend in the school system to keep students in local schools instead of sending them off to residential schools.[2]

And interpreters responded. Until this point, it had been quite common for hearing people who had some connection to the Deaf community to just help out. Perhaps what had been a solution became the perceived problem: these hearing signers usually had a close connection to the Deaf community, which is why they were able to sign in the first place. But in the increasingly public lives of Deaf people, a volunteer to help out was not the answer. Instead, interpreters who were "professional" were needed. Besides, what volunteer was going to interpret everyday in a high school or college?

Looking back, we see that many concerned individuals realized that more was needed, that the "helper model" of interpretation was no longer sufficient, and so a new era of interpretation was born. Mindess (1999) reminds us, however, that even though the potential for the helper to take and keep control was ever present, many of these interpreters were truly and genuinely appreciated for being *helpful*. Deaf people cherished an attitude of willingness and the closeness they felt to these connected interpreters. In fact, it may be argued that many of these interpreters, even though they may have felt overworked and at times taken advantage of, were connected to the Deaf community culturally, and the decisions they made were motivated by internal cultural awareness.

In 1964 a group of interpreters, Deaf people, and others met in Indiana to discuss issues related to signed language interpreting, and formed a national organization called the Registry of Interpreters for the Deaf (RID).[3] Based on the need for a standard for behaviour, the organization set out to recruit, train and accredit interpreters nationally. The Association of Visual Language Interpreters of Canada (AVLIC) was founded in 1979 upon similar principles. Although many Canadian interpreters were already RID members, AVLIC was established to address issues pertinent to interpreters working in Canada, which is an officially bilingual country (English and French), and which has sizable numbers of both ASL-English and LSQ-French interpreters.[4]

An important part of RID's original plan was to prepare a code of ethics to help ensure that interpreters' actions would not interfere with or harm the Deaf people whom they served. Besides ethical principles that guided interpreters to be confidential and to interpret faithfully, the code introduced the idea of impartiality. The original tenet, given in Quigley and Youngs (1965:9), states that "[t]he interpreter shall maintain an impartial attitude during the course of his interpreting avoiding interjecting his own views unless he is asked to do so by a party involved." This wording was later changed to state: "[i]nterpreters/transliterators shall not counsel, advise, or interject personal opinions" (Registry of Interpreters for the Deaf 1980:12). The premise was that any personal involvement on the part of the interpreter in this manner was likely to affect the outcome of the situation, and this was not the interpreter's responsibility.

In a few short years, interpreters deliberately sought to distance themselves from their clientele, motivated by an effort to empower members of the Deaf community by actively refusing to do things *for* Deaf people and instead simply interpreting to provide information so they could do things for themselves. It is during this phase that popular phrases such as "facilitating communication" and of someone being "just the interpreter" were used. The Deaf person was thought to be entirely in control. Thus during this period of time interpreters have often been characterized as working according to a "conduit" or "machine model" (see, for example, Baker-Shenk 1986). Interpreters were conduits for message transfer, nothing more.

The conduit orientation came about as interpreters grappled with achieving recognition as professionals – better trained, certified, ethical according to a set standard, and certainly not helpers. It was a bold statement to the Deaf community that interpreters would not get in the way as the community became more empowered. Many important milestones were made during this period. Interpreters began to think critically about what their role should be and to define the skills necessary to move toward professionalization. National certification standards were set in the United

States and several years later in Canada when AVLIC began certifying ASL-English interpreters in 1990. Also as a result, post-secondary training programs for interpreters began to emerge in many parts of North America.

But it is possible that interpreters generally went too far. The idea of the interpreter as conduit seems to affect two main areas of behaviour. The first, as described above, put the interpreter at arm's length from her clientele when the cultural practice in the Deaf community was to be completely open about sharing information (Mindess 1999). Thus the good intentions of interpreters (to not get in the way) created some cultural conflicts. The interpreter's goal of remaining completely neutral during interpreted interactions has recently been challenged by a number of studies on interpreted discourse. Metzger (1999), for example, studied interpretation in two medical settings, finding that the interpreters who were her subjects generated contributions to the principle participants' discourse, some of which enhanced the flow of communication while others detracted from it. Roy (2000) demonstrates (among other things) that her subject interpreter actively participated in the creation of turns. Setton's (1999) analysis includes discussion of unavoidable judgements interpreters make about the source speaker and text which impact their output texts, and Wadensjö's (1998) study of interpreted discourse shows that interpreters in practice are not bystanders but, in part because of their role as interaction coordinators, are very much participants in the overall discourse. By virtue of the interpreter being present, and being a thinking, language-mediating participant, it is impossible not to have at least some effect on the situation.

The second effect concerns the interpreter's language use directly. Because ASL and English have quite different morphological and syntactic systems, it is not possible to interpret word for word. In fact, for an interpreter to convey what is said (even at times rather simply) in the source language may mean taking a different route through the structure of the target language, and this can sometimes feel like "explaining" – something that the impartial conduit-model interpreter wanted to avoid. The reaction, according to Baker-Shenk (1986) was a retreat to transliteration, or "translating" as it was first called in this field, whereby the target message form, especially in the direction of English to ASL, looked much like the form and structure of the source language, English. Baker-Shenk makes the claim that this behaviour did not allow for ease of comprehension on the part of the Deaf audience, but they did not often object. Thus the oppression that these interpreters were hoping to alleviate was perpetuated by their own behavioural choices. Language is a crucial part of cultural identity, which means that the interpreter's language choices have little chance of being culturally neutral choices.

2.3 Interpreters as cultural mediators

In more recent years, the model of the interpreter as machine has been seen as less and less desirable. The interpreter is necessarily heavily involved in the transfer of the message because decoding and re-coding[5] draw on a host of skills and strategies that the interpreter must have (see Gile 1995 for detailed discussion, for example). Further, language use and interaction among discourse participants are complex ventures, therefore simply transferring information as unthinking machines is not a reasonable model of the interpreter at work.

Deaf people have made the strong claim that their community is best described in cultural terms, given that language and a set of social norms and traditions are what characterize this community as unique (Mindess 1999; Padden & Humphries 1988) and that numerous societal boundaries separate the Deaf and hearing experience (Padden 1996). In light of this, interpreters have sought to understand more about the cultural differences between Deaf and hearing communities and the impact this has on their communication. As a result, interpreters have come to think of their role as one of linguistic and cultural broker, using such terms as "cultural mediation", "cross-cultural", and "bilingual-bicultural" models. These labels are much more pleasing than those of "machine" or "conduit" because they are more humanizing, but because our understanding of what constitutes the cultural mind-set of Deaf people (or for that matter of hearing people; see Mindess (1999) for discussion of the American cultural psyche) is still quite limited, and because training for interpreters in cross-cultural effects has usually been *ad hoc*, it would be presumptuous to call ourselves bicultural experts even in the context of interpretation. Mindess rejects the notion of interpreters as (cultural) mediators because the work of a mediator typically goes well beyond that of the language interpreter. All in all, what providing culturally appropriate interpretation means is not very clear, and in any case, even though interpreters have a wide range of experience with the culture of the Deaf community, we have much yet to learn about the cultural component of our role as we interact situation by situation (but cf. Hoza 2003 for discussion of ethical decision making under a bilingual/multicultural framework).

2.4 Interpreters as allies

With growing dissatisfaction of the cultural mediation-type models, perhaps because they still put the interpreter at the centre of the interaction (which is not their own interaction in the first place), there has most recently been the suggestion that interpreters would do well to act as "allies" with the Deaf community (Baker-Shenk 1992). Baker-Shenk believes that one intention of the machine model approach – that the neutrality of the interpreter allowed the Deaf participants to control their own communication and thus be on an equal footing with hearing participants – ultimately failed because "by acting as if Deaf and hearing interactants were on equal footing and by not making conscious choices to help correct the imbalance of power, we help the hearing interactant maintain his/her greater power and help maintain the disempowerment of the Deaf interactant" (Baker-Shenk 1992:124). The cultural mediation model may be inadequate because the interpreter still has an inordinate amount of control (e.g., deciding what needs cultural adjusting and what doesn't) and yet attempts to treat each participant as equal within their own cultural context.

Cultural equality might be assumed, but in cross-cultural interaction, an imbalance is probable – one party or the other is likely not feeling that they are interacting on their own turf.

The interpreter as ally implies that because of the common power imbalance between Deaf and hearing people, interpreters are in a unique position to provide information about the interaction to the Deaf participants so that they can make empowered decisions on how to proceed. Perhaps even more so than with the other models discussed above, what it means to be an ally of the community is unclear. Baker-Shenk (1992) observes that being an ally begins with the attitude of not working *for* the Deaf community, but working *with* them, supporting their goals and interests as *they* see them, and not as interpreters might like to see them. Mindess (1999) notes that the ally model might be seen as a move back toward the notion of helper, but it is clear today that a paternalistic attitude would not be tolerated. If interpreters are to explore an ally philosophy of work in the coming years, success will depend on better understanding the culture and community of Deaf people, on being as bilingually fluent as possible (so that language skills do not become a barrier), on being cross-culturally savvy in their own behaviours, and on being highly knowledgeable about discourse structure, meaning, and function in two languages.

2.5 The appropriateness of models for interpreters

Models are metaphors: ways of seeing one set of behaviours in terms of some other. Of course interpreters are not, never have been, and never will be machines, but if we think of some of the good qualities of efficiently running machines, it is useful to make the analogy. Throughout our brief history we have attempted to better understand what it is we do, and how we should be doing it. As our skills and knowledge grow, we are better able to make appropriate choices. Mindess (1999) suggests that rather than discard any of the models that have characterized various periods in our history, we should consider what is valuable from each, and depending on the circumstances of a particular situation, choose the behaviour that best fits no matter which model it might be thought of as espousing. For example, if a speaker's speed is impossibly fast, with no way of having it altered for an interpreted context, many interpreters feel they have little choice but to function in an "automatic" mode. This may mean sacrificing some content or meaning, but in such cases it is likely that the source language audience isn't getting it either – it's just too fast to process. The interpreter may feel that functioning as a machine is the best coping strategy in this specific situation, even though there may be some after-effects to deal with. It does not mean, however, that this interpreter consistently operates under the conduit model.

Most importantly, it is becoming more and more obvious that cultural effects are everywhere in communication, and when people from different cultures come together to interact, cultures just might collide. Much of interpreters' decision making may be ethical in nature, but it is the underlying premise of this chapter that these decisions will most likely be perceived differently by members of different cultures, and that the interpreter's decisions will have cultural consequences.

3.   A code of conduct

The AVLIC Code of Ethics begins by stating that its purpose is *to provide guidance for interpreters, and in doing so, to ensure quality of service for all persons involved.*[6] AVLIC requires its members to uphold the tenets of the code so that a standard of practice is set and maintained across the country. In 1980, AVLIC ratified a code of ethics that was nearly identical to RID's code, but in the ensuing years, members became dissatisfied as much with the wording of what was in the code as with what wasn't in it. Both AVLIC's and RID's codes were drafted when the conduit model philosophy prevailed. AVLIC's current code, ratified in 2000, attempts to be more sensitive to cultural concerns of the communities with which interpreters work, but also stipulates expectations of ethical behaviours and professional business practices. A complete discussion of the code is not possible in this chapter. Rather, in this section we present a brief overview along with some comments on how the code addresses the cultural dimension of interpretation. In further sections our discussion highlights particular tenets of the code related to various aspects of the interpreter's practice.

The interpreter's code of conduct is intended to hold the interpreter to a high level of ethical behaviour, thus protecting 1) the public (i.e., both Deaf and hearing communities) from unfair or unethical practices, 2) the individual interpreter, who by striving to adhere to the code can expect to be treated in a professional way by her colleagues and clientele, and 3) the organization of interpreters, which claims a high standard of practice by its entire membership. AVLIC does not differentiate in its ethical expectations between certified and uncertified members.

AVLIC's code is based on five overarching values, which are *Professional Accountability, Professional Competence, Non-discrimination, Integrity in Professional Relationships*, and *Integrity in Business Practices*. The tenets specified under *Professional Accountability* are concerned with the interpreter taking responsibility for her own conduct. In other words, it is incumbent on the interpreter to ensure that information regarding clients and their situations remains confidential, that actions are not self-serving, and that the interpreter doesn't misrepresent her competencies.

Under *Professional Competence*, the AVLIC code requires that interpreters must possess the qualifications needed to practice as professionals and are accountable for the quality of their work. Of interest is article *2.1. Qualifications to Practice* which states that because interpreters work in a wide range of situations and with many clients having different needs, interpreters must *be adept at meeting the linguistic needs of consumers, the cultural dynamics of each situation, and the spirit and content of the discourse.* This general statement subsumes a huge number of skills on the part of the interpreter and, if a high level of competency is expected for a very wide range of clients and situations, a significant amount of training would be expected. This section also includes a statement regarding ongoing professional development. Because of the nature of the field and limited education opportunities for interpreters, much of this training is necessarily self-directed.

The tenets under the heading of *Non-discrimination* are most obviously directed toward cultural awareness. The general principle beginning article *3.0. Non-discrimination* reads: *Interpreters approach professional services with respect and cultural sensitivity towards all participants.* Specifically, interpreters are instructed in article *3.1.* to *respect the individuality, the right to self-determination, and the autonomy of the people with whom they work.* While nothing in this part of the code addresses inequalities between Deaf and hearing people as suggested by Baker-Shenk (1992), the wording is such that the intention is inferred. Of importance is that AVLIC has asked its members to work with an attitude of respect, discussed in Section 7 below, as a crucial element in the interpreter's approach. Article *3.3.* addresses Deaf interpreters and the need to recognize when a Deaf interpreter is recommended to be part of the interpretation team. Deaf interpreters may in fact be more important as colleagues than this article even suggests.[7] Deaf interpreters bring linguistic skills and cultural competence to the practice of interpretation that non-deaf interpreters need. It would be inconceivable in any other language combination, say English and French, to have interpreters drawn from only a native English-speaking population.[8]

The final two sections of the AVLIC code deal with professional considerations, that is, the equitable treatment of consumers and upholding professional measures. Interpreters are cautioned in article *4.2.1. Impartiality* to *remain neutral, impartial, and objective.* This suggests that even with more attention to cultural affinity, interpreters are still bound by this stringent professional requirement. This is in keeping with expectations among interpreters and translators altogether and is reflected in numerous professional organizations' codes of conduct. Schweda Nicholson (1994) includes the principle of impartiality as one of the defining features of the interpreting profession, demonstrated by its common inclusion in professional codes of ethics. Nonetheless, the principle of impartiality is one that interpreters continue to struggle with, and so we will return to this topic in Section 8 below.

The AVLIC Code of Ethics was developed to protect consumers from unprofessional and unethical behaviour. It was intended to send the message that even though interpreters are present in many sensitive situations that are really intended to be private, they can be trusted. Consumers, both Deaf and hearing, want this assurance, and want to know that their communication will be treated respectfully. Thus the code of ethical guidelines comes as a welcome safeguard. But how we wield the code can be problematic. Interpreters have often held up the code of ethics at the first hint they may be asked to compromise their principles. Even though the ASL sign CODE.OF.ETHICS (which is based on the ASL root for LAW) is meant to signal "protection", it is often read by Deaf people as "unwilling to share" or worse. In a culture where open communication and information sharing is highly valued, this can create a cultural conflict. There are many important reasons to have a set of standard practices, and interpreters must continue working to understand how a code of conduct can function alongside cultural and cross-cultural principles.

4. The role of culture in ethical practice

The original RID code of ethics begins with a tenet addressing the interpreter's own morality by stating that "[t]he interpreter shall be a person of high moral character, honest, conscientious, trustworthy, and of emotional maturity" (Quigley & Youngs 1965:9). This does not appear in later versions of RID's code nor in AVLIC's original code, but several of these personal qualities are addressed in AVLIC's current guidelines. Interpreters are asked to conduct their affairs with consumers and colleagues alike with honesty, integrity, respect, and to actively build trust. Some might argue that statements regarding the interpreter's personal character do not belong in a professional statement of ethics, but professional ethics are not likely to be maintained if the practitioner's personal moral code is lacking.

Hoza (1992) comments that during the era when the conduit model predominated, interpreters were expected to follow the code of ethics to the letter without questioning it, but that this has become unrealistic since interpreters' perception of their role has changed to acknowledge cultural considerations. Cokely (2000) claims that RID's entire code as it stands does not allow for cultural considerations and advocates for a code based on the rights of all interaction participants. Perhaps what might be said is that the expectation that interpreters' professional organizations have is that their members will unquestioningly be ethical in their practices. Adopting a philosophy of ethical behaviour means agreeing to uphold a set of values such as those set out in AVLIC's code.

How does culture come into play? It is not that one culture has some of these values and others do not, but that individual values within a set are more or less highly ranked. In this way, for example, a cultural group may value social harmony even though disagreements are possible and do occur, but because harmony is sought after, the manner of disagreeing may include a high level of indirect communication rather than confrontation (see Bond, Žegarac, & Spencer-Oatey 2000 for discussion of such variables). Bond et al. suggest that the interplay among culture-level values along with the perceptions that individual members of the culture have about individual situations help to explain variation in behaviour, something that interpreters encounter that can confound their understanding of how someone should behave. Further, Bond et al. claim that communication behaviours that reflect cultural value norms are often conventionalized as "scripts", thus members of the cultural group will recognize a script, often unconsciously, as signifying certain cultural expectations. The problem here, however, is that in a cross-cultural setting, those scripts are not likely known or perceived in the same way by members of differing cultures, even when the value behind the action is held by both. Unless the interpreter is well-versed in such scripts, she may miss the cultural significance of the discourse.

It is our belief that culturally motivated behaviours include ways of thinking, acts of communication, and the actions of the person. In this way, culture invades the behaviour of the interpreter and those whose interaction is being interpreted. This does not mean that conflict is inevitable, but quite the contrary. People often work hard to communicate effectively with others, and when people live and work in proximity to others of differing cultures and ways of life, they can and do develop a sensitivity to others' way of thinking (see, for example, the discussion of motivations for improving intercultural interaction in Cushner & Brislin 1996, 1997). Of course, the opposite may at times be true as well.

The interpreter encounters cultural considerations in interaction on at least two fronts. First, she might be faced with differences in culturally motivated approaches between the two parties for whom she is interpreting. In this case, she needs to consider her own role in bridging this cultural difference to effect clear communication without overstepping her role. Appropriate decision-making must be based upon clear understanding of the cultural principles afoot, and these decisions will be played out in the interpreter's behaviours. Second, the interpreter will experience either cultural proximity ("sameness") or cultural distance ("differentness") between herself and any given consumer. More than likely, this cannot be understood as simply polar; rather, the interpreter will be somewhere on a continuum between extreme proximity and distance with each client. And here perhaps, the importance of cultural considerations in the interpreter's decision-making and behaviour is greatest. It is in relation to the interpreter's own behavioural interaction with her clients that the most problematic ethical dilemmas will arise.

When working toward the resolution of an ethical issue, whose values are being considered? And further, are the actions and communication on the part of the interpreter conducive to a culturally appropriate resolution? The process of resolution between the interpreter and her consumer may be more successful if it follows a culturally appropriate path according to the *consumer's* culture rather than the interpreter's (if they differ). This reflects a truly culturally aware model of practice. In our discussion, we hope to demonstrate that this area too is closely tied to the cultural context where interpretation takes place.

5.   Professional considerations vs. ethical decision making

Two broad dimensions of interpreters' ethics are how interpreters conduct their business, and how they interact with others. These two dimensions are not necessarily mutually exclusive, but it is helpful to consider some guidelines for each. We begin with a brief discussion of business practices.

5.1 The interpreter in business

For many interpreters, excellent language and interpretation skills are only part of the job; they also must market these skills. Interpreters are in business. One option is to work for an agency that supplies interpretation services, in which case their work generates income for the agency (whether for-profit or not-for-profit). A second option is to work for a single employer such as for a private company, government branch, or school division. A third is working as a freelance contractor, whereby the quality and amount of work provides them their income. They may work part- or full-time. These interpreters must market their work, they negotiate fees and conditions of work, and they must abide by laws surrounding income and income taxes. Some interpreters might not see themselves as being in business to this extent. Many who work in education, for example, are employees of the school or school district, collect a salary, and need do nothing more than file their income tax statement once a year. Many of these interpreters, however, also freelance, thus have "self-employed" income on the side, and thus are in fact in business.[9]

Operating as a freelance interpreter and selling one's skills may be quite different than what one would expect when thinking of owning a business. Whereas a business owner may attract patrons through location and advertising, the freelance interpreter's product is what sells, and an interpreter with excellent skills, flexibility and a good attitude will be busy. Rather than having the benefit of a regular pay cheque that comes with full- or part-time employment, the freelance interpreter is in charge of managing all of her business transactions. She needs a system of billing, will sometimes need to track down payment, and cheques may arrive weeks later. It can be quite a challenge manipulating a schedule that is so varied from day to day, where the interpreter scheduling appointments must assess the assignment length, determine travel time to and from assignments, park, etc. It is becoming a widely accepted practice for a minimum amount of time to be billed, including the amount of time spent travelling and to account for short appointments. The freelance interpreter must maintain accurate records of appointments, receipts, and income, and may be required to charge GST[10] and submit the required fees to the federal government.

As part of day to day business, freelance interpreters must also contend with the various complexities of many different assignments. They need to be flexible and deal with diverse people from professional to para-professional to non-professional, along with discourse styles that each utilizes. Assignments can be unpredictable and a responsible freelance interpreter with a generalist skill set may need to turn down certain appointments when an interpreter with more experience or with specialized skills is a better option.

It is incumbent upon interpreters to prepare for each assignment well. Although there are times when it is appropriate and necessary to negotiate payment for time spent preparing, the onus is on interpreters to seek out information that will aid them in their work, even when that preparation time can't specifically be billed for. This can be time-consuming, but interpreters are responsible for providing the highest quality of work, and they cannot afford to "do less" and let the work slip to a mediocre level.

Good business practices are addressed in several sections of the AVLIC code. *4.0. Integrity in Professional Relationships* addresses the interpreter's business relationships with others and will be discussed as part of the interpreter's interactions below. *5.0. Integrity in Business Relationships*, however, points to a number of ethical business practices that apply to any interpreter in any situation. In a field that is by and large unregulated (e.g., there is no legal credential in Canada or in many other countries, training standards vary, and many interpreters work alone with little informed supervision), interpreters must individually determine their own day to day business practices. Organizations such as AVLIC and RID have come far in setting guidelines and attempting to regulate the behaviours of their members, for example through grievance procedures resulting from breaches of ethics, but currently there is no legal requirement that interpreters must be members of these professional organizations in order to work. At best, an agency or employer may require professional organization membership or even certification by the organization, and many do. It is still incumbent on the individual interpreter, however, to practice good business ethics.

Let's take one example of business practices, that of the interpreter's procurement, use, and disposal of preparation materials. AVLIC's code has two statements addressing materials, one of which is quite general:

§5.1.2. Members will conduct themselves in all phases of the interpreting situation in a manner befitting the profession, including negotiating work and contracts, obtaining suitable preparation material, and choice of attire and professional demeanor.

The second statement is somewhat more specific:

§5.1.4. Members shall take reasonable care of material and/or property given to them by a consumer and may not lend such or use it for purposes other than those for which it was entrusted to them.

How should someone interpret this guideline? Hopefully the interpreter has had some training in this area, can observe other professionals' behaviours, and considers what would make sense when obtaining and handling material needed for her work.

In the past, many interpreters have felt that if they are skilled, they should be able to handle interpreting an interaction "cold". Whether or not this is a throwback to conduit model thinking is unclear, but more and more interpreters accept that appropriate preparation is an important part of successful interpretation. It is rare that an interpreter is unable to find at least basic information about an assignment, and often there are print materials that may be obtained beforehand. These materials provide the interpreter with insights on the ideas to be discussed, vocabulary and spelling, level of formality, etc. Interpretation can be error-ridden because the interpreter did not take advantage of information that was in fact available beforehand. Still, an appropriate question is how much is too much – having to plough through too much material may not be economically feasible, and so the interpreter must make choices regarding the best use of time.

Some of the best preparation material is information that provides background to the content of a given interaction that is to be interpreted. For example, when preparing to interpret for a business or staff meeting at a particular company, it is helpful to find out something about what the business does, products they manufacture, the organizational chart (who's who, in other words), the mission statement, market goals, etc. This information may be available in a "new employee package" that the interpreter could obtain, or the interpreter might find pertinent information on the company's webpage.

A key issue is terminology. An interpreter might understand what is going on generally, but if she cannot understand and use the interactants' vocabulary, which is often site-specific and can be extensive, the interpretation will suffer. This problem can be acute when working from the interpreter's L2 into her L1 if the L2 speakers or signers have developed terminology that the interpreter is unaware of. If the L2 is ASL and the domain is manufacturing for example, numerous vocabulary items might be based on classifiers which would be identifiable to the interpreter, but in the context of the workplace, would correspond to some very specific and often opaque vocabulary in English. Therefore recognizing a term in one language is not enough – the interpreter must develop a repertoire of vocabulary items in two languages. This specific linguistic information may not be available in any print materials, but rather, the interpreter can benefit from some assignment-related interaction beforehand with consumers who use this vocabulary.

Materials are often useful during the interpretation as well. Interpreters who work with a signed language have the disadvantage that their hands are occupied with language production so that, unlike spoken language interpreters, they cannot as easily handle print materials as they interpret. But it is rare that a convenient surface cannot be made available, such as a table, upon which to place relevant documents. It can be somewhat of an art to manage materials while interpreting, although working in a team can certainly help. Having information available in front of the interpreter is clearly advantageous because certain facts and details, especially when they are less context-dependent (e.g., budget information, the spelling of names), do not need to be held in short-term memory. They are right there on the page. Interpreters often find themselves doing work that is more like translation than interpretation (sometimes referred to as "sight translation") when working from specifically worded documents into ASL.[11] Having access to the wording of the text both ahead of time and during the interaction is useful. Sometimes such material is available either just minutes before a meeting or not until the exchange is underway, such as policy statements being introduced or motions being read at a business meeting, but even asking for a moment to read the statement over prior to attempting an interpretation can be helpful in formulating an accurate target language rendition.

What does the interpreter do with documents once the assignment ends? Probably not toss the material into the garbage bin on the way out of the board room. Just as it is important to treat clients with respect, it reflects well on the interpreter to treat the clients' materials with respect. Especially if print information is sensitive (e.g., financial statements), it might be the best practice to return the documents to the appropriate client. No one would appreciate the interpreter walking out with material an organization means to safeguard. On the other hand, some materials are excellent to keep in an information file for future work (e.g., documents more public in nature such as human resources manuals). The interpreter may not be able to rightfully insist on doing this, but if the circumstances seem appropriate, it can be a good idea to ask for permission to retain certain documents. The interpreter should make it clear that these documents are being kept for professional, not personal, reasons and may need to give the assurance that they will be kept in a secure place in the interpreter's office, not scattered around her house. Many documents may be perceived as beneficial for an interpreter's future work, but often consumers are reluctant to turn these over to someone they do not yet trust. Also, when an individual shares materials with an interpreter that she has prepared but which were never intended to be public, the interpreter is not likely to get them to keep.

It might be argued that business practices are not clearly ethical concerns – for the most part they are what you would expect from someone with good business sense. An interpreter might be considered unethical, however, if she consistently neglected such practices or cheated in some way. If this is obvious to clients or colleagues, the interpreter will be viewed negatively, and a lack of overall trust could develop. The interpreter's actions must leave clients with the perception that her business affairs are managed carefully and that she is treating their business relationship respectfully.

Finally, even though good business practices might not seem to be determined by cultural values, how an individual carries out these practices may in fact be. In one culture, for example, an agreement made in face to face discourse can carry a lot of weight, whereas in another, nothing is certain until a written agreement is signed. In one culture, value may be placed on an exchange of services, whereas in another, monetary payment is the norm. In one culture, meeting times are fluid, with some social interaction before or after (or both) expected of everyone who participates in that culture, whereas in the other, appointments are scheduled back to back and the schedule must be maintained (see Rosaldo 1989 for a detailed discussion of similar types of conflicting cultural perspectives in an academic context). The interpreter must navigate these competing expectations among clients, and even more so, must successfully negotiate such expectations between herself and her clients when cultural perspectives are not the same.

5.2   The interpreter's interaction with clients and colleagues

The interpreter is frequently confronted by situations that demand some action or reaction falling within the domain of ethics. Ethical behaviour on the part of the interpreter should be considered the norm by interpreters and consumers alike. As previously discussed, if the interpreter has an overall philosophy of ethical business practices, she will approach her day to day business affairs with honesty and integrity. Similarly, if this philosophy extends to her interaction with consumers and colleagues, she will conduct individual interactions in an appropriate way. This does not mean that she will automatically know how to respond to each concern or conflict, but determining to be ethical from the onset can make specific resolutions easier. In other words, approaching her work from an ethical stance, understanding the parameters of her role and responsibilities, and knowing something about the effects of interaction and communication within a cultural framework will put the interpreter in an excellent position to make good decisions.

In the past, it has been thought that interpreters should adopt a "bicultural" approach to their work because they need to mediate communication between two parties who view the interaction from differing cultural perspectives. Thus for a time interpreters referred to themselves as following a "cultural mediation" model of interpretation. There is no question that the interpreter must handle communication that does not transfer directly across cultures, in which case she must make some decisions about how to reconstruct the source text into an appropriate target text that makes sense for that audience. An often used example is when a direct comment is made in the source language by a person acting according to a cultural norm of direct and non-euphemized discourse, but which must be transferred to a person whose culture encourages more indirect communication (perhaps because of some face-saving principles). The resulting text, to be successful, should best reflect the *target* cultural practice.

In cases such as this, we would argue that if any ethical question arises, it is not one of how to proceed linguistically. If anything, the ethical question is a more general one: is the interpreter committed to excellence in her work? If the interpreter does not care about the effect of her interpretation, her approach might rightfully be considered unethical. But as to the decision about the most appropriate interpretation, this is a question of applying linguistic and pragmatic knowledge, of cultural adeptness, and of creativity. Thus our position is that much of the so-called "cultural mediation" in getting from the source text to the target text falls outside the realm of ethics. Instead, ethics is about the interpreter's behaviour in interacting with others. In these interactions, cultural considerations and ethics are closely linked.

5.2.1 *Interactions during the assignment*
Numerous tenets in interpreters' codes of conduct address the stance the interpreter should take toward her work. One of the most critical principles regards using discretion in accepting work that the interpreter is qualified for, or in representing her qualifications. In other words, the interpreter should not accept work that she does not have the skill or knowledge to handle well, or if there is some mitigating circumstance that could seriously bias her work. Here the interpreter often walks a thin line, but before we address these issues, let us introduce several additional principles of an ethical nature.

In broad terms, it is expected that the interpreter will give a faithful interpretation, meaning that the message given in the source language will be an equivalent message in the target language, nothing more and nothing less. The AVLIC code states the following:

§2.2. Faithfulness of Interpretation
Every interpretation shall be faithful to and render exactly the message of the source text. A faithful interpretation should not be confused with a literal interpretation. The fidelity of an interpretation includes an adaptation to make the form, the tone, and the deeper meaning of the source text felt in the target language and culture.

And regarding bias:

§4.2. Impartiality
4.2.1. Members shall remain neutral, impartial, and objective. They will refrain from altering a message for political, religious, moral, or philosophical reasons, or any other biased or subjective consideration.

Much has been said in the literature about the faithfulness or fidelity of the message, for example Seleskovitch (1978) reminds us that the interpreter must convey the *sense* of the message without much regard to form, and Gile (1995) discusses numerous factors affecting the fidelity of the message during transfer from source to target language.[12] When working toward a faithful interpretation the interpreter must take into account the pragmatics of the situation – what the participants know already, what the goals of the interchange are, etc. Additional factors include whether or not there is a linguistic equivalent in the two languages, whether the discourse conventions of the two languages allow the message to be framed in a similar way, and even more confounding, whether or not the target culture provides a similar mental or social framework to situate the ideas (or examples, analogies, metaphors, etc.) conveyed in the source message. Since language use and language choices are always subjective in nature, an excellent interpretation has less to do with ethics than with expertise. Linguistic errors, in fact, can be made by even the most ethical of interpreters. Unethical behaviour would be the case if the interpreter were to deliberately change the message from what was intended, or not to care whether the message remained intact. This attitude may not be a conscious one, but any time an interpreter thinks "it's good enough" it might be time to re-evaluate whether or not the interpretation is falling short, or even if the interpreter has lost the motivation to do her best work.

Can an interpreter escape bias? While this question is dealt with in more detail in Section 8 below, let us say here that a completely neutral stance is likely never possible. Having opinions about things, being biased in favour of or against an idea, or treating material in a subjective manner is natural for us; in this way we humans are very much unlike machines. It is not unethical to *have* biases, but it is unethical to alter someone's message because of a bias. The best defence against letting a personal bias colour an interpretation is an interpreter's awareness of her own feelings toward the material being interpreted (or often, if the interpreter is honest, toward the person for whom she is interpreting), understanding which perspective is the speaker's and which is the interpreter's own. In this way the interpreter can separate these two views and consciously work at not including her own bias in the interpretation. Often, the difference is more distinguishable if she disagrees with the speaker or dislikes something in the message – her own feelings will be more obvious and she can work toward portraying just the intent of the message sender. More difficult are situations when she agrees with or particularly likes what is being discussed. In this case the interpreter may subtly enhance the appeal of the message. Sometimes a simple approving nod as the interpreter delivers a signed target message sends the signal that she is in agreement or supports a particular option. Here, as elsewhere, we suggest that the principles that govern ethical behaviour are broad. One of the most important questions that we can ask is whether or not the interpreter is showing respect for the message and for the participants in the situation. If so, the resulting interpretation will more remain what these participants have communicated and less what the interpreter herself would want to say.

5.2.2 *Interactions apart from the assignment*
A critical part of being an effective interpreter is the interpreter's interactions when she is not actively working. Deaf people often seek interpreters they can trust; many times something about interpreters' attitude is what makes Deaf people want to have them as interpreters almost regardless of their skill level. For many Deaf people, it isn't so much that they watch an interpreter *interpret* and conclude that they would like this person to interpret for them in the future, it is that they watch the interpreter *interact* in the community and draw this conclusion.

An important ethical practice concerns the principle of confidentiality. The underlying premise in keeping assignment-related information confidential is that the interpreter is there to allow two people who use different languages to communicate with ease. If this communication difference did not exist, the interpreter would not be there. Introducing a third party in any situation has numerous effects, so the interpreter works to minimize her presence. One way to do this is to assure the participants that the interpreter will not be the source of information being shared outside the interpreted event.

Clearly there are times when confidentiality is more critical, for example when information is sensitive. But often interpreters can be confused about when it might be permissible to talk about some assignment-related information when the event is less sensitive or more public in nature. And if interpreters are unclear, they can be sure that their consumers will be confused too. Again, it is a matter of trust. A hallmark of a profession is its members' rigorous adherence to a high standard of practice, and here it is not only the practitioner's point of view that is important. The perception of the interpreter as rigorously confidential is necessary to build and maintain trust. An interpreter with a strong sense of respect for the consumer and her communication will not have difficulty with confidentiality.

The issue of confidentiality, however, has cultural implications as well. How we communicate is intimately linked to culture. Hearing and Deaf people are both concerned about interpreters respecting their interactions. There are numerous professions where client information is not divulged outside the setting. In the Deaf community, however, people have frequently experienced situations where access to information is limited (see e.g., Foster 1998) and the culture of the Deaf community has evolved an expectation that when no communication barriers exist (i.e., interactants can sign ASL) information is shared freely and the style of exchange is often quite direct (Mindess 1999). Interpreters may therefore face frustration in this cross-cultural context.

Even though most hearing people in North America might expect that professionals' client records and client interactions are confidential, the professional status of interpreters is often nebulous, and interpreters might be expected to tell all manner of information about the Deaf person involved. Many interpreters in educational settings struggle with the boundaries of their role in this regard.

When interacting with Deaf people, many interpreters grapple with how much information they can share and what information is truly privileged. Some of an interpreter's activities might be quite well known in the community, meaning that many Deaf people know where the interpreter has been and consider that she might be an excellent and appropriate source of information. At the same time, the hearing interpreter wishes to act in a culturally appropriate way, but feels that the information is not hers to share. Interpreters still have a long way to go to learn how to negotiate these conflicts. One tactic that interpreters have often used, mentioned in Section 3 above, is to hold up the code of ethics as their defence, whereas this might be treated as an affront. A more detailed and friendly explanation may be better. The interpreter may also guide the conversation to more neutral topics, and part of the answer is for the interpreter to be more communicative generally. Mindess (1999) suggests that being available for even a few minutes before or after an assignment for some informal chatting is a culturally appropriate behaviour for Deaf people.[13] All in all interpreters need to keep exploring how to interact in cultural ways without compromising their ethical principles.

6. Effects and consequences of the interpreter's choices

6.1 Linguistic choices

It is obvious that a form-based interpretation does not provide a target text that is accessible to all participants, which means the task requires the interpreter to make some clear decisions on how to reconstruct the source text into the target language within the social context of the interaction. What is intriguing about interpretation is that given a single source text, several good interpreters would construct the target text in different ways. The challenge then, is to not stray too far from what the speaker intends.

Upon receiving the source language text, the interpreter considers what she thinks the message receiver knows or doesn't know, that is, what the given knowledge is in that specific context. Often, however, there is no definitive way of really knowing what a particular consumer would know about a topic. Instead, the interpreter must negotiate topics with consumers, delicately finding out what information they may or may not be familiar with. The choices made based on what the interpreter can determine impact the message in numerous ways both in form and flavour, such as a decision to shift the register, or to be more or less explicit regarding some part of the text but without misrepresenting the original intended message.

How can the interpreter be sure that she makes the appropriate adjustments and yet minimizes unnecessary alterations to the message? If she is knowledgeable about linguistic structures and applicable cultural norms, she will be in a better position to make effective choices, but some familiarity with the consumer(s) and the setting will help too, and consequently errors in judgement based on the interpreter's assumptions will be reduced. Here it is well worth considering working consecutively, because the benefit from increasing process time is that the interpreter can better scrutinize linguistic options and therefore the target message has a better chance of being produced with more clarity (Russell 2002, this volume).

This can be hard work. In discussing various functions that texts and parts of texts play in discourse interactions, Hatim and Mason (1990) suggest that translators (and by extension, interpreters) have a responsibility to convey the same message to the target audience that is intended for the source text audience. And yet the overall knowledge base, cultural perspective, and contextual expectations the target audience have may differ greatly from that of the source language audience. Hatim and Mason note that meaning equivalence is only drawn through the assumptions the audience can make about what the speaker must mean, that is, by inferring the meaning.[14] The translator's (or interpreter's) position is that she must make these same assumptions about the source text, and then *also* must make assumptions about what inferences the target audience is likely to make. Regarding this, the standard ethical adage that the interpreter cannot add or omit anything from the source message is on shaky ground; Hatim and Mason claim that the target audience's inferences will not necessarily be identical to those the source language audience make, and thus it is incumbent on the translator to adjust the target text to accommodate these assumed inferences, no matter how different they may be. This might be accomplished by reducing redundant information for the target audience, especially if they do not have a cultural schema to gain any sort of "equivalence" from it, or expanding an idea when necessary information is lacking in the source text.[15] So at times, the right strategy is to change something about the text. "Even in full translations [as opposed to abstract-type translation], translators can and do take responsibility for omitting information which is deemed to be of insufficient relevance to TT [target text] readers" (Hatim & Mason 1990:96). Clearly this aspect of interpretation cannot just be at the whim of the interpreter. It will be successful only when the interpreter has mastered the craft of dealing critically with the text and has a thorough understanding of the audience. Above all, knowing what linguistic choices are available and what specific effect they will have is critical if the outcome is to match what both the source speaker or signer and the interpreter intend.

6.2 Effects on the outcome of interpretation

The outcome of the interpreter's many decisions may cause subtle differences in the underlying intent, or have grave overall consequences. Depending on various factors in the setting, the interpreter may become aware of inaccuracies that occur or these may go unnoticed. There are settings where the interpreter is easily able to check her work during the process, whereas in some settings, she may be dependent on other strategies by which to monitor her work. Whatever the case may be, the interpreter will impact the message by the decisions she has made when constructing the target text, whether she is aware of it or not, and whether it is intentional or not. The consequences of interpreter errors for the consumer(s) depend on numerous factors, including the type of setting, but in every case the interpreter should make the effort to reduce this risk.

It would be helpful if there were some clear parameters in place regarding the amount of flexibility the interpreter has while inferring meaning from the source message, understanding the mind-set of the consumer, and constructing the target text, and yet sticking to the message that the *speaker* is presenting. Students of interpretation often become frustrated with attempts to find answers to their many questions either about how to interpret something well or about an ethical concern when the typical response is that "it depends". In real situations, however, the nature of interaction is that it is infinitely diverse, and the question of how much flexibility cannot escape this basic fact. But a facility in shaping an appropriate and equivalent target message comes with solid training, hard work, diligence in attending to the task the interpreter has undertaken, and respect for both the consumer and the text. And perhaps herein lies the answer: if the interpreter has carefully considered how the message is *equivalent* based on these factors, then there is a good chance that she is correct.

There isn't really much difference between the target text that results from an interpreter who takes more latitude than was rightly hers and one who lacks the skill or knowledge to choose the best linguistic structures or to provide the right mix of cultural information. The result of these effects will not be message equivalence.

Finally, the interpreter does well to consider what effect she has had on the outcome of the situation once the interaction is complete. Interpreters by and large consider that when the assignment is over, they are to take nothing with them (e.g., the AVLIC code stipulates in Section 1.3.3 that members *refrain from manipulating work situations for personal benefit or gain*). In fact, the interpreter typically works in a variety of personal and emotional situations, and once a situation is completed, the interpreter does well to leave it behind. The rationale here, of course, is that she cannot carry everyone's emotional turmoils home with her after work. However, the recipients of the interpreted exchange can be greatly affected by what transpired: it is a part of their lives. Interpreters assist communication in people's everyday affairs, and while they may feel that they can leave these situations behind and go home, the same is not true for the consumers whose situation it is. These consumers will be affected by the communication (in a very profound way, the *interpreter's* communication) and by the results and consequences of the communication. Once again, respect for consumers and their interaction is in order.

6.3 Intercultural relationships between consumers

Should the interpreter provide cultural adjustments in the interpretation, which do have an effect on the target text? Most often, yes. Adjusting for cultural considerations is just what is needed for both participants to interact successfully. This reduces the need (perceived or real) for interpreters to attempt to educate participants about each other's cultures. Mindess states that "*exposure to another culture does not automatically lead to mutual understanding*" (1999: 181, italics hers). Interpreters cannot assume that because there are Deaf people within the wider community that others will learn their culture or vice versa. Most of the time participants in an interpreted situation are interested solely in the business at hand, not in an intercultural experience. This in fact might be why they hired an interpreter: the interpretation expert is there to make the interaction go smoothly, even in the face of cultural differences. When one individual does appear interested in learning about another's culture, it might be best left up to that person to seek that knowledge, thus leaving the interpreter in her role and reducing opportunities for her to take control of this education process. If interpreters learn as much as possible about the language pairs and the community and cultures they work in and stick to what they are good at – providing access to communication – this allows for the participants to teach the aspects of culture they wish to share, and to determine if and when there is an appropriate time to do it.[16]

7.   Participation in the community and the development of trust

7.1 The Deaf community

Deaf people have long suggested that interpreters' involvement in the community is important. If interpreters are expected to be in the position of taking information, whether it be of a personal nature or not, and conveying it to another person, then a relationship of trust must be developed and maintained. It could be that the reason the community at one time accepted "helpers" to interpret for them was because these were people involved in the community. They were supportive of community values and were people the Deaf community trusted. Years ago, interpreters were not people who chose it as a career, completed a number of ASL classes, and then entered a post-secondary training program to learn how to interpret such as we see today.[17] People wanting to enter the field now still require extensive involvement in the community. Successful interpreters take the time to maintain that involvement and support throughout their careers.

There are times when it seems awkward to participate in community events, for example when some personal information is known about an individual from an earlier interpreting assignment, but having the skill and fluency to interact in a professional manner can be realized. Information the interpreter has about individuals she meets at public events is protected when she takes care in distinguishing between work environments and personal, after-work community involvement. Boundaries need to be considered and established at the onset of interpreters' careers and then rigorously kept in line with ethical standards along the way.

Once an interpreter has gained the trust of community members, Deaf people's confidence in the interpreter's abilities will grow. As her interpreting skills build, and if she maintains her involvement in the Deaf community, her reputation will also build. Other members of the community too will naturally begin to trust her.

7.2 The interpreting community

While the focus is often on interpreters interacting in the Deaf community, involvement with and interacting in the *interpreting* community can greatly aid the interpreter's work as well. In order to work successfully as a member of a team, it is necessary for interpreters to continually learn and grow. Interpreters' associations at the local and national level offer professional growth opportunities to this end. Teamwork is more effective if some of the learning takes place together and then is applied successfully in teamed situations. Interpreters have a close working relationship with one another and it is ever so clear to Deaf people when their interpreters cannot work cohesively and cooperatively.

While professional organizations as a whole strive to advance standards and working conditions and provide education on the role of the interpreter, it is the members themselves who take on these responsibilities as they work. Affiliating with other members of professional bodies provides interpreters with access to tools to better support their own working conditions and offers continual opportunities for growth as the profession evolves.

While it is important that interpreters develop a relationship of trust in the Deaf community, it is also necessary that they work to develop trust between themselves and their colleagues. In this way colleagues have the sense that the interpreter will uphold her professional standards and ethics and can be counted on when the need arises. Since the profession of interpretation is still very much evolving, trust is a critical factor when colleagues advance new ideas and practices in the field. Furthermore, the actions of one interpreter often set the tone for how future interpreters are perceived and treated at that site, thus interpreters don't just represent their own interests, but those of their colleagues and of the profession as a whole.

8.   The absence of neutrality

Ever since ASL-English interpreters have begun to organize and establish standard practices, they have worked toward providing interpretation whereby the interpreter does not interfere with the messages of the event participants. The principle of an unbiased interpretation delivered by a neutral interpreter is idealistic, but has been written into interpreters' codes of ethics since the mid-1960s. Interpreters have struggled to maintain a neutral stance even though it is often obvious that complete neutrality is not possible. Metzger (1999) calls complete neutrality for the interpreter a myth. She begins her discussion by stating that "[i]n discussions of the issue of interpreter neutrality, the anecdotes that interpreters and laypeople share suggest that the traditional perception of the interpreter's role as a neutral conduit of language is at odds with people's real-life experiences" (Metzger 1999:1).

Interpreters should not, however, throw up their hands and decide that if they can't be neutral then why bother trying. Rather, interpreters must learn about which areas they can minimize their non-neutrality and which they have less control over. Interpreters wield a great deal of power whether they like it or not, and whether they know it or not.

First, interpreters are language specialists who are brought into a situation specifically because of their language abilities. When the person interpreting does not have the language competence required for interpretation she introduces an element of control by only being able to transmit the message at her own level of language ability (and it must be remembered that often this is language use under a great deal of pressure – the message can be delivered rapidly, might be complex, etc.).

Second, the interpreter will either limit the discourse exchange or facilitate it based on her knowledge base. If she can contextualize – pragmatically, culturally, and linguistically – she will have a better chance of success. If her general knowledge base doesn't allow for this, the target message may not convey the intended meaning. Very often an interpretation falls short because the interpreter did not fully comprehend the content and context of the text.

Third, the interpreter's own biases certainly can get in the way. If she is unwilling to let go of these biases, they will inevitably pull the interpreted text toward her own take on the message and away from that of the message sender and intended receiver.

Fourth, interpreters often take charge of logistics, deciding for example where the consumers will sit or when they can speak or sign. Early on Frishberg referred to this through the metaphor of the interpreter as "traffic cop" (Frishberg 1986:28). Some of this is for good reason – if the setting or exchange is not conducive to the interpreter's understanding, the message cannot be apprehended or delivered. Still, the interpreter undeniably affects the interaction on many levels. Even if the message content is conveyed without bias, there are numerous ways the interpreter can impact the "progression of talk" (Wadensjö 1998:193) by virtue of how she manages the logistics of the interaction.

In all these cases the interpreter has exercised some control. Baker-Shenk (1992) suggests that interpreters hold too much power in these regards, and must instead work closely with consumers, and in particular Deaf consumers, to resolve these control issues.

Some issues related to neutrality are less within the interpreter's control. One such issue has to do with linguistic form. Metzger observes that certain grammatical elements available in one language are not necessarily present in a second, so that when the interpreter works between the two, she out of necessity must "alter" the message so that the target text is grammatical. One such example we can suggest is the extensive classifier system in ASL, which is not present in English. As a result, the identity of a referent is often expressed more overtly in ASL than in English. For example in English we might speak of an "object" or "thing" whereas in ASL features of the object's size and shape or its class (tube-like object, a flat surface, a vehicle, etc.) are evident from the required grammatical structure of the construction. Gile (1995) suggests that when analyzing the source message, grammatical effects such as these (and numerous others) must be noted but are not transferred if the target language does not have a grammatical equivalent. Gile classes this as one kind of "Secondary Information" that is not as critical as the "Primary Information" – the intended message itself. Thus, according to these perspectives, the interpreter has no choice but to change the text, the effects of which might be minimal or great. In this case the interpreter is wise to know explicitly what is being changed and the extent of the effect of such change rather than just blundering through. This type of knowledge goes a long way toward minimizing the interpreter's intrusive effect overall.

A second issue beyond the interpreter's control concerns the behaviour of others. Even in circumstances where the interpreter is acting as ethically and as neutrally as possible, some event participants may not act in a cooperative way, may usurp power, or a power imbalance may be part of the social structure surrounding the interaction. An interpreter may feel very much an ally to the Deaf person, but she cannot necessarily equalize power inherent in many social positions. One example is with a teacher-student relationship. Teachers may often give students a lot of leeway, but at times do not or cannot, for example restricting the privileges of students as a consequence of some unacceptable behaviour.[18] In these cases, the interpreter must be fully cognizant of majority-minority cultural relations, social mores and expectations, and the circumstances of the situation. Interpreters may not be able to neutralize such imbalances (but will undoubtedly have biases in one direction or another) but if anything, should take care not to act in ways that increase the differential.

8.1 A consumer-centred vs. interpreter-centred approach

If a person does not like to be at centre stage, being an interpreter working with a signed language is probably not a good idea. Interpreters need to be visible because signed language production must be seen by the audience of signers. Interpreters typically go to great lengths to make sure they are not obstructed from view, and a person needs to be noticed to be appreciated. Sometimes people giving the compliments do not really know what the interpreter is doing technically. Interpreters are often viewed by hearing people as doing a wonderful thing, when these people may not be in a position to judge. Rewards in the field of interpretation are not usually very tangible. Interpreters often feel overworked, underappreciated, and misunderstood. This can lead to a quest for acknowledgement from consumers and behaviours that direct attention to the interpreter rather than to recipients of the interpretation.

It is true that interpreters need certain things in order for their work to proceed smoothly, for example agendas, clarification when the message is not clear to the interpreter, and many more such things, but all too often the event begins to be about the interpretation, rather than about the actual participants. Interpreters may dislike it when it is implied that they should be "invisible" but when communication is successful, when agreements are reached, or when learning has occurred, this is all about those participants and their relationships with each other. It is not about the interpreter. Thus interpreters should be aware of behaviours that focus any attention on them and question honestly whether this behaviour serves to increase their control, or is truly a means to better facilitate others' interaction, thereby not usurping control. In short, behaviours should be consumer-centred and not interpreter-centred.

9. Conclusions

For interpreters working with a signed language, ethical practice is a basic understanding. In this chapter we have attempted not only to show why a strong sense of ethics and professionalism is fundamental, but also, and perhaps more critically, to situate ethics within the realm of cultural and cross-cultural interaction for the interpreter. Most importantly, the onus is on the interpreter herself to learn what the parameters are for ethical and professional practice, and to develop a philosophy of proactive ethical behaviour (cf. Cokely 2000) throughout her career.

In doing so, many facets of ethical and professional practice must be considered. The interpreter is not the centre of the interaction being interpreted, even though some aspects of assignments almost suggest that this is the way it is. It is tempting to think that nothing will take place at all unless mediated by the interpreter's actions and communication. In spite of this, these interactions exist only because others wish to communicate; interpreters are employed because they hold the linguistic key, but the event participants are clearly under the impression that their own interactions are the important thing, and they are right. The interpreter needs to have this in mind at all times. It is a profound respect for all consumers and for their texts and interactions that will ultimately lead to a strong sense of ethics.

Can a sense of ethics be learned? The earliest code of ethical behaviour set down by RID includes as part of its first tenet that the interpreter should be "of high moral character" (Quigley & Youngs 1965:9), which suggests that basically an ethical interpreter brings this quality to the field. Still, understanding the parameters for interpreters' ethical and professional practice will not likely be intuitive and so the budding interpreter must study, must learn from her mentors, and must become very familiar with the ways and expectations of the cultural communities within which she works.

While learning the specifics of Deaf culture, it is beneficial for interpreters to undertake a study of cultures more generally, especially cultural minorities. Courses at local colleges and universities can be taken in cross-cultural studies, linguistics, ethics, problem solving, and business practices. While the courses may cover some broader contexts, interpreters can take pertinent information and apply it to their profession. For information directly related to the field of interpretation, professional development opportunities are offered through local and national interpreting organizations.

Continuous involvement in the Deaf community is the only way to learn how to interact in culturally appropriate ways. The interpreter cannot do this from outside. Involvement in the community will also aid in setting professional boundaries, because this experience will help teach the cognizant interpreter how to interact professionally with community members as well as on a more personal level when that is expected. There are many additional benefits here. Interpreters can learn from Deaf professionals what an appropriate mix of professional and personal interactions entails, and can demonstrate to community members that they understand the boundaries of their role. Thus both study and experience together give the interpreter a well-rounded understanding of cultural norms and expectations. This is especially important for interpreters who are members of the hearing majority because majority-minority imbalances often put relations between the interpreter and Deaf consumer at risk.

Being able to recite a code of ethics might give interpreters some strategies for difficult situations, but much more is required. A thorough understanding of the intent behind ethical principles and how to apply them along with an understanding of the communities in which the interpreter works and interacts will help to guide her behaviours and lessen opportunities for principles to be compromised. The key, we suggest, to ethical success is to view these facets of the interpreter's role from a cultural perspective. Confidentiality, for example, may be valued in each culture, but the interpreter's interactions and behaviour related to maintaining confidentiality must be considered from a cultural norms and expectations perspective too.

Finally, even though the situations interpreters find themselves working in can be highly variable, and judgements often seem completely subjective, there are many strategies that interpreters can learn to apply more generally. While cultural considerations are best learned through interaction in the community, interpreters can also benefit from open dialogue with their colleagues and by seeking out valuable mentoring experiences. Interpreters can track successful progress in their careers through regular reflection on which actions and variables have led to successful outcomes and which may have led to less desirable results. This reflection is critical for interpreters to advance their skills, attitudes and knowledge in their chosen field.

Notes

1. We gratefully acknowledge our colleagues who have inspired us, and with whom we have had opportunities to discuss our ideas on ethics and culture. We appreciate the many comments we have received which have improved this chapter. Thanks to Linda Cundy, Hubert Demers, Randy Dziwenka, Judy McGuirk, Denise Murray, Brenda Nicodemus, Barbara O'Dea, Deb Russell, Barb Shaffer, Angela Stratiy, Leanne Walls, and Rick Zimmer.

2. In the United States, the passing of Public Law 94–142, The Education for All Handicapped Children Act (1975), by which children were granted the right to be educated in their local schools, is often suggested as having a major impact on education for deaf children. Many believe (e.g., Padden & Humphries 1988) that it led to devastating isolation for many deaf children who were not in environments where they could communicate easily with others. A similar effect is found in Canada. Another result, however, has been an exploding need for classroom interpreters.

3. Originally called the National Registry of Professional Interpreters and Translators for the Deaf.

4. Langue des Signes Québécoise (LSQ) is the signed language used by most Deaf people of French Canadian heritage in Quebec and elsewhere; see further details in Boudreault, this volume.

5. Wilcox and Shaffer, this volume, outline a cognitive approach to the principles behind this terminology.

6. AVLIC's Code of Ethics and Guidelines for Professional Conduct are included as Appendix A and can also be found on AVLIC's website at http:www.avlic.ca/ethics.htm. Section titles and excerpts from the AVLIC code are italicized here to set them apart.

7. See Boudreault, this volume, for more on the work of Deaf interpreters.

8. Certainly a number of excellent bicultural interpreters are those hearing interpreters who have grown up in Deaf families, and who are cherished by Deaf communities. Deaf people, however, are the only ones who truly live the Deaf experience.

9. Numerous authors have written about the differences between, and pros and cons of, working freelance or as employees. See in particular Frishberg (1986) for an early discussion of issues, Stewart, Schein and Cartwright (1998) for a more recent account, and Demers (this volume). Fischer (1998) gives details of record keeping and forms that private contractors in the US are required to regularly submit. Many business practices hinge on issues of supply and demand, for example how the interpreter markets herself, stays competitive, and builds her business. For more on this see Stewart et al.'s (1998) chapter on business practices and especially Dean and Pollard (2001).

10. Goods and Services Tax, a charge required by the Canadian government on all such services.

11. The reverse direction is not typically found. ASL does not have a written form, so documents will not be produced in "written" ASL, to be translated into spoken English. It is possible to have a prepared ASL text presented on videotape, which affords the advantage of similar preparation: the entire text can be viewed for meaning, a translation can be thought out beforehand (not memorized), and the interpreter will have more confidence in producing an accurate, cohesive target text.

12. See Janzen, this volume, Chapter 4, for more discussion on these aspects of message transfer.

13. Mindess discusses one area, that of mental health, when it is not so appropriate for the interpreter to engage the Deaf consumer in conversation just before an appointment because of the emotionally sensitive nature of the situation. It seems to us, however, that if normally this is a culturally appropriate behaviour, then at a time when the Deaf person is more vulnerable or uncertain it would be *more* important to behave in a culturally appropriate way with that person. We agree that this is a situation that requires an interpreter to have specialized skills, and perhaps can suggest that enhanced cross-cultural interaction skills should be a part of this set.

14. See Wilcox and Shaffer, this volume, on the role of inferencing in communication and interpretation.

15. Contrary to what might be understood from Lawrence (1995) on so-called "ASL expansions", this discourse process is not language specific. See Janzen and Shaffer (in press) for further discussion.

16. See Mindess (1999), especially Chapter 7 "The Interpreter's Role and Responsibilities", for further discussion on the interpreter's role in intercultural interaction.

17. It is true that early on interpreter education programs had not been established, and interpreting was not deemed something that required allocated funding, etc. In other words, the field had not yet been formalized. Nonetheless, interpretation took place, and the Deaf community had an informal cultural way of encouraging certain people to become interpreters.

18. Numerous types of relationships involving power imbalances could be discussed here, but space does not permit. This is a mammoth and important topic for interpreters to work through, and as a field we have much to learn yet.

19. Ratified July 2000. Reprinted by permission.

References

Baker-Shenk, Charlotte (1986). Characteristics of oppressed and oppressor peoples: Their effect on the interpreting context. In Marina L. McIntire (Ed.), *Interpreting: The Art of Cross-cultural Mediation* (pp. 59–71). Silver Spring, MD: RID Publications.

Baker-Shenk, Charlotte (1992). The interpreter: Machine, advocate, or ally? In Jean Plant-Moeller (Ed.), *Expanding Horizons* (pp. 120–140). Silver Spring, MD: RID Publications.

Bond, Michael Harris, Vladimir Žegarac, & Helen Spencer-Oatey (2000). Culture as an explanatory variable: Problems and possibilities. In Helen Spencer-Oatey (Ed.), *Culturally Speaking: Managing Rapport Through Talk Across Cultures* (pp. 47–71). London and New York: Continuum.

Cokely, Dennis (1992). *Interpretation: A Sociolinguistic Model*. Burtonsville, MD: Linstok Press.

Cokely, Dennis (2000). Exploring ethics: A case for revising the Code of Ethics. *Journal of Interpretation* (RID), 25–57.

Cushner, Kenneth, & Richard W. Brislin (Eds.). (1996). *Intercultural Interactions: A Practical Guide* (2nd ed.). Thousand Oaks, CA: Sage Publications.

Cushner, Kenneth, & Richard W. Brislin (Eds.). (1997). *Improving Intercultural Interactions: Modules for Cross-cultural Training Programs, Volume 2*. Thousand Oaks, CA: Sage Publications.

Dean, Robyn K., & Robert Q. Pollard, Jr. (2001). Application of Demand-Control Theory to sign language interpreting: Implications for stress and interpreter training. *Journal of Deaf Studies and Deaf Education, 6* (1), 1–14.

Fischer, Tammera J. (1998). *Establishing a Freelance Interpretation Business: Professional Guidance for Sign Language Interpreters (2nd ed.)*. Hillsboro, OR: Butte Publications.

Frishberg, Nancy (1986). *Interpreting: An Introduction*. Silver Spring, MD: RID Publications.

Foster, Susan B. (1998). Communication experiences of Deaf people: An ethnographic account. In Ila Parasnis (Ed.), *Cultural and Language Diversity and the Deaf Experience* (pp. 117–135). Cambridge: Cambridge University Press.

Gile, Daniel (1995). *Basic Concepts and Models for Interpreter and Translator Training*. Amsterdam/Philadelphia: John Benjamins.

Groce, Nora Ellen (1985). *Everyone Here Spoke Sign Language: Hereditary Deafness on Martha's Vineyard*. Cambridge, MA: Harvard University Press.

Hatim, Basil, & Ian Mason (1990). *Discourse and the Translator*. London and New York: Longman.

Hoza, Jack (1992). Doing the right thing: Interpreter role and ethics within a bilingual/bicultural model. In Laurie Swabey (Ed.), *The Challenge of the 90's: New Standards in Interpreter Education* (pp. 101–117). Conference of Interpreter Trainers.

Hoza, Jack (2003). Toward an interpreter sensibility: Three levels of ethical analysis and a comprehensive model of ethical decision-making for interpreters. *Journal of Interpretation* (RID), 1–48.

Janzen, Terry, & Barbara Shaffer (in press). Intersubjectivity in interpreted interactions: The interpreter's role in the co-construction of meaning. In Jordan Zlatev, Timothy Racine, Chris Sinha & Esa Iktonen (Eds.), *The Shared Mind: Perspectives on Intersubjectivity*. Amsterdam/Philadelphia: John Benjamins.

Lane, Harlan (1984). *When the Mind Hears: A History of the Deaf*. New York: Random House.

Lawrence, Shelley (1995). Interpreter discourse: English to ASL expansion. In Elizabeth A. Winston (Ed.), *Mapping Our Course: A Collaborative Venture, Proceedings of the Tenth National Covention*, Conference of Interpreter Trainers. October 26–29, 1994. USA: Conference of Interpreter Trainers.

Metzger, Melanie (1999). *Sign Language Interpreting: Deconstructing the Myth of Neutrality*. Washington, DC: Gallaudet University Press.

Mindess, Anna (1999). *Reading Between the Signs: Intercultural Communication for Sign Language Interpreters*. Yarmouth, ME: Intercultural Press.

Padden, Carol A. (1996). From the cultural to the bicultural: The modern Deaf community. In Ila Parasnis (Ed.), *Cultural and Language Diversity and the Deaf Experience* (pp. 79–98). Cambridge: Cambridge University Press.

Padden, Carol, & Tom Humphries (1988). *Deaf in America: Voices from a Culture*. Cambridge, MA: Harvard University Press.

Quigley, Stephen P., & Joseph P. Youngs (1965). *Interpreting for Deaf People*. Washington, DC: U.S. Department of Health, Education, and Welfare.

Registry of Interpreters for the Deaf (1980). *Introduction to Interpreting for Interpreters/ Transliterators, Hearing Impaired Consumers, Hearing Consumers*. Silver Spring, MD: Registry of Interpreters for the Deaf, Inc.

Rosaldo, Renato (1989). *Culture and Truth: The Remaking of Social Analysis*. Boston, MA: Beacon Press.

Roy, Cynthia B. (2000). *Interpreting as a Discourse Process*. New York/Oxford: Oxford University Press.

Russell, Debra L. (2002). *Interpreting in Legal Contexts: Consecutive and Simultaneous Interpretation.* Burtonsville, MD: Linstok Press.

Schweda Nicholson, Nancy (1994). Professional ethics for court and community interpreters. In Deanna L. Hammond (Ed.), *Professional Issues for Translators and Interpreters* (pp. 79–97). Amsterdam/Philadelphia: John Benjamins.

Seleskovitch, Danica (1978). *Interpreting for International Conferences.* Washington, DC: Pen and Booth.

Setton, Robin (1999). *Simultaneous Interpretation: A Cognitive-Pragmatic Analysis.* Amsterdam/Philadelphia: John Benjamins.

Stewart, David A., Jerome D. Schein, & Brenda E. Cartwright (1998). *Sign Language Interpreting: Exploring its Art and Science.* Needham Heights, MA: Allyn and Bacon.

Wadensjö, Cecilia (1998). *Interpreting as Interaction.* London and New York: Longman.

Appendix A: The Association of Visual Language Interpreters' Code of Ethics and Guidelines for Professional Conduct[19]

The purpose of the Code of Ethics is to provide guidance for interpreters, and in doing so, to ensure quality of service for all persons involved. Adherence to the following tenets are essential for maintaining national standards; professional discretion must be exercised at all times.

Association of Visual Language Interpreters of Canada

The Association of Visual Language Interpreters of Canada (AVLIC) expects its members to maintain high standards of professional conduct in their capacity and identity as an interpreter. Members are required to abide by the Code of Ethics and follow the Guidelines for Professional Conduct as a condition of membership in the organization.

This document articulates ethical principles, values, and standards of conduct to guide all members of AVLIC in their pursuit of professional practice. It is intended to provide direction to interpreters for ethical and professional decision-making in their day-to-day work. The Code of Ethics and Guidelines for Professional Conduct is the mechanism by which the public is protected in the delivery of service.

Values Underlying the Code of Ethics & Guidelines for Professional Conduct

AVLIC values:

1. Professional accountability:
Accepting responsibility for professional decisions and actions.

2. Professional competence:
Committing to provide quality professional service throughout one's practice.

3. Non-discrimination:
Approaching professional service with respect and cultural sensitivity.

4. Integrity in professional relationships:
Dealing honestly and fairly with consumers and colleagues.

5. Integrity in business practices:
Dealing honestly and ethically in all business practices.

Members are to understand that each of these core values and accompanying sections are to be considered when making ethical and professional decisions in their capacity and identity as an interpreter. These values are of equal weight and importance.

Code of Ethics and Guidelines for Professional Conduct
1.0. Professional Accountability:
Interpreters accept responsibility for all professional decisions made and actions taken.

1.1. *Confidentiality*

1.1.1. Members will respect the privacy of consumers and hold in confidence all information obtained in the course of professional service. Members may be released from this obligation only with their consumers' authorization or when ordered by law.

1.1.2. Where necessary, a member may exchange pertinent information with a colleague in order to provide consistent quality of service. This will be done in a manner that protects the information and the consumers.

1.1.3. Members need to be aware that other professional codes of conduct may impact upon their work. In such circumstances, members will make appropriate professional decisions and conduct themselves in a manner befitting the setting and the profession.

1.2. *Professional Conduct*

1.2.1. Members will hold the needs of consumers primary when making professional decisions.

1.2.2. Members shall recognize that all work undertaken by them on an individual basis, whether pro bono or paid, will ultimately reflect the integrity of themselves and of the profession.

1.2.3. Members shall conduct themselves in a professional manner at all times. They shall not badger or coerce individuals or agencies to use their professional service.

1.2.4. Members shall take into account the limitations of their abilities, knowledge and the resources available to them prior to accepting work. They will remove themselves from a given setting when they realize an inability to provide professional service.

1.2.5. Members must be aware of personal circumstances or conflict of interest that might interfere with their effectiveness. They will refrain from conduct that can lead to substandard performance and/or harm to anyone including themselves and consumers.

1.2.6. Members are accountable to AVLIC and to their local chapter affiliate for their professional and ethical conduct. Further, members are responsible to discuss and resolve, in a professional manner, issues arising from breaches of ethical or professional conduct on the part of individual colleagues after they are observed. In the case where these breaches are potentially harmful to others or chronic, and attempts to resolve the issue have not been successful, such conduct should be reported to AVLIC and/or their local chapter affiliate in a manner directed by the appropriate grievance procedure.

1.3. *Scope of Practice*

1.3.1. Members will refrain from using their professional role to perform other functions that lie beyond the scope of an interpreting assignment and the parameters of their professional duties. They will not counsel, advise, or interject personal opinions.

1.3.2. When functioning as part of a professional team (e.g., education, legal, medical and mental health settings) it is understood that members will limit their expertise to interpretation. In such settings, it may be appropriate for members to comment on the overall effectiveness of communication, the interpreting process and to suggest appropriate resources and referrals. This should be done only within the context of the professional team.

1.3.3. Members will refrain from manipulating work situations for personal benefit or gain. When working as independent contractors, members may promote their professional services within the scope of their practice. When working under the auspices of an agency or other employer, it is not ethical for the members to promote their professional services independent of the agency or employer.

1.4. *Integrity of Service*

Members will demonstrate sound professional judgement and accept responsibility for their decisions. Members will make every attempt to avoid situations that constitute a real or perceived conflict of interest. Members will ensure there is full disclosure to all parties should their ancillary interest be seen as a real or perceived conflict of interest.

2.0. Professional Competence:

Interpreters provide the highest possible quality service through all aspects of their professional practice.

2.1. *Qualifications to Practice*

Members will possess the knowledge and skills to support accurate and appropriate interpretation. It is recognized that members work in a range of settings and with a variety of consumers. This demands that members be adept at meeting the linguistic needs of consumers, the cultural dynamics of each situation, and the spirit and content of the discourse.

2.2. *Faithfulness of Interpretation*

Every interpretation shall be faithful to and render exactly the message of the source text. A faithful interpretation should not be confused with a literal interpretation. The fidelity of an interpretation includes an adaptation to make the form, the tone, and the deeper meaning of the source text felt in the target language and culture.

2.3. *Accountability for Professional Competence*

2.3.1. Members will accept full responsibility for the quality of their own work and will refrain from making inaccurate statements regarding their competence, education, experience or certification.

2.3.2. Members are responsible for properly preparing themselves for the work contracted.

2.3.3. Members will accept contracts for work only after determining they have the appropriate qualifications and can remain neutral throughout the assignment.

2.4. *Ongoing Professional Development*

2.4.1. Members will incorporate current theoretical and applied knowledge, enhance that knowledge through continuing education throughout their professional careers and will strive for AVLIC certification.

2.4.2. Members will aim to be self-directed learners, pursuing educational opportunities which are relevant to their professional practice. This could include but is not limited to peer review, collegial consultation, mentoring and regular feedback regarding specific areas of skill development.

3.0. Non-discrimination:

Interpreters approach professional services with respect and cultural sensitivity towards all participants.

3.1. *Non-discrimination*

Members will respect the individuality, the right to self-determination, and the autonomy of the people with whom they work. They will not discriminate based on ethnicity, gender, age, disability, sexual orientation, religion, personal beliefs and practices, social status or any other factor.

3.2. *Communication Preferences*
Members will respect and use the form of communication preferred by those deaf and hard of hearing consumers for whom they provide service.

3.3. *Deaf Interpreters*
The services of a Deaf interpreter may be required when working with individuals who use regional sign dialects, non-standard signs, foreign sign languages, and those with emerging language use. They may also be used with individuals who have disabling conditions that impact on communication. Members will recognize the need for a Deaf interpreter and will ensure their inclusion as a part of the professional interpreting team.

4.0. Integrity in Professional Relationships:
Interpreters deal honestly and fairly with consumers and colleagues while establishing and maintaining professional boundaries.

4.1. *Professional Relationships*
Members shall understand the difference between professional and social interactions. They will establish and maintain appropriate boundaries between themselves and consumers. Members will assume responsibility to ensure relationships with all parties involved are reasonable, fair and professional.

4.2. *Impartiality*
4.2.1. Members shall remain neutral, impartial, and objective. They will refrain from altering a message for political, religious, moral, or philosophical reasons, or any other biased or subjective consideration.

4.2.2. Should a member not be able to put aside personal biases or reactions which threaten impartiality, the member will examine options available to them. This may include not accepting the work or withdrawing their services from the assignment or contract.

4.3. *Respect for Colleagues*
4.3.1. Members will act toward colleagues in a spirit of mutual cooperation, treating and portraying them to others with respect, courtesy, fairness and good faith. Members are encouraged to share their knowledge with their colleagues in a spirit of mutual assistance.

4.3.2. Members have a professional obligation to assist and encourage new interpreting practitioners in the profession.

4.3.3. Members shall not abuse the good faith of other members or be guilty of a breach of trust or the use of unfair tactics.

4.4. *Support for Professional Associations*
Members shall support AVLIC, its affiliates, and other organizations representing the profession and the Deaf community.

5.0 Integrity in Business Relationships:
Interpreters establish and maintain professional boundaries with consumers and colleagues in a manner that is honest and fair.

5.1. *Business Practices*

5.1.1. Members will refrain from any unfair competition with their colleagues, including but not limited to: (a) engaging in comparative advertising; (b) wilfully undercutting; or (c) artificially inflating fees during times when market demand exceeds supply.

5.1.2. Members will conduct themselves in all phases of the interpreting situation in a manner befitting the profession, including negotiating work and contracts, obtaining suitable preparation material, and choice of attire and professional demeanor.

5.1.3. Members will honour professional commitments made when accepting work, and will follow through on their obligations. Members may not unilaterally terminate work or a contract unless they have fair and reasonable grounds to do so.

5.1.4. Members shall take reasonable care of material and/or property given to them by a consumer and may not lend such or use it for purposes other than those for which it was entrusted to them.

5.2. *Accurate Representation of Credentials*

5.2.1. Members shall not by any means engage in, nor allow the use of, statements that are false, misleading, incomplete, or likely to mislead consumers or members of the public.

5.2.2. Members will refrain from making inaccurate statements regarding their competence, education, experience or certification. Only members certified by AVLIC (COI) or RID (CI/CT or CSC) may use the term "certified" in printed, electronic, signed or oral transmission. This may include, but is not limited to, interpreter directories, business cards and forms, promotional materials, resumes or publications they have authored.

5.3. *Reimbursement for Services*

5.3.1. Members will bill only for services provided. Members will negotiate fees, including cancellation policies, preferably in writing or contract form before service is provided. Members will be sensitive to professional and community norms when establishing fees for services.

5.3.2. Members may also provide bartered or pro bono service in situations where the profession of interpreting and the livelihood of other practitioners will not be threatened.

PART III

Interpretation in practice

CHAPTER 8

The working interpreter

Hubert Demers
Red River College

1. Introduction[1]

In this chapter we observe the ASL-English interpreter at work. There are numerous factors to be considered if the interpreter is to do her job well. Here we will discuss the interpreter's work and some of the factors which are fundamental to her success. The chapter begins with a description of the interpreter's work, in particular the task of interpreting, who the interpreter interprets for, and the types of employment interpreters find. Interpreters wish to be considered as professionals, which brings with it some expectations both on the part of interpreters themselves and on the part of consumers of interpreting services. Interpreters find themselves included in various kinds of professional teams, and so must interact with other professionals. These factors are presented along with a general discussion of a number of skills that an interpreter requires other than those related to language use.

Following this I discuss eight steps the interpreter must undertake to interpret successfully. These steps are repeated for each and every interaction and through this cyclic process the interpreter hones her skills. The final discussion of the chapter concerns the balance of prediction skills and the time it takes to prepare for successful work. How an interpreter who is new to the profession deals with these factors will be different from how a more experienced interpreter is able to, and so we conclude with the understanding that the steps to successful interpretation, over time, not only form a structured approach to success in individual assignments, but also provide a template for professional development.

2. What ASL-English interpreters do

Interpreters work in a great variety of situations across a great variety of settings, and with a great variety of people. Any time there is an interpreter involved, there are at least two people or groups of people who wish to interact, but who do not speak the same language or share the same culture. In her introductory remarks on interpreting, Seleskovitch (1978) reminds us that this has likely been the case for a very long time: "Since man has existed, and since he has used language, he has made use of intermediaries in order to communicate from one language to another. We could say that interpretation has always existed" (Seleskovitch 1978:2).

American Sign Language (ASL)-English interpreters facilitate interactions between Deaf and non-deaf, or "hearing", people. These two groups of people use different languages and have different cultural backgrounds. In interactions where an ASL-English interpreter is present, there is at least one person who does not communicate by speaking English directly with the hearing person but rather, prefers to communicate through an interpreter. Equally, we can consider that in such interactions there is at least one non-deaf person who does not communicate by using ASL directly with the Deaf person and therefore also prefers to communicate through the interpreter. When people from these two groups interact, the interpreter is responsible for more than just facilitating the communication that takes place, she is responsible for facilitating the entirety of the participants' unique interaction in a way that neither enhances nor detracts from the participants' interaction experience.

A successful interpreter is one who conducts herself in a manner that acknowledges the humanity of those for whom she interprets (Cokely 2000). She recognizes that the interaction belongs to other participants in the event and she is able to adequately facilitate that interaction without inadvertently or purposefully imposing upon it. The presence of the interpreter cannot go so far as to make the experience similar to one where both participants are either Deaf or hearing; in other words, she cannot remove the linguistic and cultural differences that each brings to the interaction. If the interpreting goes well, it enables the participants' interaction to play out "as it should".

3.   The disparateness of consumers

ASL-English interpreters work with a broad range of hearing people and with people in the Deaf community who are culturally Deaf, as well as others who do not fully share this Deaf experience but who are audiologically deaf, hard-of-hearing, late-deafened, or Deaf-blind. For each of these groups of individuals, communication styles reflect a diverse linguistic spectrum. The term "ASL-English interpreter" is used here to refer to the interpreter who works with any of these individuals, with the understanding that she must develop linguistic skills to manage all of these communication styles and preferences (see Malcolm, this volume, for discussion of contact varieties of signed language that are included in this spectrum along with further references).

3.1 Treating consumers as individuals

Deaf, deaf, hard-of-hearing, late-deafened and Deaf-blind people all have differing life experiences and have been exposed to diverse educational philosophies and corresponding programs during their school years. Depending on these experiences and their impact on the person, the language choice of the individual may be the signed language of the Deaf community, the spoken language of the hearing majority, or some form of contact signing that combines elements of both ASL and English to a greater or lesser degree (Lucas & Valli 1992).

The interpreter must always consider that language use will vary individual by individual, and situation by situation. A single individual when interacting in different situations with others, may make use of a range of language styles (Ferguson 1994). This idea applies equally to those who have English, ASL, or a contact variety of a signed language as their primary language means. The wide linguistic spectrum that ASL-English interpreters encounter demands a vast linguistic competence so as to ensure that they can competently and ethically meet the linguistic requirements when interpreting, and so facilitate the myriad unique interactions in which they are involved. Regarding this language diversity in the Deaf community and interpreters, Lucas and Valli have this to say: "What is the best way to provide interpreters access to the complexity and diversity of language use in the American Deaf community, access they need both for assessing the situation and for interpreting? It seems that bilingualism in ASL and English will provide access to the full range" (Lucas & Valli 1992: 123).[2]

Interpreters, and particularly interpreters new to the profession, tend to focus on their responsibilities to, and relationship with, the Deaf person to the possible exclusion of their responsibilities to the hearing person. ASL-English interpreters may mistakenly think that they only interpret for Deaf people, when in reality each and every interpreted interaction requires at least two participants whose language use or preference is sufficiently different so as to need interpretation. It is interesting to note though that the interpreters in Roy's (1989, 2000) and Metzger's (1999) studies demonstrated differential treatment of Deaf and hearing interactants. In Roy's study, when overlapping discourse occurred, the interpreter consistently stopped the Deaf person but not the hearing person. Metzger found that seventy-five percent of the time the interpreter's nonrenditions (self-initiated comments or requests for clarification) were directed to the Deaf person and signed only, thus were not accessible to the hearing person. Interpreters must remember that they facilitate interactions equally for two groups of consumers. Nonetheless, competent interpreting can play a role in Deaf people enabling themselves to interact with members of the larger hearing community with more equality. When interpreters wish to have this as a goal, they must guard against developing attitudes and behaviours that are oppressive in nature (Baker-Shenk 1986, 1992). For both consumer groups, an interpreter's attitude reflects her level of professionalism, but for the Deaf community in particular, a "good attitude" is a vital quality for an interpreter to possess because it demonstrates respect for their language and culture.

4. Where interpreters work

Many Deaf and hearing people communicate with each other (with varying degrees of success) in numerous activities throughout their daily lives without any involvement of interpreters. It is often the case, however, either because of communication challenges or as a matter of convenience, that interpreters are introduced into these interactions. As a result, interpreters often find themselves in a wide range of situations on a daily basis in every type of situation imaginable. Interpreters work anywhere and everywhere. In what follows, I approach the interpreter's work by focusing on employment options the interpreter has available to her rather than the vast array of settings she might find herself working in. For discussion of these many settings, the reader is directed to works such as Frishberg (1990), Humphrey and Alcorn (2001), and Stewart, Schein, and Cartwright (1998).

4.1 Types of employment

Interpreters are typically employed in one of two ways: they are either self-employed on a freelance basis as private contactors or they work as employees of educational institutions, interpreter or service agencies, or companies. Some interpreters are employed in both ways.

The benefits and challenges that an interpreter experiences as an individual who freelances her skills are similar to those experienced by any entrepreneur in that there is no guarantee of the volume or kind of work that is available. It is thus good business practice on the part of the interpreter to consider trends in the market at any given time in her locale. When an interpreter freelances her skills, there is the benefit of greater autonomy in establishing her schedule and selecting the kind of work that is accepted than there may be for an interpreter who works as an employee for someone else. When multiple work opportunities present themselves, the freelance interpreter's autonomy enables her to select the work that falls within, or perhaps mildly stretches, her comfort zone; that is, she can select work in which she is most likely to experience success. She can also select work that she finds manageable in her professional and personal schedules and that matches her professional goals. Interpreting that is commonly provided by self-employed interpreters may be referred to as "community interpreting" which may include medical, employment, legal, religious, mental health, recreational, educational, performing arts, and the vast array of meeting situations that can range from one-on-one meetings to large group gatherings for purposes such as seminars and conferences. Some freelance interpreters frequently provide "conference interpreting" services where they work with various professional, academic, or special interest organizations, interpreting meetings and symposiums where new information is presented and discussed or debated (cf. Seleskovitch 1978). Quite often, a freelance interpreter chooses a mix of settings and types of interpreting, although some are able to specialize in one area to a certain degree. Individual contracts may last from an hour or two to several weeks or months. At times, or in locales where work is not abundant, the freelance interpreter may not feel that she has a high degree of freedom to choose her contracts, but rather, feels that she must take whatever work is available. For more on the business practices of freelance interpreters see Fischer (1998) and Humphreys (2004).

When an interpreter takes work as an employee of an institution, interpreter or service agency, or a company, she will likely find she does not have the same level of autonomy as a freelance interpreter although this may be countered by the guarantee of job security and a steady income. For many interpreters, being an employee has the advantage of leaving day to day business dealings – marketing the service, handling booking details, collecting payment, and so forth – in the hands of someone else. On the other hand, many interpreters who are employees may feel that they have less control in selecting assignments and being able to do the kind of work they would like to do. For example, while agency interpreters are also frequently engaged in community interpreting, they may wish to specialize in one or two areas but are prevented from this because of the range of requests for interpreters the agency receives. It is some interpreters' experience, however, that once they gain a good deal of experience and skills in a particular area, they find they are requested more often for work in that area of interest. As an employee, there may be occasions when the interpreter believes that ethically she is not qualified to facilitate a given interaction even though the employer feels obligated to provide service. In situations such as these, it is important for the interpreter to articulately justify her concerns to her employer while also exploring the employer's perspective. Though not always the case, the interpreter is fortunate when the employer understands her ethical concerns and is willing to consider alternatives such as re-arranging another employee's schedule so that she may take the assignment in question or hire a private contractor to provide the service.

Interpreters who are employed by educational institutions work in the kinder-garten to grade twelve (K-12) setting at the elementary and secondary level or at colleges and universities at the post-secondary level. An interpreter working in a K-12 setting is typically paired with a single student and is often the only interpreter em-ployed by that school. There are, however, K-12 programs where a small group of Deaf students are integrated at one school which then employs more than one interpreter in order to satisfy the program's requirements. Given that each of the Deaf students might be in a different classroom and that program structure and size vary, the num-ber of interpreters employed will differ accordingly. Even though interpreters in these programs typically work in different classrooms, because there is more than one inter-preter on site there is more of a likelihood that they are able to work in teams from time to time. When there is more than one interpreter on site, there is the added benefit of having a colleague close at hand with whom to debrief and network. Some schools for the Deaf employ their own interpreters (see Conrad and Stegenga, this volume, for further details on working in educational settings).

Post-secondary institutions often employ more than one interpreter, although in these settings, the number of interpreters is dependent on student enrolment and other specific circumstances. Given the nature of post-secondary education, interpreters may be employed on a part-time or contractual basis by the institution and also work in the community. Interpreters employed by these institutions experience the benefit of having colleagues close at hand with whom they can debrief and network and with whom they may at times work in teams. Because post-secondary institutions are often large and have a diversity of programs, it is common for the college or university to have an office that coordinates the scheduling and activities of interpreters. This office may also act as a resource centre for the interpreters, procuring and housing textbooks and other materials interpreters will need for the courses they interpret during any given term.

The benefits of having colleagues close at hand with whom they can work and network is also the case for interpreters employed by agencies that are large enough to require more than one interpreter on staff. Agencies that employ interpreters typically provide a range of services for Deaf clientele, such as counselling and employment services. The Canadian Hearing Society (CHS) in Ontario is the largest organization of this kind in Canada but other provinces have similar organizations. Deaf and Hard of Hearing Services (DHHS) in Calgary, Alberta, and Saskatchewan Deaf and Hard of Hearing Services with offices in both Saskatoon and Regina are two examples. As a result of services provided by the agency there are often interactions that take place either between members of the staff and their Deaf clients or between these clients and personnel at appointments they attend at other sites, such as job interviews, social service appointments, and so forth. The interpreters employed at the agency are responsible for interpreting these interactions as well as the interactions and events that occur in the community at large. The Western Institute for the Deaf and Hard of Hearing, with its head office in Vancouver, British Columbia, has a specialized service that provides interpreters specifically for medical interactions. An agency that does not provide services other than interpreting in the community is the E-Quality Communication Centre of Excellence (ECCOE), formerly known as the Independent Interpreter Referral Service, which has been operating in Winnipeg, Manitoba, since 1982. ECCOE now provides spoken language interpretation and translation and intervention services for Deaf-blind people in addition to ASL-English interpretation.

Besides educational settings and interpreter agencies, there are companies that consider it feasible to employ their own interpreter; however, most choose to retain interpreters on a contractual basis. Depending on the circumstances, such companies may choose to contract through an agency or directly with a freelance interpreter.

The employment arrangement that an interpreter chooses, either freelance or employee or a combination of the two, and the kind of work, whether educational, agency or for a company, often comes down to the interpreter finding employment that most suits her preferences and circumstances at the time. An interpreter may opt to work part-time, and thus look for an employment opportunity that suits this preference. One benefit of being in a profession that encompasses such a variety of employment options is that an interpreter may move between types of work as she moves along a career path, and as her life circumstances allow.

5.   Expectations of a professional

ASL-English interpreters are professionals who provide a service. Like other professionals, for example doctors, lawyers or mechanics, it is reasonable to believe that consumers have expectations with regard to the quality of service provided. As trained professionals, interpreters understand that ethical conduct is the cornerstone of the entire profession and is the foundation of their professional behaviour. Deaf and hearing consumers expect a certain level of interpreting competence, professional behaviour and ethical conduct from every ASL-English interpreter. The professionalism exhibited by an interpreter toward consumers enables these consumers to focus on their interaction and all that it entails without being distracted by undue attention on the interpreter or her needs. Interpreters must maintain their professionalism at all times so as to merit the trust of those who depend upon them for competent and comfortable interpreting. As such, interpreters must remember that they are responsible to all participants in the interaction and ensure that they respect each one of them.

Professionalism on the part of the interpreter contributes to consumers empowering themselves and being able to conduct their interactions with more confidence. The interpreter's professionalism, measured by a high level of competence, professional behaviour and ethical conduct, in fact, benefits both the consumer and interpreter. The consumer receives interpreting that she can be confident in from an interpreter she can trust, and the interpreter establishes a reputation that leads to her being much sought after. Furthermore, by being a member of a national professional organization, for example the Association of Visual Language Interpreters of Canada (AVLIC), the interpreter provides consumers with a formal avenue to express any potential dissatisfaction; she thus demonstrates professional humility by offering both her most professional work and a mechanism for scrutiny. Members of AVLIC agree to adhere to a far-reaching Code of Ethics and Guidelines for Professional Conduct, and are subject to a formalized Dispute Resolution Process.[3] As an AVLIC member, the interpreter acknowledges that her professionalism reflects on all interpreters, and in turn, accepts responsibility for being a representative of all ASL-English interpreters.[4]

6.   The interpreter as a team member

Interpreters frequently work alone but there may be opportunities to work as a member of a team. Interpreters can be part of two types of teams: interpreting teams or inter-disciplinary teams. Interpreting teams of two or more interpreters occur for a variety of reasons and are commonly formed for conferences and seminars that continue over an extended period of time. The teams may consist of ASL-English interpreters, a combination of hearing and Deaf interpreters, or for national level events that occur in bilingual countries such as Canada, sets of ASL-English and LSQ-French interpreters.[5] In addition to assignments that extend over a period of time, a professional interpreting team may work together in any setting because of the complexity of the interaction, the density of the information, or the sensitive nature of the assignment. Members of the team interpret in rotation, with the team member not actively interpreting typically remaining available to provide backup support, locate documents or relevant passages in the documentation being used in the interaction, and so forth. Primarily, working in teams prevents the deleterious effects of fatigue on the work. Though some research has shown that an interpreting team does not always monitor the interaction, communicate well within the team, or provide effective support (Russell 2002, this volume), a conscientious and competent interpreting team better ensures that the interpretation of the message is accurate and that the interaction is facilitated well.

The second type of team that an interpreter can become involved with is the inter-disciplinary team. This team is made up of the different professionals who come together for case advisement or to discuss issues in the setting. Two examples of situations where inter-disciplinary teams may be found are the K-12 educational setting and the mental health setting. In an educational setting, the inter-disciplinary team may discuss student progress and planning regarding an IEP (Individualized Education Plan). Ideally, a knowledgeable Deaf person should be involved on all inter-disciplinary teams to provide linguistic and cultural information; however, this ideal is not always realized. If the interpreter is the only knowledgeable person on the team regarding bilingual and bicultural issues affecting the interaction, she should be prepared to contribute to the team by providing information about how the situation might be addressed as well as information about external resources. This means that she must have the skills and knowledge to understand what is taking place in the interpreted interaction regarding communication issues, the ability to communicate these concerns to the team, knowledge of other resources, and the professional wherewithal to remain within the boundaries of her role and expertise as interpreter. Other team members are often also consumers of the interpreter's services in the setting.[6]

In terms of being a member of an inter-disciplinary therapy team in mental health settings, the interpreter works closely with the mental health service providers in an effort to ensure that they are educated about any linguistic or cultural issues that may be affecting the therapeutic interaction or the interpreter's ability to successfully interpret for the client or patient and the other members of the team. Once again the interpreter must be cognizant of the boundaries of her role in the team as well as her professional obligations to her consumers.

7.   The skills of the interpreter

Interpreters must have exceptional bilingual fluency and bicultural knowledge if they are to undertake the task of interpreting which requires that discourse information be conveyed cross-linguistically and cross-culturally (Mindess 1999), especially considering that the work is frequently complex and fast-paced. However, advanced language skills and cultural knowledge are not all that are required of a proficient interpreter. An interpreter must have many additional skills and abilities to be successful. She is a service provider who interacts with many people on a daily basis and so must possess excellent interpersonal skills (see, for example, Solow 2000); she must be both personable and professional. She is also at times required to negotiate with consumers for permission to access documents which normally would not be distributed except to a select few, or negotiate the most appropriate location in the environment to be positioned. Thus she must also be a consummate negotiator. As well, an interpreter must be able to quickly ascertain relationships: how people relate to each other, how specific bits of information relate to a topic and how each of these relates to the interaction, for example. She must be able to anticipate the manner in which variables might affect the interaction and the relationships among the participants. The interpreter must also possess keen logic, in other words, refined problem-solving skills, in order to process the many factors that often constitute complex interactions. This skill enables the interpreter to judiciously select her words or text construction,[7] or to sift through the many possible consequences of an action, for example, so as to determine the most ethical and most professional decision to make. The skill of using logic in conjunction with that of ascertaining dynamic relationships needs to, and does, become so highly developed in the interpreter that she is often able to predict with a high degree of accuracy what will transpire in a given interaction. Because she is able to anticipate in this manner, she is better prepared to respond with appropriate strategies while interpreting. These are undoubtedly only some of the skills an interpreter requires. For additional discussion of interpreters' skills, see for example Frishberg (1990), Solow (2000), and for educational settings in particular, Seal (1998).

The interpreter acquires and develops the required skills first by enrolling in an interpreter education program, and following graduation, by actively engaging in her day to day work. The process that leads to interpreting mastery is an eight step process, described in Section 8 below. Through following these steps, some of which are cyclical, the interpreter continually increases her extralinguistic knowledge (Gile 1995) and her linguistic competence, refines her ability to predict what is likely to occur during interactions, and hones her professionalism. As an interpreter moves through her career, she has the compounding benefit of completing these steps numerous times.

8.   The eight steps of successful interpreting

What follows is a discussion of eight steps that guide the interpreter toward success. Each of the steps is encountered for every interaction that an interpreter facilitates and the diligence exercised during each affects the interpreter's ability to thoroughly complete the subsequent steps. There is a cyclic nature to the interpreter's progression through these eight steps in that she will sometimes need to re-consider previously gathered information and re-frame her understanding of certain issues as she con-

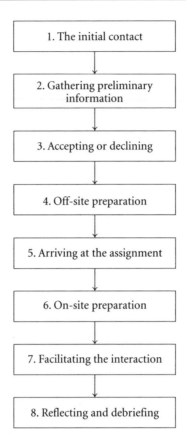

Figure 1. Eight steps of successful interpreting.

tinues toward successful interpretation. The eight steps are shown in Figure 1, and explained in Sections 8.1 to 8.8 below.

8.1 Step one: The initial contact

The first step marks the beginning of the interpreter's progression. Each time the interpreter is initially contacted with a request to interpret an interaction she begins this progression anew. The moment an interpreter is contacted, before she is even able to determine whether or not she will accept the assignment, she must respond with the utmost professionalism. Old adages become old adages because there is inherent wisdom in them. The adage "you only get to make a first impression once" is especially true in this case. Often, the first impression that an interpreter makes occurs long before she arrives at the assignment; the first impression is created with the initial contact, whether in person or by telephone, or in responding to voice mail, a text message, or a fax. This underscores the importance of remembering that one is viewed as a professional at all times. The interpreter does not always know when she is making an impression on someone and should therefore be cognizant of her conduct at every turn. When contacted, the interpreter is obligated to make a professional determination of her availability and an ethical assessment of her ability to competently facilitate the interaction for which she is being requested. Needing to ask for only minimal confidential information – the nature of the assignment along with the date, time, duration and approximate location – the interpreter should have sufficient information to determine her availability and potential suitability, and thus know whether or not to continue on to step two.

8.2 Step two: Gathering preliminary information

Having determined she is available, the interpreter will need to gather additional preliminary information so as to more accurately assess the level of knowledge of the topic, level of language fluency for this topic and the professional skills likely to be required, and thereby make an ethical determination of her ability to successfully facilitate the interaction. In order to make an honest determination, she will have to ask some additional questions of the person contacting her.

Usually, the person initiating the contact is someone knowledgeable about the circumstances of the interaction and is therefore able to answer the interpreter's questions. On some occasions, however, this person does not know much about the situation and is responsible only for securing the services of an interpreter. When this is the case, the interpreter may need to contact someone else who can provide detailed information.

The interpreter best begins by inquiring as to what the interpretation setting is, if this has not already been made clear. Settings are the broad categories used to label the various fields in which interpreters work. Some examples of settings are medical, employment, legal, religious, mental health, recreational, educational, performing arts, meetings and conferences. Each setting has some prototypical characteristics that assist the interpreter in knowing what the situation is likely to entail, what the purpose for the consumers' interaction is likely to be, and what the consequences of poor interpreting could be. For example, in a prototypical education setting an "educator" and several "learners" are gathered in one room. One person's goal, or purpose for interacting, is to teach while the other participants' goal is to learn. The consequence of poor interpreting is that the learners do not learn what is required and, as a result, "fail" to acquire information. Certainly there are many variations with regard to number of interaction participants, motivations or purposes for interacting, environments in which the education occurs, as well as the consequences of poor interpreting. However, the interpreter will have a broad mental schema for a given setting based on its most prototypical characteristics. Such schemas are formed by her experiences of interactions in these settings. At this point in the eight step process, the interpreter accesses her schema of the relevant setting to ask questions to further determine what the specific interaction may entail.

As an interpreter proceeds through her career, she gains experience and further develops her understanding of, or schemas for, interactions and the variation that can occur within them. The more experience an interpreter has, the more developed her schemas for interactions become, and the greater her knowledge is of the differences that exist in subtle variations within each setting. By eliciting further details about the specific assignment she is about to undertake, the interpreter is able to make use of a more refined mental schema for what the interaction is likely to entail, thereby giving even more focus to her subsequent questions. Continued questioning, in turn, allows her to access a more and more refined schema. This process allows the interpreter to make logical inferences as to what might occur in the pending interaction with regard to the purpose and potential dynamics. She can consider in a more refined way the knowledge of the topic she possesses or may need, terminology she is likely to encounter, and professional and ethical decisions she may need to make concerning the situation.

The purpose of asking questions to gain preliminary information is to find out as much as possible about the situation and so to more correctly determine what to expect, and what is needed of the interpreter. In the beginning, if all she knows is that it is a "medical appointment", she will only be able to make use of a very generalized schema for that circumstance which is not enough to make reasonable predictions. The range of possibilities must be narrowed. For example, if the interpreter is being requested to interpret in a "medical setting" she is aided by further finding out that it will be a "doctor's appointment" because she can evoke a schema she has for that more specific setting. But this still is not sufficient, because the scope of possible interactions that occur in a doctor's office is very broad, ranging from the very simple to the very complicated and emotional. The interpreter will be in a much better position to predict what might occur during the interaction if she learns whether a patient is having her blood pressure checked or if she is going to see her doctor to receive the results of recent cancer tests.

Thus the interpreter is able to narrow the range of interaction possibilities. The schema she now has for the more specific situation, arrived at through the series of questions she has asked and from information that has been volunteered, allows her to predict as accurately as she can what might take place. Of course, she can never be certain how the interaction will play out, and so must be prepared for a number of possibilities. She must strike a balance between reasonable predictions and being prepared for the unexpected.

The more complete the interpreter's schema is for a given situation, the more accurately she can predict what the interaction might encompass, and thus the more focus she is able to give to her questions. For interpreters who are just entering the profession, the schemas they have for various situation types are limited to their own life experiences and what they have been able to experience in the practical component of their education program rather than built up from actual interpreting experiences. Near the beginning of an interpreter's career, when she has little experience, there is a good chance that the schemas she has for many different situations are still relatively undefined. As a result, much is unknown and she might be fairly uncertain as to what she should ask. Dealing with the unknown can easily lead to feelings of anxiety and discomfort. But with more experience, the interpreter's schemas become more complete and she is better able to direct questions to the correct person and will more quickly be able to anticipate what she might encounter. These facts are discussed in section 9 below in more detail.

8.3 Step three: Accepting or declining

By gathering preliminary information as described in step two, the interpreter can compare what she believes will be the necessary knowledge, language and professional skills to complete the assignment successfully with those that she possesses, and thus determine her ability to competently facilitate the interaction for which she is being requested.

If by chance the interpreter has been unable to contact anyone who knows detailed information about the interaction, she will likely have very little information with which to make the decision of accepting or declining the assignment.

When little information is available, the interpreter is likely left with only a very generalized schema for the situation she is considering. In situations like these, the ability of an inexperienced interpreter to predict her suitability is limited and caution is recommended. On the other hand, when faced with little information, more experienced interpreters have typically developed a set of skills that enables them to be more resourceful.

Repeated experience will tell the interpreter when she has located the most knowledgeable person and has asked enough questions to make this decision without prying for more details than she actually needs for this step. The professional interpreter ethically determines whether or not to take the assignment and at some point, she will accept or decline the work. Once accepted, she can move on to step four.

8.4 Step four: Off-site preparation

Preparation is a critical factor that significantly enhances the likelihood of successfully interpreting an interaction. The need for the interpreter to be prepared for all assignments is great and remains constant throughout her career. Understanding the purpose of the interaction and its dynamics as well as correctly anticipating the information and language requirements allows an interpreter to do the work required to arrive at the site sufficiently prepared. The more accurately an interpreter has predicted what will transpire during the interaction, the more effective her preparation is.

The same information that enabled the interpreter to determine whether or not to accept the assignment is the information that guides the interpreter's preparation. The person who contacted the interpreter is usually a valuable resource for assignment information and may be able to provide documents such as agendas, reports, copies of presentations, training materials and the like which the interpreter can use to learn much about what will probably transpire. By taking advantage of these materials, she can determine what she already knows and has ready access to and becomes aware of what she still needs to learn. Following this, the interpreter must consider how she will go about acquiring the information she still needs that will put her in the best position to succeed.

The knowledge that an interpreter may need to acquire falls into two categories: it will be information about the topic or it will be regarding language that is used to discuss the topic. In all cases, the interpreter will need to access resources. One of the first things she must determine is whether the information that is needed will be available from the site itself, or is best accessed by seeking out other key resources.

With regard to information about a topic, there are two types of resources. One is the "public" type of resource such as materials found in libraries, newspapers, the Internet, and so forth. It may be the case that the interpreter has access to files and materials on commonly occurring topics, such as the resources that an agency holds if the interpreter is an employee of the agency or, as in the example of a coordination office at a college or university, copies of textbooks used in courses the interpreter is assigned to. Freelance interpreters may build a collection of resource materials regarding topics that arise frequently in the work they do, such as general guides to medical and legal terminology and procedures. The other type of resource is people – people such as colleagues or someone knowledgeable of the topic, whom the interpreter can approach with specific questions.

The best resources with regard to language usage and correct terminology are native speakers of the language who are also knowledgeable of the topic. However, good dictionaries and other guides to terminology should always be close at hand.

Often, learning something about the logistics of the situation by having asked the right questions during step two will help focus one's preparation. By way of example, learning that an information session will take the form of a round table discussion among a handful of knowledgeable professionals as opposed to a large public forum will help the interpreter prepare in more specific ways with regard to information and language.

It is quite possible that the interpreter has already facilitated an interaction that is in some way similar to the one she is preparing for, or has even interpreted for a previous interaction with the same participants regarding the same topic. When this is the case, she can prepare for the assignment quite efficiently. For example, an interpreter may work in an education setting or may regularly interpret for a certain committee or group, in which case the assignment is considered as an "ongoing" assignment. Regardless, having been there previously is not enough. The interpreter still has the need to be adequately prepared for the pending assignment, but here the interpreter's schema for the interaction can be rather precise. She will be more confident that she knows the purpose of the class or meeting and something of its dynamics, is familiar with the participants' communication styles, knows the information and language requirements, and is more able to predict what will transpire. At the onset she is much better prepared to facilitate the interaction.

Note that in a case such as this, the number of questions she must ask in step two will be greatly reduced. The experience of having interpreted previously allows the interpreter to know where to focus her questioning and preparation because the unknown variables are lessened. Still, interpreters are wise to consider that the unexpected may always take place. Thus no matter how carefully and thoroughly prepared the interpreter is, it would be a mistake to consider that her prediction about what will transpire will be the *only* version of what can possibly happen.

8.5 Step five: Arriving at the assignment

Eventually, it is time to interpret! It is important that the interpreter continue to conduct herself professionally, part of which is arriving on time to the assignment. To arrive on time is, in fact, to arrive early. The importance of this is that it is necessary for the interpreter to familiarize herself with the room, determine where participants will be located and the best place to position herself, gather any final pieces of information she might need, meet the participants, etc. (this is addressed in more detail in step six). Running in at the last minute can cause participants to be anxious as to whether or not they will be able to conduct their business, and can spell disaster for the interpreter's chances of success. However, the logistics of arriving early can vary considerably. In some Canadian cities, it is realistic to think that an interpreter can attend five or six assignments within a regular workday, given that they are each of short duration; however, in large metropolitan areas where assignments can be a great distance apart, it is more realistic to expect to book just one or two assignments in the same number of hours.

The length of time it takes to arrive at an assignment location must be realistically calculated, taking into consideration factors such as the time of day and corresponding traffic patterns, distance between assignments, and road conditions and construction. An interpreter who is unfamiliar with an assignment's location may choose to consult a map or even drive to the location the evening before so as to be confident in knowing where they need to be and how much time must be allocated for travelling.

Interpreters must also consider the availability of parking, its proximity to the assignment and its cost. It can be very expensive to park in some downtown locations and costs can vary greatly depending on where the assignment is, the time of day and duration. Parking meters are not necessarily the best option because interrupting an assignment, particularly a sensitive or heated one, to plug the parking meter so as to avoid a ticket is not likely to be viewed as professional behaviour. Parking lots and parkades are much more interpreter-friendly. It may be more palatable to regularly pay a little extra for parking than to risk being ticketed or being distracted while interpreting by the knowledge that your parking meter has run out. In some instances, it is more convenient for the interpreter to take a taxi or use an alternate form of public transit.

When accidents, unforeseen traffic conditions or parking delays are experienced, cellular telephones can be a definite asset. If delayed, a call to the person with whom contact has already been established can alleviate concerns that the interpreter will not be there. For interpreters who work for an agency, cell phones and pagers can help keep both the office personnel and interpreting staff informed of any last-minute changes to a schedule. Cell phones and pagers must be turned off, however, prior to the assignment beginning. The interpreter who responds to her cell phone or pager during an assignment is not exhibiting professional behaviour.

If the assignment is one that the interpreter has not been to before and she is not familiar with the area, a miscalculation of the time required to travel to the assignment or a delay in finding suitable parking can create a great deal of stress and even consume much or all of the time allocated for meeting consumers and doing the necessary on-site preparation.

8.6 Step six: On-site preparation

Having arrived on time, the interpreter has an opportunity to introduce herself to the participants and do the necessary on-site preparation. On-site preparation entails gathering information specific to the interaction about to occur that could not be logically inferred from the information gained in earlier steps, and the identification of elements that may affect the interaction over which the interpreter has some control.

For example, it is possible that there is a last-minute addition to an agenda for which there is a written report. Having arrived on time (i.e., early), the interpreter can prepare on-site by identifying key points in the report, or by asking the presenter what the main points are that she will be touching upon.

A critical element that affects interaction facilitation is the determination of the best location and position in which to interpret. Here, location means the place within the environment and position means whether the interpreter sits or stands. Though this may seem a trivial matter, the interpreter must seriously consider many factors in making her determination of the best location and position for the particular interaction. She must assess the physical environment and consider lines of sight and sound which can affect a consumer's or the interpreter's ability to hear everything that needs to be heard or see everything that needs to be seen. Location selection could affect the interpreter's ability to access an on-site resource and the information it holds, such as a projection screen, a document or even a team member. Lighting and amplification requirements, however, can limit location or position options.

As well, the interpreter must consider whether she will remain stationary, will re-locate at some point, or must move more than once to follow the interaction. Also, she must determine whether she will remain sitting or standing throughout, or have opportunity or need to alternate between the two. A poor decision can result in physical or psychological discomfort for either the interpreter or interaction participants. Physical or psychological discomfort could affect the interpreter's stamina or ability to focus on the task of interpreting and if so, a participant's ability to attend to the information could subsequently be hindered. Because the interpreter often works for long periods of time, physical comfort is a necessary consideration. Many interpreters suffer debilitating effects from the physical demands of the work over a long period of time such as tendonitis and Carpal Tunnel Syndrome (see Chapter 4, "Physical Factors" in Stewart et al. 1998 for further discussion, and Dean & Pollard 2001 for discussion of a wide range of work-related stressors).

In many interactions there are inherent issues of power and control. It is not uncommon for a power imbalance to exist, especially when some participants are members of a cultural or other minority. Thus it is not unusual for an interpreter to find herself working in situations where these issues are present.[8] Location and position selection can contribute to this aspect of the interaction. In essence, the location and position an interpreter chooses can reveal an alliance (or allegiance) on her part that can skew the power structure that may exist in the interaction. For interactions where there is an intentional imbalance of power, such as police interrogations and employer-employee meetings for disciplinary purposes, the interpreter will need to take care not to unduly diminish or increase the psychological impact of the experience for the participants. At other times, however, the interpreter's location and position choices can create a power imbalance when there is no call to do so. The interpreter is responsible for considering such factors when determining the best location, although there are times when the best location for the interpreter cannot rightly be negotiated. The interpreter must also be acutely aware of how this physical alliance can be reflected by who she speaks or does not speak with before the interpreted interaction or who she chooses to interpret for first if two people speak at the same time (Roy 2000).

A further issue is safety. There are times, for example in mental health or legal situations, when an interpreter must balance the issue of facilitating the experience with the issue of personal safety and so must consider this additional factor in order to judiciously select the location in which to interpret.

Because it is respectful, interpreters often consult with consumers with regard to their preference of interpreter location. This said, the interpreter remains responsible for being aware of all of the factors which must be considered, determining what is best in a given situation, and negotiating for it.

Another benefit of on-site preparation is that the interpreter could become aware of new information that leads her to further refine or even completely alter her understanding of what the purpose and dynamics of the interaction may be, and therefore change her approach. Thus on-site preparation greatly enhances the interpreter's ability to facilitate what transpires.

8.7 Step seven: Facilitating the interaction

Each and every interaction that an interpreter facilitates is unique. Despite the possibility that an interpreter has previously worked with the same consumers and may be very familiar with the topic of their interaction, some unknown factor could affect consumers or the interpreter which in turn could alter the dynamics of the current interaction. Step seven is complex because the interpreter is responsible for facilitating the entirety of the participants' interaction such that each participant's experience is as similar as possible to that of the other's. This corresponds to Nida's (1964) notion of dynamic equivalence, in which the effect the speaker has on the audience is the same for both those who understand the speaker's language and those who receive the message through interpretation.[9]

People interact principally through communicating with each other and hence, the basic expectation of the ASL-English interpreter is that she must interpret what someone says in English into ASL and what someone says in ASL into English. But in order to truly interpret well, the interpreter must convey what is *meant* by what is said; the interpreter must convey the intended "message" of a speaker, an idea discussed in depth by, for example, Seleskovitch (1978). The speaker chooses word-labels (which could be spoken words or signed words) to express the concepts she wishes to convey to the other interaction participants, and the interpreter must first understand the meaning of a speaker's words if she is to begin to understand the message. Interpreters cannot interpret what they do not understand. Here the interpreter's prediction skills based on careful preparation will help her to better understand the context within which the communication is occurring, including the purpose of the interaction.

The purpose of the interaction is the overarching reason that brings the participants together. It provides the general context within which to understand what is being said (Cokely 1992). The overall purpose of an exchange between a patient and his doctor with regard to a sore thumb, for example, could be as straightforward as the patient wishing to know whether or not his thumb is broken and the doctor wishing to assess the thumb and provide an answer to the patient's question. However, in addition to considering this overall purpose for the interaction, the interpreter must also consider the purpose of "micro-interactions" in order to ascertain the speaker's real message and to interpret this correctly.

Determining the purpose of each micro-interaction has to do with the discourse pragmatics or the "why" of the individual utterance. This element of a message conveys implicit meaning and can be much more difficult to determine than the explicit meaning based on word semantics. For example, when the doctor tells the patient with the sore thumb that he "may not be able to use his hand for one week", and the 17 year-old patient replies, "N-O W-A-Y!" it is important to determine whether the patient believes this is a good thing or not in order to intone the interpreted statement correctly, especially considering that it is likely that the source and target language expressions for such an item differ. It is imperative that the interpreter determine whether the patient is pressuring the doctor to change his opinion, as could be the case if the patient is wishing for permission to play in the divisional volleyball final or if the patient is pleased and might now be able to postpone writing an exam. When unsure of the implicit message, the interpreter will need to employ a strategy for ascertaining what it is, such as seeking clarification, so as to interpret accurately.

In order to assess the purpose of the micro-interaction and thus better understand an intended message, the interpreter must consider several additional elements of communication, such as body language, tone, intonation, gestures, as well as more generally the physical environment, the dynamics of the interaction, and the participants' similar or differing purposes for interacting. All in all, the interpreter can only attempt to convey what she understands as the source message in its source context by reconstructing what she believes to be an equivalent target message in an equivalent context – this requires inferencing on the interpreter's part.[10] As a result, there are many opportunities for the interpreter to inadvertently misconstrue what is the reality of the interaction.

When the two (or more) people interacting have the same purpose, it is typically easier for the interpreter to understand the pragmatic intent of micro-interactions and so feel more assured about the quality of her interpreting. When these purposes are different, and this is not understood by the interpreter, she may sense a lack of interpreting success as a result of the direction the discourse is taking or the outcome of the interaction. For example, the interpreter may not be aware that a patient at a doctor's office is there solely to get help with a sore abdomen but that the doctor's goal is to rid herself of a patient who keeps returning with the same complaint despite having been told that he must wait to see the specialist on a date that has been scheduled. When the interpreter does not identify that there is friction between the two interactants because of differing purposes, she experiences unease. However, if the inherent tension is perceived and conveyed, she has accurately reflected the dissonance of the interaction.

In order to successfully interpret the consumers' entire interaction well, the interpreter also must consider and manage many additional elements. In this regard, the interpreter is typically the only person aware of what is required for her to do her job well, and is therefore responsible for ensuring that she receives what she needs. She must successfully manage all of the aspects of the interaction that she is responsible for and over which she has control. This requires professionalism and often, expert negotiation.

Finally, having assessed all aspects of the situation, considered all relevant factors of the interaction, determined and negotiated the best location and position or a next best possible alternative, the interpreter facilitates the consumers' interaction.

Together, the factors outlined in steps six "On-site preparation" and seven "Facilitating the interaction" are considered to be the major factors the interpreter must be cognizant of whenever she interprets. It should be pointed out, however, that the interpreter's success is not limited to just these – there are always additional factors, not discussed here, that come into play. Nonetheless, facilitating any interaction well requires that the interpreter constantly go through the complex process of assessing the purpose of the interaction and its many elements that lead to her making the decisions she does throughout the interpretation. This process is thus cyclic, and includes the interpreter re-evaluating her decisions along the way. When she finds that her predictions are correct, she continues along, making further decisions based on this. If she finds that her understanding of something has been incorrect, she needs to re-assess her course of action, and make decisions based on this new understanding she has gained, including revising her predictions, and responding accordingly. This process is both cyclic and continual; it must be monitored constantly until the interaction comes to completion.

8.8 Step eight: Reflecting and debriefing

Having interpreted the interaction in its entirety, it is important that the interpreter reflect upon her experience. If she does not consciously consider her work and the many factors she dealt with, she does not take full advantage of an opportunity to develop professionally. Without reflecting upon the interaction, the interpreter is less likely to be aware of which decisions and corresponding actions enhanced her facilitation of the interaction and why this is the case. Similarly, should the same factors occur in a future interaction, she could potentially make the same decisions and repeat the corresponding actions that had ultimately proved to be unsuccessful.

By reflecting upon the interaction, the interpreter is able to maximize her learning. While reflecting, she may recall some portion of the message or aspect of the event that she did not fully comprehend. In situations like this, the interpreter may be unable to identify all of the factors that were affecting the interaction and her response to it, or what other strategies she could have used to manage them. In order to maximize her learning when there is something that she does not completely understand, the interpreter may choose to debrief with a colleague. It is imperative, however, that the interpreter remains ethical and professional when seeking to benefit from a colleague's knowledge and experience by ensuring that she shares only enough information to explore the point in question. To further advance her learning, the interpreter may also consider what additional resources she could investigate, such as a book or article on a particular topic or interpreting technique.

There may be occasions when an interpreter facilitates an interaction where the topic of discussion is emotionally overwhelming. She may well have understood all the factors that affected the interaction and employed correct strategies to facilitate it successfully, but in cases such as these, the interpreter may need to debrief her emotional experience and so seeks the support of an understanding colleague. The interpreter is wise to choose a colleague she knows to be ethical when participating in such a debriefing. In extreme cases, it may be essential that the interpreter seek professional assistance so as to move beyond her response to a tragic experience to which she has been privy (Harvey 2001).

As has been mentioned, an interpreter will from time to time work as part of an interpreting or inter-disciplinary team. As members of an interpreting team, the interpreters will typically debrief about the team's effectiveness in facilitating the interaction. They may discuss topics such as the efficacy of each team member's technique when providing support to the person actively interpreting and determine if there is any change in technique that could enhance the support that is provided. The team may also discuss issues relating to the management of information or resources. As a member of an inter-disciplinary team, there will be times when the interpreter will debrief with the team regarding linguistic, cultural or resource information and how the situation can be managed so that the interaction may be successfully interpreted.

The ability to reflect upon and learn from one's experience is a critical step toward providing successful interpreting because by reflecting upon each interaction and when required, debriefing with others, the interpreter is able to internalize what she has learned from both her successes and failures and expedite her growth as a professional.

9.   The marvel of interpreting experience

The marvel of the process leading to interpreting success is that it is a process through which all interpreters can proceed, and by which all interpreters can intrinsically expand their knowledge and enhance their proficiency. By successfully facilitating interactions, the interpreter gains knowledge of interaction topics, increases her language proficiency, hones professional behaviour and ethical judgement, and thereby builds the schemas she has of various situations. She becomes more aware of the many aspects that comprise an interaction while also developing strategies to manage them. Despite this fact, the need to be prepared for interpreting each and every interaction remains constant. The interpreter increases the likelihood of her future success because she cannot "un-know" what she knows; her new knowledge and enhanced proficiency greatly refines her ability to predict what will transpire during subsequent interactions.

If the knowledge of what happens in an appointment with an oncologist or during a disciplinary meeting of a unionized employee is only vague, it is challenging to predict what the unfolding discourse will be like. With the experience of completing the steps leading to interpreting success many times as outlined in Section 8 above, the interpreter's ability to predict increases. This is shown schematically in Figure 2.

Perhaps the single biggest asset that an interpreter with a great deal of experience has is that she has confronted a similar issue already and resolved it, probably more than once. She is therefore knowledgeable about what to do and confident in knowing when a similar action is likely to lead to success and when it is not.

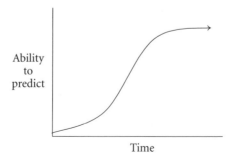

Figure 2. The interpreter's increased ability to predict over time.

The need for the interpreter to be well-prepared for all assignments remains constant throughout her career, as diagrammed in Figure 3. However, being able to accurately predict what will transpire during the interaction enables the interpreter to prepare more effectively and more efficiently.

Quite logically, interpreters with very little experience often have a sketchy set of schemas for situations that may arise. They are likely to not know which questions to ask, have less knowledge of possible purposes and dynamics of interactions, a limited understanding of the topic, limited fluency regarding the particular topic, and have limited experience accessing resources. This is because many interpreting situations fall outside of the novice interpreter's range of experiences – essentially, she is interpreting in the day to day activities *of other people's lives*. For example, she may interpret for someone undergoing a certain kind of medical test when she has never been subject to that test herself, or an arrest when she has never been present at an arrest, etc. An interpreter who has recently graduated is still learning what knowledge and language will be required and therefore has less of a schema for what to do in order to prepare. As a result, she requires a great deal of time to prepare properly. However, with the experience gained by having completed the interpreting process often, the time required to prepare typically becomes shorter, as shown in Figure 4. It should be noted

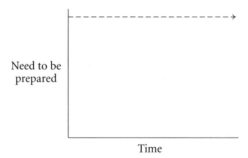

Figure 3. The interpreter's constant need to be prepared.

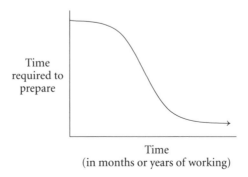

Figure 4. The decreasing time required to prepare.

that the arrows in both Figures 2 and 4 reflect tendencies and not absolutes. Even as an interpreter becomes more proficient, for example, she will still encounter complex assignments for which extensive preparation is needed. Or, for whatever reasons, there will be factors that are very difficult to predict, and these situations also require lengthy preparation time.

If the above figures reflecting the constant need for an interpreter to be prepared for facilitating an interaction, the increasing ability of the interpreter to predict what is likely to occur during an assignment, and the diminishing amount of time typically required to prepare are superimposed, the result reveals that over the duration of the interpreter's career, she can eventually better predict the knowledge and language likely to be required for the interaction, and so is better able to prepare more effectively and efficiently (see Figure 5).

The superimposition in Figure 5 also shows the nexus of the two solid arrows. When an interpreter has little experience and is not able to predict with much

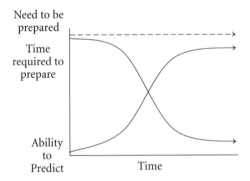

Figure 5. The combined need to be prepared, ability to predict, and time required to prepare.

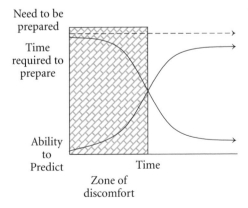

Figure 6. The zone of discomfort.

specificity, a great deal of energy and time is spent preparing for the unknown. Grappling with the unknown tends to induce anxiety for many people, and this experience of more frequent and greater anxiety is represented by the area to the left of the nexus in Figure 6. This area is referred to as the interpreter's "zone of discomfort".

At some point in every interpreter's career, regardless of the type and kind of work that she chooses, the nexus where predictability and preparedness intersect is encountered. Beyond this point, the interpreter is better able to predict what will transpire and thus can make her preparation more effective and efficient. She experiences what is here referred to as the "zone of comfort" (see Figure 7).

At some point in her career, an interpreter can anticipate moving from the zone of discomfort to the zone of comfort (although see the discussion below). This is reflected in Figure 8 which combines the elements of Figures 2 to 7.

The notion of moving from the zone of discomfort to the zone of comfort can be viewed on four levels. At its broadest level, as represented in Figure 8, the movement

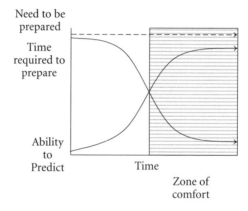

Figure 7. The zone of comfort.

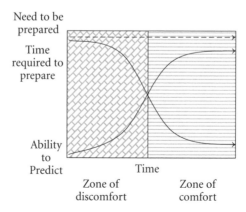

Figure 8. The interpreter' decreasing discomfort/increasing comfort over time.

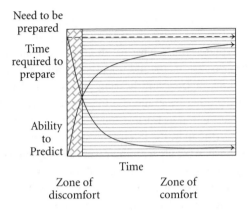

Figure 9. Moving into the zone of comfort for the experienced interpreter.

from the zone of discomfort to that of comfort reflects the interpreter's progression through her career over time as she simply becomes more comfortable with the day-to-day work of interpreting. Second, this movement between zones can also reflect the experience of any interpreter over the duration of a single assignment in that she may be quite anxious, not knowing how accurate her predictions about the interaction and corresponding preparation have been. Over the duration of the assignment, however, as she sees that she has prepared adequately and begins to experience success, she moves from the zone of discomfort into the zone of comfort. Third, the movement between zones can be further considered to occur within the assignment as the interaction moves from a general to a more specific purpose. For example, a meeting where some general discussion of familiar issues has been taking place may move to the financial report and, as a result, the interpreter may move back into the zone of discomfort until she determines that she in fact has the correct documents in front of her and is comfortable with the speaker's presentation style and pace. At the fourth level, a small wave of discomfort can wash over the interpreter when she is unsure of the speaker's perspective on a certain topic or what the purpose of the micro-interaction of his utterance is, yet she may quickly move once again into the zone of comfort when she ascertains the answer to her quandary.

It is important to note that throughout the duration of their careers, all interpreters experience both the zones of comfort and discomfort in these ways. However, as interpreters gain expertise, they find themselves moving from frequently experiencing the zone of discomfort at all levels for long periods of time to experiencing the zone of comfort at each level more often and for longer durations. This is represented in Figure 9.

10. Conclusion

An ASL-English interpreter must have exceptional bilingual skills and bicultural knowledge as well as possess many additional skills and abilities if she is to truly facilitate the interactions of Deaf and hearing people well. Upon graduation from a post-secondary interpreting program, the interpreter is ready for work, although interpreters often suggest that they learn as much again during their first several years of actual experience. Fortunately, the interpreter has the compounding benefit of the eight steps outlined above, typically with increasing success and comfort, and thereby continues to develop her knowledge, skills and abilities. The successful interpreter is aware that over time, as she becomes more proficient, she will come to experience the zone of comfort more frequently by doing what she so thoroughly enjoys.

Seleskovitch (1978) reminds us that an interpretation is much like a painting insofar as rather than capturing everything, what is of primary interest along with what is insignificant as a photograph will, a painting seeks to discover a particular meaning and highlight that. An interpreter is thus like an artist. Just as a master painter leaves the beholder to reflect on the experience of the masterpiece without ever noticing the individual brush strokes required in its creation, so too a truly competent interpreter leaves the consumers thinking about their interaction without them having ever noticed the myriad details which the interpreter has had to consider. Just as for an accomplished artist, it takes time to develop skill in interpreting.

Notes

1. I would like to express my sincere thanks to members of the Winnipeg Deaf community, colleagues and co-workers with whom I have had the honour of crossing paths, as well as the many consumers I have had the pleasure of working for; all have exercised a great deal of patience, shown tremendous support or engaged me in discussion as I have explored what is required to interpret successfully and progressed on my own journey as an interpreter. I would like to acknowledge the editor of this book and the reviewers of this chapter for their insight and guidance. I would like to say a special thank you to my family.

2. Having said this, throughout the remainder of the chapter I use the terms "Deaf", "Deaf people", etc., to designate one of the two general groups the interpreter works with (the other being non-deaf people). Much of the discussion, however, could equally apply to the other groups of individuals mentioned, i.e., deaf people who are not a part of the Deaf community, Deaf-blind people (who may or may not also be members of the Deaf community), hard-of-hearing and late-deafened people. The communication needs of each of these individuals requires the interpreter's respectful consideration.

3. These documents can be viewed on AVLIC's webpage at www.avlic.ca.

4. Many national interpreter associations in countries other than Canada, such as the Registry of Interpreters for the Deaf in the United States, have similar expectations of their members regarding ethical conduct and dispute resolution.

5. LSQ (Langue des Signes Québécoise) is a second signed language widely used in Canada.

6. Again, see Conrad and Stegenga, this volume, for more on these aspects of interpreting in educational settings specifically.

7. See Janzen, this volume, Chapter 4.

8. See Baker-Shenk (1986, 1992), Janzen and Korpiniski, this volume, and Mindess (1999) for discussions of cultural and ethical considerations on the part of the interpreter when these dynamics exist.

9. For more on this, see Janzen, this volume, Chapter 4, for language considerations; Russell, this volume, on the effects of consecutive interpreting; and Leeson, this volume, Chapter 3, for some theoretical considerations.

10. See Wilcox and Shaffer, this volume, for a detailed discussion of what this entails.

References

Baker-Shenk, Charlotte (1986). Characteristics of oppressed and oppressor peoples: Their effect on the interpreting context. In Marina L. McIntire (Ed.), *Interpreting: The Art of Cross-cultural Mediation* (pp. 59–71). Silver Spring, MD: RID Publications.

Baker-Shenk, Charlotte (1992). The interpreter: Machine, advocate, or ally? In Jean Plant-Moeller (Ed.), *Expanding Horizons* (pp. 120–140). Silver Spring, MD: RID Publications.

Cokely, Dennis (1992). *Interpretation: A Sociolinguistic Model*. Burtonsville, MD: Linstok Press.

Cokely, Dennis (2000). Exploring ethics: A case for revising the Code of Ethics. *Journal of Interpretation* (RID), 25–57.

Dean, Robyn K., & Robert Q. Pollard, Jr. (2001). Application of demand-control theory to sign language interpreting: Implications for stress and interpreter training. *Journal of Deaf Studies and Deaf Education, 6* (1), 1–14.

Ferguson, Charles A. (1994). Dialect, register, and genre: Working assumptions about conventionalization. In Douglas Biber and Edward Finegan (Eds.), *Sociolinguistic Perspectives on Register* (pp. 15–30). New York/Oxford: Oxford University Press.

Fischer, Tammera J. (1998). *Establishing a Freelance Interpretation Business: Professional Guidance for Sign Language Interpreters (2nd ed.)*. Hillsboro, OR: Butte Publications.

Frishberg, Nancy (1990). *Interpreting: An Introduction* (Revised ed.). Silver Spring, MD: Registry of Interpreters for the Deaf.

Gile, Daniel (1995). *Basic Concepts and Models for Interpreter and Translator Training*. Amsterdam/Philadelphia: John Benjamins.

Humphrey, Janice H., & Bob J. Alcorn (2001). *So You Want to Be an Interpreter?: An Introduction to Sign Language Interpreting* (3rd ed.). Amarillo, TX: H & H Publishers.

Humphreys, Linda (2004). *The Professional Sign Language Interpreter's Handbook: The Complete, Practical Manual for the Interpreting Profession (2nd ed.)*. Brentwood, CA: Sign Language Interpreting Media.

Harvey, Michael A. (2001). Vicarious emotional trauma of interpreters: A clinical psychologist's perspective. *Journal of Interpretation* (RID), 85–98.

Lucas, Ceil, & Clayton Valli (1992). *Language Contact in the American Deaf Community*. San Diego, CA: Academic Press Inc.

Metzger, Melanie (1999). *Sign Language Interpreting: Deconstructing the Myth of Neutrality*. Washington, DC: Gallaudet University Press.

Mindess, Anna (1999). *Reading Between the Signs: Intercultural Communication for Sign Language Interpreters*. Yarmouth, ME: Intercultural Press.

Nida, Eugene A. (1964). *Toward a Science of Translating*. Leiden, Netherlands: E. J. Brill.

Roy, Cynthia B. (1989). A Sociolinguistic Analysis of the Interpreter's Role in the Turn Exchanges of an Interpreted Event. PhD Dissertation. Washington, DC, Georgetown University.

Roy, Cynthia B. (2000). *Interpreting as a Discourse Process*. New York/Oxford: Oxford University Press.

Russell, Debra (2002). *Interpreting in Legal Contexts: Consecutive and Simultaneous Interpreting*. Burtonsville, MD: Linstok Press.

Seal, Brenda Chafin (1998). *Best Practices in Educational Interpreting*. Needham Heights, MA: Allyn & Bacon.

Seleskovitch, Danica (1978). *Interpreting for International Conferences*. Washington, DC: Pen and Booth.

Solow, Sharon Neumann (2000). *Sign Language Interpreting: A Basic Resource Book* (Revised ed.) Burtonsville, MD: Linstok Press.

Stewart, David A., Jerome D. Schein, & Brenda E. Cartwright (1998). *Sign Language Interpreting: Exploring its Art and Science*. Needham Heights, MA: Allyn & Bacon.

CHAPTER 9

Best practices in interpreting

A Deaf community perspective

Angela Stratiy

Edmonton, Canada

1. Introduction[1]

This chapter is about the interpreter's relationship to the Deaf community. Most interpreters begin to learn about the Deaf community around the same time they begin learning a signed language. They soon discover that the Deaf people whose language they are learning also have a culture that is unique to this community, and therefore which differs from the new signed language learner's culture. Quite often, Deaf culture is presented in terms of highly visible, material trappings and practices: how to get someone's attention, the importance of lighting, TTYs, or even the value of group consensus. But culture is more than this. It is a sense of who you are. Of roots. A connectedness with those around you who share your ways of thinking.[2] Bienvenu (1990: 12) puts it this way: "Culture is one's way of life – how one lives, thinks, eats, uses language, socializes, how one's values are defined, what belief system one adheres to, one's behaviour patterns and identity – all of these things make up cultural identity. We are a product of our culture, and our culture defines us". Those whose culture it is do not have to learn this – they live it and breathe it. But those who come to "visit" do have to learn, and those who desire to work as interpreters between members of this culture and others have to learn it well.

Some of what appears in this chapter I have discussed in an earlier article called "Interpreting and Interpreter Education: Past, Present and Future" (Stratiy 1996) based on a keynote address given at the 1994 Association of Visual Language Interpreters of Canada (AVLIC) conference. This chapter is meant as food for thought for interpreters who interact with Deaf people within the community and during their work times. I hope that interpreters will reflect on their relationship with the community, which can mean asking some important questions, such as: What do I know about Deaf culture? Do I interact appropriately with members of that culture? Which Deaf cultural characteristics should I adopt, and which belong to Deaf people themselves and not to hearing people? What expectations do members of the Deaf community have of me as a hearing person as I work professionally as an interpreter in the community?

Let's call what follows in this chapter my "wish list" for interpreters, for the interpreting community as a whole, and in fact in many ways, for the Deaf community as well. My thoughts are intended to continue us down the road of identifying best practices in the profession of interpreting, and to encourage on-going dialogue regarding issues that impact the work that we do. I have chosen to address certain issues that keep arising, but these issues are by no means the only ones that could be discussed.

The topics that I wish to cover can be divided into three overriding categories: 1) cultural considerations, 2) linguistic considerations, and 3) interpreting considerations. However, in each case, a topic in one category has implications regarding the other categories. For example, we begin by looking at the cultural practice of assigning names. But while this is clearly a cultural practice, there are linguistic implications both because of the semantic nature of name signs that often exists and because of how they are used in discourse. There are also interpreting implications related to the impact of using names and name signs during interpretation. This is just one example but as we continue, such overlapping implications will be obvious. Following discussion of a number of points under these three broad categories, I conclude with some suggestions of how the Deaf and interpreting communities can work together to find solutions to the many issues related to culture that exist.

2.   A cultural consideration: Name signs

Interpreters face cultural questions at every turn. An important aspect of any culture is how a person is referred to, and in this section we focus mainly on the use of name signs in the community and for "outsiders".

Name signs are an integral part of Deaf culture and for quite some time now I have been concerned about how they are given to individuals coming into the community who are not Deaf, about who gives them these name signs, and then about how they are used. It is not my intent, however, to blame anyone in particular when name signs have been given in a manner that goes against Deaf culture, but rather to begin a dialogue encouraging all of us – those of us who are culturally Deaf and those for whom Deaf culture is a host culture – to examine this practice.

It is my belief that a name sign should only be awarded to someone by the Deaf community and only after members of the community have had a chance to become acquainted with the individual in question. It is often the case that hearing people choose or receive name signs in a way that attaches little cultural significance to them. But in some cultures, bestowing a name is serious business. In many Native cultures, for example, the community has a time-honoured process for bestowing a name that often involves a naming ceremony. This is the case for the Menominee (Wisconsin):

During the first year of life each child must be given a name. An elder is requested to give the name, and it is bestowed at a feast given by the parents for as many people as they have food and place for. The elder gives the matter serious thought, sometimes mulling it over for several months. When he is ready, the feast is held. After the food is consumed he rises with the child in his arms and gives a talk, giving the name and explaining why it is selected and asking the spirits for a long life for the child. Sometimes the name is given in recognition of some special characteristic the elder believes he sees in the child. Other times the name of a deceased person is given in recognition of the possibility that his spirit has been born again in this child. The event is of great importance because if a child is not pleased with his name, he may depart to the spirit world from whence he came.

(Spindler & Spindler 1977:441)

While this practice is more ritualized for the Menominee than in Deaf culture, names and naming for Deaf people are not taken lightly. Supalla (1992) suggests that acquiring a name sign is a kind of rite of passage with special meaning: "A name sign is of great value to a Deaf person because, without it, this person would have no effective means for identifying himself/herself or others. ... Possessing a name sign actually marks a Deaf person's membership in the Deaf community" (Supalla 1992: 16). McKee and McKee (2000) also state that acquiring a name sign signals the person's entry into the community and that "its use reinforces the bond of shared group history and 'alternative' language use (in relation to mainstream society)" (2000: 3).

The practice of giving name signs to students in first year signed language classes goes against the Deaf community's cultural rules. These students have not yet begun to establish relationships in the community that warrant the bestowing of name signs. Often name signs are given to these students based on a distinguishing physical or personality trait to make identifying the students and calling on them in class easier. The problem, however, is two-fold. First, this practice misrepresents how name signs are given in the community in culturally appropriate ways. Second, these students do not subsequently attach any cultural significance to their name sign. A better practice would be if ASL instructors consistently fingerspelled the names of their students. This would enhance the students' expressive and receptive skills, which tend to be weak at these beginning levels. Students must wait until they become further involved in the larger Deaf community before receiving a name sign.

An additional problem I have noted is that many hearing ASL learners assume that a name sign is associated with one particular name, and not the person. For example, if someone's name is Vincent, and his name sign is a [V] that contacts the forehead, it does not mean that every other person named Vincent has the exact same name sign. ASL students sometimes make the assumption that because they have the same name as a member of the Deaf community, their name sign would also be the same. Rather, a name sign is given very individually to each person.

It may be argued that the practice of giving name signs to these beginning ASL students is similar to giving name signs to young Deaf students who attend schools for the Deaf, but this practice is not in fact the same. The Deaf students will be members of the Deaf community, have acquired (or are acquiring) ASL as their first language, and are identified by their name signs by their Deaf peers. Meadow (1977) studied ways that Deaf people acquire their name signs and found while many Deaf children receive a name sign from a teacher or counselor, a high percentage were given their name sign as children by their peers at a school for the Deaf. Meadow considers this to be a highly significant aspect of the child's socialization into the Deaf community, especially because the majority of Deaf children learn ASL from their Deaf peers at school.

Many interpreters are now in a position where they have been given a name sign either by their own peers or by ASL instructors, or have chosen a name sign for themselves. When this is the case, they must approach the use of their name sign with caution when first being introduced to the Deaf community. Most immediately, it warrants verifying with community members that the name sign the person has is not the same name sign of any member of the Deaf community. If it is, the interpreter should understand that her name sign is not likely to be accepted in the community, so she should fingerspell her name until an alternate name sign is chosen by some community member. If there is no conflict, the interpreter should be prepared to explain exactly how she got her name sign, which then may be accepted, or may eventually change. If there is any doubt about the name sign having a culturally appropriate source, fingerspelling the name might in fact be the better option.[3]

Once hearing people have attained name signs, care must still be taken regarding when, and how, they use them. Misuse may be misleading. I have been in the situation where I thought that a person I was chatting with was Deaf because she had used her name sign to introduce herself and had given me no indication that she was otherwise, and then been embarrassed to discover that she was, in fact, a hearing person.

For too long now I believe that we have misused and misunderstood the cultural practice of giving name signs, and what their use signifies in Deaf culture. I have hearing children who each have a name sign. But like our hearing counterparts whose children have nick-names that are used in familiar surroundings, those name signs are only used when I am among family, friends and members of my own community who know my family well. Otherwise, for example with my colleagues at work or in more formal situations, I use my children's full names which I fingerspell. This is common practice even for using name signs of any Deaf community member.

Similar to any aspect of Deaf culture, or to ASL signs and grammatical forms that an interpreter might be learning, the interpreter needs to ensure that she is using name signs appropriately. This means constantly watching to see how members of the community use them, and checking with community members whose culture it is as to whether or not she is using the item correctly. Interpreters must learn about culture before they begin to interpret; cultural training regarding Deaf culture must be a part of interpreters' education from the very beginning (Miller & Matthews 1986). Cultural sensitivity often ranks higher than interpreting skills in terms of what Deaf consumers are comfortable with (Bienvenu 1989). If the interpreter has culturally inappropriate ways of behaving, it will make the consumer uneasy. Problems with name signs, either inappropriately acquired or misused in interaction, suggest a lack of cultural understanding at a fairly basic level.

How one refers to another person while interacting socially, or cross-culturally while interpreting, is also worthy of consideration. McKee and McKee (2000), in discussing the Deaf community's use of name signs in New Zealand, observe that name signs are used only for third person referents. Strategies for getting someone's attention are visual and not auditory, and do not involve using that person's name sign. For speakers of English, referring to someone by her first name can be used to develop rapport between speakers. In the Deaf community, however, using a person's first name has a different purpose. Let me illustrate with an anecdote. When I was a child in school and the teacher called me by my first name, it signaled to me that I must pay strict attention to something, or that I was about to be reprimanded. Not too long ago I was called to meet with my supervisor at work and our interaction was interpreted. The interpreter began her ASL interpretation by fingerspelling my name, A-N-G-E-L-A. I froze, thinking I was in trouble for something. Quite obviously, my supervisor had begun to tell me something by addressing me by my name. What I did not realize at the time was that she had meant it as a friendly gesture, an indication of familiarity and comfort between us. This gesture, however, did not succeed cross-culturally. If the interpreter would have understood more about the use of names, she might have chosen a familiar gesture appropriate in Deaf culture, such as a polite wave of the hand and a warm facial expression.

3.   Linguistic considerations

Interpreters have an obligation not just to learn to use ASL well, but to seek out Deaf people's feedback and suggestions on how to use linguistic structures to best mean what they are attempting to convey. Here we examine several areas of language use that I think are important. Once again, this discussion may be focused on linguistic considerations, but each topic also involves cultural (and cross-cultural) considerations, and has profound implications for interpreting.

It is often the case that students make the assumption that all members of the Deaf community are alike in how they use ASL. It is imperative that second language users understand that linguistic variation exists in the Deaf community – that Deaf seniors tend to use more fingerspelling for example, or that many Deaf community members are in fact bilingual and bicultural, that some individuals are monolingual, and that children use a form of ASL that is not the same as adults' use of the language. Many people who have ASL as a second language, however, are not fluent enough to recognize these differences and to adjust their own language use accordingly. Understandably, these linguistic and sociolinguistic skills are characteristic of advanced second language learners, but certainly would be expected of anyone who suggests that she is fluent enough to work as an interpreter professionally.

In the following sections, the linguistic considerations discussed must be understood within the context of sociolinguistic variation. Most critically, second language learners should understand that there are some general rules of usage, often quite clearly related to cultural considerations, but then situation by situation, and individual by individual, variation in usage takes place.

3.1 Negotiating topics

In ASL, a topic is introduced as a piece of information that the addressee will be able to identify, in other words, something that is known to the addressee. Topics are typically marked with raised eyebrows and a slight head-tilt backwards (Baker & Cokely 1980). But sometimes whether or not the topic-marked information is completely identifiable to the addressee is not certain. In these cases the signer must negotiate the topic to make sure that this point of reference in the discourse is understood.

When people participate in discourse it is essential that they monitor each participant's use of language along with feedback they might receive about their own, if the dialogue is to be successful. When a topic is offered and participants agree that the information is familiar – that it is indeed "topical" – then the dialogue can continue. No further negotiation need occur. For example, if in a conversation with a friend I say that I have just purchased a C-O-N-D-O, fingerspelling the word, and the response I get back is a positive head nod and perhaps even a comment like "that's great!" then I can safely assume that my topic has been understood and accepted and we can continue along on our discourse path.

What does a second language ASL signer do if her topic is not accepted? If initially a topic does not consist of familiar information, the signer might check with the recipient as to whether a regional variation of a sign that she has used may be the difficulty (a more fluent signer might know that she has used an appropriate regional sign). Another possibility is to then fingerspell the item. The addressee may not recognize the sign that was used by the second language user, but a fingerspelled word might be understood. Fingerspelling might seem like an odd choice, but for several reasons, explained below, it is one I recommend. Once the addressee indicates her acceptance of the negotiated topic as identifiable information, the discourse can then continue. As an example of this negotiation process, occasionally topics in areas such as human anatomy, botany, or regarding other scientific facts may require several negotiation steps. Again, however, this depends entirely on who the discourse participant is and what background she has. Suppose the topic for some discourse is a "praying mantis" and the addressee indicates that she does not know what this is. It could be that the person is familiar with this insect, but does not recognize the sign or even the fingerspelled word, and if so, supporting information will need to be provided until the addressee does indicate an understanding.

Many times I have witnessed a person with ASL as a second language not be able to negotiate a topic well. Quite often, it is obvious that the person assumes that a topic is *not* known by a Deaf addressee, and immediately provides supporting information without having negotiated the topic in an appropriate way. To do this is very condescending on the part of a signer, even oppressive, and for an interpreter to do it is unacceptable. Yet I observe this regularly and have been on the receiving end myself. It is imperative to remember, as mentioned, that the Deaf community is a highly diverse community and thus negotiation of topics will vary with each person and within each discourse event.

I would like to discuss an example that comes from Stratiy (1996), illustrating how an extensive explanation for a topic is given when the signer makes the assumption that it will not be understood by the person she is conversing with. On one occasion I was talking with an interpreter who had experienced the death of someone close to her. I asked why this person had died. The interpreter launched into a detailed, extensive explanation of what had happened, that the person had lost a lot of weight and had progressively gotten paler and paler, and so forth. Eventually, I discovered that the individual had died of cancer. Why the interpreter had not initially just fingerspelled the word C-A-N-C-E-R was beyond me, but presumably she had the impression that because there was no ASL sign for *cancer*, I would not understand the fingerspelled word. So instead she decided on a lengthy "expansion" that was confusing. Certainly she misunderstood the discourse situation.

What should this interpreter have done instead? It is important not to make the assumption that the Deaf person will not understand a term (here I am taking for granted that the second language learner is not a beginning signer). Second, the interpreter should monitor the feedback – facial gestures, body cues, and more overt signs of understanding – given by the Deaf discourse participant. If the person indicates that the fingerspelled term is understood, then go on with the dialogue. If it is not, then further clarification would definitely be in order.

This is just as important when it occurs during interpretation. Deaf consumers are often insulted when interpreters make the assumption that English words will not be understood, therefore going into lengthy explanations for terms that could quite simply be fingerspelled.

It is also incorrect to assume that numerous supporting details of a topic must be provided when the addressee has not asked for them, even though many second language learners have the impression that this is expected in ASL. Letting the addressee know that you have simply purchased a new blouse or sweater may be all the information they need or want in order to participate in the dialogue – providing excruciating detail about the colour, material, style, etc. without being prompted by the Deaf addressee indicates that the signer is using language rules prescriptively, and not paying attention to the particular discourse situation. Once again I will stress that the interpreter needs to consider individual differences and preferences that exist within the community of Deaf people who use ASL, and that it is crucial not to overlook this fact.

3.2 Invented signs

The practice of interpreters inventing signs should be avoided. This is a practice that often occurs with no consultation with the Deaf consumers whose language it is they are interpreting into. Fingerspelling English words that do not have sign equivalents is by far the better choice.

If there is a situation where the interpreter is interpreting technical vocabulary in the classroom, then most certainly it is appropriate for the interpreter to have a discussion about this vocabulary with the Deaf student, negotiate what sign or signs can be used, and then use them in that situation. But because signs invented in this way are not part of the ASL lexicon, they should be restricted to that specific classroom in that setting only. Often, however, it appears that interpreters think that now that they have a sign for some term that they did not have previously, it can be used anywhere, including in the community. When this is the case, Deaf community members perceive that the interpreter is using signs that the community has no experience with, and that quite often these signs look more like SEE (Signing Exact English) signs rather than ASL.

It might be the case from time to time that Deaf students themselves take negotiated vocabulary items outside the classroom. If there is a reason to use this sign in the community, and it is a sign that fits the parameters of ASL, it might in certain circumstances be accepted. However, a Deaf person introducing a sign into the community and an interpreter doing so are two different things. It is rarely the case that the community will openly accept a new vocabulary item from a hearing person into their community's own language.

The interpreter thus must make it very clear to the Deaf student that she understands that the signs they are negotiating for use in the classroom setting will stay in the classroom. This shows the Deaf person (and the community as a whole) that the interpreter also understands the cultural implications of this practice, primarily that the language of ASL is a part of Deaf people's cultural identity, and must be respected as such.

3.3 Classifiers

I regularly teach workshops on ASL and interpreting around the country and have the opportunity to work with many interpreters on their ASL development. By doing so, I have come to the conclusion that hearing people who are used to thinking in and using a spoken language can have difficulty thinking visually in terms of language. Because they use spoken English, and they have learned to receive information aurally, they are used to language production in a linear fashion. When asked to explain a very simple task in ASL – like buttering a piece of bread for example – it is common for students of ASL as a second language to choose phrasing that more closely resembles a linear English phrase, and if they use a classifier, it is often not the best classifier to fit the action. As I teach, I spend quite a bit of time attempting to coax them into thinking of the actions involved in "real life" movements, and then to think of the best way to depict these actions in ASL. If the signer visualizes how to use the object or objects she wishes to discuss, and simply "shows" what it is she is doing (e.g., pouring a can of paint), then she will more than likely choose the best classifier to represent that object.

Classifiers in a signed language such as ASL have been described as follows:

> Because signed languages are perceived visually and are articulated by movements of the hands in space, signers have a rich spatial medium at their disposal to express both spatial and non-spatial information. Signers can schematize signing space to represent physical space or to represent abstract conceptual structure. For signed languages, *spatial language* – the linguistic devices used to talk about space – primarily involves the use of classifier constructions, rather than prepositions or locative affixes. ... *Classifier constructions* are complex predicates that express *motion* (e.g., "The car meandered up a hill"), *position* (e.g., "The bicycle is next to the tree"), *stative-descriptive* information (e.g., "It's long and thin"), and *handling* information (e.g., "I picked up a spherical object"....).
>
> (Emmorey 2002: 73–74)

Classifiers are the "colour" of ASL – they are rich in meaning, often quite visually iconic. If they are missing from a signer's discourse, the resulting structures are incomplete; the signer's text is "dull". Using classifiers appropriately is extremely important. When students are learning ASL, they need to think outside their comfort zones in order to expand their repertoire of sign choices. Imagine just how many ways one can "open" a window: these visual elements can go a long way in shaping language expression. Sticking with English terms will limit the signer's options.

ASL signers make extensive use of classifiers during descriptive discourse. If the interpreter is having difficulty visualizing a scene that is being described in spoken English, choosing appropriate classifiers in the ASL target text is going to be problematic. Often there is a particular classifier handshape that is most commonly used for a given item. For example, take the human heart. If an interpreter is interpreting a text from a speaker who is describing aspects of the heart, how might this be depicted clearly in ASL? If the interpreter thinks only of the heart as internal to the body, she may not be able to make the anatomy clear to the ASL observer. If, however, the interpreter uses an [S] handshape (a fist) on the non-dominant hand, perhaps first positioning the hand close to her body, but then moving it out into a more neutral space, she can then refer to the non-dominant [S] handshape by using her dominant hand, describing the lobes, position of the arteries, etc., incorporating numerous classifiers in this very visual description. The description may end with the interpreter moving the non-dominant hand back to her own chest to reiterate that the speaker has not been talking about a specimen outside the body, but of the human heart functioning within a person's entire anatomy.

Quite often, a single vocabulary item is built from several classifier "roots". In these cases, the signer must have the correct classifiers positioned in a certain orientation one to the other. An example of this is SATELLITE meaning 'satellite dish', shown in

Figure 1. SATELLITE. From Carole Sue Bailey and Kathy Dolby (2002), *The Canadian Dictionary of ASL*, p. 608. With kind permission from the University of Alberta Press.

Figure 1, with an open [C] handshape on the dominant hand and a [1] handshape on the non-dominant hand. If a palm orientation error is made on either hand, the sign is "pronounced" incorrectly. SATELLITE is a sign that is often mispronounced.

　　How can an interpreter practice the proper use of classifiers? The first and most obvious suggestion I could make is to ask a Deaf person how to make the sign. A second suggestion is to watch the communication between two Deaf people to see what their use of classifiers is like. Quite often, the use of classifiers in this conversation differs from the conversation between a Deaf and a hearing person, and this is why I suggest that watching Deaf people conversing is an excellent learning experience. A further suggestion is to ask three or four people to all demonstrate the use of a particular classifier to see if they would all choose the same construction. In doing this, sometimes a consensus as to the best way to sign something can be reached, and sometimes these signers will disagree. But once again, the second language learner should be cautioned that if this takes place, it might be because of the variation that exists among ASL signers in the community, and should not be taken as "well if *they* can't agree, how should I know what to do?" Rather, when the interpreter is using such a construction, she should monitor the addressees' feedback very carefully to make sure that she is being understood by different signers. These suggestions and other practice tips are discussed at length in the videotape *The Pursuit of ASL: Interesting Facts Using Classifiers*.[4,5]

3.4 English language intrusions in ASL

I would like to encourage second language users to become more aware of the linguistic choices they make when conversing in ASL. A linguistic feature that works in one language cannot always be carried over to the second language and hold the same function or the same meaning. For second language learners of ASL, many types of English intrusions can take place, for example English lexical words or grammatical structures. Here let me give you some examples of intrusions that are often found in discourse.

A hearing person in conversation with someone who is Deaf will often use signs that correspond to words that would be appropriate in their own native language and culture but which are not a part of ASL. This became clear to me once when I was chatting with a hearing person about how tired I was because I had had a busy day at work and had stayed up late the evening before planting in the garden. In a spoken English conversation, the person listening to this comment might respond with *right, right, right*, meaning that she completely understood my situation. However, if in ASL the addressee responded with the ASL sign that means 'right' as in "RIGHT, RIGHT" it would mean that she was there *with* the Deaf person to witness the event, that is, affirming the situation based on actual experience. This of course was not the case. Such misuse of an ASL sign can easily lead to much confusion and misunderstanding. A more appropriate response might be the sign often glossed as OH-I-SEE meaning 'I understand' (see Figure 2).

Another example of where English intrudes in ASL conversation is in the use of English *fine*. In English if you are asked if you would like something to drink you might respond with *I'm fine, thanks*, meaning that no, you would not like anything more to drink. In ASL, however, using the sign FINE can only mean that you would

Figure 2. OH-I-SEE, an ASL discourse marker meaning 'I understand'. From Carole Sue Bailey and Kathy Dolby (2002), *The Canadian Dictionary of ASL*, p. 460. With kind permission from the University of Alberta Press.

like something to drink. Another aspect of some signs, including FINE, is that the path movement and manner of movement in the sign may occur in different ways, resulting in quite different meanings. And further, often when ASL students learn a sign, the first version they learn (i.e., the first movement of the sign they learn) is the one they produce in every context. With FINE, for example, the student might first learn the sign with a sharp, fairly long, outward movement, which would be an emphatic 'that's just fine!' indicating agreement with something. But the sign can also be produced in other ways, for example with a slight tapping movement of the side of the thumb on the chest, which would be a more polite way to say 'I'm fine'.

A final example of this phenomenon is the use of NO. In English, after being told that someone has won a million dollars a person might respond with *no!* which in this case could simply mean 'really!' as an expression of surprise. In ASL if a person were to sign NO in response to the same statement, it would mean that she does not believe it is true, which would prompt the person who made the statement to go into great detail in order to convince the person that it is in fact the truth. Here again the assumed effect of the second language user's response has carried over from an English context. Items such as this are tricky to learn and to use because sometimes the meaning seems very similar across languages. NO in ASL can sometimes be used with the appropriate facial expression to mean 'you've got to be kidding!' which seems to match more closely the intent of *no!* in English to mean 'really'. But in ASL it would still carry the sense of disbelief that is not necessarily the case in English.

A final point that I would like to make in this section is that second language learners, including interpreters, often have English intrusions in their ASL because they do not know ASL grammar sufficiently and thus do not know how to phrase something appropriately, whereas many Deaf people include the occasional English word or phrase in their ASL because they are bilingual and know what they are doing linguistically. There is a difference between naïve and purposeful language mixing.

3.4.1 *Semantic choices and swear words*

I want to caution interpreters about the semantic choices they make while signing ASL, especially while interpreting when the effects of semantic errors can be serious. This topic has been discussed numerous times, but the problem is widespread and it deserves mention here. A simple example is the sign GAS (see Figure 3). This sign applies to the kind of gas you would use to fill the gas tank in your car, but you could not use it to refer to the gas that you use to heat your house. In this case it would be more appropriate to use fingerspelling, as in G-A-S.

The problem is a bit more intricate with respect to "swear" words. Often the semantics of an item in this category are not the same across languages, which means that a word might be used in one language, but its supposed equivalent in the target language does not in fact mean exactly the same thing, or it cannot be used in exactly the same way or same context. As an example, let me choose a word that has strong meaning, the word *fuck*. The sign that is typically glossed as FUCK is regularly subjected to misinterpretation when it is interpreted into English. When a

Figure 3. GAS. From Carole Sue Bailey and Kathy Dolby (2002), *The Canadian Dictionary of ASL*, p. 275. With kind permission from the University of Alberta Press.

Deaf ASL signer uses the sign in which the middle finger is extended and indexed with something,[6] perhaps an assignment that she received a bad grade on, this does not mean 'fuck this!' as might be assumed as the interpreter searches for an equivalent in English. Rather, it would be more appropriately interpreted into English as *What's up with this?* or *What's the deal here?* In the two cultures and two languages, seemingly equivalent words often do not mean the same thing or have the same impact. These are sometimes called *faux amis* or "false friends" (Gile 1995). As in the example above, the interpreter should not assume the English meaning of an "equivalent" and carry this over first into the intent of the ASL usage, and then back to the interpretation into English. The interpreter must first understand what the item means in the source language, and then find an appropriate equivalent in the target language that carries the same intent. As always, it is critical to think of the cultural implications of the interpreter's choices, and this is never so important as during interpretation. Of course there are many, many examples that could be discussed. The interpreter's best resources are members of the Deaf community who have ASL as a first language. Continued study is a must.

4. Interpreting considerations

In this section I look more directly at aspects of interpreting. Several of these considerations are about the process of interpreting generally or about the way interpreting is handled. I advocate for the increased use of consecutive interpreting and the inclusion of Deaf interpreters. It is also important to me that interpreters work closely with the

Deaf community to better understand how to communicate effectively with them as they interpret and what kind of impact their choices make on the consumer.

4.1 Simultaneous versus consecutive interpreting

I abhor simultaneous interpretation. Its effect on the Deaf consumer, quite honestly, is often much like a deer in the headlights – it knows something is coming at it (at high speed) but is unable to make sense out of what it might be. So often when I am faced with a barrage of information during simultaneous interpreting, I know that there is information there, but in my effort to sort through it, I lose the message.

I advocate for the use of consecutive interpreting in all arenas whenever possible. The process of interpreting, in and of itself, requires that the interpreter comprehend the message in the source language *before* the message in the target language can be produced. When interpretation is consecutive, the information is often produced in ASL in a way that is much clearer and, most importantly, the information is more accurate. When interpreting consecutively, the interpreter is able to take more time to sort out the meaning, and the recipient gets a more coherent message. With consecutive interpreting, I see the interpreter as more confident in portraying the source message in its entirety.

Our spoken language counterparts frequently use consecutive interpreting when working with dignitaries such as government officials as they interact with others from foreign countries. I see these interpreters taking notes, which is something I do not see with signed language interpreters. Perhaps it is time for ASL-English interpreters to follow suit. We should not be fixated on worrying about the time it takes for consecutive interpreting to occur but rather concentrate on the goals of participants and the results that are achieved through accurate transferal of information. When consecutive interpreting best facilitates these goals, it should be used.[7]

4.2 Deaf interpreters

I firmly believe that Deaf and hearing interpreters should be working together whenever possible when interpretation is required. Even top-notch, certified interpreters at times cannot entirely make the cultural bridge necessary for the target message to succeed with the audience. Teaming Deaf and hearing interpreters together can help alleviate cultural misunderstandings and gaps that do occur, and so I recommend that these teams be used more frequently than is currently the case. I am confident that if this were to take place, communication would go all the more smoothly.[8]

4.3 Using "dramatization"

I have witnessed on many occasions interpreters who, instead of using appropriate, grammatical ASL, insist on "dramatizing" a dialogue or narrative. ASL, like any language, has an array of grammatical structures and vocabulary options that speakers or signers can use to make their point. For whatever reason, many second language ASL learners have the impression that *any time* there is a descriptive passage or reported dialogue, it is best to "act it out". While there is a time and place for this sort of thing, there are often more appropriate – more linguistic – ways to convey the information. I observe that frequently when interpreters "act out" or mime a scene, it insinuates that there is no principled linguistic way to convey the same material, and this can come across as quite insulting to ASL signers. When I see someone doing this, it is obvious to me that they still have much about ASL to learn. An example or two, along with some suggestions as to why "acting out" is inappropriate, should help to clarify this.

If for example an interpreter is describing somebody who is drunk (given that they are attempting to capture the English source speaker's text), the interpreter might "become" the character and "drive" the car as if she were drunk, perhaps by using the ASL "th" mouth gesture to show a kind of careless inattentiveness, and using her signing space to demonstrate the driver driving the car haphazardly along the road. But if the interpreter has not actually *witnessed* the event, she is in fact making up what took place, and has no license to do so. She should not, therefore, act out the scene – there are other, still quite visual, means to capture the facts using principled ASL structures.

As a second example, suppose there has been an accident and the signer has actually witnessed it. If this is the case, her description of it will be much different than if she is only getting the information second hand. This is typically the case when someone is interpreting: she has not seen the actual event, and she should adjust her interpretation accordingly. Think, for example, if the speaker is describing a woman who was driving while using a cell phone and has an accident. If the interpreter acts this out, putting an imaginary cell phone up to her cheek and pretending to talk as if this is what the woman would have been doing, then swerving and crashing, etc., she will leave the impression that she knew exactly what took place because she saw it, or otherwise she is, once again, making it up. This has enormous implications both for the interpreter in a cultural sense, because she has made assumptions about "how things are done", and for the interpreted interaction, because of the way the source message is construed.

It is true that Deaf people often encourage hearing ASL learners to make their discourse more visually appealing, through extensive use of classifiers for example. But the ASL student should not then assume that any time something can be demonstrated or mimed, it should be. Learning how to use ASL well in this context takes a great deal of careful observation of Deaf ASL signers, along with considering when and where such demonstrations occur, thinking about why the person chose to do so, and discussing with ASL mentors how to do this appropriately.

4.4 The use of first and third person pronouns

A final point regarding interpreting and language use I want to make has to do with the interpreter's use of pronouns. It has long been the practice that interpretation occurs in first person, the rationale being that the interpreter is representing exactly the discourse of the source speaker, so that when the speaker uses first person, the interpreter does as well. I would like to make a suggestion however, as a Deaf person whose first language is ASL, and from the position of having watched English-ASL interpretation throughout my life. The practice of the interpreter using first person has caused Deaf consumers confusion about who the "I" is during an interpreted event.

I have had occasion to be with my mother, who is also Deaf, when she is at a doctor's appointment. The interpreter, just as she has been taught to do, carries out the interpretation using first person to represent the doctor's speech, but my mother has continually misunderstood, thinking that it must be the interpreter who will be giving her medicine, etc., and not the physician. In situations such as this, I am convinced that the interpreter should use a third person pronoun to indicate what the doctor is saying for clarity.

When I work as a Deaf interpreter I choose not to refer to the source speaker in first person in my interpreting so as to ensure comprehension on the part of the consumers I am working with. I indicate, by indexing or pointing to one person or the other that the intended action will be done by that person. I have witnessed, as I am sure many interpreters have, consumers nodding their heads to indicate their understanding when in fact they have not. This is a common form of politeness that individuals of a minority culture use in contexts where they interact with majority culture individuals and do not want to lose face (Baker-Shenk 1986; see also Friere 1970). By using third person pronouns, and by indexing who the speaker is, I believe much confusion in this area can be avoided.

Metzger (1999) found that the pronouns the interpreters in her study used did not always correspond to those either the Deaf or hearing consumer used, but Metzger's study suggests inconsistencies in the interpreters' use of pronouns. For example, in one case the doctor referred to the Deaf patient using a third person pronoun, whereas the interpreter used a second person pronoun in the interpretation. Metzger speculates that there are several reasons behind the inconsistencies in the use of pronouns, including inexperience, an unequal alignment with the Deaf and hearing consumers (thus using first person for the Deaf person's comments but third person for the hearing person's, as in "she said"), or a reflection of inconsistencies in pronoun use on the part of the consumers themselves.

I cannot offer a simple solution to this dilemma, nor do I believe that one necessarily exists. But I would encourage practitioners to begin to dialogue about this very question. Is this a case where interpreters have decided on a practice – one that seems quite logical – without considering the effect of the construction on the Deaf consumer? When the interpreter references herself, points to herself, and uses facial grammar to indicate that she is asserting something, the effect for me is that I believe *she* herself has said the thing, and it takes some conscious effort to readjust my thinking to remember that it is not the interpreter but the hearing speaker that this action or statement is attributed to. Do Deaf people just accept this because interpreters have decided that is it the way it should be? Do we need to revisit the Code of Ethics with respect to this?

4.5 Monitoring consumer feedback while interpreting

There is nothing more important to guide the interpreter's linguistic choices than feedback she gets from consumers as the interpretation continues on. Speakers introduce terms and ideas into the discourse all the time. In language generally, when new things are invented or new technology becomes popular, new lexical items get added into languages as well. When an interpreter introduces a new term or one that she suspects may be somewhat unfamiliar generally (e.g., "microwave" or "smartboard") it is important that she monitor the non-verbal feedback she receives from consumers. She should introduce the term, and if the feedback indicates understanding, she should leave it at that – stop there! Deciding off the top to go into a lengthy "expansion" insults the Deaf consumer's intelligence. Many times the Deaf person knows perfectly well what the term refers to, and no expansion is needed. I sense, however that interpreters are not looking for feedback cues, or not paying attention to them, and the Deaf community is becoming frustrated by this practice.[9]

It may be the case that sometimes a term is used that is not understood. Again I encourage interpreters to monitor their audience for non-verbal cues (e.g., a slight head shake, a brow furrow) and if such gestures are made, then and only then expand on the term and check for further feedback.

I would also caution, however, that all head nods are not created equally! A more rapid and curt head nod typically means to keep going (somewhat like the English prompt *uh-huh*), meaning that the person is still working to understand, while other more certain head nods clearly indicate "got it". And the "got it" head nod means that no further explanation (i.e., "expansion") is necessary.

One additional thing that should be noted is when Deaf consumers ask the question typically phrased YOU MEAN? Here they are not asking for a whole chunk of information to be repeated. YOU MEAN? indicates a specific point in the discourse that needs clarifying and the interpreter must monitor the discourse carefully to understand what the consumer is referring to. Going all the way back to the beginning and starting again is not called for.

These comments once more indicate that interpreters need to respect the culture of the consumer, their language, and the diversity in the community. Non-verbal cues to understanding can sometimes be subtle, but communication has often gone awry when interpreters have not appropriately monitored, understood, and respected these cues.

5.   Conclusion: Deaf and hearing communities working together

It is imperative that our communities work and learn together. It is time to enrich our learning by having Deaf people, hearing individuals who do not know ASL but who have an interest in the Deaf community, hearing ASL-English interpreters and Deaf interpreters attend workshops together on language and the interpreting process. I am confident that we would see enhanced learning outcomes from such an arrangement. Too many faulty assumptions have been made in the past about what was being achieved in learning situations where only one of the above groups attended. I have seen amazing outcomes when we have integrated these communities for workshops and classroom activities. Collaboration is the key to learning.

I organize a very interesting activity in the workshops that I teach that highlights the positive outcomes of collaboration. I have students read an interesting "snip-it" (e.g., facts, hints, etc.) and have them tell that information to a Deaf person, allowing time for questions, answers and clarification. I then ask that Deaf person to relay the same piece of information to another Deaf person, who was not present during the first exchange, and have the students watch. These students are often amazed when they observe native users of ASL impart this same piece of information. They learn so many things, for example where some information was missed that they thought had been conveyed, how to make better linguistic choices, and so forth.

I would encourage others to organize this type of learning experience as well, keeping in mind that involving Deaf people as ASL language models is the key to the success of the activity. Hearing students can see ASL modeled and Deaf participants can ask questions about English word choices for linguistic items in ASL. In other words, it is a learning opportunity for all involved.

In this chapter I have outlined a number of considerations for interpreters in how they interact with Deaf community members culturally, linguistically, and during interpreted events, and made some suggestions for how interpreters can improve the quality of their interpreting. I have discussed a number of topics related to message equivalence in interpretation, but what exactly equivalence is in ASL-English interpretation is still not always understood. We need more research in this area, and we need more in-depth training in message equivalency in interpreting programs. What should be clear is that interpreters cannot work in isolation – they need input from Deaf people in each of these areas. In fact, the suggestion has been made that the most appropriate stance interpreters and the Deaf community should take is that of being allies (Baker-Shenk 1992; Bienvenu 1990; Peery 1989).

It is the Deaf community's culture and language that the interpreter is learning about, and the community is the interpreter's greatest resource. Some of the suggestions I have made may be new to many interpreters, but I believe they reflect an honest Deaf perspective. Once again, the most important thing about collaborating is dialogue. I would like nothing more than to see these topics receive much discussion both in the classroom in interpreter education programs and among professional interpreters and community members, and if this takes place, we will undoubtedly increase our learning.

Notes

1. Much of what I have learned, and discuss in this chapter, has come from my experiences both as a Deaf Interpreter and educator. I would like to thank the anonymous reviewers for helpful comments.

2. For an in-depth discussion of Deaf people's culture, see Padden and Humphries (1988).

3. Mindess (1999) also cautions hearing people to be wary of acquiring name signs in ways that are not the norm for this practice in the Deaf community.

4. Interpreting Consolidated (1998). *The Pursuit of ASL: Interesting Facts Using Classifiers* with Angela Petrone Stratiy. Available from Interpreting Consolidated, www.aslinterpreting.com.

5. For more information on classifier systems in signed languages, readers are referred to Emmorey (2003).

6. This sign may be directed toward the item or a point in space with the palm orientation toward the signer, or the middle finger might be "pointed" directly at the item.

7. See Russell, this volume, for more on consecutive interpreting.

8. For more on Deaf interpreters, see Boudreault, this volume.

9. For further discussion of the issue of Deaf consumer feedback, see Bienvenu (1989).

References

Bailey, Carole Sue, & Kathy Dolby (2002). *The Canadian Dictionary of ASL*. Edmonton, Alberta: The University of Alberta Press.

Baker-Shenk, Charlotte (1986). Characteristics of oppressed and oppressor peoples: Their effect on the interpreting context. In Marina L. McIntire (Ed.), *Interpreting: The Art of Cross Cultural Mediation, Proceedings of the Ninth National Convention of the Registry of Interpreters for the Deaf, July 4–8, 1985* (pp. 59–71). Silver Spring, MD: RID Publications.

Baker-Shenk, Charlotte (1992). The interpreter: Machine, advocate, or ally? In Jean Plant-Moeller (Ed.), *Expanding Horizons* (pp. 120–140). Silver Spring, MD: RID Publications.

Baker, Charlotte, & Dennis Cokely (1980). *American Sign Language: A Teacher's Resource Text on Grammar and Culture*. Silver Spring, MD: T.J. Publishers.

Bienvenu, M. J. (1989). Process diagnostics: The Deaf perspective. In Sherman Wilcox (Ed.), *New Dimensions in Interpreter Education: Evaluation and Critique, Proceedings of the Seventh National Convention, Conference of Interpreter Trainers, 1988* (pp. 99–112). USA: Conference of Interpreter Trainers.

Bienvenu, M. J. (1990). Rebuilding the bridges. In Sarah MacFayden (Ed.), *Gateway to the Future: Papers from the 1990 AVLIC Conference* (pp. 7–22). Canada: Association of Visual Language Interpreters of Canada.

Emmorey, Karen (2002). *Language, Cognition, and the Brain*. Mahwah, NJ: Lawrence Erlbaum Associates.

Emmorey, Karen (Ed.). (2003). *Perspectives on Classifier Constructions in Sign Languages.* Mahwah, NJ: Lawrence Erlbaum Associates.

Freire, Paulo (1970). *Pedagogy of the Oppressed.* New York: Herder & Herder.

Gile, Daniel (1995). *Basic Concepts and Models for Interpreter and Translator Training.* Amsterdam/Philadelphia: John Benjamins.

McKee, Rachel Locker, & David McKee (2000). Name signs and identity in New Zealand Sign Language. In Melanie Metzger (Ed.), *Bilingualism and Identity in Deaf Communities* (pp. 3–40). Washington, DC: Gallaudet University Press.

Meadow, Kathryn P. (1977). Name signs as identity symbols in the Deaf community. *Sign Language Studies, 16,* 237–245.

Metzger, Melanie (1999). *Sign Language Interpreting: Deconstructing the Myth of Neutrality.* Washington, DC: Gallaudet University Press.

Miller, Mary Beth, & Deborah Matthews (1986). Warning! Crossing cultures can be hazardous to your health: A look at communication between Deaf and hearing cultures. In Marina L. McIntire (Ed.), *Interpreting: The Art of Cross Cultural Mediation. Proceedings of the Ninth National Convention of the Registry of Interpreters for the Deaf, July 4–8, 1985* (5th printing) (pp. 56–60). Silver Spring, MD: RID Publications.

Mindess, Anna (1999). *Reading Between the Signs: Intercultural Communication for Sign Language Interpreters.* Yarmouth, ME: Intercultural Press.

Padden, Carol, & Tom Humphries (1988). *Deaf in America: Voices from a Culture.* Cambridge, MA: Harvard University Press.

Peery, Patricia (1989). Interpreting: The personal, professional, and social contexts. *TBC News, 20* (The Bicultural Center), 1–2.

Spindler, George, & Louise Spindler (1977). The Menominee. In George and Louise Spindler (Eds.), *Native North American Culture: Four Cases* (pp. 361–498). New York: Holt, Rinehart and Winston.

Stratiy, Angela (1996). Interpreting and interpreter education: Past, present and future. In Terry Janzen and Hubert Demers (Eds.), *Celebrating our Roots: Papers from the 1994 AVLIC Conference* (pp. 5–16). Edmonton, Alberta: AVLIC, Inc.

Supalla, Samuel J. (1992). *The Book of Name Signs: Naming in American Sign Language.* San Diego, CA: DawnSign Press.

CHAPTER 10

Vying with variation

Interpreting language contact, gender variation and generational difference

Lorraine Leeson

Trinity College Dublin

1. Introduction[1]

This chapter considers the role that variation plays in language and the range of coping strategies that interpreters draw upon when dealing with such variation in practice. We will initially consider interpreting between one signed language, Irish Sign Language (ISL), and one spoken language, English, before exploring how variation challenges signed language interpreters across the European Union. We will begin by describing briefly the nature of the variation that arises in ISL, including gender variation, generational variation and regional variation. We will also discuss the impact of language contact on ISL, paying particular attention to the influences of a neighbouring signed language, British Sign Language (BSL), on ISL before turning to outline how professional interpreters deal with influences from BSL and as well from other signed languages. A further issue for consideration will be the role of manually coded English, or "signed English", used in the Irish Deaf community. We describe some of the strategies that professional ISL-English interpreters use in coping with variation in the Irish context. We will compare and contrast the interpreter's strategies with what Deaf people think interpreters should do in a range of situations where variation is an issue.

Finally, we consider the issue of variation across languages in the European Union, where more than 30 indigenous national signed languages are used across 27 countries. We will briefly outline the differences that arise across EU member states in terms of training opportunities for signed language interpreters before considering how pan-European meetings that require signed language interpreting are organized. Among the factors considered will be the increasing role of American Sign Language (ASL) as a signed language used for cross-European Union communication.

We begin, however, by giving a very brief socio-political overview of Ireland and its relationship with its nearest neighbour, the United Kingdom of Great Britain, in order to contextualize discussion later in the chapter regarding the relationship between Northern Ireland and the Republic of Ireland on one hand, and the Republic and mainland Britain on the other.

1.1   The Republic of Ireland – A colonial past

Ireland has been invaded by the "strong-men" of many eras including the Vikings and the Normans, and our experience is one of colonization. For more than 700 years, Ireland has had an uneasy relationship with the United Kingdom of Great Britain, whose first moves towards colonizing Ireland began in 1171 (McCrum, MacNeil, & Cran 1992). One of the most devastating effects of colonization regards the use of the indigenous spoken language Gaelic, commonly referred to as Irish. While Irish was suppressed in later periods, the Irish language and Gaelic culture were initially forces to be reckoned with. However, the use of Irish was targeted and over time, English prevailed as the prestige language. It became the dominant language, the language of success. Until the Act of Union in 1803, Irish was inextricably associated with Roman Catholicism and English with the Protestant Ascendancy. These associations still persist to a certain extent today. Our history has led to a conflation of political and religious ideology: in Northern Ireland it frequently seems that to be a Republican is to be considered a Catholic and vice versa, while to be a Unionist is to be Protestant. To understand why this is the case, we must remember that when Ireland was granted independence in 1921, the men who negotiated the treaty sought restoration of the entire thirty-two counties of Ireland. The British government conceded twenty-six, holding onto six counties that together represent the British territories in Ireland. These six counties have been the source of the long "war" that has raged between Republicans who want to see a unified Ireland and Unionists who want to remain as part of the United Kingdom. As Unionists are typically Protestant and Republicans typically Catholic, the fight for the six counties has become irrevocably associated with religious loyalty, particularly given that the Republic is considered traditionally to be a Catholic country while Britain's Protestant past has been well documented.

In the Republic, since independence, Irish has been treated as the official first language of Ireland, with English as the second official language. However, in practice, English is the working language of the state. Other languages are used in the Republic as well, but none can claim official status unless a constitutional referendum takes place in order to ratify its inclusion. This is the case for Irish Sign Language.

It is this political backdrop that frames our discussion of the variety of signed language used in parts of Northern Ireland and its potential relationship to ISL and BSL. Next we turn to look at the role of ISL-English interpreting as a professional service activity in Ireland and the consequences of the status of ISL for professional interpreters.

2.   Interpreting in Ireland – A new profession

Before the early 1990s, Irish Deaf people had no recourse to a professional interpreting service. In the mid 1980s, Deaf members of the Deaf community established the Irish Deaf Society (IDS), a self-advocacy organization of Deaf people. Primary goals of the IDS include seeking recognition of Irish Sign Language as an official language and the establishment of professional interpreter training. With this latter agenda in mind, the IDS, in partnership with the Centre for Language and Communication Studies (CLCS) at the University of Dublin's Trinity College, sought funding from the European Union's HORIZON Programme to train ten ISL-English interpreters in conjunction with the Centre for Deaf Studies at the University of Bristol from 1992–1994. There is currently (in 2005) a total of 22 accredited interpreters on the national register serving a Deaf population of 5000, but not all of these are available full-time (Leeson 2003). This compares to the Swedish situation where a population of approximately 10,000 Deaf people are served by a professional interpreting community of over 400 interpreters. Even with this degree of interpreter provision, however, access via interpretation is not guaranteed as demand continues to outweigh supply (Katarina Karlsson (STTF),[2] personal communication, 2003). Thus, for the Deaf population in Ireland, we would need approximately 200 interpreters on stream in order to provide a comparable service to that currently available in Sweden.

This lack of access to professional interpreting services was pivotal in the Irish Deaf Society's campaign to establish a permanent Centre for Deaf Studies in Ireland. Following almost a decade of lobbying, the IDS, in partnership with the University of Dublin, Trinity College, secured funding for an Irish Centre for Deaf Studies, which was established in 2001. Interpreter training is one of the core programs offered by the Centre.

A major factor in the provision of interpreting in the Irish context is that of variation, particularly variation that is based on gendered patterns of language use and gendered vocabulary choices. We shall see that language contact has also played a role in ISL. But before we turn to look at these issues in some detail, let us consider the Irish Deaf Community and the general sociolinguistic context that ISL exists within.

3.   The Irish Deaf community and Irish Sign Language

Irish Sign Language is the third language of Ireland (Burns 1998) and is used by some 5,000 Irish Deaf People (Matthews 1996), though estimates suggest that an additional 50,000 non-Deaf people know and use ISL to a greater or lesser extent.[3] Despite this, no public services are available in this language and provision of services in an accessible language in all domains of life is relatively *ad hoc*.

Since the mid 1940s, speech has been considered to be of extreme importance in the education of Deaf children in Ireland. By the 1950s, a strictly enforced segregation divided children who used a signed language and those who did not. Children were encouraged to give up signed language for Lent, the 40 days of repentance leading up to the Catholic feast of Easter. Children who were caught signing were threatened: they would be sent to the "Deaf and Dumb" section of the school, a place where those considered to be less intelligent were educated without recourse to an academic education (McDonnell & Saunders 1993). This practice continued at least until the mid 1980s, supported by individual Dominican nuns (Leeson & Grehan 2004) and is evidence of the higher status associated with the use of speech. Such attention, which focuses on normalizing Deaf people through suppression of their language, has been described as "linguistic genocide" (Skutnabb-Kangas 2000).

In contrast, the use of a signed language is greatly valued in Deaf communities. The shared experience of Deafness and the shared use of a common language create a normal context for linguistic and cultural transfer which is not immediately available to Deaf children born into families where parents and siblings can hear. For the Irish Deaf community then, the term "Deaf" has different connotations. "Deaf" means "one of us", and represents the positive shared characteristics that identify a person as a member of the Irish Deaf community. Significantly, these include the use of ISL and active participation in cultural events of the Irish Deaf community (Matthews 1996). Traditionally, attendance at a Deaf school was considered the way in which deaf children were introduced to Deaf culture and ISL – particularly for the estimated 90 to 95% of Deaf children who have hearing parents. Degree of hearing loss is not considered significant to membership of the Irish Deaf community but attitudinal factors are: to be a Deaf person, one must have pride in one's language and community (see for example Padden & Humphries 1988; Matthews 1996; Lane 2002). Indeed, we use "capital D – Deaf" to illustrate that we are talking about someone who is culturally Deaf as opposed to "lower case d – deaf" to discuss the audiological factors associated with deafness, or to describe persons who are audiologically deaf (e.g., due to old age) but who do not consider themselves members of the Deaf community (Lane 2002; Ladd 2003). Recently, Deaf researchers have begun to differentiate between these by referring the notion of shared cultural experience that is framed by the experience of being deaf as "Deafhood" (Ladd 1998, 2003).

The Deaf community is not a homogeneous community in terms of language use, however. In Ireland, evidence of this includes the many sources of variation seen in ISL. The remainder of the chapter discusses these along with implications for interpreters.

3.1 Variation in Irish Sign Language: Gendered signing, Gay Sign Variation (GSV) and regional variation

In this section we discuss the types of variation that have been identified as occurring in Irish Sign Language. We begin by briefly considering the role of gender.

3.1.1 *Gender variation*
There has been longstanding variation based on gender in ISL, arising as a result of the strict segregation of Deaf boys and girls in the schools for the Deaf. As a small

country with a population of approximately 3.5 million, Ireland did not (and still does not) have a large number of Deaf schools. There is one major school for Deaf boys, St. Joseph's, and one for girls, St. Mary's. The gender variation that exists for a particular generation of now elderly signers has been described in a number of papers by Le Master and Dwyer (1991) and Le Master (1990, 1999–2000, 2002). The details of gender variation in ISL deserve greater attention than this overview of variation types in Section 3.1. This topic is thus expanded upon in Section 4 below.

3.1.2 *Gay Sign Variation*

Sexual identity may also influence a signer's use of ISL. A Gay Sign Variation (GSV) has been posited for Irish Sign Language, though to date, only two tentative discussions of the subject exist (Murray 2002; Fitzgerald 2004). Generally, GSV in ISL is used by some Deaf gay men and is considered to be predominantly lexical in nature. GSV appears to be made up of a range of vocabulary items and phrases, many of which are in fact borrowed from the gendered generational female variety (Fitzgerald 2004), and for "standard" ISL items, the movement path may be elongated and some handshape components altered, leading to a recognizable stylized articulation which could be described as being "camp". There is a clear need for a descriptive analysis of GSV in ISL. In the interim, interpreters deal with GSV in a small range of specific environments, notably at gay community events.

While protection is offered to members of the gay community on the basis of legal instruments such as Article 13 of The Amsterdam Treaty (1997) of the European Union and the body of Equality Legislation that has been introduced in Ireland, including the Equal Status Act (2000), there is still a tension that exists in Irish society regarding sexuality, and this tension extends to gay members of the Deaf community. This may lead to Deaf men using GSV only in contexts where they are open about their sexuality, probably within gay community settings. In other situations they may use a more standard form of ISL. For interpreters too, these tensions exist. For example, there may be gay and lesbian interpreters who have not disclosed their sexual identity to the wider interpreting and Deaf communities, thus they may minimize demonstrating their knowledge of GSV (if they are in fact knowledgeable about this variety) in certain contexts to maintain their own privacy.

The appropriateness of interpreters using certain varieties is another issue for consideration: while variety exists across languages, it is not always appropriate for all members of a language community to use all varieties, even though they may know and understand them. Some varieties may be commensurate with "insider status", which may result in a reluctance to share specific terms with non-deaf people (e.g., Kleinfeld & Warner 1996). Given the dearth of information about GSV in the Irish Deaf community, we cannot make presumptions about how and when signers wish for interpreters to use GSV. Some Deaf people may expect that interpreters simply understand their variety and adequately represent them in the target language without feeling compelled to use a "camp" accent (particularly if the interpreter is not gay). On the other hand, some signers may feel that interpreters should both understand and be able to produce a specific variety, including GSV.

3.1.3 *British Sign Language as a language of influence*
ISL operates within a complex sociolinguistic context. While ISL is quite distinct from our nearest neighbouring signed language, BSL, there are many influences from BSL on ISL. This stems from access to televised BSL programs, a longstanding migration of Irish Deaf people to the UK for post-secondary training and employment, and the co-operation of organizations of Deaf people in the UK and the Republic. These influences are discussed in some detail in sections that follow.

3.1.4 *Regional variation*
While regional variation is not a prominent sociolinguistic characteristic of ISL, there is a growing consideration of the possibility that there exists a distinct Northern Irish variety of Irish Sign Language (NISL). The relationship of NISL to ISL appears to be at the syntactic level, while the lexicon is BSL based (Ó hEorpa 2003). Ó hEorpa suggests that NISL signers seem to be "signing BSL using the ISL grammar when in Belfast" (2003:8), but notes that NISL is recognized by BSL users in the UK as being "different" from standard BSL. While research is needed to document the nature of the variety used in Northern Ireland, specifically in terms of identifying just how similar or different NISL is from ISL and BSL, we can note that the intuitions of practicing interpreters support those of Deaf NISL users. Ó hEorpa cites two interpreters from Bristol, a city situated in the South East of England where signed language interpreters have been trained for almost 25 years. One interpreter was originally from Northern Ireland, but trained as a BSL-English interpreter at Bristol University. These two interpreters noted that while they learned BSL at Bristol, they "learned nothing about the language we use here!" (i.e., in Northern Ireland) (Ó hEorpa 2003:8). The second BSL interpreter noted that he could not follow NISL signers as "they do not use BSL" (Ó hEorpa 2003:8). Indeed, Ó hEorpa, who is himself a Deaf interpreter working between ISL and BSL, notes that he finds that he "understands ISL interpreters better than England's BSL interpreters" (Ó hEorpa 2003:8).

However, Ó hEorpa also reports that many "Anglo-Irish" Northern Irish signers argue against the use of the acronym NISL and believe that while their variety is distinct, it is still a part of British Sign Language. This has led to the somewhat tongue in cheek suggestion that the acronym BSL be used to refer to Belfast Sign Language.[4]

All of this suggests that there is an interesting Northern Irish variety to be explored and documented from a sociolinguistic perspective, and that a good deal of exploration is needed with regard to what interpreters should be learning about this variety. As it stands, interpreters working with NISL are typically local to the area. When NISL users travel to the UK, they report that they modify their signing somewhat in order to be understood by BSL users and BSL-English interpreters. Where possible, they use Northern Irish interpreters who have relocated to the UK mainland (Ó hEorpa, personal communication). With a corpus-based research project commencing in the UK (including Northern Ireland) in late 2007 (Adam Schembri, personal communication), we hope to gain a clearer understanding of the relationship between the variety of signed language used in Northern Ireland and those used elsewhere in the UK.

We can also suggest that as more and more Deaf children are educated in Partially Hearing Units (PHUs) rather than at schools for the Deaf, that is, in special units for Deaf and hard of hearing children attached to local schools, an increased degree of variation may occur, with local varieties, particularly at the lexical level, potentially emerging from local schools and increasingly localized Deaf communities. However, it is fair to say that to date, regional variation has not been identified as a major characteristic of contemporary ISL given the traditional centralization of educational services in the Republic's capital, Dublin. As a result, no attempts to fully describe regional variation exist at present for ISL.

In contrast, gender variation *has* been identified as an important issue in ISL. Thus, the next section focuses on this topic. We begin with a review of the literature in this area.

4.   Gender and generation in Irish Sign Language

In this section, we begin by briefly reviewing the work that has been carried out on gender and generation in ISL, most notably through the work of Le Master and Dwyer (1991) and Le Master (1990, 1999–2000, 2002). We describe the evolution of lexical variation in ISL that is associated with male and female signers of a specific generation. We also consider questions such as: Does gender variation occur in ISL beyond the lexical level? Why do signers aged 20–60 years suggest that gender continues to play a role in the way Deaf men and women sign today? If gender variation plays a role in contemporary ISL across the generations, how is this expressed (i.e., only at the lexical level, in quasi-idiomatic expression, or in the form or frequency of specific grammatical or pragmatic structures)? And finally, what is the impact of this variation on interpreters, and how should interpreters respond?

We will see how the age of the signer conflates to some extent with gender variation for male and female varieties when we come to talk about "generation and gender in ISL".

4.1   Gender as an influencing factor

The Dublin Deaf community has a history of distinct sex-differentiated vocabularies that spans more than a hundred years (Le Master & Dwyer 1991). The two major schools for the Deaf in Ireland are based in Dublin, less than a mile from each other. Like many other religious-run schools in Ireland, the schools for the Deaf are segregated according to gender.

In establishing the Catholic schools in the 1840s, it became clear that the Dominican Sisters who would manage and run the first school for Catholic Deaf girls would have to develop a system for teaching Deaf children. To this end, two Dominican nuns travelled with two Deaf girls, Agnes Beedan and Mary Ann Dougherty, aged eight and nine respectively, to Caen in France to study teaching methods that utilized signed language (McDonnell 1979; Matthews 1996; Crean 1997; Coogan 2002). The Dominican Sisters adapted the French methodical signing system to one suited to teaching English to those attending St. Mary's School for Deaf Girls. Ten years later, when St. Joseph's School for Deaf Boys was established, the Christian Brothers used the same signing system as the Dominicans, though alterations were made to the form of many signs. Crean (1997) suggests that the Christian Brothers at St. Joseph's School drew on published references to American Sign Language in their preparations for teaching Deaf boys. Folk belief has it that the Christian Brothers wished to make the signs they learned from the Dominican Sisters less feminine and more masculine so as to be appropriate to the teaching of young boys (Leeson & Grehan 2004).

Even though the schools were located close to one another, students did not have the opportunity to mix socially (Le Master & Dwyer 1991). Over time, this segregation, along with the intentional alteration to several signed forms, led to the evolution of distinctive gender biased signed vocabularies that were to some degree mutually unintelligible (Le Master 2002). Even when students left school, they were discouraged from socializing together or marrying each other. McDonnell and Saunders (1993) describe reports from Deaf women that Dominican nuns at St. Mary's school would advise employers with more than one Deaf member of staff to minimize opportunities where Deaf staff members could communicate through sign. These attempts at segregation seem to have played a role in allowing for the evolution of widespread lexical differences which became entrenched in the respective vocabularies, and as Leeson and Grehan (2004) suggest, also in the prototypical grammars of male and female signers.

4.1.1 Gender and generation in Irish Sign Language: The role of the lexicon

Le Master (1990) conducted a study on differences in women's and men's signing within an older population of ISL signers. Her study focused on women who left school around 1946 and men who left school around 1957. The early to mid 20th century was a time when signed language was still openly used in the education of Deaf children in Ireland. The oral philosophy was not implemented until the late 1940s and became entrenched as policy after the publication of a 1972 government paper on the education of children handicapped by impaired hearing. All of Le Master's informants were active members of the Dublin Deaf community, who had continued access to gender varied signs that they had used when at school through social interaction with their peers.

Le Master (1990) analyzed 106 different male and female signs, finding that 63% of these signs used by male and female signers were related to each other in some way (the remainder were not related). For example, related signs may share the same handshape but be articulated in a different location or have a movement that differs. Le Master (1990) argues that as such a high percentage of the vocabulary she analyzed was in fact related, one would expect some degree of mutual intelligibility between male and female signers using these related signs. This was not the case. Le Master found that men and women both reported that they had to actively learn the vocabulary used by the opposite sex. Interestingly, this contrasts with comments made by Foran (1979), a leading member of the Deaf community at the time. Foran was also a member of the "unified sign language committee" responsible for the preparation of the 1979 Dictionary of Irish Sign Language, and he states that gender-based variation did *not* cause confusion among members of the Deaf community, but did hinder hearing people who were learning this signed language.

Le Master evaluated semantic lists for gender variation and demonstrated the occurrence of variation across all lexical categories analyzed (e.g., GIRL (noun), WORK (verb) and YELLOW (adjective)) (Le Master 2002:8). However, Le Master's informants also reported that female signs were no longer in use as women adopted the male variety as the standard form for daily interaction, suggesting that male signs were more accessible to both male and female signers than were female signs (Le Master 2002). Other writers suggest that this move is a form of patriarchy within the Deaf community (Coogan 2003; Leeson 2004a).

4.1.2 Contemporary ISL: Do gender and generation continue to conflate?

Leeson and Grehan (2004) suggest that while the widespread lexical differences described by Le Master do seem to have a corollary in generation, (i.e., they are not generally used by younger signers), contemporary signers have another lexicon of gendered signs. The signs that Leeson and Grehan refer to are lexical items that co-occur with compulsory oral (mouthed) elements. The obligatory multi-layered components that make up these signs differentiate them somewhat from the signs referred to by Le Master. Leeson and Grehan note that these signs typically had their origins in the segregated schools for the Deaf in Cabra, but many of them made it past the school-gate and continue to be used today by Deaf women ranging in age from their mid twenties to their late fifties. Figure 1 is an example of such a female sign. This sign can be glossed as DON'T-ANNOY-ME and is used by Deaf women in contexts where they do not wish to respond to an interlocutor. Deaf men would not normally use this sign. Further, Leonard (2005) found that gendered signs are not only confined to the age-group reported on by Leeson and Grehan (2004). He interviewed six signers aged 18–30 and found that they too use gendered signs, some of which they use in common with older signers, and some of which seem to have been created by younger cohorts of signers. This clearly demonstrates that gender based variation remains in ISL and that interpreters need to be aware of the range and type of gendered variation that occurs.

This sign, along with others described by Leeson and Grehan, is typically used in all-female company in informal settings. It is highly unlikely that a Deaf woman would use it in a mixed gender conversation or in a formal context, such as at a conference.

Figure 1. DON'T-ANNOY-ME. A contemporary gendered sign in Irish Sign Language.

Indeed, Leeson and Grehan looked for examples of gendered signs in a video recording of a day-long Deaf women's conference organized by the Irish Deaf Women's Group and found only one example. On this basis, we might think: well, maybe interpreters will not come across these signs in practice – do they really need to know them? On putting this question to several Deaf women who are students at the Centre for Deaf Studies at Trinity College, however, the unequivocal answer was that interpreters must, at the very least, understand these signs.

On a practical note, we should bear in mind that interpreters are most likely to meet these signs in predominantly female or all-female semi-formal environments such as women's group meetings, assertiveness training courses, and mother and toddler group sessions. However, male interpreters have also reported coming across gendered signs in mixed settings. These facts clearly indicate that interpreters need to understand these signs, even in cases where they are unlikely to use them themselves.

4.2 Beyond the lexicon: Does gender play a role?

The gender divide also seems to have had an impact on the form and the frequency in which male and female signers produce certain constructions in ISL. Preliminary research has focused on two specific structures, namely simultaneous constructions and topic-comment structures (Leeson & Grehan 2004).

4.2.1 *Simultaneous constructions and gender in ISL*
Signed languages make use of two manual articulators, the hands, which operate in three-dimensional space. Given this fact, we expect that signers will use structures

involving both hands to establish the relative location of two objects or actors in their signing space or to introduce and hold one item on one hand and then refer to it using the other hand. Miller (1994) provides a good overview of the kinds of simultaneous constructions found in signed languages.

In looking at simultaneous constructions in ISL, Leeson and Saeed (2004) found a difference in how frequently male and female signers produced such constructions used to establish locative relations between entities. In terms of structure, male and female signers seemed to uphold certain underlying cognitive principles relating to what information was introduced on the dominant and non-dominant hand respectively. Generally, male and female signers alike used the non-dominant hand to present information that was backgrounded (or "old") information and the dominant hand to present foregrounded (or "new") information.

Building on this work, Leeson and Grehan (2004) analyzed a corpus of ISL data contributed by twenty-seven Deaf ISL signers. In considering eight hundred and seventy-five lines of glossed text of authentic ISL data that included excerpts from conference presentations, lectures, TV interviews and story-telling sessions, they found a total of thirty-five simultaneous constructions that were used to establish locative relations. Sixteen of these constructions were produced by female signers and nineteen by male signers. What is interesting, however, is that male signers produced nearly *double* the number of lines of text produced by Deaf women. This means that Deaf women are in fact producing almost twice as many simultaneous constructions to mark locative constructions as their male counterparts.

4.2.2 *Topic constructions and gender in ISL*
Topic constructions also appear to be influenced by gender. Leeson (2001a) reports a qualitative difference in how men and women mark topic constructions in Irish Sign Language. This contrasts with Ó Baoill and Matthews (2000) who suggest that topic constructions are very frequent in ISL, being used to highlight certain elements within discourse or to bring an element into focus. Ó Baoill and Matthews propose that the discourse topic is always nominal and that the main non-manual features associated with topic constructions in ISL are the head, which is tilted back slightly, and raised eyebrows accompanying the articulation of the topic. This is followed by a head-nod, while the eyebrows remain raised. They report that the eyebrows return to a neutral position during the articulation of the comment.

Leeson (2001a) found that while this description was adequate for prototypical topic-comment constructions in ISL, it did not account for the non-manual features in the majority of topic constructions found in her Irish Sign Language data. Instead, she proposes a continuum of prototypicality for topic constructions in ISL where, in the typical instance, the signer's head is tilted back and eyebrows are raised, and the offset of the topic is marked by an eyeblink, which could be described as an intonation break, following Wilbur (1994) for ASL and Rosenstein (2000) for Israeli Sign Language. In less typical constructions, signers can omit either or both the backwards tilt of the head and the eyeblink at the offset of the topic. While some

ISL data exhibits a clearly identifiable head-nod at the offset of topic, this does not seem obligatory. Leeson suggests that male signers are most likely to make use of the prototypical topic construction while female signers are most likely to omit the backward head tilt component of the non-manual marking on the topic, marking it only with raised brows.

4.2.3 *The impact of variation on the interpreter's task*

If signed language varieties have not been described by linguists, and lexical items typical of certain varieties are not listed in any dictionaries of ISL, then how can students of ISL, including interpreters, acquire an understanding of these forms? If signed language tutors teach only what are considered "standardized" forms of ISL, then again, where do students learn the varieties that exist? And as well, if professional, qualified ISL tutors are, as has been the case in Ireland over the past decade, typically male, then how are students to gain access to varieties that these teachers themselves may not know, or to stigmatized varieties that the teachers do know but feel are inappropriate for teaching in a formal context?

The facts given above regarding gendered differences suggest that ISL-English interpreters must develop increased sensitivity to the gender variation that exists within ISL, primarily through recognition of the types of gendered variation that exist, and secondly, through considering the strategies they might use when working into ISL in all female situations, all male situations and in mixed gender contexts, and the consequences that these strategies have on their interpreting. For example, should interpreters alter their use of certain structures when working into ISL for an all female audience? Should they include gendered signs? Do they understand the range of functions that these gendered signs play? What should they do in a mixed environment? Should male interpreters know and use gendered signs? How do the decisions that interpreters make for coping with challenges related to variation impact on their performance? These are just some of the important questions that we will address throughout the remainder of the chapter.

5. Language contact, signed languages and interpreters

When languages come in contact, a range of outcomes is possible. These include bilingualism, diglossia, code-switching and code mixing, borrowing, convergence and divergence, interference, foreigner talk, the development of lingua francas, and the evolution of pidgins and Creoles (Holmes 2001; Fromkin, Rodman & Hyams 2003). These terms have also been applied to signed language communities but researchers are increasingly becoming more guarded in their use of such terms when describing signed languages (for example see Cokely 1983; Lucas & Valli 1992 for the appropriateness of discussing signed languages as pidgins).

While we cannot include a complete discussion of the range of contact outcomes that have arisen for ISL in this section, we can focus on a number that are of direct relevance to our discussion of variation. These include borrowing, convergence and divergence, interference, and the use of lingua francas.

5.1 Borrowing

Borrowing occurs when one language takes a lexical item from another language and incorporates it into its own system. In spoken languages, borrowing is frequent. For example, English has borrowed the word *pizza* from Italian, while the word *bazaar* is borrowed from Arabic (McCrum et al. 1992). Signed languages also borrow from each other (e.g., ISL has borrowed vocabulary from other signed languages including the one handed BSL sign HAVE). Signed languages also borrow from spoken languages (e.g., compounds used by ISL signers such as HOME^WORK, BOY^FRIEND, etc.). While often also described as borrowed items, fingerspelling and the initialization of signs should be considered as "unique phenomena" according to Valli and Lucas (1992) and Blumenthall-Kelly (1995).

5.2 Convergence and divergence

Convergence occurs when a signer or speaker of a language uses the language or language variety of her interlocutor in order to appear friendly or to help with communication. Divergence occurs when the signer or speaker does not use the language or language variety of the other interlocutor, deliberately avoiding using the other person's language (Holmes 2001).

Use of divergent or convergent interaction can also be used to mark insider or outsider status. Divergent interaction may indicate a status differential between two varieties, which may indicate that the interlocutors are not members of the same social or linguistic group (see, for example, Holmes 2001). On the other hand, speakers or signers may recognize that they are from the same sociolinguistic group and this recognition is marked through the use of convergent discourse. In the past, it has been thought that when North American Deaf people met, their language converged around use of ASL, whereas when interacting with non-deaf people, convergence would occur in a different direction insofar as Deaf people would switch to a manually coded variety of English to accommodate their hearing interlocutors. However, Lucas and Valli (1992) demonstrate that this is not exactly the case all the time. Indeed, it seems that convergence and divergence are phenomena that occur as much between varieties of the same language as between discrete languages.

In consideration of interpretation, we could say that the need for interpreters arises in divergent situations: in such situations, people typically do not know each others' languages or do not speak them well enough for interaction to occur fluidly unassisted. Another possibility is that people do not wish to use their addressee's language even though they may know it. This can happen for several reasons. For example, the speaker may have political reasons for not using the language of their interlocutor, such as those of Flemish speakers who speak their own language rather than French in Brussels because, they argue, Brussels is the bilingual capital of Belgium and therefore all services should be available in both French and Flemish. Indeed, many Belgian companies hire interpreters working between Flemish and French to interpret meetings (Peter Van Den Steene, personal communication).

Other reasons for choosing to use one's own language may be related to a speaker's wish to publicly promote that language. For example, a minority language may be used such as Irish in the Dáil (the Irish parliament) even though English is the normative language for interaction. In other situations, languages may be of equal status and interpretation is provided, such as in the European Union's Parliament. A special instance of divergence may be that of signed language users who are typically bilingual in the majority language of their country to a certain degree, but who may not be able to follow spoken language interaction in mixed groups because of constraints on lip-reading,[5] or because they do not lip-read, or because they prefer to use an indigenous signed language.

5.3 Interference

Another outcome of language contact is interference. This occurs when a bilingual person uses her second (typically non-native) language, but her first language creeps in unconsciously or "interferes" with the structure or grammaticality of target language production (Holmes 2001). For example, a native speaker of French may use the word *sensible* in English (but which means 'sensitive' in French) and she may intend the French meaning. Because a speaker of English will understand *sensible* to mean someone who is not being rash rather than someone who is sensitive, miscommunication can easily occur. The issue of interference is always present for interpreters, and it represents one of the reasons why organizations of spoken language conference interpreters advocate that interpreters only work into their mother tongue. Baker (1992) notes that interpreters should have total control of the idiomatic expression of a language before they can claim to be truly fluent in that language. This is the degree of fluency demanded by the Translators Guild of Great Britain (which has been superseded by the Institute of Translators and Interpreters (ITI)) of translators working into any given language (Baker 1992). If fluency is not acquired to a "mother tongue" level, the language is understood to be used passively, that is, the interpreter can work from this language into her active languages, but cannot work into this language.

Given that many signed language interpreters learn ISL as a second (or subsequent) language, we can expect that when they work into ISL there may often be evidence of English language interference in their output. Similarly, it is possible that where interpreters have ISL as a first language, their English output will show evidence of ISL intrusion. Unlike many spoken language interpreters and translators, it is simply not possible to minimize mother-tongue intrusion on signed language interpreting by advising interpreters to solely work into their mother tongue, as this would make it impossible for Deaf people to go about their business in interpreted domains. For this very reason signed language interpreters need to take intrusion seriously. Being aware of what constitutes source language intrusion and strategizing to minimize the effects of intrusion are important skills for all signed language interpreters to develop.

5.4 Lingua francas

Lingua francas are another interesting outcome of language contact. When several communities, each with their own language, also share a common language with which they can communicate with the other communities around them, this language common to them all is known as a lingua franca (Crystal 1997). In this way we can say that a lingua franca may typically be a language that some people know as a native language (e.g., English for some Europeans), or a language that no-one in a particular community has as a first language, or it can be one that no-one uses as a daily language any more (e.g., Latin in Europe). A lingua franca can also be an artificial language (e.g., Esperanto or Gestuno). In Deaf communities, lingua francas are used in international settings. While people refer frequently to "International Sign", it is important to note that research has demonstrated that when signers interact, they actually maintain quite a significant amount of their primary language in the interaction (Sutton-Spence & Woll 1999). We will discuss the use of International Sign along with the potential for, and restrictions on, interpreting in International Sign in Section 9.4 below. First, let us consider the outcomes of language contact between ISL and BSL.

5.5 British Sign Language and Irish Sign Language

We noted at the outset of this chapter that ISL has been influenced by its nearest neighbour, British Sign Language. Indeed, the earliest schools for the Deaf in Ireland were established while Ireland was still a colony of the British Empire. The earliest school for the Deaf was established in 1816 in Dublin. The Smithfield Penitentiary School (later known as the Claremont School) was a Protestant school which sent a teacher, Mr. Joseph Humhreys, to study the methods employed by the Braidwoods in Scotland, who pioneered what became known as the Braidwood System, a combined system that made use of manual signs and speech components. Matthews notes:

> When Humphreys returned to Ireland to teach deaf children at the Claremont School, it is reasonable to assume that he may have actually brought back and used in his teaching, many features of British Sign Language. Some elderly deaf people who attended the Protestant School in Ireland use the British two-handed manual alphabet to this day, supporting this theory.   (Matthews 1996:71)

In more recent times, BSL has continued to have an influence via educational experience: many Northern Irish Catholic Deaf children have traditionally been sent to the Dublin Catholic schools for their education. When children returned to the North of Ireland and settled into a Deaf community that was not segregated on the basis of religious difference, the situation was ripe for language contact, with the possibility that a new variety emerged that drew on elements of both ISL and BSL, leading to what has been called Northern Irish Sign Language by some (Ó hEorpa 2003).

Despite the nationalist/unionist divide in Northern Ireland, the Deaf communities in Northern Ireland and the Republic of Ireland have engaged in co-operative activities for many decades, particularly in the sporting arena. This again allows for opportunities for BSL and ISL to come into contact.

However, the major factors influencing language contact between BSL and ISL in recent times are probably emigration and television. For much of the 20th century, Ireland suffered from an economic downturn with resulting mass unemployment. As a result, many Irish people emigrated, seeking employment or training in the UK, United States, Australia and Canada. Given the geographic proximity, many went to the UK. In the 1990s, the economy in Ireland boomed and the "Celtic Tiger" economy was born. For the first time, Ireland was a land of returning émigrés, and among this group were returning Deaf people who now brought with them British Sign Language. Many did not return to Ireland, however, having settled into a relatively more empowered British Deaf community. The tendency for Irish Deaf people to migrate to specific regions of the United Kingdom has had an impact on the variety of language used in those communities too. It has been noted that in areas of the UK where there are significant communities of Irish Deaf people, ISL has had an influence on BSL, for example in Liverpool and London (Brennan 1992; Sutton-Spence & Woll 1999).

Coupled with this economic history, we must bear in mind that educational opportunity also gave rise to language contact possibilities. Given that there was no professional interpreting service in Ireland until the mid 1990s, many Deaf people chose to study in the UK, where they had a greater opportunity to access a wide range of courses. In the early and late 1990s, European Union funding allowed for the establishment of interpreter tutor training via partnerships between Irish and British universities. These opportunities, along with increasing possibilities to study Deaf Studies in UK universities, meant that Irish Deaf people often found themselves in British contexts studying Deaf related issues through the medium of BSL and presenting coursework and assignments in that language. Indeed, given the lexical gaps that existed in ISL for certain vocabulary during this period (e.g., for "linguistics"), a good deal of BSL vocabulary was borrowed into ISL. Some of these lexical items have remained close to the original BSL forms while other items have altered over time to meet the phonetic and phonological constraints of ISL, thus truly becoming part of ISL.

Irish Sign Language has also experienced contact with American Sign Language and French Sign Language (LSF). Given the global dominance of ASL, it is somewhat surprising that there currently seems to be less vocabulary borrowing from ASL than from BSL. In part this may be a result of the fact that Deaf people have tended to travel more frequently between Britain and Ireland than they have travelled to the United States and Canada. However, given increased participation in international organizations and events where the lexicon of ASL is highly influential (e.g., the World

Federation of the Deaf and the European Union of the Deaf), it is possible that the global influence of ASL may become more prominent in the future in influencing which lingua franca ISL signers use when conducting international business.

While language contact with ASL might be considered a recent development by many, Crean (1997) suggests that there was contact between the two languages in the 19th century. Fr. John Burke, the chaplain considered responsible for developing a manual code of English based on de l'Epée's French methodical system (in Ireland) may have borrowed ASL vocabulary from documents published by the Rochester Institute for the Deaf in the mid 1800s.

This American connection is tenuous, but the contact with LSF and methodical French signs is well documented, particularly regarding the involvement of Fr. Burke in adapting the established methodical French system (Matthews 1996). His system was eventually implemented in the Catholic schools for the Deaf in Dublin. Besides this, we have already noted that two Irish Deaf girls accompanied the Dominican Sisters who first went to Normandy to study the French approach to Deaf education, thus the connection to LSF is well established.

While the contact situation with BSL, LSF and ASL has led to borrowing into ISL, this almost pales into insignificance when compared with the relationship that has existed between ISL as a minority natural language and signed English, the codified form of the "global" language, English, since the dawn of education of the Deaf in Ireland. In the next section, we explore this relationship in more detail.

5.6 Signed English as a prestige variety

Given the suppression of natural signed languages across the western world, coupled with educationalists' attempts to present spoken languages in visual forms, it comes as no surprise that in Ireland, a manually coded form of English also exists. It is known as "signed English" or "manually coded English". McDonnell (1997) says that a central aim in Deaf education in Ireland has always been the teaching of English, and that manually coded systems of English were specifically designed to assist in achieving this aim. We have seen that in the mid 1800s, the Catholic chaplain to St. Mary's School for Deaf Girls, Fr. Burke, assisted in the task of developing a methodical system of signs to represent the grammar of English based on the French methodical system used by the Abbé de l'Epée (Matthews 1996). A century later, in the 1960s and 1970s, signed English was revived as part of the move towards "Total Communication" (McDonnell 1997).

In the 1950s, Ireland adopted a strong pro-oralism approach, which became the normative approach to Deaf education in the 1970s with the Government Report "The Education of Children Who Are Handicapped by Impaired Hearing". While the report proposed that if a child proved unsuccessful in an oral environment, she should be moved to a class where a manual system could be used, many writers have noted that in practice, such children were seen as failures, both orally and academically (Matthews 1996; Crean 1997; Leeson & Matthews 2002). Matthews (1996) notes that while the report suggested that children could be transferred to a section of a school for the Deaf where education was delivered through signed language, "in reality it often did not happen. The vast majority of deaf children remained in the oral section of the schools. And even when the children were unable to lip-read or understand much of the educational material being imparted, they remained in that system and were not transferred to a unit to be taught through manual communication" (1996:79).

The schools undermined the status of signed language by associating its overt use with lack of ability. Children who were educated via signed language were typically those with multiple disabilities, which often included learning disorders; they did not sit state examinations and were typically trained in the trades, with little attention given to their academic education (McDonnell 1979; McDonnell & Saunders 1993; Matthews 1996; Crean 1997; Coogan 2003).

Given the strict policy of segregation advocated by the 1972 report,[6] children who used a signed language were educated in a separate section of the school's campus from children who were educated orally. Those who were oral successes were discouraged from communicating with children who used signed language, and punished if they repeatedly flouted the "no sign language" policy. Punishment included being sent to the "deaf and dumb" school, and threatened that they would not be allowed to return to the oral section of the school if they did not cooperate (McDonnell & Saunders 1993).

Outcomes included a diminished status for the use of a signed language in educational establishments. With the demise of this academic association and the removal of significant numbers of Deaf teachers from the schools, ISL became the language of the oral failures, the less able and the uncooperative. This led to ambivalence in the Deaf community about the value of ISL, with many Deaf people unaware that their means of communication constituted a legitimate natural language. Indeed, the Deaf community only began calling their language "Irish Sign Language" in the 1980s, previously referring to it as "the Deaf way" or "the sign language" (Leeson 2003; Leeson & Matthews 2002).

Even when non-deaf people became interested in learning a signed language, Deaf people felt that they could not teach ISL, which they saw as lacking grammar and as an impoverished form of signed English. Instead, they argued that signed English should be taught as it followed the patterns of grammar known to their English speaking students, making it easier for them to learn than "the Deaf way" of signing.

Attempts in the late 1980s and early 1990s to teach ISL were met with resistance by those teaching signed English (Patrick A. Matthews, personal communication). Even today, with increased recognition of the role that ISL plays in the Deaf community, there is still a reluctance in some quarters to move toward teaching ISL, perhaps because there are still so few professionally trained ISL tutors in the field. But as this domain becomes professionalized, attitudes toward teaching ISL and the subsequent standards of ISL achieved by students attending classes can be expected to rise. This status issue can be considered as under review today with a recently introduced state examination in Irish Sign Language (Leaving Certificate Applied examination), a reference to Irish Sign Language in the Education Act of 1998, and the steadily increasing awareness of the existence of ISL as a language in its own right among the general population with commensurate rights for Deaf people to access information via Irish Sign Language (e.g., via the provision of ISL-English interpreters, information on TV in ISL, or via video materials provided by the Irish Deaf Society).

6. Vying with variation: The challenge for ISL interpreters

Leeson (this volume, Chapter 3) notes that interpreters have to make decisions. As professionals they make decisions about the intent of the speaker or signer, the desired effect of their comments, the pragmatics of an event, the sincerity of the speaker, and the degree of definiteness in their utterances, among other things (e.g., Baker 1992; Gile 1995; Robinson 1997). Some of these decisions are influenced by what is said or signed, others by inferences made, and yet other decisions are formulated in response to the context that the interpreting occurs in, framed in part by the individual speakers and signers that interpreters find themselves working with.

The Irish context poses significant challenges to interpreters. An understanding of the interactive nature of interpreting is essential if interpreters are to come to terms with the challenges that this degree of variation poses, with the consequences that certain strategic decisions may have for the interpreting process, and with the outcomes of interpreted interaction.

In this section, we look at a range of issues including: what does an interpreter do when faced with a mixed audience whose language choices might include Irish Sign Language, signed English, gendered varieties, generational gendered varieties, and evidence of language contact with BSL, ASL and International Sign? Do interpreters make strategic decisions about how they will deal with such contexts? And perhaps most importantly, what are the consequences of certain strategies on the subsequent interpreting performance?

Another important question that is often left unasked in this context is: can we reasonably expect a single interpreter to learn how to skilfully handle all this variation in an undergraduate training program or should we be looking at the strengths of interpreters in the field, both individually and collectively, in responding to the patterns of variation that exist? Perhaps rather than expecting one interpreter to deal with the entire gamut of variation, we should be considering the strengths of the existing interpreting community vis-à-vis the task at hand. Indeed, the Deaf community itself serves to identify through trial and error which interpreters function best in which contexts, with the result that interpreters are requested to work in particular settings where they are known to participants as having the skills required to function successfully. For example, interpreters who grew up in Deaf families are typically much more familiar with gendered generational variants of ISL than their colleagues who are not from Deaf families. Younger interpreters are more familiar with the vocabulary used by recent school-leavers than are older interpreters. And as mentioned earlier, Northern Irish interpreters are familiar with the Northern Irish variety while their southern Irish and mainland UK counterparts typically are not. This issue of matching interpreters to their domains of strength is a point that we will consider again later.

In what follows, we also build on the range of coping strategies that are used by interpreters and translators generally, as discussed in Leeson (this volume, Chapter 3), when considering specific strategies used by ISL interpreters to deal with the challenges of variation. Our discussion of the impact of strategies used on interpreting performance is framed in Gile's (1995) Effort Models of interpreting, also outlined in Chapter 3.

6.1 Strategies used by ISL interpreters to deal with variation

Many strategies used by ISL-English interpreters faced with variation are in fact extensions of those used by interpreters generally, or are related to the general strategies discussed in Chapter 3 of this volume.

We begin by considering strategies that interpreters can and do apply during their preparation phase prior to an interpreting event. Here it is important to note that in Section 7 we discuss Deaf community members' feelings toward some of these very same strategies, and it is obvious that reactions can differ greatly. In some cases, the strategies discussed below are those that interpreters *are* using (perhaps as opposed to *should be* using), and we would be well advised to consider the impact they make on the client. Regarding the interpreter's ability to prepare, and to strategize during this phase, we acknowledge that interpreters do not often have all the information that they should ideally have prior to an interpreting assignment. Despite this, interpreters can use their background knowledge of the community they work with when preparing to deal with language variation. A key preparatory task is that of getting to know your audience.

6.1.1 *Knowing your audience*
Knowing the audience is a strategic move when a community of language users is diverse. This is key to successful interpreting in Ireland. If you are not aware of the sociolinguistic characteristics and socio-political attitudes held by members of your audience, it is very difficult to make informed decisions about how to present information vis-à-vis how much fingerspelling to incorporate, how much initialized signs should be used as opposed to choosing to paraphrase, or whether to seek a more "free" interpretation (Napier 2002) of the source language, for example. Without knowing the audience, the interpreter will not be able to predict the degree of gendered signing that may arise, or the extent of mouthing that will be used, which tends to co-occur with use of cued-speech influenced vocabulary items in a segment of the female Deaf population (e.g., the index finger extended to the lips in the sign for SHOES that is sometimes used; the little finger extended to the lips in an occasionally used sign for CORK, etc.).

With regard to fingerspelling, knowing the audience can assist in predicting how much fingerspelling to expect and who might use a good deal of fingerspelling without any accompanying lip-patterns (typically these are older male participants). Recent research suggests that fingerspelling may exhibit variation for gender in other signed languages too, for example, ASL (Mulrooney 2002). No research exists to date on whether fingerspelling in ISL is qualitatively different between genders, though as noted above, there appears to be a difference in terms of frequency of use. Knowing the audience means knowing that older male signers approximately fifty years of age and above are most likely to use fingerspelling even in situations where there are established ISL signs, some examples of which are BACK, TWINS, etc. It means knowing that male and female signers aged sixty years and above are less likely to have experienced an oral education and are thus less likely to use mouthed lip-patterns in their communication, and perhaps are also less likely to be able to decode this receptively in the way that younger signers who have experienced an oral education would. These older signers are most likely to use the gendered signs that Le Master reports. They are also more likely to use initialized signs and to express a preference for signed English, which may be influenced by the high status associated with using signed English that has been part of their experience.

Also regarding gendered differences, female signers may use more simultaneous constructions than male signers and young male signers are more likely to use certain non-manual features to mark topics than female signers.

Knowing the audience means recognizing that younger signers will probably incorporate mouthing into their production of ISL and use a greater number of agreement verbs than their older counterparts. For example, older signers often use the verb TO-TELEPHONE as a plain (i.e., uninflecting, often body-anchored) verb while younger signers inflect this verb to mark agreement with a subject and object. In other words, younger signers mark certain verbs as agreement verbs while older signers do not (McDonnell 1996, 2004).

This information is needed to formulate decisions about an interpretation. Of course, such decisions do not occur in isolation, but are often framed by the function of the interpretation taking place. For example, it may be necessary to fingerspell new terminology in an educational environment to maximize opportunities for the Deaf student to operate in a bilingual setting where lectures are translated into ISL but all course materials, including the core texts, are in English. Other reasons for fingerspelling may be to bridge a lexical gap in ISL without attempting to create a new sign.

6.1.2 Nonce signs

While the use of fingerspelling can be extremely useful for interpreters, alternative strategies also exist. For example, an interpreter may introduce a "nonce" sign for the duration of an event or series of events (Davis 1989). This nonce sign may be negotiated with a client prior to the event or may be introduced while the interpreter is on-task. Typically these signs are introduced by fingerspelling the word that the nonce sign will represent, then producing the sign. A repetition of the fingerspelled item may then occur, though this does not seem to be obligatory. The use of nonce signs is widely reported by interpreters and seems to be successful insofar as the practice is not usually considered as an attempt to create "new" signs by the Deaf community. Instead, these signs seem to be accepted as a strategy for maximizing understanding of a concept which currently does not have an established lexical sign, but only for the duration of a conference or a lecture or even a course of study.[7]

It is possible that individual nonce signs have made it into wider circulation. This may happen if a student relates some discourse about a topic that they have studied to other Deaf friends, then this sign may become a more widely used sign for a specific concept among their group. An example of a nonce sign for a specialized concept that has lived beyond the context of its creation is that of "SEMANTICS". In ISL this sign is a compound of MEAN+DEEP. It was developed by Deaf students who were studying linguistics in the early 1990s. Given that further opportunities arose for Deaf students in the area of linguistics, sometimes with these original Deaf students acting as tutors, lecturers or mentors, this sign became the established ISL sign for 'semantics' and is widely used by students and researchers in the area of linguistics today (e.g., at the Centre for Deaf Studies and the Centre for Language and Communication Studies, Trinity College, Dublin).[8]

It goes without saying that interpreters should set out to expand their knowledge base first by consulting with their Deaf clients, who, as participants in the context where an interpreter is working, are the most likely people to know existing signs for concepts that arise. We will return to this point in Section 7 where we discuss strategies suggested by Deaf consultants for maximizing interpreters' efficiency in dealing with variation.

6.1.3 *Repetition using a variety of vocabulary as a strategy*
This strategy is typically used in situations where the interpreter is aware that members of an audience use more than one sign for a particular concept. For example, one sign may be iconic while another takes an initialized handshape. Or, there may be female and male variants of the sign or generational differences that arise, for example there are contemporary signs for EASTER in the community and another sign for EASTER used by older female signers of approximately 60 years of age and above, as reported by Le Master and Dwyer (1991). In such settings an interpreter may choose to present a range of signs that they know for the individual concept in order to maximize understanding for different audience members. A sociolinguistic correlate of this decision making process includes recognition of the fact that this strategy affirms the varieties used by different members of a diverse community.

The downside to including more than one such vocabulary item is the fact that the interpreter typically is attempting to accommodate this diversity *while* interpreting simultaneously. Being this mindful of the audience through the use of multiple varieties in the output increases lag time and processing energy. If an interpreter is focusing her attention on the vocabulary items that she is producing, this then shifts attention away from negotiating meaning in the incoming message. However, no research has looked at this issue to date.

We should also consider the pressure this strategy places on the Memory Effort (see Gile 1995). In situations such as these, the interpreter is increasing the demand on short-term memory and is probably going to end up in a position where she must simplify or omit parts (or all) of the subsequent message to make up for having accommodated the audience at the lexical level. Some questions thus arise. Is this lexical accommodation an equal pay-off for loss of part or all of a subsequent message? Is the audience aware that the potential loss of a subsequent message is a possible consequence of interpreter decision-making in this regard? Of course, we could ask whether interpreters themselves fully consider the consequences of this strategy.

Similarly, lag time effect is heightened for the interpreter through repetition of a message segment (i.e., articulation of multiple lexical items that carry the same meaning. Cokely (1992) demonstrates that both shortened lag time and lag time that is extended beyond optimal length impact the quality of target language output. He shows that interpreters with a lag of just two to four seconds have an increased likelihood for the production of substitutions and other anomalies. Miscues are extremely frequent in interpreted pieces where lag time is in this range. Cokely's study shows that interpreters with a two-second average lag time generally had more than twice the total number of miscues than interpreters with a four-second average lag time. Further, the interpreters with four-second lag time had twice as many miscue errors as interpreters with a six-second average lag time. Conversely, optimal lag time in the range of six seconds minimizes the likelihood for these miscues to occur. Interpreters with a lag time beyond this level tend to experience miscues that derive from overburdening short-term memory.

6.1.4 *Finding equivalence: The role of inference and paraphrasing*
The gender of the interpreter may be a factor for Deaf people in terms of their expectations of what interpreters should know. While we might expect that female interpreters would be expected to know and use female varieties, we might not have the same expectations of male interpreters. However, male interpreters may choose to mirror gendered vocabulary use in specific contexts. Male interpreters relate that they have interpreted in situations where gender specific vocabulary was used, noting that the problem is not so much in identifying the vocabulary item as gender specific, but finding an appropriate equivalent in English. Sometimes this is not as necessary as context carries the inferred intention or attitude of the signer (Tony Dolan, personal communication).

When working from English, interpreters may use a range of strategies including paraphrasing information in a number of ways. For example, if there is a mixed audience of male and female signers across age groups with different signing style preferences, interpreters may begin by using a style that incorporates more features of signed English such as elements for adverbials, continuous aspect or past tense like -LY, -ING, -ED, etc. As their performance continues, they will gradually reduce the number of explicit signed English items and increase the frequency of core Irish Sign Language features such as non-manual features to mark adverbials, use of space to mark time, aspectual modification of agreement verbs, etc. In such contexts, interpreters may not pay attention to gender related issues because stylistic features take precedence. One interpreter I spoke with referred to this strategy as the "demonstrate that the interpreter knows and can deliver the signer's preferred variety" strategy.

While this may facilitate a relationship with certain members of the audience, the consequences of such a strategy may include minimizing access for members of the audience who do not make use of signed English. At the very least, a move toward transliteration places increased responsibility for recovering meaning on the audience members. In effect, they are left in a position where they must seek to reformulate the (signed) English-like production into a comprehensible ISL message.

If this strategy is chosen at the outset of an interpreting assignment it may leave an ISL user who knows little English at a disadvantage in terms of tracking referents through the discourse, particularly where key concepts may have been outlined in a speaker's introductory comments. Of course, choosing *not* to accommodate a signer who prefers a style approximating signed English, or which incorporates elements of signed English, excludes them from the interpreted event and alienates them. An attempt to accommodate the ISL signer that moves from a more signed English styled presentation towards a more typical ISL presentation affirms their inclusion in the event without creating tensions along the socio-political linguistic divide.

6.1.5 *Affirming variation while on-task*

Another strategy is that of affirming variation while on-task or "Affirming the Dissenter!" This strategy was reported by a very experienced interpreter who finds that when interpreting in mixed audiences, there is great potential for conflict arising from vocabulary choice. In such instances, if the interpreter chooses a vocabulary item that is challenged from the floor, maybe explicitly or through use of a negative headshake, the interpreter will then ask the dissenter what their sign for the particular concept is, take it on board, but also explicitly ask the other Deaf members of the mixed audience if they saw the alternative provided, seek feedback from the audience that this alternative sign is acceptable, and then incorporate the dissenter's sign into her target text production.

The benefits of this strategy include the fact that the interpreter is affirming the Deaf client's right to variation and demonstrating the flexibility to incorporate alternative vocabulary. This strategy also indicates that the interpreter is willing to take constructive feedback while still ensuring that other members of the mixed audience have an opportunity to agree or disagree with the dissenter in their midst.

The negative outcome of such a practice again is such that the interpreter is required to focus attention on negotiating with her audience rather than attending to the incoming message. This may lead to a consequent gap in the message that is transmitted to the target language audience.

6.1.6 *Omission of certain items from the target language text*
Leeson (this volume, Chapter 3) notes that the omission of part of the source language message from the target language output while interpreting has been described as a miscue in some analyses (Cokely 1992), but is recognized by other authors as constituting a strategic approach (Baker 1992; Gile 1995; Napier 2002; Napier & Barker 2004). In dealing with variation in ISL, interpreters report that they can often omit a specific gendered item from their interpretation by finding a way to express the pragmatic intention of the lexical item in the target text. Indeed, professional ISL interpreters note that the very difficulty inherent in interpreting these gendered items is the fact that they are so culturally embedded in ISL and that they do not have ready-made English equivalents that offer the same content and gender-specific "feel" of the source element. Therefore, there is effectively no one-to-one mapping possible between ISL gendered signs and spoken English, which does not have a lexicon of idiomatic items used exclusively by women to the same extent.

7. The Deaf perspective: Let the interpreter beware!

In this section, we consider strategies for coping with variation that were suggested by a number of Deaf informants.[9] These perspectives are synthesized below.

7.1 Knowing a variety versus using a variety

Deaf informants suggested that while interpreters need to know the signs that make up a particular variety, especially gendered variants, they should not feel obliged to *use* these variants. Indeed, Deaf people reported that it is sometimes not appropriate for a signer to use a particular variety, for example Deaf men do not typically use female variants and may not in fact understand many of them. When asked about how an interpreter could learn when it is appropriate to use a certain variety and when it is not appropriate, given that this is not information that has been recorded or published, some suggested that perhaps only trial and error will tell the interpreter the answer. We might therefore consider this learning approach as: "Let the interpreter beware!"

7.2 Affirming variation while on-task

Deaf informants suggested that if an audience member disagrees with the sign an interpreter is using, the interpreter should use the sign the Deaf person suggests, providing this is acceptable to other members of the audience. This is clearly in line with the strategy outlined in Section 6.1.5 above. However, it would be interesting to see if Deaf people are aware of the interpreting performance outcomes that such negotiation creates, and if so, whether they are willing to trade content for increased comfort. Exploration of these issues, perhaps through experimental research and discussion regarding the consequences of implementing this strategy, would clearly enrich the understanding between Deaf people who regularly work with interpreters and the interpreting community.

7.3 Ask the Deaf person for advice

Deaf informants suggested that when an interpreter does not know a specialized vocabulary item in ISL or a preferred variety of a lexical item, they should consult the Deaf client directly. Deaf informants felt that their knowledge of their own language and of the concepts being discussed was often overlooked. They reported situations where interpreters turned to colleagues for assistance regarding vocabulary choice but overlooked the fact that Deaf persons may be the most qualified to offer such ISL advice, particularly if they are students of a subject, and have developed vocabulary items to overcome lexical gaps in ISL.

This would be an ideal strategy for use in preparation for events, but also during the event taking place when individual lexical items "fed" from Deaf clients could be incorporated into the target text by an interpreter quite easily without any critical impact on performance. Problems may arise if there is more than one Deaf client and they disagree over terminology or variants, however. Then, problems arise for the interpreter in coordinating the target language message. As well, at the participant interaction level, tensions may arise between clients or between a client and the interpreter.

7.4 When in doubt, use ISL

Deaf informants suggested that most users of signed English understand ISL, but not all ISL users understand signed English. They argued that as the interpreter's task is to work between two distinct languages, namely Irish Sign Language and English, this is exactly what the interpreter should do. They suggested that the Deaf person who has a preference for signed English has a responsibility to express this to a meeting or conference organizer prior to an event to ensure that they are facilitated maximally. The expectation of these Deaf informants thus suggests that the interpreter's strategy of beginning to interpret at an event using signed English would create a conflict.

7.5 Don't use foreign vocabulary

While signers may use foreign vocabulary in their production of ISL, Deaf people were very clear that signed language interpreters should not mirror this approach. They thus advocated a divergent approach in suggesting that interpreters avoid using foreign vocabulary. Instead, they suggested that interpreters could fingerspell an item instead of borrowing a foreign language term for it. Interpreters could then paraphrase the meaning of the concept in ISL. Some informants went further in suggesting that if an

ISL signer uses a foreign item, the interpreter should point out to them that this was not an ISL term. In discussion, however, most Deaf informants felt that this was not in fact an appropriate role for the interpreter, recognizing that the primary task of the interpreter is to comprehend a source language message and produce an acceptable target language equivalent.

8.   Comparison of approaches: The interpreter and the Deaf consultant

We have seen that many of the strategies used by ISL-English interpreters are in line with the strategies put forward by Deaf consultants. These include being aware of variation and understanding a particular variety that exists without necessarily using it oneself. It includes acknowledging a variant that is presented to the interpreter while on-task, although we have problematized this strategy somewhat and suggested that further analysis of its consequences must be considered.

What is surprising is that no-one specifically suggested that only interpreters who are familiar with certain varieties should work in contexts where those varieties are likely to be used. It may be that this is a foregone conclusion on the part of both interpreters and Deaf people alike. As mentioned earlier, the market itself may handle who works in specific contexts: because the interpreting community is so small, individual interpreters are known to the Deaf community, and those who are known to cope well with specific variation (e.g., interpreters who are knowledgeable about use of gendered generational variation because they grew up with Deaf parents who used gendered signs specific to their generation), are requested for that circumstance. We noted that in the Northern Irish context, local interpreters are preferred over non-locals. This preference is likely guided by the knowledge that locals are familiar with the variety being used. This common sense approach to interpreter choice does mean that ISL interpreters are not obliged at present to demonstrate efficiency across all varieties, although there are expectations from sections of the Deaf community that an interpreter *should* be able to deal with all kinds of variation.

Such expectations are more idealistic than realistic given the current situation. At present there is no standardized route to learning ISL in Ireland. There are fewer than twenty professionally trained tutors of ISL. The Centre for Deaf Studies in Dublin offers the only full-time classes in the country. Thus, opportunity for learning what we might refer to as "standard" ISL is very limited and as yet, no specialist courses focusing on variation exist. In a bid to alleviate this problem for prospective interpreters, the Centre for Deaf Studies makes every effort to teach interpreting students to become sociolinguistically sensitive, sharing what is known about variation in ISL and the reasons for its existence. We also attempt to balance gender regarding the ISL tutors who teach at the Centre and ask the tutors to incorporate discussion of variation into their classes. Further we encourage students to interact with members of the Deaf community whose signing styles differ from those of their tutors and fellow Deaf students. This is reinforced through placement opportunities where students get to meet Deaf people in a range of settings and observe and work with experienced interpreters in the field.

Another restriction on access to variability is interpreters' experience in certain domains but not others. Interpreting students from Deaf families are typically very competent in informal styles of ISL when they come to training, but may not be as familiar with more formal styles that exist. Contrary to this, students from non-Deaf backgrounds may have learned ISL in formal classes and may not be as knowledgeable about less formal styles of interaction. Of course, some interpreting students have acquired their ISL informally too – from friends, neighbours, colleagues, or children. This degree of variability in interpreters' backgrounds makes it necessary for programs to attempt to offer a "one-stop shop" approach to interpreter training. It is hoped that future developments in the delivery of ISL classes in the wider community, along with specialist pre-interpreter programs, will increase the entry-level ISL skills that student interpreters possess. This would allow training programs to move beyond the need for continued teaching of the language and instead focus on more advanced skills dealing with specific domains and particular challenges, such as those posed by variation.

Finally, there is a clear role for Deaf interpreters in this story of variation. In many situations, most notably those that are legal in nature, Deaf and non-deaf interpreters work alongside each other in a bid to maximize the mediation of information. In Ireland, no training is currently available for Deaf interpreters, which means that they are not formally trained in simultaneous interpretation management strategies and the consequences of decision-making processes (such as the consequences of miscues; the strategic use of additions, omissions, etc.). Relayed interpreting between any two languages can lead to a reduction in equivalence between source and the ultimate target languages, which is important specifically in legal and para-legal contexts where Deaf interpreters work most frequently. Thus, while the inclusion of Deaf interpreters is another means of managing variation, their inclusion is not unproblematic. Deaf interpreters are conscious of this fact and many are seeking training to better equip themselves to deal with the challenges that their particular role brings.

While the examples given thus far have focused on the Irish situation, it is clearly the case that the regional socio-cultural backdrop frames interpretations. To extend this theme, in the next section we look at the broader European picture, considering interpreting in the European Union.

9.   Signed language interpreting in the European Union

In this section, we will set the scene by considering the political infrastructure of Europe and the policies that offer support to languages at official and minority levels, both nationally and regionally. We will look at the resolutions recognizing signed languages that have been passed by European institutions and consider the possibility for recognizing signed languages under the auspices of the Council of Europe's Charter for Regional or Minority Languages (CRML) (1992). From there, we will outline the current lack of standardization in signed language interpreter education in the European Union and explore what this means for "International Sign" interpreting in a European context, paying particular attention to the issue of variability. We start by considering the two major political entities, the European Union and the Council of Europe.

9.1 The European Union and the Council of Europe: Recognition and protection of languages in Europe

The European Union (EU) was established after World War II. Following a call from France to establish the "first concrete foundation of a European federation" (www.europa.eu.int/abc/index_en.htm), the process of European integration began in May, 1950. Having expanded from a point where the European Community comprised six Member States, the EU currently has twenty-seven Member States (http://www.eurunion.org/states/home.htm). The European Union is a democratic entity where Member States "delegate sovereignty to common institutions representing the interests of the Union as a whole on questions of joint interest. All decisions and procedures are derived from the basic treaties ratified by the Member States" (www.europa.eu.int/abc/index_en.htm). Many issues are covered by the principle of subsidiarity: if a policy area does not fall within the remit of one of the European Union Treaties, then Member States have the freedom to implement their own policies at the national level. For European Union purposes, the recognition of minority languages falls into this category.

Within the EU, there are currently twenty-three official languages.[10] These are the languages in which meetings are interpreted and official documents translated. Minority languages such as Basque, Breton or Gaelic are not official languages. Minority languages of the European Union are not protected under any current European Treaty, meaning that funding for activities related to minority languages is dependent on Member State level support. This can be problematic, as in some countries there is a lack of willingness to recognize or support certain indigenous or immigrant languages. In a bid to raise awareness of the specific cultural values that these languages embody, the European Bureau for Lesser Used Languages (EBLUL) was established. EBLUL is a non-governmental organization that promotes EU policy-making in favour of minority and regional languages and aims to safeguard the languages of an estimated 40 million plus speakers of minority languages in the EU (http://www.eblul.org).

One of the protections available to indigenous languages in Europe is the Charter for Regional or Minority Languages (CRML). The CRML is an instrument of the Council of Europe. It is worth briefly introducing the Council here in order to contextualize the role of the CRML.

The Council of Europe is a separate political entity from the European Union, comprising 47 Member States and using two official languages, English and French (though the Council's Parliamentary Assembly also uses German, Russian and Ital-

ian as working languages) (http://www.coe.int/T/E/Com/About_Coe/Member_states/
default.asp). All EU Member States are also members of the Council of Europe. The
Council of Europe territories comprise some 800 million citizens.

Language is of importance to both the Council of Europe and the EU: both institutions aim to promote plurilingualism and pluriculturism among their citizens in
order to combat intolerance and xenophobia through improved cultural relations
(http://www.coe.int/T/E/Cultural_Co-operation/education/Languages/). This promotion of plurilingualism led to the highly successful European Year of Languages 2001,
which was jointly sponsored by the European Union and the Council of Europe. Financial support for linguistic activities was made available regarding official languages,
minority languages and signed languages. The Council of Europe's commitment to
languages and language learning has resulted in the establishment of the European
Centre for Modern Languages (http://www.ecml.at/aboutus/aboutus.asp?t=mission)
and the Common European Framework of Reference for Languages (CEFR)
(http://www.coe.int/t/dg4/linguistic/CADRE_EN.asp). The CEFR has been applied to
a growing number of European signed languages, including Irish Sign Language.

While the Council of Europe has only two official languages and the EU 23, there
remain many other languages, spoken and signed, which do not fall under the day
to day protection offered by national or international organizations and institutions.
To alleviate this problem, the Council of Europe developed the Charter for Regional
or Minority Languages (1992). This Charter, which has the status of a treaty, aims
to "protect and promote the historical regional or minority languages of Europe. It
was adopted, on the one hand, in order to maintain and develop Europe's cultural
traditions and heritage, and on the other, to respect an inalienable and commonly
recognized right to use a regional or minority language in private and public life"
(http://conventions.coe.int/Treaty/en/Summaries/Html/148.htm).

The CRML opened for signatories in 1998. Countries outline the native indigenous languages of minorities or of particular geographic regions that they will protect
under the terms of the treaty, along with identifying which aspects of the treaty they
will adopt. This is an important point to bear in mind for when we later discuss the
recognition of signed languages under the CRML.

9.2 The European Union of the Deaf (EUD)

The European Union of the Deaf (EUD) is a non-governmental body representing
organizations of Deaf people across the European Union. The EUD works in partnership with umbrella organizations of Deaf people in Central Europe through the
World Federation of the Deaf's Central European Regional Secretariat (CERS) and, in
the Eastern Europe/Asia border areas, through the Eastern Europe and Middle Asia
Regional Secretariat (EEMARS) when consulting with the Council of Europe, given
that the territories of the Council include countries represented by these regional
secretariats.

Since its establishment, the EUD has lobbied for the recognition of signed languages at the EU level. This has culminated in two resolutions on signed languages from the European Parliament (EU) in 1988 and 1998 and one resolution on signed languages from the Council of Europe's Parliamentary Assembly in 2001.[11] All of these resolutions, recognizing the principle of subsidiarity, call on their respective Member States to recognize the indigenous signed languages of their territories at the national level.

At the national level, the diversity of legal instruments that protect languages across the Union complicates the issue of such recognition. For example, some countries have constitutions (e.g., Ireland, Greece) while others do not (e.g., United Kingdom). This makes it difficult for an EU-wide call for constitutional recognition of signed languages. However, some countries have attained recognition of their native signed language(s) within their constitution, such as Sweden (Krausneker 2001; Leeson 2004b). Some countries have already implemented legislation that makes reference to signed languages and the right to a signed language interpreter in a range of settings (e.g., Italy, Ireland, Portugal) (Krausneker 2001), while others have *de facto* recognition of their languages, as is the case with British Sign Language following the British government's announcements to recognize BSL as a language in its own right, although it currently has no legal status as such.[12]

Given the fact that recognition of signed languages varies from country to country within the EU,[13] it is not surprising that the EUD has advocated seeking protection for signed languages under the auspices of the Charter for Regional or Minority Languages. Sweden, the UK and Denmark have each lobbied for the inclusion of their respective signed languages in each country's ratification of the CRML, although none has been successful to date. Lawyers for the Council of Europe have argued that signed languages are not natural languages, but rather "created" or "artificial" and also that they have not been established long enough to be considered "historically indigenous" to a region or territory. Eminent linguists from across the EU territories refuted these claims, which in 2000 led to the publication of the Flensburg Recommendations which advocate that, "The Council of Europe and other international organisations should consider the desirability and feasibility of preparing a legal instrument to safeguard these languages [signed languages] and the rights of their users. Likewise, the European Commission is requested to sympathetically consider the inclusion of actions to support Sign Languages in their language programmes" (European Centre for Minority Languages 2000: Par. 18).

The EUD held a meeting of members in 2001 to consider the path forward for signed languages and the CRML. The question asked was: should the EUD lobby for inclusion of signed languages under the CRML, or should they lobby for a new treaty that would focus protection on signed languages only? The membership was overwhelmingly in favour of the inclusion of signed languages under the current CRML, perhaps by seeking an annex to the original treaty to allow for those countries already signed up to the CRML to ratify the treaty for signed languages. This is the path currently being followed. Since then, a number of key players at the EU have commented publicly that the decision to exclude signed languages seems to have been ill advised given that signed language users consider themselves as linguistic minorities. To date, however, no country has included a signed language as one of the languages under their ratification of the CRML, but the profile of signed languages and signed language users has clearly risen in these European institutions.

9.3 Training of signed language interpreters across the European Union

Signed language interpreter training has been in place in parts of the EU for more than 30 years, though approaches to training and program duration varies significantly from country to country. Sweden was the first to introduce a formal program of training in the late 1960s. Initial training courses constituted a two-week program, but over time, this has developed to current levels whereby the majority of full-time interpreter training programs in the EU range between two and four years in length. Some of these are undergraduate programs leading to diplomas or Bachelors degrees, or equivalent levels of qualification. Other programs lead to a Masters degree. Some programs are run at university level, others at vocational training institutes, and others are run through Deaf organizations, with many programs (frequently part-time or evening courses) having no state accreditation.

This variability demonstrates that there is no standardization regarding how signed language interpreters are trained or what the minimum standard for performance on completion of training should be. In many EU countries only part-time training options exist at present (e.g., Belgium), and in some countries, no ongoing program exists (e.g., Luxembourg). This contrasts with training in Denmark, for example, where a national three and a half year program for signed language interpreters is in place. To date, many European countries have depended on financial support from the EU, for example through the HORIZON Programme, to establish pilot training programs. Unfortunately, when EU funding ran out for these ventures, national governments did not always step in to take responsibility for the training of signed language interpreters at the national level, despite the severe shortage of interpreters in every country. With continued lobbying of national governments by Deaf organizations, change has occurred in some countries, such as the establishment of the Centre for Deaf Studies at the University of Dublin, Trinity College, in 2001.

Leeson (2002b) notes that in Europe, the average signed language interpreter is typically female and learns the signed language of her region or country as a second language. The average signed language interpreter does not have a second working signed language or spoken language, though in order to work at the European level, knowledge of English is necessary. Leeson notes that in recent years, there has been an increase in the number of interpreters who do work with more than one spoken and one signed language, though this is not yet the norm. Training programs have not typically moved to offer more than one spoken and one signed language to students, although Tècnic superior en interpretació del llenguatge de signes in Catalonia is an exception, offering spoken Catalan and Spanish, Catalan Sign Language, and

Spanish Sign Language (Maria Josep Jarque, personal communication). Primary focus is typically placed on skill development in the one signed language being taught. As the European Deaf community becomes more multilingual in their signed language use, this will probably need to change.

Despite the lack of training standards at the EU level, there is an increased sense of cohesion and professionalism among signed language interpreters. Almost every EU country has an association of professional signed language interpreters, and these form the membership body of EFSLI, The European Forum of Sign Language Interpreters. Interpreters and interpreter program instructors have the opportunity to come together annually to discuss matters of interest to the profession and the development of standards and best practices in interpreting. However, training opportunities for signed language interpreters are not yet on a par with those for spoken language interpreters across the EU. For this to occur, a common standard of training will need to be agreed upon by the profession and the relevant training bodies that falls in line with EU conventions. Further, greater recognition must still be afforded to the signed languages of Europe and subsequently, to the profession of signed language interpreting.

9.4 Communicating at pan-European Union meetings

When Deaf Europeans meet to discuss the business of the EUD, they communicate freely even though they do not share a "mother tongue" nor do they depend on interpreting into their national signed language. Instead, they use a system of communication that has evolved as a lingua franca among Deaf people who attend these international meetings. At these meetings, there is no shared working language (such as Catalan Sign Language or Swedish Sign Language) but instead, what is referred to as "International Sign" has been used. International Sign is not a natural language but a system for communication. It does not have a fixed grammar or lexicon, does not have a community of users who acquire it as a first language, and it is recognized as being partly based in language and partly based in gestural communication. International Sign has been described as "a mixture of mime, international gestures that are mutually known (perhaps borrowed from another language or perhaps not) and signs made up for that encounter only and with meaning only in that context" (Sutton-Spence & Woll 1999: 32).

While meaning is negotiable in such an international exchange, Sutton-Spence and Woll (1999) found that up to 70% of signs used by a British Sign Language signer when communicating in International Sign were in fact BSL signs. As a result, they propose that International Sign could be described as a situational variant of *each* of the signed languages in contact during a given international communication event.

Meaning in International Sign encounters is typically negotiated. Signers can seek clarification from their interlocutors regarding particular lexical items or ask for an example to elucidate the meaning of a concept. This factor is a major issue to contend with when proposing that "interpretation" into International Sign be provided at international meetings.

Leeson (2002b) lists a number of points for consideration regarding the potential for interpreting into International Sign at pan-European events:

1. International Sign is not a language but a communication system. We do not normally talk about "interpreting" between non-languages.
2. Meaning is typically negotiated in International Sign. Given the nature of simultaneous interpreting there is no time for such negotiation to occur during the process of transfer between the source language and the target language or system.
3. International Sign is heavily influenced by the native signed language of the signer. This is especially relevant when providing "International Sign" interpretation for signers who have different signed languages from the interpreter's.
4. Because International Sign is not an established language and does not have a fixed grammar or lexicon, interpreters are not typically trained in International Sign, although some short workshops have been offered. This has implications for quality assurance in interpreting provision.
5. Signed Language interpreters frequently have their working signed language as a second language. This can have implications for fluency (most especially in terms of idiomatic expression) in their national signed language, not to mention another signed language or International Sign.

These are some of the reasons why the European Union of the Deaf advocates the provision of interpretation from and into natural national signed languages when Deaf people attend European Union institutional events (Leeson 2001b). Other reasons also influence this EUD recommendation: Deaf people attending the EUD congress in 2001 reported that they would prefer interpretation into their national signed languages rather than into International Sign as they felt that they could have negotiated meaning in a clearer way in their respective national languages.[14]

Until a solution can be reached, Deaf people attending European level meetings prefer to work with a national signed language and thus seek out professionals from their own country to accompany them, providing their interpreter also speaks the working spoken language of the meeting. Another alternative is to use a second signed language, for example, BSL or ASL and draw on the population of interpreters who use these languages as active languages and who are based at or near the location of the EU meeting. Because many Deaf Europeans have studied in the United States, many are familiar with ASL. Thus, ASL is frequently chosen as the lingua franca for interaction and as the preferred signed language for many meetings where the working spoken language is English. Where International Sign is used, the vocabulary that arises is frequently heavily influenced by ASL. However, with the growth of the European Union from 2005–2007 (bringing the number of Member States from 15 to 27), the increased level of inclusion of eastern European Deaf people at the European level may result in the increased use of Deaf interpreters to work between signed languages at international events.

9.5 Towards international working signed languages?

We are at a crossroads in the development of the signed language interpreting profession in Europe. As Deaf people gain greater access in numerous domains, their demands regarding the core skills of the interpreters who facilitate their participation increases – and rightly so. For example, while ten years ago there were only a handful of Deaf graduate students across the EU, today an increasing number of Deaf individuals are pursuing academic goals and practicing professionally in domains that earlier generations would never have even imagined to be options, such as in social work, law, social policy, linguistics, etc. Consequently, signed language interpreters are dealing with languages and language varieties that are developing in line with the new domains that they too find themselves in. These interpreters also find that their professional skills are expected to match the setting.

A further consequence of change is globalization. For the European Deaf community this brings many opportunities, particularly in terms of education and career choices. Deaf people are travelling to other countries to study, and when they do, they acquire new languages. For many, these languages are BSL, ASL and LSF. This opportunity for bilingualism is increasing and contributes to developments in the provision of bilingual education in preschool, primary and secondary levels of education across parts of the EU. In Sweden, some schools for the Deaf offer ASL as a language option (Therese Rollven, personal communication).

Over time, it is possible that in Europe it will be normative for Deaf people to know more than one signed language and that one or more of these indigenous signed languages will function as a "working language" for EU purposes (Leeson 2001b). For now, however, this is far from the reality, with many Deaf children across the EU fighting for an accessible and appropriate education in their national signed language. Currently, Deaf people chosen to represent their national associations are frequently those who have studied abroad, know English, and probably know some BSL, LSF or ASL. Interpreting teams best equipped to deal with the variability that arises in such European contexts are teams made up of interpreters whose skills compliment one another's well. Such teams would ideally include interpreters who, in addition to sharing the working spoken and signed languages of the meeting, know at least one other signed language and come from culturally diverse regions. This would allow the team to better identify cultural references that arise in the interaction, for example the various systems of government and education that operate across the EU, and as well, deal effectively with different fingerspelling systems, such as one-handed versus two-handed systems. However, with the growth of the EU, we see that some Eastern European Deaf people have had greater exposure to Russian as a second language (instead of English) and this will present additional challenges for interpreting teams who will not be able to depend on points of reference that may have been more culturally shared in the "old" European setting. As in the Irish context, this suggests that one interpreter cannot be expected to be able to deal with the entire range of diversity she may face at the European level. Rather, different interpreters bring different strengths to the task and these strengths can only be maximally utilized when working in teams.

9.6 Looking forward

As we move towards an increasingly plurilingual European Deaf community, interpreters must plan professionally. Demand for interpreting services increases to outstrip the number of interpreters coming on stream each year. Deaf people are taking their rightful place as full participants in society, but in many cases, this requires access via interpreting. Currently there simply are not enough interpreters to go around. And as the Deaf community becomes increasingly mobile, interpreters will need to be prepared for further challenges in their work. There will be more language contact between diverse signed languages, meaning that there is the potential for greater degrees of borrowing into people's national signed languages. This will create challenges for interpreters in the Deaf person's home country because of an influx of new "foreign" vocabulary, and for interpreters working in a host country, where a foreign Deaf person uses that country's signed language as a second language with all the problems that potentially brings, including non-native pronunciation.

Increases in contact between cultures inevitably bring opportunities for cultural conflict. Until now, at the national level, interpreters have talked about Deaf culture versus "hearing" culture, but in a plurilingual European Deaf community, interpreters are beginning to deal with the diverse cultural experiences of people from twenty-five states with very different political experiences, what it means to be Deaf in Europe, etc. Variation clearly brings challenges – and these challenges will remain with us for a long time to come.

10. Summary

This chapter has been about variation. We looked at the kinds of variation that can occur in a language and at how interpreters must deal with it, with particular reference to the consequences of the decisions they make, be this in one country or in an international setting. We saw that decision making is central to the task of the interpreter. The kinds of decisions that interpreters are required to make in the course of their professional activities can be categorized along a linguistic-interactive continuum. We should note that the list of decision types below is not meant to be taken as a complete listing (we could add many others, including, for example, ethical decisions):

–   **Purely linguistic decisions** (e.g., decisions regarding available lexical or syntactic choices);
–   **Discourse structure decisions** (e.g., the interpreter may consider radical changes to the structure of a message in order to make it more readily meet the discourse norms of the target language);

- Sociolinguistic-driven decisions (e.g., the choice of specific gendered items or the use of GSV vocabulary in certain situations but not in others; at the European level, the choice of a language-specific example or the use of a second language term – the use of the term "commune" to refer to the local government in Belgium or a more generic term like "town council", for example);
- Reparative decisions (e.g., decisions made by an interpreter to repair an earlier target language production which may have included errors or been incomplete in capturing the focus of the source language message; specific strategies to get back "on-track", for example strategic omissions, lengthening or shortening of lag time for strategic purposes, etc.); and
- Interactive/participant-driven decisions (e.g., making decisions to affirm the client through acceptance of vocabulary items suggested from the floor; negotiating meaning while working on-line).

From Leeson's (this volume, Chapter 3) discussion of the kinds of strategies used by interpreters, we see that professionals reflect on the decisions that they make. We also note that these decisions are typically driven by two factors which co-occur and create a tension, namely the tension between processing constraints and interactive constraints. Processing constraints apply to interpreting performance, outlined in Gile's (1995) Effort Model of simultaneous interpreting (Leeson, this volume, Chapter 3). Here, we have applied the model to the strategies used by ISL interpreters.

In terms of interactive constraints, we noted that the Irish Deaf community is small and close-knit. The interpreting community is even smaller. Maintaining good relations and carefully considering Deaf community perspectives when preparing and delivering an interpretation is important for the ISL interpreter. But as we have seen, this special set of circumstances can lead to dilemmas for the interpreter. Does one choose to give precedence to the interactive factors in order to maintain good working relations with clients? This may be at the expense of accuracy in the production of target language texts because this interaction takes time. Or, does one strive to minimize interactive engagement and focus on delivering a highly processed, comprehensive target language output, even if this occurs at the expense of smooth working relations with the Deaf audience? These constraints also hold at the European level, where working between signed languages creates a similar potential for interpreter-client on-task interaction (to build and maintain clarity) as does the need to address a broad range of variation, as in the Irish context.

This tension between accuracy and interaction is a conundrum faced by all interpreters to a certain degree. For signed language interpreters, I suggest that the tension between these facets is increased, though to the best of my knowledge, no research has been conducted to look critically at this aspect of interpreted interaction to date. Thus, the answers are fuzzy: while the interpreting task – the transfer of information from a source to a target language – is clear cut, the fact that we operate in a context where sociolinguistic variability is rife suggests that the "purity" of our language transfer task is confounded in a profound way.

But consider that the community is rich and diverse. This brings special challenges to the signed language interpreting field that may not exist to the same degree in other branches of interpreting. Challenges demand a response, and such a response entails reflection on what we do as professionals, seeking reasons for why these challenges occur, and questioning how we can do better. As a developing profession, such challenges develop our mettle and ensure that we never presume that we can stop learning. Robinson (1997) asserts that we are constantly in the process of *becoming* interpreters. I couldn't agree more.

Notes

1. Many thanks to the following for their contributions to discussion regarding how interpreters do, could or might deal with variation: John Bosco Conama, Tony Dolan, Bernadette Ferguson, Susan Foley-Cave, Alvean Jones, Shane Ó hEorpa, Carmel Grehan, Patrick A. Matthews, Evelyn Nolan-Conroy, and interpreting and ISL tutor students at the Centre for Deaf Studies, 2001–2003. Thanks also to Katarina Karlsson of the Association of Sign Language Interpreters in Sweden (STTF) for her assistance regarding the current situation in Sweden.

2. STTF is the association of signed language interpreters in Sweden affiliated to the European Forum of Sign Language Interpreters (EFSLI).

3. This may be because their parents or siblings are Deaf, because they are teachers of the Deaf, because they attended signed language classes, or because they are interpreters, etc. This gives us an approximate total population of 55,000 people who know and use ISL in Ireland (Leeson 2001a, following Bergman 2001 for Swedish Sign Language users).

4. Belfast is the capital city of the six Northern Irish counties that remain a part of the United Kingdom of Great Britain.

5. Lip-reading is frequently referred to as "lip-speaking" in Europe.

6. While the 1972 report officially sanctioned the oral approach, the schools – particularly St. Mary's School for Deaf Girls – had implemented oral policies in the late 1940s and early 1950s. By the 1970s the oral approach was normative and allowed for stricter enforcement of oral policies in the schools.

7. See Stratiy (this volume) for another view on this issue.

8. See Leeson and Foley-Cave (in press) for a discussion of some of the challenges of interpreting in a university linguistics classroom.

9. This group consisted of Deaf people with numerous experiences with interpreters and Deaf instructors at the Centre for Deaf Studies, Trinity College, Dublin.

10. See http://europa.eu.int/comm/education

11. The texts of these resolutions can be viewed at the European Union of the Deaf website (www.eudnet.org).

12. Federation of Deaf People press release, 18 March 2003.

13. See the EUD Update March 2001 for an overview of the status of signed languages in each of the European Union Member States. This can be viewed at www.eudnet.org.

14. Feedback from EUD Congress participants, 2001.

References

Baker, Mona (1992). *In Other Words. A Coursebook on Translation*. London and New York: Routeledge.

Blumenthal-Kelly, Arlene (1995). Fingerspelling interaction: A set of Deaf parents and their Deaf daughter. In Ceil Lucas (Ed.), *Sociolinguistics in Deaf Communities*. Washington, DC: Gallaudet University Press.

Brennan, Mary (1992). The visual world of BSL: An introduction. In David Brien (Ed.), *Dictionary of British Sign Language/English* (pp. 2–133). London: Faber and Faber.

Bergman, Brita (2001). Sign languages. Paper presented at the Official Opening of the European Union/Council of Europe Year of Languages, "The Challenge of Linguistic Diversity in Europe", Lund, Sweden, February 18–20, 2001.

Burns, Sarah E. (1998). Irish Sign Language: Ireland's second minority language. In Ceil Lucas (Ed.), *Pinky Extension and Eye Gaze: Language Use in Deaf Communities* (pp. 233–273). Washington, DC: Gallaudet University Press.

Cokely, Dennis (1983). When is a pidgin not a pidgin? An alternate analysis of the ASL-English contact situation. *Sign Language Studies, 38*, 1–24.

Cokely, Dennis (1992). *Interpretation: A Sociolinguistic Model*. Burtonsville, MD: Linstok Press.

Coogan, Anne (2002). Why does history matter: From a Deaf woman's perspective. Paper Presented at the "Deaf, Woman, Proud" Conference, University of Dublin, Trinity College. Irish Deaf Women's Group. 28 September 2002.

Coogan, Anne (2003). Irish Deaf Women: The Appropriateness of their Education? Unpublished M. Phil Dissertation. Centre for Gender and Women's Studies: University of Dublin, Trinity College.

Crean, Edward J. (1997). *Breaking the Silence: The Education of the Deaf in Ireland 1816–1996*. Dublin: Irish Deaf Society.

Crystal, David (1997). *The Cambridge Encyclopedia of Language* (2nd ed.). Cambridge: Cambridge University Press.

Davis, Jeffery (1989). Distinguishing language contact phenomena in ASL interpretation. In Ceil Lucas (Ed.), *The Sociolinguistics of the Deaf Community* (pp. 85–102). San Diego, CA: Academic Press.

European Centre for Minority Languages (2000). *Flensburg Recommendations on the Implementation of Policy Measures for Regional or Minority Languages*. Flensburg, Germany: ECMI.

Fitzgerald, Angela (2004). Gay Sign Variation in ISL. Essay presented in part-fulfillment of requirements for the Diploma in Irish Sign Language /English Interpreting. CDS, Trinity College Dublin.

Foran, Stanislus (1979). Preface. *The Irish Sign Language*. Dublin: National Association for the Deaf.

Fromkin, Victoria, Robert Rodman, & Nina M. Hyams (2003). *An Introduction to Language* (7th ed.). Boston: Thomson/Heinle.

Gile, Daniel (1995). *Basic Concepts and Models for Interpreter and Translator Training*. Amsterdam/Philadelphia: John Benjamins.

Holmes, Janet (2001). *An Introduction to Sociolinguistics* (2nd ed.). London and New York: Longman.

Humphrey, Janice H., & Bob J. Alcorn (1996). *So You Want to Be an Interpreter: An Introduction to Sign Language Interpreting* (2nd ed.). Amarillo, TX: H & H Publishers.

Kleinfeld, Mala Silverman, & Noni Warner (1996). Variation in the Deaf community: Gay, lesbian, and bisexual signs. In Ceil Lucas (Ed.), *Multicultural Aspects of Sociolinguistics in Deaf Communities* (pp. 3–35). Washington, DC: Gallaudet University Press.

Krausneker, Verena (2001). Sign languages of Europe – Future chances. In Lorraine Leeson (Ed.), *Looking Forward. EUD in the 3rd Millenium – The Deaf Citizen in the 21st Century* (pp. 64–73). Coleford: Douglas McLean.

Ladd, Paddy (1998). In Search of Deafhood: Towards an Understanding of British Deaf Culture. Unpublished doctoral dissertation, Centre for Deaf Studies, University of Bristol, UK.

Ladd, Paddy (2003). *Understanding Deaf Culture: In Search of Deafhood*. Clevedon: Multilingual Matters.

Lane, Harlan (2002). Do Deaf people have a disability? *Sign Language Studies, 2* (4), 356–379.

Leeson, Lorraine (2001a). Aspects of Verbal Valency in Irish Sign Language. Unpublished doctoral dissertation. Centre for Language and Communication Studies, University of Dublin, Trinity College.

Leeson, Lorraine (2001b). The provision of sign language interpreters at European institution meetings: Some points for consideration. Unpublished paper. Brussels: European Union of the Deaf.

Leeson, Lorraine (2003). Sign language interpreters: Agents of social change in Ireland? In Michael Cronin & Cormac O'Chuilleanain (Eds.), *The Languages of Ireland* (pp. 148–166). Dublin: Four Courts Press.

Leeson, Lorraine (2004a). Being powerful: An exploration of why Irish Deaf women do not have access to processes of power in Ireland. Essay presented in part-fulfillment of the requirements of the Women's Political Development Programme. Feminist Approaches to Politics, the State and the Economy in Ireland. University College, Dublin.

Leeson, Lorraine (2004b). Signs of change in Europe: European developments on the status of signed languages. In Patrick McDonnell (Ed.), *Deaf Studies in Ireland: An Introduction* (pp. 172–197). Coleford: Douglas McLean.

Leeson, Lorraine, & Susan Foley-Cave (in press). Deep and meaningful conversation: Challenging interpreter impartiality in the semantics and pragmatics classroom. In Melanie Metzger & Earl Fleetwood (Eds.). *Translation, Sociolinguistic, and Consumer Issues in Interpreting*. Washington, DC: Gallaudet University Press.

Leeson, Lorraine, & Carmel Grehan (2004). To the lexicon and beyond: The effect of gender on variation in Irish Sign Language. In Mieke Van Herreweghe and Myriam Veermerbergen (Eds.), *To the Lexicon and Beyond: The Sociolinguistics of European Deaf Communities* (pp. 39–73). Washington, DC: Gallaudet University Press.

Leeson, Lorraine, & Patrick A. Matthews (2002). Centre for Deaf Studies Submission to the Advisory Committee on Deaf Education. Dublin: Centre for Deaf Studies, University of Dublin, Trinity College.

Leeson, Lorraine, & John I. Saeed (2004). Windowing of attention in simultaneous constructions in Irish Sign Language. In Terry Cameron, Christopher Shank, & Keri Holley (Eds.), *The Proceedings of the Fifth Annual High Desert Linguistics Society Conference, November 1st & 2nd, 2002, University of New Mexico, Albuquerque, New Mexico* (pp. 1–17). Albuquerque, NM: High Desert Linguistic Society.

Le Master, Barbara (1990). The Maintenance and Loss of Female and Male Signs in the Dublin Deaf Community. Unpublished doctoral dissertation. UCLA.

Le Master, Barbara (1999–2000). Reappropriation of gendered Irish Sign Language in one family. *Visual Anthropology Review, 15* (2), 1–15.

Le Master, Barbara (2002). What difference does difference make? Negotiating gender and generation in Irish Sign Language. In Sarah Benor, Mary Rose, Devyani Sharma, Julie Sweetland, & Qing Zhang (Eds.), *Gendered Practices in Language* (pp. 309–338). Stanford, CA: CSLI Publications.

Le Master, Barbara, & John P. Dwyer (1991). Knowing and using female and male signs in Dublin. *Sign Language Studies, 73,* 361–396.

Leonard, Cormac (2005). Signs of diversity: Use and recognition of gendered signs among young Irish Deaf people. *Deaf Worlds, 21* (2), 62–77.

Lucas, Ceil, & Clayton Valli (1992). *Language Contact in the American Deaf Community.* San Diego, CA: Academic Press.

Matthews, Patrick A. (1996). *The Irish Deaf Community, Volume 1.* Dublin: ITE.

McCrum, Robert, Robert MacNeil, & William Cran (1992). *The Story of English* (New and revised ed.). London and Boston: Faber and Faber.

McDonnell, Joseph (1997). The lexicon and vocabulary of Signed English or Manually Coded English: *Teanga 17.* Dublin: ITE.

McDonnell, Patrick (1979). The establishment and operation of institutions for the education of the Deaf in Ireland, 1816–1889. Unpublished essay, Education Department, University College Dublin.

McDonnell, Patrick (1996). Verb Categories in Irish Sign Language. Unpublished doctoral dissertation. Centre for Language and Communication Studies, University of Dublin, Trinity College.

McDonnell, Patrick (2004). Verb categories in Irish Sign Language. In Patrick McDonell (Ed.), *Deaf studies in Ireland: An Introduction* (pp. 116–134). Coleford, England: Douglas McLean.

McDonnell, Patrick, & Helena Saunders (1993). Sit on your hands: Strategies to prevent signing. In Renata Fischer & Harlan Lane (Eds.), *Looking Back: A Reader on the History of Deaf Communities and their Sign Languages* (pp. 255–260). Hamburg: Signum Verlag.

Miller, Christopher (1994). Simultaneous constructions in Quebec Sign Language. In Mary Brennan & Graham H. Turner (Eds.), *Word Order Issues in Sign Language. Working Papers* (pp. 89–112). Durham: International Sign Linguistics Association.

Mulrooney, Kristin J. (2002). Variation in ASL fingerspelling. In Ceil Lucas (Ed.), *Turn-taking, Fingerspelling, and Contact in Signed Languages.* Washington, DC: Gallaudet University Press.

Murray, Edwina (Snr.). (2002). Gay Sign Variation in Irish Sign Language. Video document presented in part-fulfilment of the requirements for the Diploma in Irish Sign Language Teaching. Dublin: Centre for Deaf Studies, University of Dublin, Trinity College.

Napier, Jemina (2002). *Sign Language Interpreting: Linguistic Coping Strategies.* Coleford, England: Douglas McLean.

Napier, Jemina, & Roz Barker (2004). Sign language interpreting: The relationship between metalinguistic awareness and the production of interpreting omissions. *Sign Language Studies, 4* (4), 369–393.

Ó Baoill, Dónall P., & Patrick A. Matthews (2000). *The Irish Deaf Community, Volume 2: The Structure of Irish Sign Language.* Dublin: ITE.

Ó hEorpa, Shane (2003). What is NISL? A Northern Ireland Sign Language? *IASLI Newsletter, 4* (3). Dublin: Irish Association of Sign Language Interpreters.

Padden, Carol, & Tom Humphries (1988). *Deaf in America: Voices from a Culture.* Cambridge, MA: Harvard University Press.

Robinson, Douglas (1997). *Becoming a Translator: An Accelerated Course.* London and New York: Routeledge.

Rosenstein, Ofra (2000). Is ISL (Israeli Sign Language) a Topic Prominent Language? Poster presented at TISLR 7, Amsterdam, 23–27 July 2000.

Skutnabb-Kangas, Tove (2000). *Linguistic Genocide in Education – Or Worldwide Diversity and Human Rights?* Mahwah, NJ: Lawrence Erlbaum.

Sutton-Spence, Rachel, & Bencie Woll (1999). *The Linguistics of British Sign Language: An Introduction.* Cambridge: Cambridge University Press.

Valli, Clayton and Ceil Lucas (1992). *Linguistics of American Sign Language.* Washington, DC: Gallaudet University Press.

Wilbur, Ronnie B. (1994). Foregrounding structures in American Sign Language. *Journal of Pragmatics, 22,* 674–672.

Web-sites of Interest:

Centre for Deaf Studies, School of Linguistic, Speech and Communication Science, Trinity College Dublin: http://www.tcd.ie/slscs/cds/

Council of Europe: www.coe.int

European Bureau of Lesser Used Languages: www.eblul.org

European Forum of Sign Language Interpreters: www.efsli.org.uk

European Union: http://europa.eu.int

European Union of the Deaf: www.eudnet.org

Irish Deaf Society: www.irishdeafsociety.org

STTF: The Association of Sign Language Interpreters in Sweden: www.sttf.just.nu

World Federation of the Deaf: www.wfdnews.org

CHAPTER 11

Case studies in education

Practical application of ethics and role

Patricia Conrad and Susan Stegenga

St. Albert, Alberta, Canada / Calgary, Canada

1. Introduction[1]

The presence of interpreters in educational settings is relatively new, dating back a matter of decades. Prior to the 1960s, the need for educational interpreters was virtually non-existent, since the majority of Canadian Deaf students were educated at residential schools for the Deaf. Teachers communicated directly with their students, via signed language, fingerspelling, or oral methods, and the children seldom, if ever, had the opportunity to interact with hearing peers (Stewart 1988). Upon completion of school, many young Deaf graduates found jobs on factory assembly lines, in the trades or in manual labor. Others became farmers and homemakers. It was a rare individual who went on to attend a community college or university.

Much has changed since then. In the 1970s, ground-breaking American legislation, such as the Vocational Rehabilitation Act Amendments (Public Law 95–602, Section 504) and the Education for all Handicapped Children Act (Public Law 94–142), paved the way for professional interpreters to enter the educational realm (Witter-Merithew & Dirst 1982; Stewart 1988). Similar legislation came later in Canada, beginning with Ontario's Education Amendment Act (Bill 82) of 1980, which dictated the right to an appropriate education for all exceptional children (Winzer, Rogow & David 1987).

Such legislation, coupled with the trend toward inclusion,[2] increased the demand for educational interpreters (Stewart 1988). Today, growing numbers of Deaf children attend their local schools. Even those who attend schools for the Deaf may take some classes at a nearby public school. Upon graduation, many choose to pursue further education at colleges, universities, technical institutes, or business and trade schools.

As educational choices open up to Deaf individuals, so do opportunities for signed language interpreters. While some Deaf students prefer to have notetakers or real-time captioning for communication access, most will choose the services of an interpreter. In fact, educational facilities are among the largest employers of interpreters today, with an outlook that promises continued expansion (Stewart, Schein, & Cartwright 1998).

Interpreting in educational settings, by its broadest definition, refers to facilitating communication in any and all settings where learning takes place. Settings that first come to mind are elementary and secondary levels; however, educational interpreting may include everything from pre-school classes, first-aid seminars and non-credit evening classes to national computer conferences and graduate-level university courses.

For practical reasons – because we cannot cover everything within the constraints of one chapter – our discussion here will address interpreting issues in formal, ongoing educational programs. The basic tenets of effective interpreting, however, generally apply even to less formal settings of shorter duration. We will address interpreter roles and responsibilities, classroom language issues, issues of power and control, ethical decision-making, perspectives on interpreting within the educational setting, and resources for interpreters. Finally, we offer a short self-assessment tool to help determine employment suitability in this realm.

It is not our intent to discuss educational philosophy or the benefits of specific placement decisions in this chapter. However, in those situations where the decision has been made in favour of mainstreamed education, it is our belief that the employment of top-calibre signed language interpreters affords the Deaf student a greater chance of success; *true* accessibility demands nothing less.

We will address all levels, from kindergarten to graduate school, where the interpreter's primary daily employment is within an educational institution. In doing so, we will introduce a pool of hypothetical interpreters, and lead you, the reader, through a variety of reality-based scenarios. Each of these interpreters makes judgments during the course of their work, and each decision has a different outcome. Some of their judgments may be similar to those you might make, while others may be very different. As we examine each interpreter's choices and their consequences, we offer ideas to ponder and explore further.

We offer one caution here: there is never a single choice that is *always* right. Given the enormous diversity of situations and individuals, personalities and experiences, it is not feasible to create a single, generally applicable template, nor is it possible to reliably predict the outcome of any particular choice. What might seem the best decision in one instance may not work the next time, or with another student. There is no answer key at the end of this chapter, but then nor is there in life. So file away any *a priori* notions of right or wrong along with the impossible pursuit of perfection, and strive instead toward a more achievable goal, that of making thoughtful decisions that lead to a more effective interpreting performance.

2.   Roles and responsibilities of the interpreter

2.1   Single versus multiple roles

The function of interpreters in educational settings is to facilitate communication between those in the school who are Deaf and those who are hearing. Although our task may appear straightforward and easily defined, it rarely is. The notion of role is a complex one, laden with misconstrued expectations and rife with ambiguity.

Some job postings call for "interpreter-aide", others "interpreter-tutor" or even "signing assistant" – a designation often intended to encompass any task that might arise in the classroom. Add to this "mother-figure", "disciplinarian", "buddy" and "signed-language model", and we have a fairly accurate picture of the implicit expectation in some elementary settings.

Formal job descriptions, created by individuals such as the school principal, teacher(s) of the Deaf or Human Resources personnel, are often designed to accommodate the perceived needs of the school, the Deaf student and the classroom teacher. In reality, however, these job titles may also lead to misconceptions about the student's abilities.

In school settings where aides are hired to tend to the physical needs of specific disabled students, for instance, the title of interpreter-aide may lead to the perception that the Deaf student is more dependent than her classmates. Consequently, those classmates, their parents, the teacher and even the student herself may, consciously or otherwise, lower their expectations of that student.

Ideally, the position title would simply be "interpreter" or "communication facilitator", with the inherent natural boundaries of a single, clearly-outlined role. Multi-role positions are, by their nature, complex. Frishberg (1986) suggests the importance of role clarification for interpreters, with descriptions of appropriate behaviour for each role. Accordingly, Stewart (1988) proposes a flexible framework to assist school programs in scheduling duties for individual interpreters that include a variety of functions, from interpreter, tutor and classroom aide, to liaison and public relations coordinator. Such a framework, he suggests, could be adjusted yearly according to the needs of the program's Deaf students.

The interpreter's challenge, then, is to reconcile role behaviours in a way that reduces confusion for the student, teacher, and school community. For example, an interpreter-tutor might function as interpreter in the classroom, and tutor only outside class time. Avoiding the temptation to overlap roles may be difficult in some settings, and we urge interpreters to carefully assess their own abilities to maintain role distinctions before accepting multi-role positions.

In current practice, interpreters employed in secondary and post-secondary levels are more likely to maintain a single-role function, if only because students at more advanced levels are usually recognized as independent and competent consumers. For many interpreters, this reality adds to the appeal of employment at these levels, where boundaries are more easily defined and less ambiguous.

In some school settings, especially where only one interpreter is employed, tutoring is an explicit expectation. This is a point that needs to be brought to the table during the hiring process. Some interpreters simply are not comfortable with such a dual role, and would be wise to decline this type of position.

Not every interpreter functions well as a tutor, since tutoring is a distinct role with a skill set that differs from that of interpreting. If an interpreter is interested in accepting a position that involves tutoring, she must take a critical look at her own teaching skills beforehand, as well as her ability to separate the two functions. Coursework in education is advisable for someone wishing to gain skills in tutoring as part of her work.

Preparation time for tutoring may be scheduled during the workday, or alternatively, the interpreter may be compensated for the time. Either way, the issue needs to be negotiated beforehand. Tutoring without preparation is much like flying without fuel: it's a gamble no one can afford.

2.2 Interpreter qualifications

"Historically, schools have been the place for newly graduated interpreters to get their feet wet" notes one RID-certified interpreter, in a plea for more stringent interpreting standards in the classroom (Radatz 1994: 1). Wilcox, Santiago and Sanderson concur that educational interpreting has long been viewed as "the stepchild of interpreting – a place to send people who are not ready for 'real' interpreting" (1992: 175).

Today the practice of hiring novice interpreters for school settings persists, lending unwarranted credence to fallacies that educational settings are the best starting point for new interpreters, and that younger Deaf students can cope with less skilled interpreters. As much as we work to refute these false beliefs, the more disturbing concern is that such misconceptions survive.

Perhaps some school districts[3] have lower standards for classroom interpreters than those espoused by Deaf and interpreting communities. In certain cases, inadequate assessment tools may be at fault, making it difficult to evaluate an interpreter's performance. Perhaps too, Deaf children are less demanding than adults of their right to quality access. Indeed, any or all of the above may be true, and this is no less alarming. Radatz stresses that "mainstream classrooms of Deaf and Hard of Hearing children can no longer be used as the training ground for interpreters who are not qualified to work with adults" (1994: 1).

Ideally, in order to be effective in educational settings, interpreters must demonstrate the following qualifications:

– Completion of an interpreter education program (or the equivalent in life experience, professional development and interpreting credentials)[4]
– Proficiency in both ASL and English

- Demonstrated ability to interpret between English and ASL, preferably through national certification, and minimally, through the use of a screening or assessment tool administered by competent individuals who have the appropriate credentials
- A degree in a related field (e.g., linguistics, education, psychology)
- Knowledge of Deaf culture
- Knowledge of ethical guidelines for interpreters
- Affiliation with local and national professional interpreting associations
- Excellent interpersonal, oral and written communication skills
- Demonstrated organizational and time management skills

Further, relating to her own experience, Radatz notes that "there were skills and knowledge unique to educational interpreting that I also needed to do my job well. But that knowledge and those skills were needed *in addition* to my language and interpreting skills, *not in place* of them" (1994: 22; italics hers). At the elementary and secondary levels, for instance, a talent for interacting well with parents, administrators and counselors, as well as the Deaf student and classroom teacher, is vital. An interpreter who displays resiliency and confidence, a good understanding of how students learn, creative thinking, a broad knowledge base, and a desire for lifelong learning will certainly have an extra edge on the competition.

Reality, unfortunately, is less than ideal. In many school district job advertisements, interpreting ability is overlooked altogether. Signing skills are assumed to be sufficient. Stewart, Schein and Cartwright note that "a few schools do not even mention ability to sign, and most do not emphasize *quality* interpreting" (1998: 192, italics theirs). Worse yet, many overlook the need for formal interpreting education and certification, awareness of cultural features, knowledge of ethical guidelines, or affiliation with professional interpreting associations.

Once hired by a school district, interpreters may face further ambiguity. Within the school setting, they may be deemed support staff, professional staff, or possibly para-professionals. More often than not, the labels interpreters would choose for themselves and the labels bestowed by the school have little in common.

The picture is not entirely bleak, however. Progressive school districts continue to adjust position expectations and job categories to reflect the real objectives of interpreting, due to the ongoing efforts of forward-thinking interpreters and Deaf communities. Interpreters contemplating jobs in the educational realm do well to seek positions where the job description is clear-cut, desired credentials reflect national professional standards, a reliable screening or evaluation tool is part of the hiring process, and points of concern are open to collective negotiation.

Post-secondary settings consistently hire more qualified interpreters. At institutes of higher learning, the standard of qualifications for all professionals tends to be of a higher calibre. In this setting the primary consumers of interpreting services are adult students, typically proactive in expressing their preferences directly, rather than through a parent or teacher. They demand quality access and tend not to settle for less.

2.3 Interpreting for children

Interpreting in primary and elementary classrooms poses challenges rarely found with secondary or post-secondary students. An interpreter considering employment at these earlier levels would benefit from first undertaking a study of children's cognitive development and language learning processes as a foundation before working with this consumer group.

Understandably, the complexity of the interpreting process may be a mystery beyond a young child's comprehension. From her perspective, it is difficult to grasp that the message from one adult's mouth comes via another's hands, or that when one scowls, it is actually the other who is angry. The child's developmental level can lead her to perceive the interpreted message as originating with the interpreter rather than her teacher. To rectify such misperceptions, the interpreter and teacher may need to work together on clarifying their roles, and the interpreting process as a whole, to both hearing and Deaf students. Strategies such as role-playing can be useful.

The interpreter may also choose to use third person during the interpretation to reinforce the Deaf student's understanding of role differences, as in, "She said, (pointing to the teacher)..." Interpreters are taught to interpret in first person, given that using third person in the interpretation creates a perception of distance between consumers. In the case of working with small children, however, the interpreter assumes some responsibility for teaching them about the roles of the teacher and interpreter in the classroom, and the distinction between the two, hence the decision to use third person.[5]

Expectations placed on interpreters by young children go far beyond communication access. Humphrey and Alcorn suggest that "a five-year-old cannot distinguish between a teacher and an interpreter – all s/he sees is a 'big person' " (1995:299). For Deaf and hearing students alike, the presence of a second adult in the classroom may signal that another authority figure is available to them. Accordingly, the interpreter needs to be prepared with an appropriate response when a young child races up with a scraped knee or a complaint of bullying by another youngster. In these instances, a response of "I can't do anything about that – I'm just the interpreter" is woefully inadequate. It may require a little creativity to frame oneself not only as the interpreter but also as a caring adult and human being.

Expectations placed on interpreters by the parents of Deaf children may also extend beyond their designated function. Some parents may rely on the interpreter rather than the teacher as the expert on Deaf children, signed language, and education specific to Deaf children, inadvertently creating role conflicts within the classroom. It is worthwhile for both teacher and interpreter to meet together with the parents to clarify role boundaries and, in some cases, to suggest other resources for the information sought.

2.4 Responsibilities within the classroom

The interpreter's primary responsibility in the classroom is, of course, to provide communication access. This involves direct interpreting between the teacher or professor and the student, or between students, and may include interpreting lectures, class discussions, group work, lab activities, and so forth.

Once the interpreter's role has been clearly established, the onus is on all participants – the interpreter, the Deaf student and the instructor – to work together in arranging the physical space in a manner that will satisfy all. The goal here is to accommodate visual accessibility for the student, while not unnecessarily altering the teacher's instructional style or use of classroom space. If there is frequent movement in the classroom by the teacher or others, success in this regard may call for considerable innovation.

Facilitating classroom interaction entails a dual competency on the part of the interpreter, relaying in spoken English what the Deaf student is signing, and signing to the Deaf student what the teacher and other hearing participants are saying. The overall goal is clear communication between those who do not share the same language. Acting as an intermediary in this regard requires excellent interpersonal skills, along with the ability to both detect when communication problems are occurring, and assist in their resolution without making autocratic decisions.

Let's now look at the case of one hypothetical student as she works with several interpreters. As you read through the scenario, ask yourself what you would do, given a similar situation.

> Hillary is a Deaf high school student who likes to use her own voice when communicating with non-deaf people. Abby, our first interpreter, simply smiles and nods when Hillary indicates her preference. For Abby, the Deaf student's wishes take priority. Accordingly, she provides English to ASL interpreting, and remains silent when it's Hillary's turn to talk. This works fine most of the time, but Abby notices that some teachers occasionally have a hard time understanding Hillary's speech. In fact, one teacher avoids calling on her in class because he doesn't understand her responses. *Too bad,* Abby thinks, *he'll just have to get used to her speech. I'm not getting involved.* She says nothing to either the student or the teacher, and the teacher-student relationship continues to deteriorate.
>
> Blaine, our second interpreter, becomes concerned when he notices the teacher's difficulty understanding Hillary. Since Blaine is used to Deaf speech, he has no problem understanding her. Feeling sorry for the teacher and wanting to improve the communication, Blaine decides to interpret into English for the teacher whenever Hillary talks. The first time he does this, Hillary gives him an odd look and raises her volume. The teacher, however, seems relieved. Eventually, Blaine finds himself almost shouting to be heard over Hillary. Afterwards, the student angrily accuses him of taking over. He attempts to justify

his behaviour, and they get into an argument over who should be making such decisions.

Our third interpreter, Cass, handles the situation differently. Noting the teacher's struggle to understand Hillary's speech, Cass leans over and quietly asks if he would prefer an English interpretation. When he responds affirmatively, she alerts the student to the problem and makes a simple suggestion for its resolution. Both quickly agree to Cass's remedy. Hillary will continue to speak for herself, but if the teacher has difficulty, he will cue the interpreter that he needs her help. Hillary, pleased with the interpreter's approach, immediately lowers her voice whenever she sees Cass begin the English interpretation. As he becomes more used to Hillary's speech, the teacher indicates that he requires less intervention by the interpreter, and Cass responds by interpreting over the student's voice much less frequently.

Abby's approach, though initially respectful of the student's choice, is overly rigid when an unexpected difficulty arises. As intermediaries, interpreters are in a prime position to detect communication problems, and when they do, it is up to them to assist in resolving the issue. By assuming a detached stance, Abby shirks this responsibility and ultimately exacerbates the problem.

Blaine, faced with the same dilemma, hastens to rescue the teacher. By making an autocratic decision without input from either consumer, he manages to satisfy one while offending the other. Even when the solution seems obvious, interpreters must be wary of this approach. Deciding what is best without consulting with consumers may be construed as oppressive.

We are reminded here that the interpreter is only one of several participants in the communication process. In the third example, Cass takes the lead by initiating a solution that involves all participants and strives for mutual agreement. Sensitivity toward all perspectives remains a vital consideration in decision-making, and ongoing communication is key. Indeed, there are many instances within the educational setting where Deaf students are encouraged by parents, teachers of the Deaf or speech therapists to practice their speech skills, and this pursuit deserves the same respect as any other.

Another of the interpreter's classroom responsibilities is to provide the Deaf student(s) with access to environmental information, which often includes disruptive hallway noises and public address announcements. When relaying *all* information becomes counterproductive, however, the interpreter requires the sensitivity to modify this practice. Below, we examine this issue in another common scenario.

Damien interprets for three Deaf students in a Grade 10 classroom where the teacher often assigns seatwork to be completed in class. During these work periods, the teacher likes to share stories of his extracurricular pursuits. He is an avid snowboarder and often relates tales of his feats on the slopes. The hearing students are able to enjoy his stories while they continue to work. The Deaf students are not, however, because they cannot simultaneously watch the interpreter and attend to their work. Damien feels strongly that the Deaf students should be privy to the same information as the others. Whenever the teacher begins his digression, Damien waves to get their attention and interprets everything. On days the teacher is especially verbose, the Deaf students fall behind in their work, and are sometimes reprimanded. Damien feels bad for them, but he doesn't know what else to do.

Conversely, Ellie believes that the Deaf students have the same right to quality work time as the non-deaf students. When the teacher begins his usual digression during work periods, Ellie simply ignores it. Occasionally one of the Deaf students looks up, notices the teacher talking, and gives the interpreter a puzzled look. Ellie reassures him that the teacher's monologue is irrelevant to their work, and this is usually accepted. When hearing students ask, "Why do you interpret some things, and not others?" Ellie replies, "I just omit what's not important." Once, one of the Deaf students noticed the whole class laughing at a teacher's joke and asked what was going on. When Ellie replied with her customary response, the student became angry, and later accused her of excluding them.

Farrah's approach offers the choice back to the Deaf students. Initially, whenever the teacher began his side commentary during work sessions, she simply continued interpreting. The students could choose to watch or not, she reasoned. The Deaf students occasionally glanced up, but soon realized it was an irrelevant story and went back to their work. She continued to do this until the day one of the Deaf students told her not to bother interpreting the teacher's stories during work sessions, and the others nodded in agreement. From that point on, she hasn't. Once in awhile, especially if there is laughter, one or more of the Deaf students will turn to her, curious. On these occasions Farrah asks, "Do you want me to interpret?" If the answer is yes, she does a quick summary to catch them up, and then continues to interpret to the end of the story.

The variable here is control. Who has control, and who *should* have it? Even though interpreters are in the classroom to facilitate communication access, their specific decisions and actions will be influenced by one of several interpreting models (e.g., helper, conduit, communication facilitator, bilingual-bicultural broker) that are available. Each model reflects a particular purpose, and although widespread use of earlier models has declined, there may still be occasions where their use is warranted. In brief, any of the models will serve effectively when consciously chosen as the best fit for variables presented. Among other factors, consumer age and ability level, desired outcome of the interpreting and any number of unique circumstances influence the selection of an appropriate interpreting model to guide the interpreter's behaviour.[6]

Damien, a subscriber to the conduit model in the above example, insists on interpreting everything regardless of the situation, and the students suffer for it. Ellie, while operating under the guise of being supportive to the students' needs, has unintentionally adopted the behaviour of an oppressor by blatantly declining to interpret what is taking place. Both interpreters, by making their decisions independently, have neglected the crucial step of consulting with both sets of consumers to reach a mutually satisfying resolution.

Farrah's approach is a well-intentioned compromise, although she fails to include the teacher in resolving the issue. As a result, the teacher remains unaware of the problem and is deprived of a chance to offer input. Thus the opportunity for cooperative negotiation is lost. Simultaneous listening and writing, or talking and writing, is a basic human capability as long as hearing is intact (Johnson 1991). For Deaf people, however, this is not the case for practical reasons. Unless the teacher is made aware of such cultural variations, relationships between the teacher and Deaf student(s), and between the teacher and interpreter, are in danger of faltering. Interpreting decisions based on the bilingual-bicultural model, in which the interpreter functions as a cultural broker, would likely be most effective here.

While providing communication access, interpreters "must decide when interpreting is unnecessary, intrusive, or excessive" (Stewart, Schein, & Cartwright 1998:201). If this seems like a hopeless contradiction, remember that the key is balance. Interpreting a private teacher-student conversation two rows away from the Deaf student, for instance, may be unnecessary while the rest of the math class is working. When the teacher tags on a comment directed to the whole class, however, it should be relayed to the student. Interpreting all the other students' gossip and laughter during a lecture may be intrusive, although the Deaf student needs to know why the instructor is pausing and glaring at certain individuals. Finally, when considering the many other sounds in the classroom environment, calling the Deaf student's attention to the furnace each time it grumbles, for example, may be excessive unless it's loud enough to disrupt the class.

In some instances, the student's right to access conflicts with school or classroom rules (e.g., when the student is subversively plotting mischief with classmates, and expects the interpreter not to divulge the information). If the interpreter has taken a proactive approach at the outset, clarifying her professional role and its inherent obligations to both school and student, problems will more easily be circumvented. If that has not been done, a discussion with either the interpreting supervisor or principal is warranted, even if it takes place after the fact. Role clarification, including what is *not* part of an interpreter's responsibility, is crucial to preventing misunderstandings and their resulting difficulties.

A particular challenge in most educational settings is the interpreter's role in interpreting exams. In cases where the student's reading level does not allow adequate access to written English, the interpreter may be approached to interpret test questions into ASL. And when the student has difficulty writing English, the interpreter may be called upon to transcribe the student's signed responses to the exam questions.

Seal notes that "decisions about the interpreter's role, if that role is to be extended beyond interpreting directions and incidental interruptions, should be made by the child's educational team" (1998:99). Whenever required to interpret an exam, the interpreter must strive to faithfully interpret the meaning, without inadvertently giving away answers due to the visual nature of ASL.

Clearly, interpreting in the classroom calls for a balance of thoughtful deliberation and instant judgment, skills refined through professional training and years of experience. Accordingly, interpreters must commit themselves to being lifelong students, and avail themselves of the knowledge and wisdom of interpreting instructors, mentors and more seasoned colleagues.

2.5 Responsibilities beyond the classroom

Outside the classroom, the interpreter may be expected to facilitate communication for any number of extracurricular activities, such as counseling sessions, travel clubs and sports activities. Interpreters are wise to anticipate all possibilities in negotiating a manageable schedule and fair compensation at the outset.

A further responsibility is adequate preparation, essential for any interpreter who wishes to remain effective in the classroom. Scheduled time and pay for preparation may need to be negotiated into the contract as well.

Aside from reading textbooks, assignments and lecture notes beforehand, it is useful to have a look at curriculum guides, if they are available. E-mail contact with instructors is another worthwhile practice, increasingly popular in today's age of technology. With a simple keystroke, lessons and unit plans can be sent to interpreters as e-mail attachments, with minimal inconvenience to the instructor.

Previewing movies and videotapes, too, allows more accurate prediction when interpreting. Once the interpreter is familiar with the selection, she can usually fill in gaps even when audio quality is poor. Some interpreters routinely meet with the instructor before each class to better understand their teaching goals and to get clarification on key concepts that will be taught. This is an excellent way to ensure that classroom interpreting supports instructor objectives. Collaborative preparation, often with the student as well as the teacher, is paramount to effective interpreting.

At the secondary level, encouraging appropriate "consumer" behaviour in students may become a further responsibility of the interpreter (Witter-Merithew & Dirst 1982). As a Deaf student becomes more independent, she is expected to take a more active role in alerting the interpreter or teacher when she doesn't understand a concept, for instance, without being asked to do so. The interpreter who consistently demonstrates integrity, impartiality and confidentiality in daily practice reinforces Deaf students' appropriate use of interpreters (Witter-Merithew & Dirst 1982; Seal 1998). Modeling appropriate behaviors will educate not only the Deaf student but hearing consumers as well, and their responses to interpreted situations will be conducive to successful interaction.

2.6 The interpreter as part of an educational team

Within an elementary or secondary school setting, the interpreter is often expected to function as a member of the educational team along with professionals such as the student's teachers, counselor and audiologist. For interpreters who adhere to a narrow, rigid role definition, this expectation may signal an ethical breach and be met with anxiety or resistance. At the other end of the spectrum, interpreters who adopt a multi-role function (e.g., interpreter-teaching assistant) without a clear sense of boundaries may also encounter difficulty. Often, the inclination is to overstep one's bounds of expertise in offering input, which may appear to be a less difficult route than to assert professional role constraints.

Either of the two approaches above can, despite good intentions, lead to problems. In the scenario that follows, we explore how interpreters' philosophies regarding their role affect the choices they make.

> When asked for her thoughts at a team meeting, Ginny, our first interpreter, protests with, "My opinion isn't relevant here. I can't discuss a consumer." Consequently, other members see her as overly rigid and not helpful at all, and this creates a rift in the team. They eventually stop inviting her to meetings, and thus she misses out on vital information about the student's progress.
>
> Hal, on the other hand, wants to be helpful. He freely offers his opinion on any aspect of the student's file, including some derogatory comments about her psychological maturity and extracurricular social habits. Not only are his comments subjective, they are beyond his field of expertise. As a result, the team's perception of the Deaf student becomes skewed.

A compromise may offer the best solution here. While a number of topics, such as cognitive and psychological abilities, are outside the interpreter's realm, she may be the *only* team member who "is fully capable of commenting on the student's language preference, language skills and the appropriateness of interpreting services within a particular educational placement" (Humphrey & Alcorn 1995:305). Further, Witter-Merithew and Dirst suggest that "the interpreter would also be able to describe other behaviors...such as attention span, motivation, peer interactions, and comprehension of various parts of the classroom activities" (1982:402).

> Ina, our third interpreter, realizes this, respects the confidentiality that guides the entire team, and confines her remarks to issues related to communication and interpreting. She is in an ideal position to relay information about an interpreter's preparatory needs and the interpreting process. She also is able to offer ideas to resolve the student's communicative challenges.

Unlike Ginny, who resists involvement by citing role constraints, or Hal, who portrays himself as a general expert, Ina takes a more balanced approach, recognizing that her input is valuable to the team while limiting her comments to her own area of knowledge. When requests are made beyond her scope of expertise (e.g., could she teach signed language?), Ina responds whenever possible with referrals back to the student or an appropriate community resource. By using the team meeting as an opportunity to educate colleagues and by being open to their questions, Ina is able to offer ideas that foster a more effective learning environment for the student and demonstrate her own value as a team player. Her comments also provide the team with a deeper appreciation of the impact of quality interpreting on the student's education.

3.   Language issues in the classroom

Interpreters in the educational milieu are faced with myriad communication choices. When interpreting to the Deaf student, options include ASL, fingerspelling, any one of a variety of English-based sign systems,[7] or potentially a combination of these. When dealing with a student who presents a mixed communication profile, "interpreters must be able to assess the student's interpreting needs and respond to those needs with the most appropriate interpreting mode, code, or recommendation for an alternative communication system" (Seal 1998: 101).

At post-secondary (and sometimes secondary) levels, the choice is easier, since the Deaf student usually expresses a clear preference. At primary and elementary levels, however, the decision becomes more involved. Though the Deaf child's need remains straightforward – to understand and be understood – the school's language policy and parental preferences are key factors here. In choosing the language of interpretation, a classroom interpreter is often confronted with the additional challenge of satisfying not only parents and educators, but the Deaf community as well.

In their description of a model program for the education of Deaf children, Johnson, Liddell and Erting assert that "the first language of Deaf children should be a natural language, ASL" (1989: 15).[8] In the school setting, Stewart (1988) notes that interpreters are often an important source of linguistic input for the Deaf child. Hence the interpreter's role may, in some cases, extend to that of ASL language model, a responsibility that is understandably daunting for many interpreters.

It is our belief that the child's exposure to ASL ideally occurs through interaction with Deaf peers or adults, though in reality such interaction is not always realized. Accordingly, interpreters may choose to share information at school about upcoming Deaf community events, or suggest Deaf contacts who may be available as potential resources for classroom activities.

In situations where no Deaf ASL models are available, the task of modeling appropriate language use for the child may fall to the interpreter, whether or not she has the degree of ASL fluency to warrant such a significant undertaking. Even if she does, Winston (1994) suggests that the expectation that a Deaf child will achieve language competency through interpretation is a fallacy, and cautions that language acquisition requires "interaction and direct communication" (1994: 56). Interpretation of a message does not qualify as direct communication, since the message conveyed does not originate with the interpreter. Nor does interaction occur directly between the Deaf student and the hearing person during interpretation, since the two do not share a common language. The interaction that does take place is facilitated through the interpreter, thus is deemed indirect.

Winston further challenges the whole premise of an interpreted education, questioning whether it in fact leads to inclusion or exclusion of Deaf students. In so doing, she raises a point of controversy with no simple solution. Detailed discussion of this complex issue is beyond the scope of this chapter, but we urge interpreters to dialogue with Deaf community members, school personnel and other stakeholders, where appropriate, regarding such concerns. In settings where Deaf education liaisons, specialists or coordinators are available as resources, consultation with these experts is certainly warranted. Interpreting program instructors, Deaf mentors and ASL instructors in the community are also excellent resources, as are veteran interpreters and language experts. Further research and reading in the area of first and second language development will be useful as well when considering Winston's fundamental question.

Schick (2001) notes that teachers' communication with young children is different than with adults. The teacher's use of prosody and the interpreter's accurate interpretation of it are essential to a Deaf student's grasp of language in the classroom. "In other words, you construct meaning in a message from both what you say and how you say it" (Schick 2001:10). This is especially important when working with Deaf children who are not native users of ASL. The pace may need to be slowed, points emphasized and vocabulary simplified to accommodate their needs.

Message equivalency remains all-important. For a naive interpreter, equivalency may be perceived as volume or quantity. This interpreter will strive to produce as many ASL signs as there are English words in the original message. Humphrey and Alcorn suggest, however, that "producing a multitude of signs to match the English volume tires the eyes of the Deaf participants, and generally fails to provide equivalent and accessible information" (1995:212). Seal (1998) agrees, noting that if anything, the interpreter's task is to expose the simplicity of target and source languages, not to further complicate the message being conveyed. For the Deaf student, this critical distinction between *quantity* and *simplicity* may signify the difference between confusion and comprehension; such is the influence of the interpreter's performance on a student's academic growth.

When successfully interpreting, a skilled interpreter glides smoothly between languages, manipulating ASL spatial relationships, adding English mouthing when necessary, fingerspelling new vocabulary, and being as innovative as required to clarify a message. Success in the task requires both talent and experience. Seal (1998) suggests a variety of strategies that interpreters might use to make a message more meaningful, including the use of temporal pausing, postural shifts, and the use of space to indicate sequence or chronology. Quality interpreting demands first that the interpreter be fluent in ASL. With fluency, creativity in articulating concepts from a variety of angles comes more easily.

When interpreting for several Deaf students in one class, the interpreter's challenge is to accommodate varied language needs and preferences at the same time. Where the task falls to a single interpreter, appropriate judgment is essential in finding acceptable compromises in the communication. Minor adjustments and reiterations can then be made to accommodate individual needs within the range. It is no simple task, but a resilient and resourceful interpreter can often make it work.

4.   Issues of power and control

As in all other interpreting venues, interpreters in this environment must remain sensitive to power imbalances and the role they might play in tipping the scales in one direction or the other, especially in light of the Deaf community's long history as an oppressed minority. Non-deaf, English-speaking interpreters hold power simply by virtue of their membership in a majority culture, whether or not this is their intent. The hearing community is much larger than the Deaf community and thereby has the potential to wield more influence.

Accordingly, interpreters must be wary of further disempowering members of the minority Deaf culture by speaking for them. In school settings where they encounter questions about ASL as a language, or about Deaf culture, a best-practice response would be to refer those interested to ASL classes or to Deaf consultants as the best resource.

For interpreters who work with minors, the adult-child dynamic comes into play. The mere fact of the interpreter's *adulthood* carries a perception of authority for Deaf children, exacerbating an already skewed balance of power. Even at the college level, the interpreter's role as *professional* puts her into the same perceived category as instructors, differentiating her from the student population.

Since she carries this inherent power with her into any classroom, the interpreter's task is first to recognize her own potentially oppressive behaviors, then to rectify apparent imbalances as much as she is able. Her first impulse may be a defensive one, since few interpreters would readily admit to oppressive behaviours. Yet if interpreters examine common interpreting practices in educational settings and ask themselves some hard questions, they may uncover some enlightening, albeit disheartening, truths.

For instance, the deliberate use of more English-like signing while interpreting when this has not been expressed as a consumer preference forces the Deaf student to accept a quasi-English message when they would rather have an ASL version. An interpreter's lack of fluency in ASL has the same effect. Either of these could be construed as an oppressive behaviour, in ranking the interpreter's own comfort level above consumer preference or need.

For some interpreters, the choice is not a conscious one. They are doing the best they can with their language skills. Conversely, an interpreter may be fluent in ASL but unable to adjust her interpreting toward a more English structure, supplemented with English mouthing, for a Deaf student who prefers a signed variety of English.

When an interpreter has not mastered a full range of communication modes and is either unwilling or unable to accommodate a consumer's preference, the best choice is to simply decline the job. These are issues to be addressed during the interview process prior to accepting a position. At that stage, it is crucial for the interpreter to self-assess her abilities to meet the requirements of the position. If this is not done at the interview stage and a dilemma arises later, the interpreter's options are more limited. She can strive for improvement in the area of need, or resign the position.

Clearly, the selection of language mode for interpreting in the classroom is not always the Deaf student's choice. As mentioned earlier, school policy, parents or teachers may dictate these decisions, often when neither interpreter nor student would make the same choice. When an English-based mode of signing is designated for classroom use despite a student's preference for ASL, the interpreter's innovative talent is truly put to the test. Some interpreters will strive to satisfy all stakeholders, creatively blending ASL signs and features within an English structural framework. Again, the interpreter is wise to discuss, and be comfortable with, expectations before accepting a position.

4.1   A self-check on issues of control

Interpreters have a duty to examine their own personal biases and inadvertent oppressive tendencies, since these can be changed only after they are recognized. The following list of questions can serve as a self-check, and we suggest that interpreters consider the potential consequences of each response. It would be of benefit to discuss these questions with colleagues or mentors. Keep in mind that options may vary depending on the age of the consumer.

– As an interpreter, who do I align myself with in the educational setting – the educators or the Deaf student? Am I able to keep my own biases in check?
– Can I be an advocate for the Deaf student's needs? If so, how does this shift the power balance?
– When the Deaf student and her teacher (or another classmate) begin a comment or question at the same time, which message do I choose to interpret first, and why?
– Do I always offer to interpret extracurricular events, or do I expect the Deaf student to ask me when the need arises?
– When a Deaf student arrives late to class, do I recap what was missed? Or do I expect that she will seek out the missed information (from the instructor or a classmate) if she wishes to do so?
– How much editing do I do when I interpret, and for what reasons? Do I ever edit hurtful comments from my interpretation to protect the Deaf student's feelings?
– Do I find myself answering a student's questions rather than relaying them to the teacher? If so, why?
– Do I ever make decisions for a Deaf student rather than allowing her to choose? Are there times when I nudge her in a direction that I believe will benefit her?

Ironically, an interpreter's well-intentioned desire to help Deaf students can often lead to the greatest imbalance of power. Fostering dependency on the interpreter ultimately robs students of their right to make autonomous choices, to develop responsible decision-making skills, and to gain a sense of control over their own lives. It may also diminish the student's self-confidence.

Though an interpreter might be tempted to justify such behaviour as nurturing or helpful, it can be far more detrimental than she realizes. Even a Deaf student has the right to fail, and an interpreter who goes overboard to prevent this is doing the student a major disservice in the long run. According to Humphrey and Alcorn, "The role from which we can most appropriately operate is that of ally – one who supports, undergirds, and fosters Deaf individuals in their own struggle for liberation" (1995:75).

For further discussion on the complex issue of oppression, we refer readers to Paulo Freire's (1972) *Pedagogy of the Oppressed* and Charlotte Baker-Shenk's (1986) article "Characteristics of oppressed and oppressor peoples: Their effect on the interpreting context".

5. Ethical decision making in the educational setting

Educated interpreters know the basic ethical principles that guide their profession, including professional accountability, impartiality, integrity and respect for consumers. Implementing them in daily practice, however, may be more difficult. How professional ethics are applied in educational settings depends on far more than simple knowledge. Personal ethics, individual values and a sense of integrity all play vital roles in shaping the decisions interpreters make everyday in the workplace.

With every decision made or action taken, interpreters do more than resolve their own dilemmas. They also set precedents for colleagues who follow in their footsteps. With each chosen course of action, one interpreter creates an impression of all interpreters and of the entire profession. In many instances, her decisions will also shape someone's impression of a Deaf student.

Although adaptations to interpreters' general codes of ethics have been proposed from time to time for specific use in educational settings, it is our stance that such adaptations are unnecessary. The Association of Visual Language Interpreters of Canada's current Code of Ethics and Guidelines for Professional Conduct, ratified in 2000, offers sufficient scope and flexibility for application across the entire spectrum of settings, despite the differences in each.

As school personnel, educational interpreters are expected to follow the same school policy guidelines (e.g., a freedom of information policy) as any other employee. Concerns relating to safety, allegations of sexual abuse, or suspicion of illicit drug use are legally required to be reported to the proper authorities. Reconciling the desired confidentiality and neutrality of the interpreting role with such employee obligations may seem daunting, yet the resiliency to do so is essential to working in educational settings.

While we are not able to address all of the ethical quandaries common to educational settings, we touch on three of these below, and explore the decisions of several interpreters.

5.1 Professional boundaries

In a setting where interpreters work daily with the same consumers, they are faced with the dilemma of whether or not to socialize with them. For many interpreters, especially those working at college and university levels, this issue is rife with contradictions. Effective interpreting requires a trust relationship between interpreter and consumer, for example, but it also demands professional distance. Working long term with a Deaf student offers plentiful opportunities for shared confidences, particularly when interpreter and student are close in age, which might be the case in a post-secondary setting.

Where to draw the line between a professional relationship and a personal friendship, and the consequences of not making this distinction, are addressed in the next scenario. Again, there are no simple answers. In defining her professional bounds, the interpreter is driven by factors such as professional ethics, a sense of morality, personal comfort, and just as importantly, external perceptions.

But is there anything wrong, for instance, in going for a drink with a couple of Deaf students after a difficult college exam they've just written?

> Our first interpreter, Jenna, doesn't think so. In fact, she's so relaxed with them that she has one drink too many and begins to giggle, flirt, and slur her signs. She is embarrassed later, and not sure how to face the students the next morning.
>
> Kees declines the invitation for drinks; he doesn't think it's appropriate. The Deaf students appear somewhat insulted by his decision, but they go anyway. They don't invite him again, which suits him just fine.
>
> Layla, modeling her behaviour on that of other professionals at the college, firmly believes she can be friendly without being friends. She decides to join the students at the pub for a finite period of time, an hour or so, and orders a non-alcoholic beverage instead of beer. She steers the conversation in a direction that she's comfortable with – light and friendly, but not overly personal – and excuses herself when they order a second round.

Now let's take a closer look at the potential outcome of each interpreter's choice. Jenna blatantly ignores professional boundaries in favour of personal friendship with the students. Chances are, they'll expect her to continue in that role. Her neutrality has been compromised, as most likely has any respect the students would have had for her as a professional. Kees places his role at the other end of the spectrum, distancing the students as a result. Being professional doesn't necessarily mean being cold or uncaring. Interpreters can be personable within a professional relationship.

Layla has the right idea in following the example of other college faculty. By doing so, she has maintained a professional standard, yet avoided alienating the students. Should the conversation veer toward a discussion of the exam, she would be wise to remember that she is in that social setting as a professional, not as a peer or a friend. If the students have concerns about the exam, suggesting that they take these back to the instructor avoids any potential role ambiguity.

5.2 Error management

Interpreters, like everyone else, are imperfect beings, and despite their best efforts, will make mistakes at some point. "[M]iscues do occur and certain types of miscues may occur despite preparation and conscious effort on the part of the interpreter to avoid them" (Cokely 1992: 160).

If interpreters accept that mistakes and miscues are inevitable, adopting sensible strategies for error management can become a significant part of their professional approach, especially in the educational setting where interpreting performance directly affects a Deaf student's success. A conscientious interpreter will consistently self-monitor for errors, correct them as needed, and arrange for periodic evaluation of her skills by a colleague, senior interpreter or coordinator. This is rarely included as part of a job description, yet it is a crucial element of professional development. And regarding the student, Seal comments that "[w]hen learning is at stake, interpreter mistakes can be serious" (1998: 179).

Assuming that interpreters realize errors are going to occur, how they choose to handle them is critical. Involving consumers is a first step. Consumers can offer valuable feedback to an interpreter if they are made aware of specific areas of concern and, when given, this input must not be overlooked. Secondary and post-secondary Deaf students in particular may set explicit guidelines for how they would like the interpreter's errors to be managed.

As one Deaf graduate student explains, "if the interpreter misses something, I think it's the interpreter's responsibility to interrupt the teacher and ask for a repetition. But, if I don't understand something, if I missed it, then I will interrupt the professor and ask for a repetition" (Seal 1998: 185). This is the ideal strategy. Not only does it strengthen the direct professor-student relationship, it removes any guesswork on the part of the interpreter.

However, not all consumers operate so decisively; a student's age and experience are important factors for how interpreters approach their work. Provided they are guided by interpreting models such as the communication facilitator or bilingual-bicultural model, an interpreter's role can be readily adapted based on consumer variables.

Though consumer preferences will undoubtedly vary, all underscore the need for agreement between the interpreter, student, and in many cases the instructor, on how errors and omissions are to be managed. Consensus depends on open communication among participants. Strategies decided upon by the interpreter alone may result in failure.

5.3 Use of down time

In most classroom settings, there is a certain amount of down time during which no interpreting is required. Students may be writing an exam, for instance, or doing homework, or working on individual projects. Whatever the reason, the interpreter is still at work and must do something to occupy her time in the classroom.

> For our first interpreter, Mariah, this is an issue easily resolved. On the days she anticipates down time, she brings along a diversion such as a magazine, crossword puzzle or novel. She decides to remain in the classroom so that either the Deaf student or the instructor may call on her to interpret if necessary. However, since she is clearly occupied with an activity, she hopes the student will not be tempted to talk with her during this time. Mariah is generally satisfied with this solution, although she is sometimes perturbed by instructor and student reactions. "Tough job!" the teacher said to her once as she was leaving for the day. The Deaf student's jibe was similar. "Easy job," he signed to Mariah, "You earn money for doing nothing!"
> Nadia, though she agrees she should stay in the classroom during down time to be available to interpret, is at the same time concerned about negative perceptions. She doesn't want to appear idle or frivolously occupied during working hours, so she usually brings along prep materials to review. Reading ahead in the textbook will free up some designated prep time later. On the days she doesn't feel like preparing, she brings along a book to peruse in order to broaden her mind with something academic rather than merely passing the time. The students eye her books curiously once in awhile, but rarely comment.
> Oscar, our third interpreter, makes a point of leaving the classroom during down time. Sitting idle is, in his opinion, not an appropriate use of his time. He lets the Deaf student and the teacher know that he'll return periodically to see if he's needed, and then heads back to the interpreting office to read or do preparation. Occasionally, upon his return, the student will indicate that she missed some spontaneous comments or explanations. Whenever that happens, Oscar attempts to find out what was said so he can relay the missed information to the student, but this is not always possible.

The above options are only three of many. There is seldom an absolutely correct or ideal choice. The decisions an interpreter makes on how to manage down time will often be shaped by school expectations and personal comfort level.

The inevitability of down time in schools is likely one reason that school administrators may insist on combining the interpreting role with another, such as aide or tutor. Those whose sole role is that of classroom interpreter may need to justify how their down time is to be managed. Relieving a colleague in another class while she takes a short break, for instance, or joining that colleague to team-interpret her class are two of many sensible options for using down time when more than one interpreter works in the same school. "Indeed, two heads can be better than one when it comes to representing the verbal information of a challenging classroom or educational setting" (Seal 1998: 179).

When striving to resolve *any* ethical quandary – and there will be many – there are several key questions to ask. For instance, what is your conscience telling you to do? If the whole world were watching – colleagues, interpreting instructors, mentors and the Deaf community – what move would you make? How will your decision affect other interpreters who find themselves in a similar quandary? Are you fostering a desirable perception of interpreters as professionals, or the opposite? Decisions based on honest answers to these important questions will usually lead to the best solution for the circumstance. See Janzen and Korpiniski (this volume) for further discussion of ethical practices generally.

6. Perspectives on interpreting in educational settings

Interpreting in educational settings is not without its controversies. In this section we discuss the perspectives of three groups of stakeholders: the Deaf community, instructors, and interpreters themselves.

6.1 Deaf community perspectives

Any interpreter considering employment in mainstream educational settings may first wish to explore Deaf community views on the issue. Inclusion of Deaf children in the regular school system remains highly controversial in the Deaf community, with many Deaf leaders citing academic failure, a lack of Deaf role models, minimal ASL exposure, and separation of the Deaf child from her cultural peers as downfalls of the practice. "Whereas interpreters generally encounter appreciation and affirmation from members of the Deaf community, those in mainstreamed elementary educational settings may encounter negative responses" (Humphrey & Alcorn 1995: 307). This is especially true of centres where a school for the Deaf exists as a nearby alternative.

A number of interpreters have, over the years, decided against working in mainstream settings, deeming it culturally inappropriate. Others believe, however, that when this stance is taken by qualified interpreters, it subjects the Deaf student to *less* qualified interpreters or even "signers" who have no training in interpreting, and hence *reduces* their chances for academic success. Thus interpreters considering this employment choice are wise to weigh all factors carefully in order to make fully informed decisions.

In addition to Deaf community views, interpreters encounter various perceptions from Deaf students themselves. Creating an accurate perception of interpreters for a school-age Deaf child poses a challenge when her first exposure to them is in the classroom. Most often, the task of teaching a young Deaf student how to work with an interpreter falls by default to the classroom interpreter. Depending on what they have been taught and their level of awareness, Deaf students may view the interpreter as helper, buddy, support person, counselor, communication facilitator, bicultural advisor, or translation machine. While some of these labels are at least partially accurate, others indicate an obvious misunderstanding of the interpreter's true function.

If possible, workshops for mainstreamed Deaf students on how to work with interpreters are a good option, preferably with the involvement of Deaf mentors or senior Deaf students as facilitators. Such workshops have frequently been suggested either by interpreters or the Deaf community, and some progressive school districts have made them a regular part of student orientation. How often they are implemented in other settings, particularly in rural schools, remains uncertain.

By the time a Deaf student reaches the post-secondary level, she has more than likely worked with several interpreters in the community as well as in the school, and thus brings a deeper understanding of the interpreter's role with her into the educational setting.

6.2 Instructors' perspectives

Every teacher and professor reacts differently to having an interpreter in the classroom. Whether interpreters are pointedly ignored, eyed with skepticism, or welcomed as classroom colleagues, one fact is certain: their presence does make a difference to most instructors.

Some instructors admit to trepidation when faced with the new experience of having an interpreter and Deaf student in their class. One Canadian interpreter who conducted an informal survey in her school division reports that for teachers, having another adult in the classroom is a great source of anxiety (Brosseau 1997). This may be surprising, but if a teacher lacks confidence in her ability to manage the class, the interpreter, witness to every fumble or hesitation, may be perceived as a threat. If the instructor has never met a Deaf student, knows little about deafness and even less about the interpreter's role, there may be fear of the unknown. Further, if these factors are combined with not being given any choice in having a Deaf student and interpreter in the classroom, there may be an added measure of frustration.

Alternatively, a teacher may be excited about having a Deaf student in the class, eager to work closely with the interpreter, and open to learning as much as possible about deafness and interpreting.

In most cases, instructors arrive in the classroom with preconceived notions, based either on sketchy information or past experiences, which shape their approach to the Deaf student and the interpreter. Some will perceive the Deaf student as disabled, while others will view her as an individual of different ability. Instructor attitude will be reflected not only in behaviour toward the student and interpreter, but in the expectations placed on both as well.

The instructor's fears can usually be allayed through education. When an interpreter takes the time to explain the interpreting role and duties, she "creates an atmosphere of mutual trust and cooperation" (Brosseau 1997:1). It will quickly become evident that she has no wish to usurp the instructor's place in the classroom, nor is she there to evaluate instructor performance. This helps set the stage for a positive learning environment.

In post-secondary (and sometimes even in secondary) settings, astute Deaf students will often opt to relieve the interpreter of this task and orient the instructor themselves, especially about the everyday realities of deafness. At some universities, too, student service centres deliver orientation packages to prepare professors who are slated to have Deaf students and interpreters in their classes.

At lower grade levels, however, the interpreter, again by default, often becomes the educator-advocate, a role many would happily relinquish, given a suitable alternative. In many cases, however, the interpreter is the only one within the setting able to provide relevant, accurate and current information to school personnel.

6.3 Interpreters' perspectives

How an interpreter's colleagues view her decision to work in educational settings is of concern to many educational interpreters, especially if this setting is viewed as a second-best alternative for those who falter as community interpreters. The perception that working in education signifies lesser interpreting skills, or is somehow easier than freelance work, certainly does exist. Yet many hold the opposite view. Brosseau, a classroom veteran herself, describes interpreting in the educational setting as "no less professional than community interpretation or conference interpretation. It is simply a matter of different clients and different knowledge bases and skills" (Brosseau 1997:1). Because educational interpreting offers a more reliable income than freelance work, many interpreters choose to combine community work with one or more educational contracts, thus balancing variety with stability.

Negative perceptions directed toward interpreters working exclusively in mainstream educational settings usually have more to do with an interpreter's professional behaviour (or lack of) than the setting itself. If an interpreter isolates herself from the Deaf community, neglects regular professional development, or demonstrates an inadequate skill level for the setting, negative reactions may ensue. Conversely, if the interpreter interacts with the Deaf community enough to maintain ASL fluency and familiarity with cultural protocol, and portrays a professional demeanor that reflects well on the profession, a collegial response is more likely to be supportive. If an interpreter is respected as a true professional in terms of skills and behaviour, this view is likely to be held no matter where the interpreter works.

How interpreters view themselves within educational settings is equally significant. If they are there because they love children and welcome the challenges of the classroom, have examined their own qualifications for that particular setting and decided they can manage the role effectively, they will more likely succeed. If they are committed to doing their best, they will take the time for self-reflection, assessing their motives and honestly appraising their personal suitability for an educational setting.

7.   Finding resources

Often, interpreters working in educational settings find themselves working in isolation. When questions and dilemmas arise, it may be time to seek guidance from an external source. Below we have listed some resources that many interpreters have found helpful.

– *The Deaf community*
Members of the Deaf community are the foremost resource on issues of cultural conflict, ASL usage versus other sign variations, and the consumer perspective. Moreover, Deaf faculty in interpreter education programs can offer keen insights into the concerns of interpreters.

– *Mentors*
Who better than a fellow interpreter to offer wisdom based on experience, or a shoulder to cry on when needed? Most interpreters, novice or otherwise, know a few seasoned colleagues working in similar situations who would willingly offer the wisdom of their experience or serve as coaches if asked. Interpreting program instructors, too, make ideal mentors. Choose someone whose judgment you trust, and with whom you have a good rapport.

– *Colleagues*
Consider using your school's professional development days to visit interpreters in other schools, or to meet with colleagues to share interpreting strategies for similar settings.

– *Professional development*
Local and national interpreting associations offer valuable opportunities for enhancing skills and knowledge. Get involved, connect with your colleagues, and learn. As well, consider taking courses in public speaking and public relations, since educating the public is an integral part of the interpreter's role. A study of linguistics will certainly assist in addressing language-related concerns.

– Current literature
The profession of signed language interpreting is growing rapidly. With new research being undertaken and information being published regularly, there is a wealth of reference material that our predecessors did not have, from interpreting textbooks and journals to articles and newsletters. We need only skim the bibliographies of current textbooks and articles to discover more readings on a topic. Building a resource library for interpreters at the school, including subscribing to a selection of interpreting periodicals, is an excellent way to stay updated in the field.

Several books in particular are worth mentioning. These are:

> *Best Practices in Educational Interpreting* by Brenda Chafin Seal (1998).
> This book takes a comprehensive look at the practice of interpreting in various educational settings, and works well as a practical guide for interpreters. Seal focuses on real-life situations and offers best-practice solutions along with questions for further analysis and reflection.

> *So You Want to Be an Interpreter? An Introduction to Sign Language Interpreting* by Janice H. Humphrey & Bob J. Alcorn (1995); 3rd edition (2001).
> Described as consumer friendly, this book is suited to both novice and seasoned practitioners. Humphrey and Alcorn offer a text that contains an abundance of useful information. Though it is not specifically geared to interpreters working in the educational realm, it is broad enough in its approach to be applicable to the setting.

> *Sign Language Interpreting: Exploring its Art and Science* by David A. Stewart, Jerome D. Schein, & Brenda E. Cartwright (1998); 2nd edition (2004).
> While this text addresses interpreting in educational settings in one chapter only, the information overall is relevant to interpreting issues in a range of venues. Of particular interest is the "Encounters with Reality" section, an opportunity to read about situations experienced by colleagues and to reflect upon our own choices and decisions in similar situations.

– Interpreter education programs
Both recent graduates and working interpreters will benefit from continued access to a program's resource materials and the experience of its faculty. This link should be maintained.

– Professional associations
"During my educational work, I sometimes felt isolated. I became involved in MAVLI and that helped me to feel connected to my colleagues and more grounded in the field" (Barker & Lahner 1998:13).[9] This quote from an educational interpreter shows the obvious benefit of professional affiliation. Interpreters may find value in affiliating not only with local and national interpreting associations, but also with Deaf organizations and associations for educators of the Deaf.

– Monitoring skills

An external evaluation by a qualified interpreting diagnostician is an ideal way to get feedback. When this is not possible, an interpreter might seek permission from participants in a setting to videotape herself at work, and from that conduct a self-assessment. There is, though, a drawback with an assessment after the fact, in that miscues are detected only after the interpretation has been completed (Cokely 1992). Nonetheless, if the interpreter can learn from viewing these mistakes, self-assessment is an excellent tool for improving future performance (see Section 8 below for more details on self-assessment).

Where there are several interpreters at one location, regular observation or monitoring by colleagues is a feasible and desirable option. Study groups, too, are an excellent way of lending collegial support and of learning from each other.

– University courses

An adequate background in linguistics and language development, child development, learning styles and strategies, education in general and the particulars of education for Deaf children, is vital. If an interpreter lacks this foundation, we urge post-secondary study in relevant disciplines. With enhanced education, the interpreter will not only be more effective in school settings, she may prove herself more worthy of professional status.

By the same token, a solid grasp of course content is a prerequisite for interpreting in college and university settings. Though some interpreters are able to compensate with extensive preparation, most require formal study in a subject area to be truly effective as interpreters.

Critically, we believe that any interpreter interested in working in the post-secondary environment should first attain the basic credential expected of *any* professional in such a setting, namely a post-secondary education. Not until interpreters have the necessary academic qualifications can they realistically foster a positive perception of the field, nor can they claim the right to a professional title.

– Networking via technology

In today's world of technological advances, we have an international network at our fingertips. E-mail discussion groups, interpreting associations and Deaf-related links on the World Wide Web, interpreting chat rooms, on-line job advertisements and distance learning technology are a few among countless possibilities. Below are several excellent websites, although there are numerous others that are of interest as well.

> www.avlic.ca (The Association of Visual Language Interpreters of Canada)
> www.rid.org (The Registry of Interpreters for the Deaf (USA))
> www.terpsnet.com
> www.deafworldweb.org
> www.deafplanet.com

8.   Self-assessing employment suitability

Is interpreting in an educational setting the right choice for you? To help you decide, we offer the following questions to ponder. This self-assessment may also be useful to those who have been working in the setting for some time; our goal here is to have interpreters consider carefully the demands and challenges of the educational environment.

We would suggest taking some time to go through the list on your own, or meeting with a colleague or mentor to see what emerges from this exercise.

– What are my motives for choosing to work in an educational setting?
– Do I want a routine schedule or would I prefer the variety of freelance work?
– Am I more comfortable working with young children, teenagers, or adults?
– Do I prefer working in a team environment or on my own? If I am the only interpreter in a school or community, how well do I work in isolation? Do I have the stamina to work alone for long periods of time? Or, how well do I work in a team, if I am one of several interpreters in the same setting?
– How effectively do I handle the inevitable politics of working within an educational institution?
– How well do I function in a school team with other professionals? Am I prepared to advocate for Deaf students when the need arises?
– Am I comfortable interpreting in settings with large audiences (e.g., school assemblies)? Or would I prefer to work only with individuals or small groups?
– How comfortable am I with a multi-role position, if this is required? Do I have the ability to clearly delineate the designated roles, and offer input only within the bounds of each? Am I able to function effectively in several roles in the school without confusing consumers?
– Am I comfortable making quick decisions, or am I at my best when given time to contemplate before responding?
– Am I astute enough to recognize when communication is failing, and proactive enough to offer creative solutions? Do I have the confidence to assert myself in order to manage difficult situations effectively?
– Am I able to maintain a neutral position, yet remain sensitive to both participants during an emotional communication exchange?
– Do I endorse, and practice, a philosophy of lifelong learning?
– Do I have a solid foundation of the skills I will need in the setting? For instance, do I have a sufficient understanding of how students of all ages learn? Is my knowledge base broad enough to handle a full range of course content?
– Are my ASL skills strong enough to serve as a language model for those Deaf students with no exposure to ASL beyond the classroom? Or do I expect to increase my ASL fluency on the job by learning from older Deaf students?
– If an alternate communication mode is required, are my skills sufficient? Philosophically, is that mode a comfortable fit for me?

- Is my spoken English fluent enough to accurately represent the communication style of Deaf students? Is my command of English such that I can articulate the complex nuances of my role to school personnel, and respond appropriately to questions?
- Do I have the interpersonal skills to interact effectively with Deaf students, teachers, parents and school administrators?
- Do I interact regularly with the Deaf community to enhance my skills, update my knowledge of current issues, and feel comfortable with cultural protocol so I can interact with Deaf students in culturally appropriate ways?
- Do I have post-secondary (i.e., university or college) background? If not, can I work effectively in post-secondary settings? Am I willing to upgrade my own education, if necessary, to become more effective?
- Finally, am I willing to step into what will be a significant role in a Deaf student's academic life?

9. Conclusion

A single chapter cannot fully address all the issues and concerns facing interpreters working in educational settings. Certainly the field is ripe for further research. For instance, a longitudinal study that tracks students receiving an "interpreted education", profiling learner perspectives and success rates, would offer a wealth of information to school personnel, the Deaf community, and interpreters working in such settings. Also of interest would be a look at the impact of interpreters as "language models" for young deaf students, and how that influences language development over the long term.

In the meantime, we hope we have provided enough information, and asked enough questions, for interpreters to begin making some decisions about their place in the profession.

As with every career choice, interpreting in educational settings has its challenges, and we have noted many throughout the chapter. The complexity of multiple roles in some settings and the many expectations arising as a result can certainly cause dilemmas for interpreters. The lack of understanding of interpreting roles at times and the reluctance of some teachers to accommodate interpreting needs are common sources of frustration. A further challenge comes with the diversity in course content encountered by interpreters.

For many in the educational setting, however, the rewards outnumber the deterrents. The interpreter can count on a secure income, a regular pay cheque and a predictable schedule. In addition, there is the comfort of working with the same group of Deaf and hearing consumers over a period of time, there is opportunity to work with exceptional instructors, and interpreters often reap the benefits of mental stimulation that come with involvement in a teaching and learning milieu. Perhaps the greatest reward of all, though, is the feeling of complete satisfaction that comes with a student's graduation, whether that student is a child moving into Grade 2, an adolescent who has just finished high school, or a university student who has earned a graduate degree. Moments like these, more than anything else, reinforce the true value of the work done by interpreters in educational settings.

Notes

1. The authors would like to thank Debra Russell and Kirk Ferguson for their editing prowess, Diana Kay for allowing us to raid her professional library, and all our colleagues who have mentored and supported us on our journey as interpreters working in educational settings.

2. Inclusion may alternatively be referred to as integration or mainstreaming.

3. We use this term in its broadest sense to indicate any educational board, department or authority responsible for decisions relating to interpreting services in the schools.

4. While this is becoming less accepted, we recognize that some interpreters in our field began their practice prior to the advent of formal interpreter education programs.

5. See Stratiy, this volume, for further discussion of using third person versus first person in other interpreting contexts.

6. See Mindess (1999) and Janzen and Korpiniski, this volume, for more discussion of the appropriateness, and overlap, of these models that have guided the field over time.

7. This general term is used in this context to encompass the range of signed English-based codes (e.g., Sign Supported English, etc.) developed for use in teaching Deaf and hard-of-hearing children.

8. "Natural language" refers to any language learned spontaneously and easily through normal language acquisition processes, with exposure at an early age, but in this context, Johnson et al. refer specifically to ASL.

9. MAVLI is the Manitoba Association of Visual Language Interpreters.

References

Baker-Shenk, Charlotte (1986). Characteristics of oppressed and oppressor peoples: Their effect on the interpreting context. In Marina L. McIntire (Ed.), *Interpreting: The Art of Cross Cultural Mediation* (pp. 59–71). Silver Spring, MD: RID Publications.

Barker, Bonnie-Lyn, & Christine Lahner (1998). A conversation about the COI. In *The AVLIC News*, Volume IX, No. 4, Winter (pp. 13–14). Edmonton, Alberta: The Association of Visual Language Interpreters of Canada.

Brosseau, Nathalie (1997). An educational interpreter prepares for work. In *The AVLIC News*, Volume XIII, No. 3 & 4, Fall & Winter (pp. 1–3). Edmonton, Alberta: The Association of Visual Language Interpreters of Canada.

Cokely, Dennis (1992). *Interpretation: A Sociolinguistic Model.* Burtonsville, MD: Linstok Press.

Freire, Paulo (1972). *Pedagogy of the Oppressed.* New York: Herder & Herder.

Frishberg, Nancy (1986). *Interpreting: An Introduction.* Silver Spring, MD: RID Publications.

Humphrey, Janice H., & Bob J. Alcorn (1995). *So You Want to Be an Interpreter? An Introduction to Sign Language Interpreting.* Amarillo, TX: H & H Publishers.

Johnson, Kristen (1991). Miscommunication in interpreted classroom interaction. *Sign Language Studies, 70,* 1–27.

Johnson, Robert E., Scott K. Liddell, & Carol J. Erting (1989). *Unlocking the Curriculum: Principles for Achieving Access in Deaf Education.* Gallaudet Research Institute Working Paper 89–3, Gallaudet University, Washington, DC.

Mindess, Anna (1999). *Reading Between the Signs: Intercultural Communication for Sign Language Interpreters.* Yarmouth, ME: Intercultural Press.

Radatz, Jan (1994). Professional standards for interpreters working in educational settings. *RID Views, 11* (2), 1–22.

Schick, Brenda (2001). Interpreting for children: How it's different. *Odyssey,* Winter/Spring 2001 (pp. 8–11). Washington, DC: Laurent Clerc National Deaf Education Center, Gallaudet University.

Seal, Brenda Chafin (1998). *Best Practices in Educational Interpreting.* Needham Heights, MA: Allyn & Bacon.

Stewart, David A. (1988). Educational interpreting for the hearing impaired. *British Columbia Journal of Special Education, 12* (3), 273–279.

Stewart, David A., Jerome D. Schein, & Brenda E. Cartwright (1998). *Sign Language Interpreting: Exploring its Art and Science.* Needham Heights, MA: Allyn & Bacon.

Wilcox, Phyllis, Jo Santiago, & Gary Sanderson (1992). Triangulation of interpreting relationships: A model for connecting educational interpreter standards. In Jean Plant-Moeller (Ed.), *Expanding Horizons: Proceedings of the 1991 RID Convention* (pp. 166–176). Silver Spring, MD: RID Publications.

Winston, Elizabeth (1994). An interpreted education: Inclusion or exclusion? In Robert C. Johnson & Oscar P. Cohen (Eds.), *Implications and Complications for Deaf Students of the Full Inclusion Movement: A Joint Publication of the Conference of Educational Administrators Serving the Deaf, and the Gallaudet Research Institute* (pp. 55–63). Washington, DC: Gallaudet Research Institute.

Winzer, Margret, Sally Rogow, & Charlotte David (1987). *Exceptional Children in Canada.* Scarborough, Ontario: Prentice-Hall.

Witter-Merithew, Anna, & Richard Dirst (1982). Preparation and use of educational interpreters. In Donald G. Sims, Gerard G. Walter, & Robert L. Whitehead. (Eds.), *Deafness and Communication: Assessment and Training* (pp. 395–406). Baltimore, MD: Williams & Wilkis.

CHAPTER 12

Deaf interpreters

Patrick Boudreault
California State University, Northridge

1. Introduction[1]

> *"How can a Deaf person be a signed language interpreter in
> your own Deaf community? It can't be. You're Deaf!"*

This was once said by a Deaf community member to a Deaf interpreter. He argued
that there are already many qualified hearing interpreters to handle communication
access, that it is futile to have Deaf interpreters since they cannot perform as hearing
interpreters do. The fact is that many Deaf people who encounter a Deaf interpreter for
the first time assume that she is hearing, and when they find out that she is Deaf, they
are suspicious and confused. But the Deaf community and hearing interpreters are
now learning how Deaf interpreters contribute significantly in many areas of signed
language interpreting and communication. There is a new trend around the world
for the Deaf interpreter service provider to be an integral part of Deaf life. However,
there is very little information on Deaf interpreters in the signed language interpreting
literature. One rare exception to this is the comparative analysis between "direct"
and "intermediary" interpretation in American Sign Language conducted by Carolyn
Ressler (1999). Because of this lack of information, a chapter on Deaf interpreters
in this volume is essential. The description of various Deaf interpreter (DI) tasks
and roles will give practitioners and consumers a better understanding of this new
profession. This chapter is written expressly for Deaf and hearing individuals in the
field of interpreting and is intended as a source of information about the many DI
issues that exist.

Throughout this chapter, the main languages used in examples are American
Sign Language (ASL), Langue des Signes Québécoise (LSQ), English and French.
These languages are the most commonly used languages of the Deaf community in
Canada. However, this discussion can be applied to other language users around the
world as well.

The chapter is divided into several main sections, beginning with some history and
a description of the roles of DIs, which will be elaborated before presenting different

models of DI arrangements. A discussion of ethics and DI training programs follows this, and finally, some conclusions are drawn.

2.   Deaf interpreters

Spoken to signed language interpreting is a common form of communication access between Deaf and hearing communities and is extensively described in the literature (e.g., Cokely 1992; Frishberg 1990; Humphrey & Alcorn 2001; Mindess 1999; Solow 2000; Stewart, Schein, & Cartwright 1998; Taylor 1993, 2002). Deaf individuals, however, who act as interpreters for Deaf members of their own community are faced with many challenges that must be addressed. Below, the roles that DIs play in the community are discussed within historical, socio-linguistic and educational contexts. These factors are introduced in order to understand more clearly how the Deaf community views DIs and why these interpreters are necessary.

2.1 Deaf interpreters within the Deaf community

There are many possibilities for informal interpreting within the Deaf community where some members of the community possess numerous skills to act as communication facilitators. The context can be within a Deaf school, the workplace or when meeting professional hearing people such as lawyers, doctors, etc. This DI process can involve voicing, gesturing, writing, or using other signed languages. In Section 2.1.1 below are several examples of the circumstances in which bilingual Deaf individuals act informally and naturally as DIs. This type of interpreting began to take place much before any certification for DIs was implemented.

2.1.1 Deaf bilinguals
A Deaf bilingual with skills in at least one written and one signed language can be an interpreter or translator even if she is unable to hear or speak. Kannapell (1993) defines these "balanced-bilinguals" as individuals who function comfortably in two languages and cultures. A very common situation in a classroom at a school for the Deaf or even in a higher education context is that the hearing teachers do not communicate or transmit their ideas clearly. Their signed language abilities are quite often underdeveloped and may contain a confusing mixture of vocabulary and grammar from a natural signed language and from systems invented to code a spoken language. When there is a no clearly established form of communication that is accessible to Deaf students, there can be huge linguistic gaps between these instructors and the students. A Deaf student in the classroom frequently acts, informally or without expressly being asked, as a "relay" or "facilitator" between the teacher and the others in the class. Often there is at least one Deaf student who possesses the skills to grasp the teacher's ideas because she is highly proficient in the signed language and

has a good mastery of her second language (written or spoken), and thus shares the teacher's message with the rest of her classmates.

A similar situation may occur in classrooms in mainstream settings where a small number of Deaf students are grouped in the same class. In this case, it is more usual for them to have a hearing interpreter in the classroom, but from time to time, one of the Deaf students may still interpret or translate information for other Deaf students.

In other instances, a Deaf person might act as a facilitator between another Deaf person who is uncomfortable communicating by writing and a hearing person who is not used to ways of communicating with the Deaf person. The bilingual facilitator will communicate with the hearing person using written language and translate this into signed language, and vice versa.

Many communication situations such as those described above are possible for the bilingual Deaf person, but these bilinguals are generally unaware of a code of ethics in these "DI" situations and they frequently behave as "helpers". These interpreters may also become advocates for Deaf people as they act as their interpreters.

In every Deaf community, there are some individuals who are culturally Deaf but have some residual ability to hear or to speak. They are often labeled as "hard-of-hearing" but yet they are considered primarily as "Deaf" people when they have strong links to the Deaf community. These bilinguals are frequently called upon to facilitate communication between hearing and Deaf people. This interpreting process is generally consecutive in nature. Also, these bilinguals can act as "communication facilitators"[2] between hearing people who can sign only in a restricted range of registers and a Deaf person who is considered semilingual (Cummins 1979, 2000; Skutnabb-Kangas 1981)[3] or monolingual. The DI plays an important role, even if informally, in this communication process by ensuring that the Deaf person grasps the message transmitted by the hearing person who is unable to convey her ideas clearly and grammatically in a visual and spatial medium.

The interpreting by Deaf bilinguals described above may not necessarily be considered professional. Professional status for DIs was not considered until the 1970s in the United States (Bienvenu & Colonomos 1992) and it is still virtually non-existent in Canada. But DIs should be expected to work as professionals and to do this, they need to gain more training and experience. The next section describes Deaf interpreters' rise to the professional level.

2.2 Deaf interpreters as professionals

The professional status of DIs began when the Registry of Interpreters for the Deaf (RID), a United States organization equivalent to the Association of Visual Language Interpreters of Canada (AVLIC), formally recognized the role of the DI by establishing the Reverse Skills Certificate (RSC) in 1972. However, the RSC was most often granted to hard-of-hearing individuals whose preferred means of communication was spoken English and who were generally not greatly involved with the Deaf community. This early RSC certification allowed these individuals to be members of evaluation teams for screening and certification processes for hearing interpreters. Thus it is somewhat misleading to assume that there was true certification for DIs during that period (Bienvenu & Colonomos 1992).

In the 1980s, United States legislation mandated communication accessibility in legal and medical services. This increased the need for RSC interpreters to ensure effective communication between Deaf consumers who use idiosyncratic signs and gestures or who are semilingual (or even monolingual in some cases), and hearing interpreters. The Deaf caucus of RID proposed that the RSC title be changed to "Relay Interpreter Certificate". In this period, we see an emergence of relay interpreting services provided by Deaf people themselves. Practitioners in the field of signed language interpreting began to realize the importance of having DIs in the field for as many situations as possible when hearing interpreters have difficulty in performing their task for a number of reasons. Teaming the hearing interpreter with a DI increases the quality of interpretation for everyone. This does not translate necessarily to the idea that hearing interpreters are incompetent, but is more a question of the many factors that lead to the recognition of including a DI as a part of the team (Bienvenu & Colonomos 1992; Mindess 1999; Stewart et al. 1998). These points will be discussed further throughout the remainder of this chapter.

In the late 1990s, RID more formally promoted certification for DIs by establishing a provisional certificate (CDI-P) to allow DIs to perform professionally until a permanent evaluation tool could be fully implemented. The term "relay interpreter" proposed in 1980s was not used any longer. Then in 1998, full DI certification (CDI) was offered by RID. A Deaf person interested in certification must take a two-part exam: a written exam and an interpreting performance exam. After gaining certification, DIs are required to take ongoing training in order to maintain their certification similar to their hearing colleagues who hold the Certificate of Interpretation (CI) or Certificate of Transliteration (CT) (Gouby 2003).[4]

There were several attempts to establish a certification process for DIs in the 1990s in Canada where there are a number of Deaf individuals who act as DIs in various situations, and a small number of DIs who have had an opportunity to receive training, especially in British Columbia, Manitoba and Ontario. During the national AVLIC conference in 1996 there was an attempt to set up a DI branch within the organization but it never materialized formally and no certification for DIs in Canada exists as of yet. However, there has been a great demand within the Canadian Deaf community for ASL-LSQ interpreting services during national conventions or at festivals since the mid-1990s. There is one company owned by a Deaf person in Montreal that offers services in interpreting between two signed languages as well as "mirror interpreting" (Boudreault & Scully 2001) (see Section 3.2.1 below). As the demand increases for DI services across North America, and because there is a better understanding of the importance of DI services, certifying DIs in Canada is the next logical step to ensure that a high level of interpretation quality is maintained.

3.   Description and roles of Deaf interpreters

Definitions of the role of Deaf Interpreters have generally not been clearly established either within the Deaf community or for signed language interpreters in Canada, although there is a general assumption that a DI is considered as a "language facilitator" or a "mirroring" interpreter. We tend to think of spoken to signed language interpreters as "hearing" interpreters, so perhaps we might consider "Deaf" interpreters to be those who just happen to be Deaf. However, many people assume that Deaf interpreters can only do certain specific tasks. This often leads to the misconception that a DI's role is limited. There is a general misunderstanding among members of the Deaf community and many hearing people that the DI's task only involves relaying between a certified hearing interpreter and a Deaf consumer, compensating for differences in language use, given the Deaf consumer's educational and language background.

In Sections 3.1 and 3.2 below, the various possible tasks of DIs are introduced. There are two main categories of DI: those who work primarily with two languages and those who work primarily within one language. In order to understand the need for the various roles of DIs in Canada, an historical overview must be considered.

3.1   Working with two languages

In Canada and in many others countries around the world where there are two or more official spoken languages (e.g., Switzerland, Ireland, etc.), these countries are considered as a whole to be bilingual or multilingual. Along with more than one official spoken language in these countries, we usually see the emergence of two Deaf communities, often in parallel with the language regions of the hearing community, even in a single city.[5] Deaf Schools are typically established that coincide regionally with the parents' spoken language. The language of education in these schools is primarily that of the parents' first spoken and written language, even when these parents are Deaf, for example French if the parents live in a French-speaking community. Often the natural signed language in each region is considered only as an option or an alternate method of communication in Deaf education (Chamberlain & Boudreault 1998).

In Canada there are two official spoken and written languages, French and English. There are, however, many other languages spoken in Canada, such as native languages and other allophone communities.[6] When it comes to the Deaf community, there are two signed languages formally recognized by the Canadian Association of the Deaf: Langue des Signes Québécoise (LSQ or Quebec Sign Language) used in the Francophone community and American Sign Language (ASL) used in the Anglophone community (CAD 2002). Both signed languages are closely related in origin and share many similar linguistic features, yet they are two separate languages found within their own cultural contexts and reflecting their own community of users' ways of thinking. Each has its own grammar, and each experiences at least some influence from the spoken (and written) language of the region. Sometimes, however, their apparent similarities lead to serious misunderstandings when Deaf members of both communities communicate with each other.

3.1.1 *ASL-LSQ DIs*

Given the cultural, educational and linguistic characteristics of the Canadian Deaf community, there is a need for ASL-LSQ DIs to assist the two linguistic groups in interacting and communicating with each other. Despite many years of partial linguistic segregation, contact between the two signed languages is now increasing continually, but increased contact between the two linguistic communities does not mean that each individual has become bilingual.

The ASL-LSQ interpreting process is similar to that encountered by hearing signed language interpreters except that the ASL-LSQ interpreter may need to work with an additional DI (in a process of mirroring) depending on several factors. This requirement will be discussed further in sections below regarding the working environment. ASL-LSQ interpreters also need to be very efficient visually, keeping track of multiple contextual and linguistic pieces of information all at once and relaying the multiplicity of meanings into either signed language as the target language. But knowing two signed languages is not sufficient. ASL-LSQ DIs also need to be proficient in two written languages: English and French. ASL uses more fingerspelling and abbreviated signs or acronyms compared to LSQ. There is a need to understand English in order to identify the sources of these items, and thus to find the correct equivalent in French or LSQ. As an example, during a board meeting with ASL-LSQ interpreters present, the board president signed "O-O-O". The ASL-LSQ DI, however, did not know this acronym, and needed to ask for clarification. The DI learned that it was an abbreviation of "Out of Order" and had to look up the semantic equivalent in French before signing the concept in LSQ where there is no such abbreviation. Another common example is that LSQ tends to make use of mouthing a word along with signing the first (fingerspelled) letter of the word to designate a proper noun or technical term, whereas ASL will spell the word out. Therefore the interpreter must first understand the word in French and translate into English before constructing the message in ASL, where either an ASL sign or fingerspelling may be the appropriate target choice.

This presents a greater challenge for ASL-LSQ DIs in coping with multi-cultural and multilingual information all at once to ensure that meanings are properly trans-mitted between two parties. Occasionally, ASL-LSQ DIs must interrupt Deaf partici-pants during meetings or when discussion is heated, since both ASL and LSQ signing participants tend to assume that they are understanding each other without paying attention to the interpreter and the interpreter's message, when the interpreter in fact has detected semantic differences in the participants' signing that causes confusion between them. This can take place because ASL and LSQ share numerous common grammatical structures and assumptions in this regard can lead to a great deal of mis-understanding. The ASL-LSQ DI bears the responsibility to ensure that both parties do have the same understanding of each other's messages, and so must constantly be prepared to deal with linguistic items stemming from all languages involved.

3.1.2 *ASL-LSQ interpreting and Deaf–blind people*

In addition to ASL-LSQ DI tasks such as those described above, DIs work with individuals who are Deaf-blind or who have severely limited vision. In general, there are four types of Deaf-blind people: those with Usher's Syndrome, those with congenital blindness, those born of maternal Rubella, and those who experience the loss of sight in later life (Atwood, Clarkson, & Laba 1992; Collins 1993). The ASL-LSQ DI will interpret tactilely for a Deaf-blind person or sign in a smaller, restricted area and closer to the person with limited vision. The interpretation will include both the discourse message and visual information regarding the surrounding area. It is a colossal task to ensure that the Deaf-blind individual is able to follow discussions or presentations delivered in another signed language, with the least restriction possible (Collins & Petronio 1998; Petronio 1995; Smith 1994). A detailed description of turn-taking in signed conversations of Deaf-Blind individuals can be found in Mesch (2001). The Deaf interpreter is best suited to perform this task since she will have the linguistic ability to convert spatial information to a non-visually dependent form, into a smaller space, or tactilely, which results in the highest quality of interpreting for Deaf-blind consumers.

3.2 Working within one language

The DI can function in several capacities where she only deals with one language. In technical terms, then, how can we consider the DI to be an "interpreter" in these cases? For the DI, the work does not necessarily always involve two languages but instead can mean working from one language to some other form of communication, such as gesturing, drawing, using props, idiosyncratic signs, International Sign, etc., which are not considered as actual language systems. In other cases, the DI's source language (the language she receives) is identical to the target language (the output language), that is, during "mirroring" (see Section 3.2.1 below). The main concern is that the Deaf interpreter needs some time lag to process all the incoming information to be transmitted in each of these different formats. There are three categories of the DI working within one language. These are mirroring (DI-M), working in the capacity of facilitator (DI-F), and interpreting using International Sign (DI-IS). The DI interpreting for a Deaf-blind person can be considered as an additional area of competency for each of these three tasks.

3.2.1 *Mirroring*

Mirroring can sometimes also be called "shadowing" or "shadow interpreting". The term "mirroring" is more suitable, however, since it generally refers to a setup in which the DI faces the signer (the source input). The DI who is mirroring (DI-M) has the task of replicating every grammatical feature of the message signed by the presenter, someone in the audience, or even by another ASL-LSQ DI or hearing interpreter. The DI-M is most often used during a question period when a large number of participants are present, such as an assembly or conference, and where the majority of the participants are Deaf. In order to maintain communication efficiency in terms of both fluency and time management for all members of the audience, the DI-M enables Deaf participants to simply stand and ask a question without needing to go up to the front or on the stage. The DI-M will replicate all the information from the signer by signing the lexical material and the non-manual features. The DI-M may need to have some lag time to ensure enough time to process the message and sign it clearly without omitting important grammatical items. The DI-M must have outstanding language imitation skills and the ability to rapidly process information to succeed. If the mirroring is not clear, Deaf audience members will likely attempt to locate the source of the message somewhere in the room, but this can lead to confusion (e.g., the source signer is hard to locate, difficult to see, has already finished asking the question, etc.). Occasionally, the lack of message clarity is not caused by the DI-M, but occurs when the source message signer is not expressing herself clearly. In such cases the DI-M may not understand or may include additional information where the source message is vague. Most of the time, however, the DI-M transmits the message verbatim as it is seen, thus acting much like a "conduit" or as a messenger conveying another person's message.

Another type of situation where a DI-M is used is in conjunction with an ASL-LSQ DI. In these situations, the ASL-LSQ DI sits across from an ASL or LSQ presenter and the DI-M mirrors the ASL-LSQ DI's target message. Figures 2 to 6 and 7a, appearing later in the chapter, include a DI-M in this capacity in the configurations the figures address; readers might wish to refer to these figures at this point. An ASL-LSQ DI teamed with a DI-M is a common combination of interpreters to ensure the transmission of the message when the audience cannot see the ASL-LSQ DI's interpretation because this interpreter faces the presenter along with the audience. A DI working with two languages may switch roles between acting as an ASL-LSQ DI and a DI-M on-site during the interpreting process in order to maintain the message flow. This is an interesting aspect of interpreting performance since the interpreter needs to be very versatile and flexible in her use of language and regarding conscious cognitive processing tasks. Further examples of this are described below.

Unfortunately, once in a while the DI may be caught inadvertently mixing up her languages during such role switching. For example, the interpreter acting as ASL-LSQ DI might be signing LSQ as the target language while the presenter signs ASL to the audience. The DI might have to switch rapidly into the role of DI-M when someone in the audience poses a question in LSQ, which is interpreted into ASL by the (original) DI-M, and which now must be mirrored to the presenter. After the question is asked and interpreted, when the presenter answers, this interpreter returns again to her role as ASL-LSQ DI to interpret the response. The problem is that in situations where this complex language switching has been taking place, the DI has been known to begin to sign ASL *exactly as the presenter is*. In one instance when this took place, luckily a member of the interpreting team sitting across from the confused DI caught the error and alerted the team. This type of error can happen when fatigue sets in after a long day of interpreting.[7]

On some occasions, the DI-M works with a hearing interpreter as a team member. In these cases, the DI-M stands on the stage facing the audience while the hearing interpreter works from a spoken language such as English as the source into a signed language such as ASL. The DI-M then takes this ASL text as her source, but because the DI is a native signer of ASL, she will be able to sign the target message in very clear and fluid ASL. This is a possibility that is used for special occasions where the majority of the audience is Deaf. In this role, the DI-M expands and improves visual aspects in the target text from a potentially more limited or rigid register produced by the hearing interpreter. The target language is signed with a richer, more complete use of grammatical facial expression and greater use of grammatical space. The DI-M can also incorporate cultural and linguistic information based on a Deaf view of the material. Audiences report enjoying this kind of team interpreting, but unfortunately, it does not take place frequently.

3.2.2 The DI as facilitator

In this chapter, the term "facilitator" is used instead of the more popular terms "relay" or "intermediary" interpreter.[8] However all the terms are considered similar and in-dicate the same task. The emergence of the DI Facilitator (DI-F) came about when hearing interpreters began to acknowledge that they were confronting major diffi-culties in comprehending some Deaf consumers' signing. This may be due to many factors such as the educational, language and cultural backgrounds of these consumers that result in the person being virtually without a formal language system to being "semilingual" as discussed in the literature on bilingualism (Cummins 1979, 2000; Skutnabb-Kangas 1981). The individual may possess limited or minimal communica-tion and inter-cultural interaction skills. Based on these factors, hearing interpreters began to realize that they needed to team up with a Deaf individual to ensure the quality of communication was being maintained throughout the interpreting process.

The population we are concerned with here are those whose language acquisition was delayed or the quality and quantity of language input was insufficient for them to develop fully into proficient ASL or LSQ signers (Boudreault 1999; Morford & Mayberry 2000), thus they are considered as semilingual. There are also some isolated individuals who have rudimentary forms of signed communication because they have been withheld from any formal education, or because they have not had opportunities to interact and communicate with many other people over the years. These people use mainly home-signs or gestures, and typically only a very few individuals would understand what they are communicating. As an example of where such an individual might encounter an interpreter would be if she were being questioned by someone in the justice system to find out if she knew a certain individual or relative. Quite possibly, the person might be unable to understand the name that is fingerspelled by the interpreter or even ASL signs such as MOM or SISTER. The person may have developed her own gesture to identify a specific individual (or concept), so "sister" may be signed or gestured as "LONG HAIR FRECKLES" instead of the conventional ASL sign SISTER that begins with a hand configuration located at the chin and ends with this hand contacting the side of the other hand. This poses a tremendous challenge for the interpreter to figure out a message signed, or even gestured, by that person. The participation of a DI-F is essential for this extraordinary circumstance because the trained DI-F can more readily establish a rapport with this person and tap into the communication system she uses by learning her home-signs, or communicate by other means such as gestures, drawing and figuring out visual ways to represent abstract ideas. Clarity is important because in the legal system, there are numerous abstractions that are challenging for the DI-F to convey in visual, more concrete terms when conventional language is not a fully reliable option. Section 4 below offers a number of models of interaction involving a DI that suggest ideal positioning. Readers are referred especially to Figures 8 and 9 in that section for suggestions on how to set up a one-to-one interview and Figure 10 regarding how to position the DI in a courtroom situation.

The term "semilingual" is one of several that describe the language profile of Deaf people who generally possess a small vocabulary and produce incorrect grammar, and whose language production is not automatic. Some other labels that have been used are "minimal language skills", "limited general knowledge" or "highly visual language" (see, for example, Frishberg 1990; Gouby 2003; Humphrey & Alcorn 2001; Stewart et al. 1998). The communication of a semilingual Deaf person may sometimes also be referred to as "survival communication", meaning that this person's limited communication enables her to get what she needs, but not much more. It should be noted here that it is very important for us to be able to refer to the Deaf person's linguistic status or communication abilities humanely and with respect and not by assigning denigrating labels.

Clearly identifying the requirements of semilingual Deaf persons is also important when explaining to service providers, government officials, courtroom and legal authorities, etc., what type of interpretation is appropriate so that the Deaf person will be able to understand and express herself comfortably. Many times this includes needing to explain why a DI-F should be part of the interpreting team. The most common explanation is that the hearing interpreter, even when certified, needs to work with a DI-F as the only way to ensure that communication for all participants will be successful. In the legal system, the need to include a DI-F is often recognized by legal workers since full understanding of communication during all steps of the legal process is critical (Bienvenu & Colonomos 1992; Frishberg 1990; Gouby 2003).

Regarding persons who are semilingual or who have no conventional language at all, interpreters must remember that language and communication abilities can vary greatly from person to person. It is possible that the Deaf person with a language limitation may still watch the ASL-English (hearing) interpreter but once in a while have a difficult time following all the linguistic and cultural nuances. This can be the case even when the interpreter is certified and highly skilled. The consumer will depend on the DI-F to greatly aid her understanding if she knows how to use the DI-F properly. For example, there may be a situation where the consumer must describe an event that occurred the previous day. She may instead begin to describe events that took place several weeks prior, however, in order to put the more recent event into context. Because the DI-F functions as an "interpreter-facilitator" she will work with the consumer to focus her attention just on the information being requested, and by assisting the consumer to frame her response to match the conventions of the setting.[9] Teaming a hearing interpreter with a DI-F can thus be seen as a great asset in facilitating the communication process.

Apart from the language barriers, there are other factors that have a significant impact such as culture (other than Canadian, American, or Deaf culture, because Deaf members of minority ethnic groups may be in situations where they require interpretation and some of these people will not be fluent in ASL or LSQ), different social or economic status, and dialects (vernacular language use, regional variants, school for the Deaf communication methods, age group factors, etc.). The DI-F should be attentive and sensitive with respect to consumer background and should expect the diversity of individual experiences that can lead to unique language usage case by case.

The Registry of Interpreters for the Deaf (RID) evaluates Deaf interpreters and offers a certificate called the Certified Deaf Interpreter (CDI). A CDI is defined as follows:

> A Certified Deaf Interpreter (CDI) is an individual who is deaf or hard of hearing and has been certified by the Registry of Interpreters for the Deaf as an interpreter.
>
> In addition to excellent general communication skills and general interpreter training, the CDI may also have specialized training and/or experience in use of gesture, mime, props, drawings and other tools to enhance communication. The CDI has an extensive knowledge and understanding of deafness, the deaf community, and/or Deaf culture which combined with excellent communication skills, can bring added expertise into booth [sic] routine and uniquely difficult interpreting situations. (RID Standard Practice Paper: Use of a Certified Deaf Interpreter; www.rid.org)

The field of Deaf interpreters has only come into being very recently and RID's definition of the CDI does not provide us with clear, detailed descriptions of the various roles of the DI as discussed in this chapter. The definition provided by RID seems mainly focused on the DI-F role. RID's Standard Practice Paper on CDIs briefly outlines several additional functions and possible tasks of the CDI, so it is clear that the definition can be broadened beyond the function of facilitator to include categories such as mirroring and interpreting for Deaf-blind people (as RID suggests), interpreting between two signed languages, and so forth.

3.2.3 *Working with International Sign*
The International Sign interpreting situation is very similar to the ASL-LSQ DI model introduced in Section 3.1.1 above. A significant difference, however, is that Interna-

tional Sign is not considered to be a natural or native signed language associated with a specific Deaf community of users. Thus, I consider it here as part of Section 3.2 "Working within one language" because it entails interpreting between a natural signed language and a system of signing that is not a natural language or a native language of any Deaf community members. This system includes a combination of gestures, loan signs from various existing signed languages, and "pidgin" signs created specifically for particular interpreted situations such as international conferences (e.g., Deaf Way II), Deaflympics, or international meetings where Deaf individuals using various signed languages are involved. Previously called "Gestuno", meaning the unity of sign languages and intended as the equivalent to the spoken international "language" Esperanto (Moody 1987), it was mandated by the World Federation of the Deaf which commissioned a basic dictionary of approximately 1500 Gestuno signs, published by the British Deaf Association (World Federation of the Deaf 1975). The term currently used instead of Gestuno, however, is International Sign. It is used in language contact situations for specific communication among the participants at the event, but as mentioned, it does not have a complex and complete set of grammatical features compared to natural signed languages such as ASL and LSQ. However, it is important to recall that International Sign is based on natural and visual principles of grammar, thus it is often the case that signers feel very comfortable using this communication format. Very often Deaf people have looked at International Sign as one of the natural signed languages but in fact it is not. Nonetheless, the Deaf interpreter using International Sign (DI-IS) is a great asset for an international audience knowledgeable in International Sign by making the information accessible using the most widely understood international signs.

3.2.4 *Working with Deaf-blind people within one language*

Along with the DI working with a single language in the functions of DI-M, DI-F and DI-IS, DIs also work with Deaf-blind people. In Section 3.1.2 above, I discussed the process of working with a Deaf-blind consumer when two languages, such as ASL and LSQ, are involved. In the case of working with only a single language, much about the process is similar other than the transfer of information from one source language to a different target language. Here, the DI working with a Deaf-blind consumer relies on the source input from a signing presenter, another DI or a hearing interpreter, and conveys that information using a form of communication that is understandable to that Deaf-blind consumer, but only one language is involved. One difference between this and the other functions of DI-M, DI-F and DI-IS is that the DI has to be positioned near to the Deaf-blind or limited vision consumer, although this positioning arrangement may take many forms depending upon the consumer's preference (Petronio 1995; Mesch 2001). These consumers may pose significant challenges since they cannot make use of drawing or ready-made pictures – in other words visual media can be used only minimally if at all. The DI must be prepared to overcome these communication difficulties and be skilled communicators with a variety of Deaf-blind individuals (Smith 1994).

3.2.5 *Summary*

The professionally trained DI is well suited to perform the various tasks discussed above in Section 3.1.2. The important factor leading to the DI's success is to be sensitive to the language and communication diversity of the Deaf population by considering their use of foreign signed languages, gestures, individual (and highly variable) home-sign systems, etc. The DI who works with communities in Canada using ASL and LSQ must be multilingual, with skills in these two signed languages and in the written forms of English and French, and multi-cultural, so she can move swiftly among these multiple dimensions of language use to ensure message accuracy. For those DIs working in areas where only one signed language, for example ASL, and one major written language such as English are used, the DI should be bilingual in these two languages. The major advantage of including DIs is that they are first language users of the signed language of the region and share the Deaf experience with the Deaf consumer; this "sameness" is an important factor in establishing rapport and communicating effectively. The DI can be an advocate for the process of understanding and communication for Deaf consumers within the limits of the code of ethics (Bienvenu & Colonomos 1992), which is discussed further in Section 5 below. The psychological impact of the DI's presence on the Deaf consumer can be very positive since the DI and the consumer can relate to each other based on their experiential "sameness" and cultural identification. This can generate a sense of empowerment within the Deaf consumer with which to express her thoughts to other people whom she could not previously communicate with or access (Bienvenu & Colonomos 1992; Gouby 2003; Humphrey & Alcorn 2001).

A real interpreting case serves as an excellent example of this. In this situation, a hearing interpreter was working with a Deaf woman who was presented with the possibility of giving up her child to adoption (Gouby 2003). The interpreter began to believe that there was a communication issue with the consumer because she seemed quite willing to have her child adopted and yet, given the circumstances, this willingness was illogical. Fearing that a communication barrier was a factor, the hearing interpreter decided to request bringing in a DI-F to ensure that the consumer understood all legal implications of giving up her child. The DI-F joined them and began to interpret the interaction, including the issues involved in the case, and verifying that she understood the legal implications of the judge's rendering the final decision. The woman only then understood that she had the right to decline the suggestion of adoption and could argue her case for keeping her child. In the end, it dramatically changed the course of events in the courtroom. This is an example of empowerment in the decision making process that can take place because the Deaf consumer can relate to and trust another member of her own Deaf community. In this way she had the opportunity to express herself freely instead of being alone and psychologically overwhelmed by the hearing people that surrounded her. Thus the DI can play a profound role in terms of psychological factors in enabling the communication process through interpretation.

4.   Models of Deaf interpreter positioning and arrangement

In this section, a number of models of DI arrangements and language transmission possibilities are illustrated. Readers should keep in mind that in these scenarios there are four languages possible: ASL, LSQ, English (spoken or written) and French (spoken or written). The aim is to have the most efficient configuration to transmit the message from source language to target language with the least number of "chained" transmissions as possible to avoid losing the original message meaning. There are several partial models suggested in this chapter but these should not be taken as a fixed set; there is always the possibility that additional models may be found based on interpreter team agreement or negotiation with consumers.

4.1 ASL-LSQ DI, DI-M and DI-IS models

There are several models of possible arrangements for ASL-LSQ DIs. These are: 1) the one-to-one or small group model, 2) a model where mirroring takes place, 3) a model of teaming with a hearing interpreter, and 4) an audio-visual support model. The ASL-LSQ DI can work solo or in a team of two DIs (for the ASL-LSQ DI or DI-M or DI-IS models) or more, depending on the situation and visual access requirements. The DI-IS interpreting process can also take place with respect to the models presented below when signed languages such as ASL and LSQ are either the source or target language.

4.1.1 *The DI working solo*
For situations such as one-to-one conversations or discussions involving a small group, the ASL-LSQ DI can work alone and the process will be either consecutively or simultaneously interpreted. The DI is positioned between the source and target language signers, as shown in Figure 1. An advantage to this situation is that the DI has a great deal of flexibility and can be more mobile – moving to whatever positioning arrangement is most conducive to the best facilitation of communication, given the specifics of the space and setting in which the interchange takes place. One

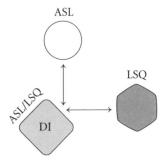

Figure 1. A model of the ASL-LSQ DI working solo between ASL and LSQ consumers.

disadvantage, however, is that the DI does not have support from other DI colleagues, because she is working alone. A second disadvantage to working alone is that she cannot take a break that rotation would allow if the interpreting exceeds more than 30 minutes, and can become fatigued.

4.1.2 *DIs working as a team*

In situations with a larger audience where there are two signed languages involved such as ASL and LSQ, the ASL-LSQ DIs require working as a team of three. There are two main reasons for this. First, during each rotation, one interpreter acts as the ASL-LSQ DI, the second acts as the DI-M and the third rests until the next rotation, although this third interpreter may act as a support to the team as needed. Therefore throughout the day, each interpreter works in the two roles of ASL-LSQ DI and DI-M. Second, conferences, seminars and workshops are usually more than one or two hours long, and rotation every 20 minutes is recommended both as a preventative health measure and to avoid language processing breakdown. Thus each interpreter works 40 minutes out of every hour.

Figure 2 illustrates a model for this type of setting where the presenter is signing in ASL (the arrow labeled "1") and using overheads with English text. The ASL-LSQ DI sits facing the ASL presenter and, shown as the arrow labeled "2", produces an interpretation from ASL to LSQ (or even from English to LSQ, or English to French then to LSQ if the presenter did not include a French version of the text on the overhead). The DI-M on the stage next to the ASL presenter mirrors the LSQ from the ASL-LSQ DI sitting directly across. The DI-M may improve the target text and correct some of potential language contact effects produced during the interpreting process on the part of the ASL-LSQ DI, and may insert or expand grammatical non-manual features to make the final target message clear and complete. A third DI (not shown

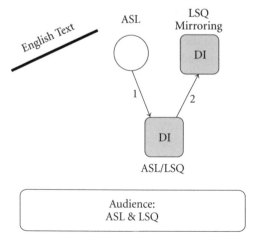

Figure 2. The ASL-LSQ DI model, in this case with an ASL presenter.

in the figure) typically sits next to the ASL-LSQ DI so she can provide feedback and support if needed. When the opportunity for rotation is presented, usually when there is a pause in the source message or at the completion of a sub-section of the source message, the third interpreter will walk up to the stage to replace the DI-M, the DI-M will take over the ASL-LSQ DI role, and the ASL-LSQ DI takes her turn to rest. This arrangement should take place approximately every 15–20 minutes.[10] This model of interpreting generally assumes that the interpretation is performed simultaneously.

The advantages are tremendous with this model. The interpreters in the team tend to feel supported by their colleagues and are less exhausted at the end of an assignment because of the rotation system. The ASL-LSQ DI is able to focus on language process-ing from the source signed and written language, including the contextual information and cultural subtleties of the message, instead of also paying attention to the audience feedback. This is because the ASL-LSQ DI is sending the information via her inter-pretation to the DI-M only. As mentioned, the DI-M can correct the interpreted text if necessary and improve the message quality for the target audience without losing meaning, and can also look to the third interpreter for feedback in case this interpreter notices any errors. The process occurs simultaneously instead of consecutively, which means that even though the target message flow may be lagged somewhat behind the source message, it proceeds smoothly without interruption compared to certain sit-uations where a DI-F[11] is involved.[12] The disadvantage with this model is the cost incurred in having three interpreters present compared to two hearing signed language interpreters.[13] Even with the additional cost, however, the quality of interpreting when three DIs work together is much more assured for every participant involved in the event. The use of English text by the presenter without signing the text in ASL can frequently cause difficulty because many members of the LSQ audience will likely be unable to understand the written English. A pause initiated by the ASL-LSQ DI is nec-essary to gain some additional time to translate the English text into LSQ before the presenter can continue with the presentation. Generally the team will try to sensitize the presenter in advance by informing her that by adding a translated French text along with the English will benefit the audience directly and assist the DI process as well.

Using the model presented in Figure 3, let us consider what happens when a member of the LSQ audience poses a question to the ASL presenter. When this takes place there is a logistic implication to ensuring that everyone has access to the questioner's message. First of all, there usually needs to be a short pause to allow the ASL-LSQ DI sitting across from the presenter time to walk up on the stage to act as a DI-M from the LSQ questioner to the rest of the LSQ audience. In Figure 3, arrow 1 along with a dashed line signifies that the DI has moved into the mirroring position, receiving the LSQ message (arrow 2) from the audience member. The DI-M who was already on the stage will switch into the ASL-LSQ DI role to interpret the LSQ question (a second arrow 2 in the figure) into ASL. The presenter will need to turn to look at this LSQ to ASL interpretation of the audience member's question (shown as arrow 3). When the ASL presenter then answers the question, usually the third interpreter, if present, will take over the ASL-LSQ DI task while sitting across

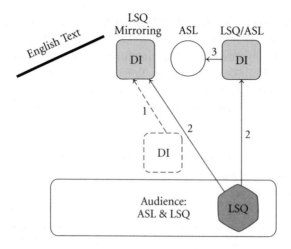

Figure 3. The ASL-LSQ DI model showing the interpretation of an LSQ audience member's question to the ASL presenter.

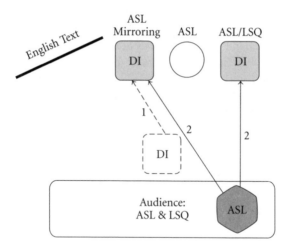

Figure 4. The ASL-LSQ DI model showing an ASL signer's question to the ASL presenter.

from the presenter, while the ASL-LSQ DI on the stage waits to interpret the next question. This requires swift coordination to make the necessary changes in DI roles and positioning. The team needs to guard against creating confusion since everyone may wonder which DI will interpret what, and which language each will be using. The solution is simply to begin by stating which language the questioner is using and informing the audience which role and language each interpreter will use consistently throughout the question period. This arrangement is very well designed for a team of three DIs working together. The process is usually simultaneous, but can possibly be consecutive depending on factors such as the level of complexity of the audience member's question.

The process for interpreting an ASL question to the ASL presenter is quite similar as that just presented in Figure 3. The only differences are that the ASL presenter does not need to turn to look at the ASL-LSQ DI, and this interpreter now works from ASL to LSQ for the audience. The ASL presenter can look at the questioner directly (see Figure 4).

4.1.3 *The DI working with hearing interpreters*

Teaming one or more hearing signed language interpreters with ASL-LSQ DIs results in an arrangement similar to the models discussed above. The difference is that this takes place when the presenter herself is, for example, a non-Deaf French speaker with a trilingual audience: French, ASL and LSQ. This is shown in Figure 5. Because the source language is spoken French, the first step in the interpreting process will be for the hearing interpreter to interpret from French into LSQ in front of the audience, represented by arrow 1 in the figure. The ASL-LSQ DI who is sitting across from the LSQ-French interpreter will interpret from LSQ into ASL (arrow 3) which is relayed by the DI-M on the stage who signs in ASL for the ASL audience. This procedure requires more processing time since it involves one extra step compared to the Deaf presenter arrangement illustrated in Figure 2. This may be somewhat problematic since the ASL-LSQ DI's eye contact with the DI-M is reduced to minimal because she must maintain eye contact with the LSQ-French interpreter along with watching the French text at the same time she is producing the ASL target message. However, a third interpreter sitting next to the ASL-LSQ DI can usually give appropriate feedback and support if

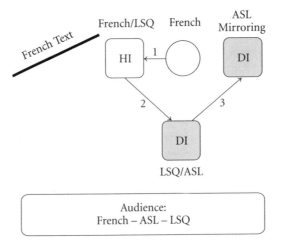

Figure 5. The team consisting of an ASL-LSQ DI, DI-M, and LSQ-French hearing interpreter, with a presenter speaking French.

there is message breakdown or if misinterpretation occurs. The interpreting process is generally simultaneous in this arrangement as well.

During a question period, the model for interpreting an LSQ questioner is based on the model in Figure 3 and for an ASL questioner the arrangement is based on Figure 4, described above. The difference with this approach when a hearing interpreter is involved, however, is that there may be three interpreters on the stage instead of two (a hearing interpreter, an ASL-LSQ DI and a DI-M). The interpreters will have to work together in advance to locate the optimal positions they should take on the stage to avoid bumping into each other when repositioning during the question period. When a French-speaking audience member asks a question directly to the presenter with the hearing interpreter conveying the message in LSQ, the ASL-LSQ DI receives this message from the hearing interpreter and interprets from LSQ into ASL for the DI-M. The DI-M then conveys the ASL message to the audience. This model also may require a much longer delivery time along with changes of positioning, but once repositioning has taken place the interpreting will proceed simultaneously and fluidly. This is a very efficient process compared to interpreting between two spoken languages, which in a similar situation (without electronic equipment and a booth), will need to be consecutive to avoid spoken language interference.

4.1.4 *Audio-visual support*

Working with language is a very complex and challenging task. The interpreter must cope with many factors at once such as two grammars, semantic equivalents, the context surrounding the message, continuous language processing during interpretation, teamwork and so forth. Working with colleagues is always reassuring because they can be supportive in case of interpreting errors or other complications, and the interpreters can work together to maintain the quality of the message output. In some circumstances, however, the number of highly qualified DIs available can be very limited or the financial situation of the client does not permit having a team of three DIs as suggested in the discussion above. When this is the case, the introduction of audio-visual support provides one possible alternative model.

Figure 6 shows the arrangement of interpreters when only two interpreters make up the team, using video equipment as part of the interpreting process. The video camera and TV should be set up in the room prior to the beginning of the event. The ASL presenter (as an example) must be informed beforehand that there are two important considerations that will enable the ASL-LSQ DIs to be successful: 1) the presenter should remain in place in front of the camera and face the audience while signing and not turn to the side or move around the stage, and 2) since the camera will be focused only on the ASL presenter (dotted line 1 in Figure 6), the projected English text on an overhead, chart or PowerPoint slide will not be on camera. The ASL presenter should be asked to sign all the written information appearing on the screen if it is to be interpreted for the target audience, or add a translation of the information in the second language (e.g., if in English, then include a French translation) if the audience composition is such that some people read English and some read French. If

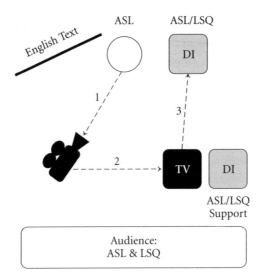

Figure 6. ASL-LSQ DIs with A-V support.

the event includes an international audience but English is an official language of the event, meaning that delegates would be expected to read the English text, the DI-IS (i.e., using International Sign) can focus just on the ASL presenter's content instead of worrying about interpreting the written text message as well. If it becomes clear that the English text needs to be interpreted, an option is to have the second interpreter (who at that point would be taking a break but potentially acting as a support) move up onto the stage to translate from the English written text into LSQ. This means, however, that the second ASL-LSQ DI will be unable to get any break between her previous and next rotations of interpreting from ASL to LSQ on the stage.

As illustrated in Figure 6, the ASL-LSQ DI on the stage watches the TV screen on which the image of the presenter is shown. This is advantageous because the DI does not need to look sideways at the presenter on the stage, and the audience can see the DI clearly (the DI faces both the TV and the audience). If possible, the TV should be larger than 32 inches, but this depends on the distance between the DI and TV screen (dotted line 3 in the figure). The chain of interpreting in this model is reduced to a minimum (i.e., one) compared to models that include a DI-M, where two steps in the chain of interpreting are required. This results in a shorter overall transmission time.

The DIs will always be nervous about A-V breakdown, the quality of the TV image, or if the camera might generate a blurry or unclear image. These are technical problems that would affect their interpreting performance. In addition, the use of video equipment requires more space to set up without obstructing the audience's view of the stage. This model is often considered as the least desirable and should be avoided whenever possible.

A further option, also incorporating video technology, is to project the ASL-LSQ DI or DI-IS on a large screen with an LCD projector. This is a very popular option when the audience is larger, for example more than one or two thousand Deaf people. The audience thus has more visual access to a large screen image rather than watching a distant DI on the stage. This option has been used successfully during national or international gatherings such as Deaf Way II or the World Federation of the Deaf Congress opening ceremonies and keynote addresses. Focusing a video camera on the DI on stage and retransmitting the image onto a large screen behind or above the DI can be applied to several models such as those illustrated in Figures 2, 5, and 6 for large audiences.

4.1.5 Board meetings

Typical situations in Canada, where two official signed languages are used and ASL-LSQ DIs and DI-Ms work in teams, are the board meetings and Annual General Meetings (AGMs) of most national Deaf organizations. There are two models that have been used since the first board meetings were facilitated by ASL-LSQ DIs in the mid 1990s. One model is where the number of users of each of the two signed languages is more or less equal and they are dispersed around the meeting table as in Figure 7(a). A second option is employed when one of the signed languages is under-represented or when a small group of users of one signed language are located at only one part of the meeting table as in Figure 7(b).

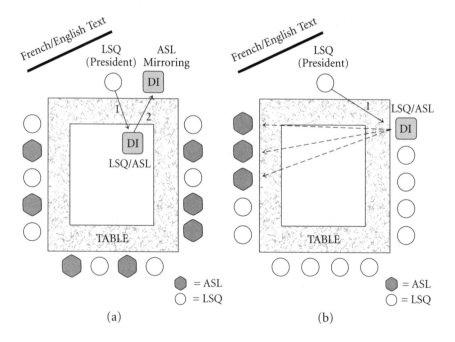

Figure 7. (a) ASL-LSQ DIs positioned for a board meeting, with a Board of Directors consisting of a mix of ASL and LSQ signers around the table, and (b) ASL and LSQ board members grouped.

The president of the organization, who might be for example an LSQ user, typically sits at the head of the table, with the best position for the ASL-LSQ DI being to sit inside the circle of the table so that this DI can clearly see the president running the meeting. In Figure 7(a) the DI-M is shown standing next to the LSQ president, mirroring the target language, ASL, from the ASL-LSQ DI (arrow 2). This model usually includes a third DI to the side who is taking a break until her next rotation (not shown in Figure 7). The ASL and LSQ board members can sit practically anywhere around the meeting table, with the interpretation facilitating the opportunity for the two linguistic and cultural communities to mingle as they wish.

When it comes to questions or a discussion period for the board as a whole, there are two options that the president chooses from, usually at the beginning of the meeting: 1) the members must walk up to the front next to the president where the DI and other board members can see them, or 2) members must raise their hand to take a turn, with the president controlling the turn taking communication. This second approach forces the DI-M, positioned next to the president, to alternate between the role of DI-M and ASL-LSQ DI.

The second model of DIs interpreting a board meeting is to group the users of one signed language together in one location where they can all see the ASL-LSQ DI directly. This works best if the DI is seated between the president and the other board members as shown in Figure 7(b). This model allows the interpreting team to consist of two ASL-LSQ DIs instead of three. These models allow for simultaneous processing most of time, with consecutive interpreting used when necessary.

4.2 Models of the DI-Facilitator[14]

As described in Section 3.2.2 above regarding the need for a DI-F for Deaf consumers who are semilingual or without any conventional language, DI-Fs usually work along with certified hearing signed language interpreters to ensure the communication process is successful. There are two possibilities for the arrangement of interpreters to facilitate the Deaf consumer communicating with a hearing person who does not know any signed language. The first model, illustrated in Figure 8, shows that the hearing French speaker is interpreted by an LSQ-French hearing interpreter (arrow 1). The Deaf consumer may understand the hearing interpreter most of the time (arrow 2) but the DI-F sits next to the hearing interpreter, monitoring the communication process to ensure that the message is being clearly understood. The DI-F can intervene if she believes that the Deaf person is misunderstanding or being misunderstood (arrow 3). This model indicates that the hearing interpreter is considered as handling the primary communication access. Nonetheless, the arrangement in Figure 8 empowers the Deaf consumer because she has a choice between accessing information through either the hearing or Deaf interpreter. For this to take place, the DI-F must build trust and show support to ensure that the communication with every participant involved is successful.

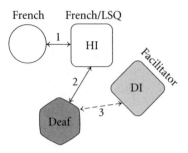

Figure 8. A DI-F working with an LSQ-French interpreter, through whom the Deaf consumer has primary communication access.

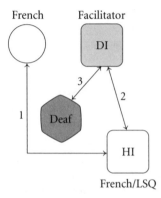

Figure 9. A DI-F with an LSQ-French interpreter, where the DI-F acts as the only communication access for the Deaf consumer.

However, some Deaf consumers really do have a difficult time communicating or understanding through standard interpretation channels, with mild to severe effects. The model presented in Figure 9 may represent the best approach for these Deaf consumers since they are likely to be unable to understand clearly, especially if the interpreting is maintained simultaneously. At times the process requires the information to be rendered into highly visual and more concrete ways through other means of communication such as gestures and so forth. The DI-F is positioned right next to hearing French speaker so the Deaf consumer will see the DI and not the hearing interpreter who is sitting to the side and behind the consumer. This avoids multiple language inputs that may confuse the Deaf person in this situation. This model allows the hearing client to have more direct contact with the Deaf consumer and it can also facilitate more confidence and represents a higher respect for the Deaf person during the communication process. The DI-F can develop a strong communication bond based on linguistic and cultural sameness which will promote successful communication.

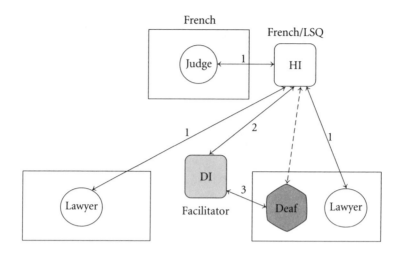

Figure 10. A DI-F with an LSQ-French interpreter in a courtroom.

DI-Fs frequently work in legal situations because communication access and clarity are critical. A basic model of the DI-F process in a courtroom is illustrated in Figure 10, although the model can be adapted in numerous ways depending on the actual situation and courtroom setup. The communication dynamics of this setting are different from most other interpreting assignments, and the DI-F must ensure that the Deaf consumer is able to follow the courtroom communication without a feeling of being overwhelmed. A hearing interpreter usually stands next to (or near) the judge and interprets the messages of each party (e.g., the judge, the client's lawyer, prosecuting lawyer, etc.; see the three arrows labeled "1" in Figure 10). The DI-F tends to stand or sit fairly close to the Deaf consumer but is positioned to be able to follow the hearing interpreter as well (in the figure, this is shown in the combination of arrows 2 and 3). The interpreting process must be consecutive and allow for contextual elaboration using highly visual means. Because it is consecutive, the Deaf consumer can first watch the hearing interpreter to attempt to understand the message (the dashed line in the figure), which is then followed by a consecutive interpretation by the DI-F to ensure message reception and comprehension by the Deaf consumer. This may require more time compared to that needed for a bicultural and bilingual Deaf consumer for whom simultaneous interpreting may be used, but the process will ensure that everyone understands correctly and in the long run it will save time and financial costs by avoiding repeat appearances or errors in judges' decisions.

4.3 Written text to signed language

Another trend in DI services is to have DIs translate from written text to signed language. Translation can be from closed or open captioning on video material or from textbooks for educational purposes and for general information. The final translated product is generally in video format (e.g., VHS, DVD or online video streaming) or vice-versa. This task is considered more as a translation process rather than interpreting because the translator has the time to analyze the text, consider meaning, and conduct contextual research regarding the source material before the final target text is produced. The translator is allowed to practice and refine the final text to make it as perfect as possible before finalizing a fixed product (such as a DVD). This is different from the more traditional "on-site" interpreting where numerous errors, corrected or not, can occur. Such translation products often have the aim of increasing Deaf people's access to informational material, which many Deaf people prefer to be produced in their first language by a Deaf user of that signed language who has mastered the art of communication in this format.

There are several possible forms of translation: 1) a written language text to signed language (e.g., French to LSQ or English to ASL), 2) from one signed language to another (e.g., ASL to LSQ) where one or both texts are in a recorded format, 3) a signed language to International Sign (similarly recorded), and 4) from a signed text to a simplified format with additional context for Deaf individuals who are semilingual or without conventional language. This assists in empowering members of the Deaf community by providing materials in their own language and by increasing their knowledge. Recorded translated texts are convenient communication tools in this era of video streaming technology, which enables communication to take place efficiently and at a low distribution cost. The major advantage of this translation approach is that discourse content can be modified to fit Deaf ways of expressing ideas and structuring discourse.

5.   Ethics

A code of ethics and professional conduct is considered as a safeguard for both professionals and community members, and this is especially true for signed language interpreters. The tenets in AVLIC's and RID's codes of ethics may need further consideration regarding DI issues since these tenets were developed from a hearing perspective. However, DIs are a part of the Deaf community, and the close bonds they have and the cultural sameness they share with the community create a different dynamic than most hearing interpreters[15] experience in the Deaf community. DIs are deeply connected to the Deaf community but even so, they will remain as ethical as possible and maintain an appropriate professional distance both during and outside of their interpreting assignments. For example, when a DI is on an out-of-town assignment with a national Deaf organization, some difficulty may occur if the DI is invited to join the Deaf board of directors for lunch or dinner, not in the capacity of DI, but just as a member of the Deaf community. She may also be asked to join local Deaf community events along with the members of the visiting board of directors. In these cases, the DI will interact socially with the board as a member of the Deaf community, but needs to maintain a professional distance in terms of the Deaf organization's issues. This may be awkward for everyone in the beginning since as a member of the Deaf community the DI is entitled to express her views and opinions, but the DI and her consumers must understand what ethical limits the DI professional has in a very close-knit community. The DI makes decisions based on her best professional judgment regarding whether she can or cannot be involved in discussions related to the interpreting assignment. Delicate situations can be created if the DI pushes ethical boundaries beyond what it is generally expected in this field. Thus new ethical questions arise such as whether there are different ethical values that need to be considered when viewed from a Deaf community perspective.

Another situation that involves serious ethical considerations has to do with switching in and out of the DI role. This can happen, for example, when an ASL-LSQ DI also happens to be knowledgeable about the linguistics of both signed languages. In one instance, during a meeting the board president asked the ASL-LSQ DI to switch roles momentarily to discuss some issues as an expert in linguistics. This poses an ethical dilemma for the ASL-LSQ DI. A similar dilemma arises if the board contacts this very same interpreter for assistance on linguistic questions outside of the interpreting assignment. This may interfere with Sections 1.3.1 and 4.1 of the AVLIC Code of Ethics and Guidelines for Professional Conduct:[16]

> *§1.3.1. Members will refrain from using their professional role to perform other functions that lie beyond the scope of an interpreting assignment and the parameters of their professional duties. They will not counsel, advise, or interject personal opinions.*
>
> *§4.1. Professional Relationships*
> *Members shall understand the difference between professional and social interactions. They will establish and maintain professional boundaries between themselves and consumers.*

Section 1.3.1 of the code clearly states that the interpreter mentioned above should not have switched out of her role as interpreter during the assignment, and Section 4.1 cautions interpreters to maintain professional distance and approach social interaction with consumers carefully. Based on Deaf cultural norms, however, *not* establishing rapport on a personal level is generally unacceptable, causing social and professional tension among Deaf members of the Deaf community. Developing relationships through social interaction in accordance with the norms of Deaf culture is appropriate even though the code of ethics does not promote this (Bienvenu & Colonomos 1992). However, the DI must be aware that she can draw certain boundaries between her role of DI and her participation in the community as a Deaf community member. She must explore this distinction based on a Deaf cultural perspective without causing tension.

There is a more complex situation that a DI may face which may take place in a legal setting such as in the courtroom where a case involves two Deaf clients, one a defendant and the other a plaintiff. The DI may feel uncomfortable not greeting or having conversations with one of the Deaf consumers, but this may be the protocol if the DI has been hired to interpret for only *one* Deaf consumer in the case. It is common for the interpreter not to handle interpretation for both sides of the case when the two consumers are opposing, but the DI may feel that such one-sided actions go against Deaf cultural norms regarding social expectations. This may present conflicts on two levels: 1) Deaf community norms, and 2) standard interpreting practices in the courtroom. This situation deserves much further ethical consideration (Gouby 2003).

The AVLIC Code of Ethics and Guidelines for Professional Conduct allows the interpreter some flexibility in order to perform her task appropriately:

EXAMPLE 1: INFORMATION SHARING

> *§1.1.2. Where necessary, a member may exchange pertinent information with a colleague in order to provide consistent quality of service. This will be done in a manner that protects the information and the consumers.*

The DI-F may certainly benefit from consulting with other DI-Fs who have previously worked with a Deaf consumer to gain valuable information, and may consult the consumer file if one is accessible. But sometimes the DI-F needs to consult with other professional resources or even relatives to learn home-signs, gestures, or idiosyncratic signs the consumer uses, or to learn something of the background of the consumer. This, however, is much beyond the boundaries of the interpreter in the traditional sense.

EXAMPLE 2: IMPARTIALITY

> *§4.2.1. Members shall remain neutral, impartial, and objective. They will refrain from altering a message for political, religious, moral, or philosophical reasons, or any other biased or subjective consideration.*

As discussed above, advocacy, based on cultural and political values, may be needed because of the right of the Deaf individual to have full access to communication. This presents a problem regarding impartiality since the DI is bound to cross the line of what would normally be thought of as an impartial stance. Does this section of the code apply literally to the DI situation? The concept of impartiality is somewhat easier to describe on paper than to put into practice, especially for the DI.

Section 3.3 of the AVLIC code states that hearing interpreters must be aware that a Deaf consumer may need to work with a DI to facilitate the communication process:

> *§3.3 Deaf Interpreters*
> *The services of a Deaf interpreter may be required when working with individuals who use regional sign dialects, non-standard signs, foreign sign languages, and those with emerging language use. They may also be used with individuals who have disabling conditions that impact on communication. Members will recognize the need for a Deaf interpreter and will ensure their inclusion as a part of the professional interpreting team.*

This is a very important section that AVLIC has included in their code of ethics to ensure that the hearing interpreter recognizes her own limitations in these circumstances. However, as mentioned, implementing a certification process for DIs is necessary to give this field formal professional status. As well, it is recommended that additional sections of the code of ethics be included that are specially designed for situations involving a DI where an appropriate Deaf cultural perspective is considered along with "hearing" culture. In any case, DIs should be members of professional interpreting organizations so as to have protection in their work equally with their hearing peers.

6. Deaf interpreter training programs

The Deaf community is a heterogeneous community – its members are linguistically and culturally diverse, determined by each person's educational and life experiences. Not every Deaf member is exposed to a natural language early such as ASL or LSQ; instead they might be exposed to various means of "coded" communication at school or at home, such as signed English or French or oral language. In addition to the lack of opportunities for proper language input during their formative years, they usually do not take ASL or LSQ grammar classes as compared to their hearing counterparts who take English or French grammar classes throughout their education. As for becoming qualified DIs, they need to strengthen their language foundation in both signed and written language before they can begin learning how to undertake both translation and interpreting processes. Apart from a basic knowledge of the language, most Deaf individuals do not possess a sufficient theoretical knowledge of linguistics, cultural studies and communication skills for interpreting, even if they grew up within the Deaf community. They may be regular consumers of interpreting services throughout their lives but rarely get the chance to experience the interpreting task first hand. Deaf individuals should not become interpreters "on the job" or just by taking a few workshops, or by being mentored briefly and then passing a certification exam. They need more extensive and rigorous training to attain the degree of excellence that is desired in the field of interpreting.

Even though DI services have grown steadily in the last several years in North America and around the world, there are no current formal interpreter training programs at colleges or universities that fully meet the training needs of DIs. However, as an example of DI training that has taken place, the interpreting training program at Northeastern University offered DI training twice in the 1990s. This program consisted of nine courses offered monthly over three years. The Northeastern program still offers some DI training, and some other interpreting programs in North America currently offer similar courses (Cathy Cogen, Interpreter Education Project for New England, Northeastern University, personal communication). As well, occasional workshops are offered, but this is rare in Canada. As for RID, this organization requires Deaf members to take two workshops of eight hours each approved by RID prior to taking the CDI test. These workshops topics are: 1) roles and responsibility of Deaf interpreters, and

2) the code of ethics. This, however, is largely insufficient compared to the skills needed for the actual task. Theoretical parts of current curricula in training programs for hearing interpreters would be suitable for DIs,[17] but the practical training currently offered in interpreting between English and ASL or French and LSQ is not appropriate since DIs have different tasks to perform.

Implementation of a Deaf interpreter training curriculum is necessary in order to create a truly qualified pool of DIs. DI training could be combined with training for hearing signed language interpreters for certain courses such as ASL linguistics, theory of interpreting, Deaf culture, etc., while other courses would need to be offered separately, such as those developing International Sign skills, alternative communication for individuals who are semilingual or without language, Deaf-blind interpreting, mirroring, and ASL-LSQ interpreting, each with full consideration of the interpreter being *Deaf* and a member of the cultural community of Deaf people. As well, specific courses on interpreting in the legal system could be developed so that the DI is equipped to handle legal terminology and has all the tools needed to translate these into other means of communication, as discussed in earlier sections of this chapter. Deaf and hearing individuals bring very different linguistic and cultural experiences to their training, and as has been suggested (e.g., hearing students have studied language structure – often including ASL or LSQ – while Deaf people have not), there is an inherent imbalance of knowledge and power (Bienvenu & Colonomos 1992). Deaf students may not come to a program with theoretical knowledge of language and cultural studies but importantly, they do have an innate knowledge of Deaf culture. This is the primary reason for the suggestion that training programs should offer some courses to the two groups of students separately. In this way the students are learning based on their differing backgrounds of having a signed language as their first or second language.

Providing a course on the role and tasks of the DI to hearing signed language interpreters is essential too. This way, they will be more prepared to work effectively with a DI as a team. This will allow them to be more aware of and prepared to use DI services when the communication between Deaf and hearing consumers becomes uncertain or difficult. Hearing interpreters should not feel unqualified because they cannot perform the task, but with opportunities for working with DIs in the professional preparation program, they will be more comfortable with the DI role and apt to work with them to ensure communication efficiency (Bienvenu & Colonomos 1992; Frishberg 1990).

A formal professional preparation program for DIs will allow Deaf members of the Deaf community to be more aware of this field as a career possibility. Formal preparation would include structured learning and mentoring for DIs instead of relying on learning on the job. Structured training would also mean that consumers could be more confident that they are getting professionally trained DIs in the future.

7. Conclusion

The existence of DIs dates back to the emergence of Deaf communities and to the beginnings of Deaf education. Today, DIs continue to meet the communicative needs of the Deaf community in many different ways. The main function of the DI is to ensure that communication is clearly transmitted and understood by all participants involved in an interaction, but especially for Deaf consumers. Beyond the traditional range of interpreting tasks, DIs face new challenges such as promoting empowerment in the Deaf consumer during communication exchanges, based on respect for that Deaf community member. Qualified DIs possess the linguistic and cognitive adaptability to generate and transmit messages that satisfy a wide variety of Deaf consumers with a range of communication abilities. More so, the DI is not only responsible for the linguistic information itself but also for understanding and mediating cross-cultural differences from a Deaf perspective, which is a very crucial aspect of the successful communication process.

Employment possibilities for DIs are unlimited. A number of these possibilities have been mentioned in this chapter, but DIs could as well work in the education system, particularly in mainstream settings along with the signed language interpreters who are already there. The more we understand how beneficial DIs are, the more we will see DIs spread to other areas where Deaf people must interact with the hearing community.

This chapter has demonstrated the importance of having DIs in the field of interpreting. The DI is a tremendous addition to the field of signed language interpreting because of what she can offer. Although this chapter has covered many of the fundamental principles of the Deaf interpreter's work, there are certainly many other important issues that deserve careful consideration, such as ethical concerns for DIs when viewed from Deaf people's perspectives and the implementation of formal DI training comparable to that for hearing signed language interpreters. Formal, in-depth research in these areas is needed along with research on the identification and features of language varieties of Deaf consumers who are semilingual or monolingual.

Notes

1. This chapter would not be possible without constant encouragement and support from the editor of this book, Terry Janzen. I also am very grateful to the Deaf community and my DI colleagues with whom I have worked in the past few years for their valuable input, and to the anonymous reviewers for comments and suggestions. Also, thanks to Lawrence Fleischer for his wonderful comments and discussions pertaining to DI issues, and to my wife, Genie Gertz, for her continuous support for me in my writing.

2. The term "communication facilitator" is discussed in more detail in Section 3.2.2.

3. See Section 3.2.2 below for details on the use of this term.

4. See also the description of certificates and other pertinent information on the Registry of Interpreters for the Deaf website at www.rid.org.

5. See Leeson (this volume, Chapter 10) for a discussion of this situation in Ireland. Two distinct Deaf communities each with their own signed language may not be the case in Ireland as it is in Canada, but it is clear that signed language usage in Ireland is characterized by a large degree of variation.

6. "Allophone" is defined as "Se dit d'une personne ou d'un groupe, dont la langue d'usage est autre que la ou les langues officielles du pays où il se trouve." (www.granddictionnaire.com), that is, 'This refers to a person or group who uses a language other than the official languages of their country or surrounding area.'

7. Hearing interpreters sometimes report a similar fatigue effect where they find themselves "interpreting" in the very same language as the source speaker or signer is using.

8. The term "facilitator" used here is not intended to reflect an older definition in this field that may imply simplifying or making the communication somehow easier for one party. It is clear that this term is not widely accepted but here I am attempting to make a distinction between the different roles of the DI. This word seems to best capture the task described in Section 3.2.2. The DI-F performs her role as interpreter to ensure that the communication process is successful just as the hearing interpreter does, nothing less and nothing more.

9. See Mindess (1999) for discussion of cultural framing and contextualizing in this regard. Specifically, Mindess suggests that such framing for Deaf ASL signers and hearing English speakers can differ greatly.

10. There is no fixed convention in rotation time and frequency, leaving the team to decide what is best and to determine when to switch during the process.

11. See Section 4.2 below for details.

12. This should not be taken to mean that simultaneous interpreting is always better than consecutive interpreting, since Russell (2002; this volume) demonstrates that accuracy can increase when interpreters use the consecutive mode (see also Stratiy, this volume). In a lecture or seminar, however, as shown in this model of interpreting with DIs, it is more likely that the situation is best facilitated by simultaneous interpreting.

13. Although note that it is not uncommon for spoken language interpreters to work in teams of three in similar settings.

14. Once again, note that this term is used here to help distinguish between the various roles of the DI for this discussion. Generally, however, no matter which role the Deaf interpreter has technically, she can be referred to simply as a "DI".

15. This may be not the case for most CODA interpreters since they are part of the Deaf community.

16. The AVLIC Code of Ethics can be found at the general AVLIC website at www.avlic.ca. The full Code of Ethics text is also found in Appendix A, Janzen and Korpiniski, this volume.

17. Many programs say that their doors are open to hearing *and* Deaf students. The truth is that Deaf people rarely go through an entire interpreting program alongside their hearing peers, although in Canada, several DIs have done this.

References

Atwood, Alan A., John D. Clarkson, & Charlene R. Laba (1992). *Deaf-blindness.* Washington, DC: Gallaudet University Press.

Bienvenu, M. J., & Betty Colonomos (1992). Relay interpreting in the 90's. In Laurie Swabey (Ed.), *The Challenge of the 90's: New Standards in Interpreter Education, Proceedings of the Eighth National Convention, Conference of Interpreter Trainers* (pp. 69–80). United States: Conference of Interpreter Trainers.

Boudreault, Patrick (1999). Grammatical Processing in American Sign Language: Effects of Age of Acquisition and Syntactic Complexity. Unpublished Master's thesis, McGill University, Montreal, Quebec.

Boudreault, Patrick, & Liz Scully (2001). DEAF Pt-2? Sign Language Interpreters Who are Deaf. Paper presented at Critical Link III, Montreal, Quebec, May 2001.

CAD (Canadian Association of the Deaf) (2002). CAD's Position on Official Languages. http://www.cad.ca/index2.php?lid=e&cid=12&pid=16. Retrieved April 29, 2005.

Chamberlain, Charlene, & Patrick Boudreault (1998). Biliteracy and Bilingual Signed Language Acquisition of the Deaf in Canada. Paper presented at the Canadian Association of the Deaf Conference, Ottawa, Ontario.

Cokely, Dennis (1992). *Interpretation: A Sociolinguistic Model.* Burtonsville, MD: Linstok Press.

Collins, Steven D. (1993). Deaf-Blind Interpreting: The Structure of ASL and The Interpreting Process. Elizabeth A. Winston, Coordinator, Gallaudet University Communication Forum, Vol. 2. W. Moses, Acting Dean, Publisher.

Collins, Steven D., & Karen Petronio (1998). What happens in tactile ASL? In Ceil Lucas (Ed.), *Pinky Extension & Eye Gaze: Language Use in Deaf Communities* (pp. 18–37). Washington, DC: Gallaudet University Press.

Cummins, Jim (1979). Cognitive/academic language proficiency, linguistic interdependence, the optimum age question and some other matters. *Working Papers on Bilingualism, 19,* 121–129.

Cummins, Jim (2000). *Language, Power and Pedagogy: Bilingual Children in the Crossfire.* Buffalo, NY: Multilingual Matters Ltd.

Frishberg, Nancy (1990). *Interpreting: An Introduction* (Revised ed.). Silver Spring, MD: RID Publications.

Gouby, Gino (2003). Role and Responsibilities of the CDI. Workshop presented by SCRID, Oxnard College, April 12, 2003.

Humphrey, Janice H., & Bob J. Alcorn (2001). *So You Want to Be an Interpreter? An Introduction to Sign Language Interpreting* (3rd ed.). Amarillo, TX: H & H Publishers.

Kannapell, Barbara (1993). *Language Choice – Identity Choice.* Burtonsville, MD: Linstok Press.

Mesch, Johanna (2001). *Tactile Sign Language: Turn Taking and Questions in Signed Conversations of Deaf-blind People.* Hamburg: Signum.

Mindess, Anna (1999). *Reading Between the Signs: Intercultural Communication for Sign Language Interpreters.* Yarmouth, ME: Intercultural Press.

Moody, Bill (1987). International gestures. In John V. Van Cleve (Ed.), *Gallaudet Encyclopedia of Deaf People and Deafness,* Vol. 3 (pp. 81–82). New York: McGraw Hill.

Morford, Jill P., & Rachel I. Mayberry (2000). A reexamination of "early exposure" and its implications for language acquisition by eye. In Charlene Chamberlain, Jill P. Morford, & Rachel I. Mayberry (Eds.), *Language Acquisition by Eye* (pp. 111–127). Mahwah, NJ: Lawrence Erlbaum.

Petronio, Karen (1995). Interpreting for Deaf-blind students: Factors to consider. In Kathleen M. Huebner, Jeanne G. Prickett, Therese R. Welch, & Elga Joffe (Eds.), *Hand in Hand: Selected Reprints and Annotated Bibliography on Working with Students Who are Deaf-Blind* (pp. 37–40). New York: AFB Press.

Ressler, Carolyn I. (1999). A comparative analysis of a direct interpretation and an intermediary interpretation in American Sign Language. *Journal of Interpretation* (RID), 71–102.

Russell, Debra (2002). *Interpreting in Legal Contexts: Consecutive and Simultaneous Interpreting.* Burtonsville, MD: Linstok Press.

Skutnabb-Kangas, Tove (1981). *Bilingualism or Not: The Education of Minorities.* Clevedon: Multilingual Matters Ltd.

Smith, Theresa B. (1994). *Guidelines: Practical Tips for Working and Socializing with Deaf-blind People.* Burtonsville, MD: Sign Media Inc.

Solow, Sharon Neumann (2000). *Sign Language Interpreting: A Basic Resource Book* (Revised ed.). Burtonsville, MD: Linstok Press.

Stewart, David A., Jerome D. Schein, & Brenda E. Cartwright (1998). *Sign Language Interpreting: Exploring its Art and Science.* Needham Heights, MA: Allyn & Bacon.

Taylor, Marty M. (1993). *Interpretation Skills: English to American Sign Language.* Edmonton, Alberta: Interpreting Consolidated.

Taylor, Marty M. (2002). *Interpretation Skills: American Sign Language to English.* Edmonton, Alberta: Interpreting Consolidated.

World Federation of the Deaf. Unification of Signs Commission (WFD). (1975). *Gestuno: International Sign Language of the Deaf. The Revised and Enlarged Book of Signs Agreed and Adopted by the Unification of Signs Commission of the World Federation of the Deaf.* Carlisle, England: British Deaf Association, for the World Federation of the Deaf.

Name index

Subject index

Benjamins Translation Library

A complete list of titles in this series can be found on *www.benjamins.com*

74 WOLF, Michaela and Alexandra FUKARI (eds.): Constructing a Sociology of Translation. 2007. vi, 226 pp.
73 GOUADEC, Daniel: Translation as a Profession. 2007. xvi, 396 pp.
72 GAMBIER, Yves, Miriam SHLESINGER and Radegundis STOLZE (eds.): Doubts and Directions in Translation Studies. Selected contributions from the EST Congress, Lisbon 2004. 2007. xii, 362 pp. [EST Subseries 4]
71 ST-PIERRE, Paul and Prafulla C. KAR (eds.): In Translation – Reflections, Refractions, Transformations. 2007. xvi, 313 pp.
70 WADENSJÖ, Cecilia, Birgitta ENGLUND DIMITROVA and Anna-Lena NILSSON (eds.): The Critical Link 4. Professionalisation of interpreting in the community. Selected papers from the 4th International Conference on Interpreting in Legal, Health and Social Service Settings, Stockholm, Sweden, 20-23 May 2004. 2007. x, 314 pp.
69 DELABASTITA, Dirk, Lieven D'HULST and Reine MEYLAERTS (eds.): Functional Approaches to Culture and Translation. Selected papers by José Lambert. 2006. xxviii, 226 pp.
68 DUARTE, João Ferreira, Alexandra ASSIS ROSA and Teresa SERUYA (eds.): Translation Studies at the Interface of Disciplines. 2006. vi, 207 pp.
67 PYM, Anthony, Miriam SHLESINGER and Zuzana JETTMAROVÁ (eds.): Sociocultural Aspects of Translating and Interpreting. 2006. viii, 255 pp.
66 SNELL-HORNBY, Mary: The Turns of Translation Studies. New paradigms or shifting viewpoints? 2006. xi, 205 pp.
65 DOHERTY, Monika: Structural Propensities. Translating nominal word groups from English into German. 2006. xxii, 196 pp.
64 ENGLUND DIMITROVA, Birgitta: Expertise and Explicitation in the Translation Process. 2005. xx, 295 pp.
63 JANZEN, Terry (ed.): Topics in Signed Language Interpreting. Theory and practice. 2005. xii, 362 pp.
62 POKORN, Nike K.: Challenging the Traditional Axioms. Translation into a non-mother tongue. 2005. xii, 166 pp. [EST Subseries 3]
61 HUNG, Eva (ed.): Translation and Cultural Change. Studies in history, norms and image-projection. 2005. xvi, 195 pp.
60 TENNENT, Martha (ed.): Training for the New Millennium. Pedagogies for translation and interpreting. 2005. xxvi, 276 pp.
59 MALMKJÆR, Kirsten (ed.): Translation in Undergraduate Degree Programmes. 2004. vi, 202 pp.
58 BRANCHADELL, Albert and Lovell Margaret WEST (eds.): Less Translated Languages. 2005. viii, 416 pp.
57 CHERNOV, Ghelly V.: Inference and Anticipation in Simultaneous Interpreting. A probability-prediction model. Edited with a critical foreword by Robin Setton and Adelina Hild. 2004. xxx, 268 pp. [EST Subseries 2]
56 ORERO, Pilar (ed.): Topics in Audiovisual Translation. 2004. xiv, 227 pp.
55 ANGELELLI, Claudia V.: Revisiting the Interpreter's Role. A study of conference, court, and medical interpreters in Canada, Mexico, and the United States. 2004. xvi, 127 pp.
54 GONZÁLEZ DAVIES, Maria: Multiple Voices in the Translation Classroom. Activities, tasks and projects. 2004. x, 262 pp.
53 DIRIKER, Ebru: De-/Re-Contextualizing Conference Interpreting. Interpreters in the Ivory Tower? 2004. x, 223 pp.
52 HALE, Sandra: The Discourse of Court Interpreting. Discourse practices of the law, the witness and the interpreter. 2004. xviii, 267 pp.
51 CHAN, Leo Tak-hung: Twentieth-Century Chinese Translation Theory. Modes, issues and debates. 2004. xvi, 277 pp.
50 HANSEN, Gyde, Kirsten MALMKJÆR and Daniel GILE (eds.): Claims, Changes and Challenges in Translation Studies. Selected contributions from the EST Congress, Copenhagen 2001. 2004. xiv, 320 pp. [EST Subseries 1]
49 PYM, Anthony: The Moving Text. Localization, translation, and distribution. 2004. xviii, 223 pp.
48 MAURANEN, Anna and Pekka KUJAMÄKI (eds.): Translation Universals. Do they exist? 2004. vi, 224 pp.

47 SAWYER, David B.: Fundamental Aspects of Interpreter Education. Curriculum and Assessment. 2004. xviii, 312 pp.

46 BRUNETTE, Louise, Georges BASTIN, Isabelle HEMLIN and Heather CLARKE (eds.): The Critical Link 3. Interpreters in the Community. Selected papers from the Third International Conference on Interpreting in Legal, Health and Social Service Settings, Montréal, Quebec, Canada 22–26 May 2001. 2003. xii, 359 pp.

45 ALVES, Fabio (ed.): Triangulating Translation. Perspectives in process oriented research. 2003. x, 165 pp.

44 SINGERMAN, Robert: Jewish Translation History. A bibliography of bibliographies and studies. With an introductory essay by Gideon Toury. 2002. xxxvi, 420 pp.

43 GARZONE, Giuliana and Maurizio VIEZZI (eds.): Interpreting in the 21st Century. Challenges and opportunities. 2002. x, 337 pp.

42 HUNG, Eva (ed.): Teaching Translation and Interpreting 4. Building bridges. 2002. xii, 243 pp.

41 NIDA, Eugene A.: Contexts in Translating. 2002. x, 127 pp.

40 ENGLUND DIMITROVA, Birgitta and Kenneth HYLTENSTAM (eds.): Language Processing and Simultaneous Interpreting. Interdisciplinary perspectives. 2000. xvi, 164 pp.

39 CHESTERMAN, Andrew, Natividad GALLARDO SAN SALVADOR and Yves GAMBIER (eds.): Translation in Context. Selected papers from the EST Congress, Granada 1998. 2000. x, 393 pp.

38 SCHÄFFNER, Christina and Beverly ADAB (eds.): Developing Translation Competence. 2000. xvi, 244 pp.

37 TIRKKONEN-CONDIT, Sonja and Riitta JÄÄSKELÄINEN (eds.): Tapping and Mapping the Processes of Translation and Interpreting. Outlooks on empirical research. 2000. x, 176 pp.

36 SCHMID, Monika S.: Translating the Elusive. Marked word order and subjectivity in English-German translation. 1999. xii, 174 pp.

35 SOMERS, Harold (ed.): Computers and Translation. A translator's guide. 2003. xvi, 351 pp.

34 GAMBIER, Yves and Henrik GOTTLIEB (eds.): (Multi) Media Translation. Concepts, practices, and research. 2001. xx, 300 pp.

33 GILE, Daniel, Helle V. DAM, Friedel DUBSLAFF, Bodil MARTINSEN and Anne SCHJOLDAGER (eds.): Getting Started in Interpreting Research. Methodological reflections, personal accounts and advice for beginners. 2001. xiv, 255 pp.

32 BEEBY, Allison, Doris ENSINGER and Marisa PRESAS (eds.): Investigating Translation. Selected papers from the 4th International Congress on Translation, Barcelona, 1998. 2000. xiv, 296 pp.

31 ROBERTS, Roda P., Silvana E. CARR, Diana ABRAHAM and Aideen DUFOUR (eds.): The Critical Link 2: Interpreters in the Community. Selected papers from the Second International Conference on Interpreting in legal, health and social service settings, Vancouver, BC, Canada, 19–23 May 1998. 2000. vii, 316 pp.

30 DOLLERUP, Cay: Tales and Translation. The Grimm Tales from Pan-Germanic narratives to shared international fairytales. 1999. xiv, 384 pp.

29 WILSS, Wolfram: Translation and Interpreting in the 20th Century. Focus on German. 1999. xiii, 256 pp.

28 SETTON, Robin: Simultaneous Interpretation. A cognitive-pragmatic analysis. 1999. xvi, 397 pp.

27 BEYLARD-OZEROFF, Ann, Jana KRÁLOVÁ and Barbara MOSER-MERCER (eds.): Translators' Strategies and Creativity. Selected Papers from the 9th International Conference on Translation and Interpreting, Prague, September 1995. In honor of Jiří Levý and Anton Popovič. 1998. xiv, 230 pp.

26 TROSBORG, Anna (ed.): Text Typology and Translation. 1997. xvi, 342 pp.

25 POLLARD, David E. (ed.): Translation and Creation. Readings of Western Literature in Early Modern China, 1840–1918. 1998. vi, 336 pp.

24 ORERO, Pilar and Juan C. SAGER (eds.): The Translator's Dialogue. Giovanni Pontiero. 1997. xiv, 252 pp.

23 GAMBIER, Yves, Daniel GILE and Christopher TAYLOR (eds.): Conference Interpreting: Current Trends in Research. Proceedings of the International Conference on Interpreting: What do we know and how? 1997. iv, 246 pp.

22 CHESTERMAN, Andrew: Memes of Translation. The spread of ideas in translation theory. 1997. vii, 219 pp.

21 BUSH, Peter and Kirsten MALMKJÆR (eds.): Rimbaud's Rainbow. Literary translation in higher education. 1998. x, 200 pp.

20 SNELL-HORNBY, Mary, Zuzana JETTMAROVÁ and Klaus KAINDL (eds.): Translation as Intercultural Communication. Selected papers from the EST Congress, Prague 1995. 1997. x, 354 pp.